KEEP IT MOVING

KEEP IT MOVING

BAJA
BY CANOE

VALERIE FONS

The Mountaineers • Seattle

THE MOUNTAINEERS: Organized 1906 "... to encourage a spirit of good fellowship among all lovers of outdoor life."

© 1986 by Valerie Fons

Published by The Mountaineers
306 2nd Avenue West, Seattle, Washington 98119

Published simultaneously in Canada by Douglas & McIntyre Ltd.
1615 Venables Street, Vancouver, B.C. V5L 2H1

Manufactured in the United States of America

Edited by Sharon Bryan
Cover design by Elizabeth Watson
Map by Newell Cartographics
Large cover photo by Lloyd Fons

Library of Congress Cataloging in Publication Data

Fons, Valerie, 1951–
    Keep it moving.

    1. Sea kayaking—Mexico—Baja California. 2. Baja California (Mexico)—Description and travel. I. Title.
GV788.5.F66 1986   797.1'4'09722   86-18146
ISBN 0-89886-101-2

0 9 8   7   6

5   4   3   2   1

Dedicated as an offering
of the first fruits

Contents

Acknowledgments

Thanks to: My sponsor, Eddie Bauer Expedition Outfitters, which joined the expedition through its support, including accepting my collect calls from "where in Mexico?" Merchandise manager Jim Wheat, who gave me two boxes of Eddie Bauer equipment and said, as he helped me carry it to the car, "I hope it all fits in the boat." Camplite Foods, whose donations taught me the meaning of powdered cheese, and Mad River Canoes which had the good sense to build Kruger-designed Monarch canoes.

Also: My father, Lloyd Fons, who flew to the West Coast the day of my return to accompany me to the waiting family celebration. My mother, Venita Fons, who recognized the miracle that brought us safely home. And my friends, whose thoughts and prayers were with us all the way.

Special thanks to: My brother, John Fons, whose persistence in following his dream to be a writer encouraged my own progress with this book. Marianne Fons, my sister-in-law and first editor, who sat long hours after her children were in bed, sharing the Baja adventure with me. Also, the many talented people at Mountaineers Books who steered the manuscript to the finish.

My Baja journey would never have been completed without my partner, Verlen Kruger, who wouldn't let me quit, and the people of Baja who loved us as their own.

Foreword

Amazing—truly amazing—that seems to be the best word I can find, but it is still inadequate to describe the Baja experience. Baja was the most exciting—and dangerous—portion of my 28,000-mile canoeing odyssey around the North American continent.

By the time I met Valerie Fons, Steve Landick and I had paddled 20,000 miles of our 3½ year journey. In all those miles across the continent, I met what I consider to be some of this country's most interesting people—those who are full of life and have the courage to live their dreams. Unique even among those was Valerie, who had boundless energy and a great boldness.

People who have the boldness to pursue their dreams seem to attract one another, so when Steve had to temporarily drop out of our trip, I turned to Valerie to be my partner. We may have seemed a strange, unlikely combination, but we shared strong explorer instincts and a great zest for discovery. It seemed destined that we should share a special portion of life.

The west coast of Baja is not canoe country—the Pacific Ocean from the viewpoint of a solo canoe is awesome. To make matters worse, we got caught in the year of "El Niño," when the weather patterns of the entire Pacific went haywire. Unpredictable storm after storm, huge waves, and crashing surf were continual problems.

In all our research before we left Long Beach, California, we found no account of anyone who had paddled completely around the Baja Peninsula. Valerie's achievement was significant, not only for adventurers, but for womankind as well. As for myself, I had the pleasure of being there, and by the time I got to Yuma, I knew I had discovered a modern-day heroine.

This book tells the story of our Baja journey in a way that every adventurer can share, and Valerie's story proves that skill and strength are less important than spirit when facing the unknown. If we have the courage to keep it moving and follow our dreams—the best is yet to come!

Verlen Kruger
April 1986

xi

ONE

Inergia

My decision to paddle around the Baja Peninsula with Verlen Kruger was not difficult. Beginnings have always been easy for me. There is a Hebrew word for explosive energy: *inergia,* like a firecracker going off. That was my style. A short fuse with a big bang is never boring.

The idea of taking an ocean canoe journey ignited my imagination, but the reality of climbing into a solo canoe and joining a legendary man on the most dangerous portion of his 28,000-mile Ultimate Canoe Challenge was life changing. Paddling 2,411 miles along the desert coast of Baja was to be my own ultimate challenge, resulting in an adventure that cultivated within me a different sort of energy—an energy of endurance from beginning to end.

In this beginning, Verlen Kruger was standing on a floating dock at the south end of Green Lake, in Seattle, Washington. He leaned on his canoe paddle as if the stick were a marathon dancing partner. His rough-hewn hands were folded over the handle that reached just under his chin and disappeared beneath a full white beard. A bevy of curiosity seekers was gathered at Verlen's elbow. The *Seattle Times* newspaper had sent a photographer and reporter for a story.

"The idea sort of grew," he explained. "I guess I read too many adventure stories when I was a kid. Lewis, Clark, and Daniel Boone were my heroes."

"Were you born too late?" the reporter quizzed.

"No," Verlen said. "This is my time. I belong here and now. The canoe opened up North America and the canoe is still a legitimate vehicle for exploring a continent. I'm discovering for myself."

1

Verlen was at ease, even with a camera pointed at him and a microphone stuck in his face. He showed off the canoe that he had designed and built himself and talked to the crowd about his big trip. He and his partner, Steve Landick, were passing through Seattle on the route of their Ultimate Canoe Challenge.

When I arrived at the dock, I had never heard of these two men and so didn't pay any attention to them. This was the first race of June at the Seattle Canoe Club, and the excitement of the event held all my interest.

Many boats were already in the water when I got to the lake. Pulling a numbered racing bib over my head, I hurried down to the dock, looking around for a partner with muscle. Because I had arrived late, I was teamed with a skinny girl and the heaviest canoe on the racks. Even so, I was happy just to be there, my pent-up energy waiting to be released by the starting gun.

When my racing partner and I walked to the end of the dock to put our canoe in the water, the white-bearded explorer moved out of the way. He leaned over and held the gunwale of our boat as we positioned ourselves into the seats. When I looked up to say thanks, he stared down with the merriest blue eyes I'd ever seen shaded beneath the bill of a sun-faded denim captain's hat.

My partner and I pushed off the dock and joined the other canoes in the line-up. I didn't look at the other boats, but stared straight ahead toward the first turn on the course. There was a pause as I held my paddle in the air, then the signal for the start went off with a bang.

I lowered my head and dug my paddle into the water. There was a wild eruption of energy as frantic racers dug their paddles into the lake, shoveling with their blades. I worked my arms at 60 strokes per minute, slicing down and pulling back hard. All of me was driving forward, straining to overtake the canoes already pulling away from us. Our effort equaled motion but our motion was a little slower than the other boats.

After 10 minutes the pace settled into a steady grind as each team concentrated on the finish. The distance between the boats on the course lengthened. We sprinted hard, but we were still falling behind. After completing three laps during more than an hour of gut-straining paddling, we finished last.

We paddled back to the dock and pulled the heavy boat out of the water. I shook hands with my partner, reminded myself that this was just the beginning of racing season, and vowed to do better next time. The salty looking visitor was still by the dock, patiently demonstrating his boat to the crowd of viewers.

"Who's that?" I asked a bystander who was listening intently to what the man was saying.

"Verlen Kruger. And, that's his son-in-law, Steve Landick, over there." He spoke almost reverently. "These are the two guys on the 28,000-mile canoe odyssey." I edged closer to hear.

"The canoe is my home," Verlen was saying. "All of America is my home. Wherever I am, I'm comfortable and happy. It isn't just a canoe trip anymore, this is my life." Standing in a tripod pose with his paddle, he didn't seem concerned about impressing any of us. He pushed his paddle blade into the soft wood of the dock as if to anchor his restlessness and told his story. It was clear that he thrived on what he was doing—his eyes shone as if he were sharing a marvelous secret with us.

"I'm a traveling man," he explained. "I'm happiest when I'm moving."

The other half of the Ultimate Canoe Challenge, Steve Landick, was sitting quietly at the far end of the dock. He seemed to be about my age. I didn't want to sound like another interviewer, but I was curious to know who he was. The 28,000-mile wasn't easy to comprehend—all I knew was that it was a long way. Steve knew the meaning of the distance—he had paddled it one stroke at a time. I decided to sit down and ask him what it was like.

During our conversation I began to understand that mileage figures were inadequate to describe their journey. Big sacrifices had been necessary for this trip, and Steve didn't appear as thrilled with the adventure as Verlen was. He seemed instead to be waiting patiently for the journey to end. He mentioned his wife, Sarah, who was waiting at home.

Verlen was the one who handed out printed information with a map of their trip. Verlen and Steve had already paddled 18,583 miles, and were passing through Seattle on their way south. Their fact sheet was a glossy testament to their commitment: "Surpassing the distance around the earth . . . " it read. Their trip would be over three times the length of the current world record. In two one-person canoes, they would cover the entire route under their own power. No motors, no guides, no follow-up crew or support team on land or water. The canoes would be their homes for three years as they traveled through nearly every type of terrain, waterway, and climate North America had to offer.

Their trip was an exploration of North America that had begun in late April of 1980 at Red Rock, Montana, close to the source of the Missouri River. The team had paddled downstream on the Missouri to St. Louis, up the Mississippi and the full length of the Illinois to Lake Michigan, then crossed four great lakes and followed the Erie Canal and Lake Champlain through New York State. The Saint Lawrence floated them to Quebec City, and from there they headed up the Chaudière and portaged over the height of land into Maine. Early in October of the first year they reached the Bay of Fundy, then paddled on the North Atlantic before entering the

Intercoastal Waterway south of New York City. And this was just the warm-up!

Their route had been planned to keep them paddling south during the winter months. Both men agreed that racking up miles had little to do with choosing the route. They had set out to see North America by canoe, following the waterways and the seasons. Connecting this route between places they wanted to go and things they wanted to see sometimes took them on some dangerous waters and many times had them pointed upstream.

The first winter they circumnavigated Florida and part of the Gulf of Mexico before beginning a trek up the entire length of the Mississippi River. At Lake Itasca, Minnesota, the headwaters of the Mississippi, they paddled and portaged into Canada, then picked up an old fur trade route on Lake Winnipeg and traveled to Great Slave Lake, where they followed Mackenzie's historic route down the river that bears his name. After passing Tuktoyaktuk on the Arctic Ocean, they headed for Alaska. Up the Rat River, through McDougall Pass, they paddled downstream to the Yukon. After paddling upstream on the Yukon they arrived at Chilkoot Pass in mid-October of the second year.

They spent the winter of 1981–1982 at home in Michigan with their families, raising money to continue their journey. In March they returned to the Chilkoot Trail and picked up where they had left off. Then they followed the coastline of Canada and made an unscheduled stop in Seattle for a national media meeting.

After Seattle they would tackle the exposed Pacific Coast, certainly the most dangerous portion of the journey, then navigate the treacherous Baja Peninsula before starting up the Colorado River. They planned to paddle upstream through the Grand Canyon and upper canyons into the Green River.

Their longest portage, 66 miles, would carry them over the continental divide through the 7,400-foot South Pass into the Bighorn watershed in Wyoming. From there they would be paddling downstream for the first time in two years. Portaging again from the Missouri to the Souris River, they would follow the historic route of the French Canadian *voyageurs* through Minnesota and Ontario and into Lake Superior. Paddling up the Au Train and down the Whitefish rivers, they would traverse Michigan's upper peninsula. The Grand River from Lake Michigan to Lansing would be the last leg of the journey. The men planned to finish at Verlen's home on the Grand River in November of 1983.

Verlen and Steve had literally criss-crossed the continent on a route that included all five of the Great Lakes, three of the world's oceans, 44 states and eight Canadian provinces and territories. They were a couple of travel-

4

ing men going south on the coast, picking up sponsors and supporters as their journey gained credibility through time and distance.

I listened with interest to the details of the journey, just like all the other people crowded on the dock and the many people who would read the news in the morning paper. I didn't know then that the Ultimate Canoe Challenge would change my life.

By midafternoon the races had concluded for the day and the president of the canoe club announced that the Ultimate Canoe Challenge team would be crossing Elliott Bay on Monday. A national television crew that was coming to film a documentary of the two explorers had requested background paddlers to form an official escort for the team as they headed into Seattle. I made plans with a friend to borrow a club boat and join the festivities.

Driving home from the races, I remembered the first time I'd walked into the boat house two months before. I had seen a race announcement and had arrived at the dock in jeans, carrying a life jacket and straight river paddle. One of the club members sized me up as a landlubber, but he took the time to hand me a bent-shaft racing paddle and give me a little instruction. I wedged my feet into the bow of a tippy marathon racing canoe, and with the first stroke at the water I was hooked: the 32-pound racer glided as if jet propelled. Right then and there canoeing started to take over my life.

I had never thought of myself as a canoe racer, much less a canoe explorer. I had a beautiful home set high on a hill with a view of the Olympic Mountains. The address was Woodinville, but I could see the Seattle Space Needle some 20 miles away from my front door. The house was a "fixer-upper" that I had found several years before, when I was working as a real estate broker. I had spent a year hanging sheetrock and wallpaper, laying carpet, and setting ceramic tile. I gave my heart to the house and it showed.

A lot of dreams went into the making of that house. There was an over-sized French lop-eared rabbit in the backyard, waiting for children to play with. A pool table in the basement had balls racked for future teenagers and two friendly Newfoundland dogs stood by to lick and nanny my envisioned family, even though at 31 I didn't have any children and wasn't married. Many small projects were still unfinished at the house, but I had lost my motivation. The house had become a drain on my attention and a constant reminder that my life was not working out as I had hoped.

But I was busy and active. I had a full-time job doing map work and calculations for a geologist. My latest business project was raising financing to drill an exploratory well in hopes of finding hydrocarbons. I also wrote a short column for the local newspaper, participated in church functions, and was a prize-winning quilter. But paddling was becoming my favorite pastime and seemed to provide the spark of excitement that had been missing. No matter how busy I was, I went to the lake every day after work and exchanged my dress and high heels for a bathing suit and paddle. My new vitality was in canoe sport, sustained by training, friends, and scheduled races.

After the race that day in June, it was particularly difficult to go home. With my adrenaline still pumping, the silence in my house was oppressive. Settling my body into an easy chair was impossible.

The next afternoon, 60 local paddlers unloaded their multicolored boats in a scramble of barking dogs, life jackets being strapped on, and a shuffle of smiling friends revolving around the Ultimate Canoe Challenge celebrities.

We formed a parade from Shilshole Bay to Alki Point. Mount Rainier was on its best behavior, majestically visible to the south. The clouds had lifted their skirts and the skyline of Seattle was crystal clear. The sky spread out and the water was large around us. When the film crew arrived aboard a large powerboat, they wanted all the paddlers to circle the canoes and wave. We grabbed onto each other's gunwales, knocking hulls and trying to stay upright in the bounce. As the television camera focused on Verlen and Steve, the heroes shepherded their flock across Elliott Bay.

Something happened to me that afternoon. I was no longer on a river or a placid lake, and for the first time I could feel a movement beneath me that came up through hundreds of feet of water. There was an exhilaration, as if life itself were centered in that space. The big water had an energy that thrilled me. I was made complete yet charged with the sparks of excitement that promised more.

I had been in a sailboat on Puget Sound before, but the perspective from a canoe was different. The canoe was so close to the water that I felt a part of the liquid. The canoe moved with each rise and fall as if it were undulating in rhythm with the heartbeat of the sea. With each paddle stroke, I touched the water with my fingers, dipping into the diamonds formed by the sun's reflection on the surface.

Verlen and Steve hadn't told me about these feelings. Their route on the map hadn't spoken to me the way the water did as it pushed against my canoe. Once I was experiencing for myself the life and energy in the moving water, I understood why these men were on a long-distance canoe trip. And I knew I belonged there, too.

The sun was setting at Alki beach when we landed. As Verlen stood by his canoe, the light seemed to gather within his eyes. He was a soft-spoken man who made me want to listen. He didn't seem to be in a hurry, yet his words were urgent.

"I'm an explorer," he said. The waves lapped on the sand in agreement. "As the wild goose must fly south in the winter, and the compass must point north, an explorer must explore." His face was profiled against the sky as he looked out to sea and talked with the group about his love of water travel. "There came a time when I had to go. Reach out," he said, motioning to the world around us. "If there is a spark within you, let it grow."

I listened but most of what I heard were my own feelings inside, waking up and bursting out in a new dimension.

"I sure would like to go with them," said a man standing next to me to no one in particular.

Driving home, my head was spinning. There was no silence in my house that night—I was making a racket equal to the hallelujah chorus. In an effort to discharge my enthusiasm, I phoned a friend. By the sound of his voice, I knew immediately I had awakened him. Undaunted, I poured out my story.

"You should have been there," I raved. "It was fantastic. The water, the sky, what an abundant feeling of life! I've got this idea—I'm going to sell everything and go on a canoe trip."

"This sounds like another of your harebrained schemes," he said patiently. "Like the time you wanted to milk goats at the Puyallup Fair for world hunger."

"That would have worked," I argued. "But we didn't have a team effort. That's what I like about this guy Verlen. He's a real participant."

"What's he like?" my friend questioned.

"He's over 60 and he's shorter than I am."

"Doesn't really sound like your type," he interrupted.

"No, it's not him. He's married with 9 kids and 21 grandchildren. It's the canoe—the romance of the canoe," I continued. "But I do like his energy. Verlen's a compact bundle of life, and he kept talking about a spark within us."

"Well, that does seem exciting, but eleven o'clock at night is not the time for an explosion. Just what would this accomplish in your life?" he asked. "Settle down and go to sleep," he suggested as he hung up.

Given a touch of reason, I was finally able to go to bed, but I couldn't forget the Ultimate Canoe Challenge. And as it turned out, circumstances were not going to let me.

As I set about my weekly shopping the next morning, I noticed a box of stationery near the check-out counter. Across the top of each page were the words "40 Days and 40 Notes," and below that an ark full of smiling animals rode a row of stylized waves. I was so moved by the men's adventure that I bought the paper, and when I got home I wrote 40 short notes of encouragement, tied the bundle with a red ribbon, and decided to present the package to Verlen when the team left Seattle.

On June 17th, I went to see the men off at Edmonds beach. It was a quiet afternoon and there were few indications that history was being made—just the two men, their canoes, a pile of gear, and a few well-wishers.

The Ultimate Canoe Challenge team was headed toward the west coast of Washington, where they would paddle 3,000 miles south on the Pacific Ocean to the tip of Baja. Before they left, Verlen accepted my gift of notes and declared we must be kindred spirits. I asked him to open one note each day.

"Thanks," he said. "I may need some encouragement. No one has ever canoed the entire West Coast, and it could be pretty rough. I sure do appreciate these notes," he said with a smile. "If you feel like writing more, send a letter to one of our mail drops." He handed me a schedule.

After consulting compass and visual headings, Verlen and Steve launched their canoes and paddled into the distance, aiming for Admiralty Inlet and the Pacific Ocean. I waited until I couldn't see their boats anymore. Then, as I walked back to my car, instead of feeling longing, I felt relief. They were gone, and I could go back to normal. Thank goodness this temptation of upheaval was paddling into the sunset. Writing the notes had apparently satisfied my need to participate. I stuffed the printed schedule into my pocket and drove home, putting the Ultimate Canoe Challenge out of my mind.

I was sitting at my desk plotting points on a geological survey map when Verlen called on June 25th. He and Steve had paddled 260 miles and were in Westport, Washington. Verlen told me how much he was enjoying the notes and said that the weather was socked in, so they were waiting for better conditions. He said that a small group of paddlers, including the editor of *Canoe* magazine, was driving out to Grays Harbor to meet them and spend a day paddling around the sheltered water. He wondered if I wanted to come. I was very glad to hear from Verlen, but I had work to do. I couldn't possibly go. In fact, I didn't even own my own boat.

When I hung up I looked back down at my map work. But the figures didn't make sense anymore. Within a few hours, I had abandoned my chores, packed, and was driving the 150 miles to the coast with a borrowed solo canoe.

Verlen and Steve were a little startled to see me, and I was surprised to be there. Since I arrived with a canoe on top of my car, they could see I intended to paddle with the rest of the group. I tagged after them as they went inside a Westport cafe for pancakes.

"Have you ever paddled on the ocean before?" Steve asked.

I shook my head no. Wearing my enthusiasm like a badge, I hoped to get past the gate. I kept looking down at my plate, eating pancakes and wondering what I was getting myself into. I had never even been in a solo boat before.

"How much paddling experience have you had?" Steve asked. I gulped.

"I just started paddling seriously in April, when I began race training at the club, but I used a canoe when I was a Camp Fire Girl about 20 years ago, and I spent a summer on Babine Lake in Canada."

Steve was skeptical.

"Two years ago I paddled the Bowren Lake chain in British Columbia," I added.

"Well," began Verlen, noticing Steve's hesitation. "We won't actually be on the ocean today. It's too rough out there. After breakfast we'll head out to explore Grays Harbor."

Steve didn't answer. In fact, he didn't go with us as his mother had arrived from Michigan for a visit. Verlen led the way to the marina and I joined the others—a magazine editor, a writer, and an experienced sea kayaker—to paddle in the harbor.

It was Verlen's day off from the route and it would have been understandable if he had wanted to rest but he was just as excited as the four of us to see another corner of the harbor where he had never been and paddle a few more miles of new territory.

I was a little worried that I wouldn't be able to keep up, but my lack of experience didn't hinder me at all. The race training I had been doing had put me in good shape, but the energy I felt came from my spirit more than any physical conditioning. I felt a total rightness about where I was.

The solo canoe was a new experience for me but it seemed to suit my nature. Piloting my own boat was the height of independence, since I was both captain and crew. Every move was my responsibility, and I became intensely aware of the continual movement generated by the sea and the wind. There were a few waves to compete with, but the harbor was relatively calm. My borrowed canoe was the same design as Verlen's, and as I paddled next to him I felt like a twin. Certainly Verlen's experience was far out of my league, but I could feel the same joy that had driven him to the water. As I concentrated on matching his consistent, even stroke, I felt as if I could paddle forever.

The other paddlers were calling their boats kayaks and using double-bladed paddles. Verlen and I used a single-blade paddle, and he called his boat a canoe. As we paddled side-by-side, I asked Verlen to explain the difference in styles.

"A kayak is an Eskimo canoe. It's a boat you wear, built so you can wedge your knees under the deck and roll over and up without falling out," he explained. "I call my boat a canoe and I believe it's more comfortable. I'm sitting up off the floor, so I can sit here longer because my legs are in a comfortable position. I'm not set up to roll like a kayak, but I've got more stability and greater carrying capacity designed into the boat.

"I've used those double blades quite a bit," he continued. "But, I'm interested in distance. The double-bladed paddle will tear you up on a long haul. You can paddle faster on a short stretch with the double blade, but the single allows one side of the body to rest as you exchange sides. Single-bladed paddlers are drier too. You're continually dripping water onto yourself and wetting down any person paddling next to your boat if you're windmilling a double blade. I can't abide the splash."

"Is the single blade as safe on the ocean?" I asked. "What about when you need to brace to keep from capsizing? It seems pretty handy to have a double blade with the capability of bracing on either side when you need it."

"You'd have no problem bracing with a single blade. I saw you racing. You paddle more than 60 strokes per minute and changed sides at least every 5 strokes. You could easily put your paddle in the water on whatever side you needed to to keep from going over."

The other paddlers fell behind as Verlen and I charged ahead, talking all the while. At lunchtime we waited for the group at the abutment of a highway bridge. Birds flew out from beneath the beams of the bridge as our canoes nudged together around the base. When the other paddlers arrived, we passed a gorp jar and baloney stick across the cockpits, listening to the cars going by overhead.

The weather had cleared so Verlen and Steve were leaving the following day to travel 20 miles south to the next harbor. I wanted to paddle with them on the big water, but Steve warned me about the problems that could arise. The special Ultimate Canoe Challenge boats had been designed and built by Verlen with a covered deck for ocean travel. My loaner canoe was a manufactured copy of Verlen's design, but it lacked the attached deck and wasn't even outfitted with a spray cover.

Steve described what might go wrong. "If the waves get rough the ocean will swamp your canoe," he said. "You would be forced to make a surf entry and we would be going on. I'd hate to see you try a surf landing alone, but our survival depends on paddling to the next harbor before dark. You probably won't be able to keep up with our pace, either."

Steve was right. I didn't belong on the ocean: all the enthusiasm in the world doesn't make up for experience. The Ultimate Canoe Challenge team was continuing south, but I would go home. Perhaps now I could go back to work and quit dreaming about the big water.

I drove back to Woodinville, and when I opened the door to my quiet house, my familiar belongings welcomed me home. Early Monday morning I went back to work on my maps. Several normal weeks went by before the Ultimate Canoe Challenge interrupted my life again.

Most of my days began with a call from my neighbor. Usually Marie just wanted to chat, but when she called the morning of July 22nd she had important news.

"Valerie, those guys you were telling me about. I just heard on the news that one of them capsized in the Pacific Ocean. He's in Oregon somewhere, in a hospital." I was sitting up now, wide awake.

"What exactly did you hear?" I questioned her, trying to get the story straight.

"On the news this morning," she repeated. "One of those men on the Ultimate Canoe Challenge capsized in the ocean and lost his canoe. They say he's all right."

"What channel? Where did you hear this?" I grabbed at a pencil.

A call to the television station confirmed the news: Verlen had capsized. I quickly looked through the schedule information he had left with me. There was a mail drop in Coos Bay, Oregon, and a phone number. Taking a chance, I called.

The woman who answered the phone sounded calm. "Yes, we brought him in last night from the hospital. His body temperature had gone down to 91 degrees by the time the Coast Guard had lifted him out of the water."

Verlen got on the line.

"How are you?" I asked.

"Glad to be alive," his voice was reassuring. "Steve and I got caught in a sudden thermal squall with 60-mile-an-hour winds. We didn't have the boats catamaraned, and a wave bounced me the wrong way. My boat turned, and when I grabbed for it another wave came and took it faster than I could reach. All I was touching was the smooth bottom of my canoe. I've lost my boat." His voice caught with emotion. "My Loon had been with me all the way." He paused. "Everything, even my pants, were gone when the helicopter picked me out of the water." Then he laughed, and I realized he was all right.

"I climbed up on the stern of Steve's canoe and he began paddling to shore. We set off an emergency radio beacon given to us by a sponsor just last week. Only two places on the entire West Coast were equipped to receive that emergency transmission, and we were within range of one. The good Lord was watching over me."

"Verlen, if there is anything I can do, please let me know."

"Maybe you can help," he said. "I'm coming back to Seattle to regroup."

11

After we finished talking I hung up the phone and let the news of his rescue sink in. Giving into impulse, I sent a telegram to the Oregon address: "With you I celebrate the miracle of life."

Verlen arrived the next Saturday at the Seattle bus station with no luggage, looking as out of place as a beached whale. All the expedition trademarks were gone. He had no paddle to lean on and the familiar red expedition T-shirt was missing. He was wearing discount clothing chosen to cover his body until he could resupply.

When I met him I could see that the ocean dunk had not daunted his spirit; his smile was as bright as ever and he was excited about beginning again. Verlen was full of plans to re-outfit himself and put back into the ocean where the waves had turned him over.

Verlen's preparations for the Ultimate Canoe Challenge had been so elaborate that he had even designed and built another boat as a spare, and he made arrangements to have that one sent from his home in Michigan. While Steve took a two-week vacation, Verlen eased himself back into the water, purchasing and ordering new equipment and working on the boat. Though he had lost all his belongings in the Pacific, Verlen didn't feel sorry for himself. He was anxious to be paddling again and cheerfully went about the task of regrouping.

His biggest job was getting the spare canoe ready for ocean travel. This new one was a larger volume design called a Monarch that needed an ocean-going deck and a bulkhead installed behind the seat to make the stern of the canoe into a watertight compartment. When a Seattle canoe dealer offered the use of his shop facilities for modifying the boat, Verlen was in business.

After work each day I drove to the canoe shop to watch and help. Verlen had no molds or patterns to work from, but he knew what to do. Using a tough woven fabric called Kevlar and a special vinyl ester resin, he constructed a kayak-style deck. To reduce his cockpit opening, he added a bright yellow cockpit rim and a stern hatch cover made from surplus aluminum. Verlen worked meticulously, knowing full well that the quality of his boat was critical to his survival.

When the new equipment was assembled and the boat complete, I offered Verlen a ride back to Coos Bay. The very day we arrived at the beach, the Coast Guard reported that Verlen's original Loon had been found floating 8 miles offshore and some 80 miles south of the accident. A fisherman pulled the canoe out of the ocean and alerted the authorities after hearing of Verlen's loss on the television and learning that one of Verlen's sponsors had offered a $2,000 reward.

This incredible turn of events enabled Verlen to resume the voyage in his original canoe, and I found myself driving back home with a new ocean-ready Monarch on top of my car. Verlen was sure that the Monarch was a better design than the Loon because he had incorporated some improvements into this new model. But he wanted to continue the journey in his original Loon and his sponsors were interested in knowing whether his construction materials would hold up for 28,000 miles. Verlen instructed me to take good care of the Monarch in case he needed it.

With the boat stored in my garage, I couldn't put the Ultimate Canoe Challenge out of my mind. Every time I walked into my garage I stared at the beautiful canoe sitting beside my car. It was built to move. There were no straight lines or flat spots on the smooth body. It looked like a living thing just begging to float.

I began taking the new Monarch out for water practice on weekends, working in the surf on the coast and paddling in Puget Sound. I was floating the deluxe cruiser every chance I could get. The more time I spent with the canoe, the more my eagerness for an ocean journey grew.

What did I have to lose? By letter, I made a formal proposal to the Ultimate Canoe Challenge team to join their expedition. I sent the request to their next mail drop and waited. The answer came within a week: no. Their main reason was their commitment to each other. No one else could be a part of their journey. Steve also added that my lack of experience eliminated me as a candidate. I respected their partnership and knew that Steve was right about my limited experience, but there was something inside me that understood their journey as if it were my own.

I kept paddling. I entered many local races that summer, and as I became more successful a sporting goods company in Redmond began to sponsor my racing, paying my expenses and supplying clothing and gear. The Ultimate Canoe Challenge might rule the Pacific, but there was water near my own backyard I could conquer.

Early in October my telephone rang.

"Valerie?" It was Verlen.

"Where are you?" The last I had heard, the two explorers had been in southern California.

"I'm home in Michigan."

"You've got to be kidding. The Pacific Ocean is miles away," I said. "Are you ahead of schedule?"

"No, our progress has been stopped." He paused. "Steve's child, my granddaughter, Saba Dawn, has died."

I remembered seeing a taped interview in which a San Francisco reporter asked Steve to name the most beautiful thing he had seen on his journey. Steve had smiled into the camera and said without hesitation, "my little baby daughter." Now Saba was gone. She had died of Sudden Infant Death

Syndrome the morning after Steve had arrived home for a visit. He had seen his baby daughter for only a few days during her three months of life. Suddenly, the Ultimate Canoe Challenge was not the first priority.

"Steve has decided to stay home with his wife. He's not going to continue the trip at this time," Verlen said. I listened carefully.

"Steve suggests that I go on ahead with the journey. If he decides to come later, he'll try to catch up with me somewhere along the route, but he can't give me a date now. I'm facing the most hazardous portion of the Ultimate Canoe Challenge, but I have to go on. There are over 2,000 miles of wild, remote salt water between Long Beach, California, and Yuma, Arizona. No one has ever paddled around the entire Baja Peninsula in a canoe. About 1,300 miles of the route is unprotected coastline between Long Beach and Cabo San Lucas, the southern tip of Baja. The area is notorious for unpredictable storms, few harbors, and the largest surf on the West Coast. It isn't safe for me to do this section alone."

I began to see where his conversation was leading.

"My strategy for survival on the Pacific Coast is to have someone with me to hook two canoes together catamaran-style when the water gets rough. That's proved to be my best safety factor. But it seems impossible to find someone capable both mentally and physically who can be ready to go by the end of this month." He paused. "Do you still want to go to the ocean?"

I didn't hesitate. I probably could have phoned him back. I should have thought about the consequences, but immediately I said "yes."

TWO

Departures

There was no crowd to say good-bye. On October 25, 1982, when Verlen and I unloaded our two canoes and a truckload of gear onto the Long Beach, California, Coast Guard dock, only a few government workers stared from their office windows. My canoe sat heavy on the planking, the nose jutting over the edge of the dock like a springboard above the salt water.

Deliberately, I began to stow supplies. Each piece of gear had to be positioned for convenience of storage and balance during the journey. I tied a stuff sack with signal flares to the right of my seat and attached a series of small zipper bags to the inside of the canoe. I filled these handy compartments with suntan lotion, a first-aid kit, strobe light, sunglasses, candy, pocketknife, and waterproof matches. Under my seat I wedged a plastic hand pump, rubberized wetsuit, bleach bottle bailer, and an item called a sea sock, designed to keep the cockpit dry during a surf entry. Behind the seat I stacked water bags and a personal pack crammed with hat, tissues, whistle, pencils, paper, bathing suit, windbreaker, and my Bible. As we prepared for take off Verlen asked me again. "You know we're a team, why don't you let me carry the heavy stuff?" We both knew there was plenty of bulky, lightweight gear that could fill my boat.

"No way, I want to carry my share," I exclaimed.

An example of self-sufficiency, I continued to arrange my belongings. I had everything I needed for my own independence, even though Verlen was packing many pieces of identical equipment. At that time I hadn't begun to grasp the concept of a team. I was in a one-person canoe and my boatload of belongings gave me a sense of security. I had a lot to learn.

15

The canoe was covered with a hard-shell deck that reduced the open area to a kayak-size cockpit. In order to pack the bow of the canoe, I set all items on the floor in front of the seat and shoved them forward under the deck. A seven-inch round screw-on hatch cover interrupted the smooth surface of the deck. From this opening I could stick my hand down into the boat and push gear farther to the front. In this manner I loaded the bow with swim fins, snorkel, and mask. Then I added a spare parts bag bulging with extra shock cords, canned goods, sacks of dry food, and a fish net.

Next I packed a stuff sack of plastic bottles filled with vitamins, cocoa, cornmeal, rice, powdered milk, pancake mix, and fruit drink where it would be within easy reach. I also stowed my sleeping bag in the bow, protected in a waterproof stuff sack. A stainless cook kit rested just ahead of the foot brace. There was barely enough room left for me.

Newspaper reporters who arrived at the dock devoted most of their attention to Verlen. As my partner leaned over his canoe, fitting in each package, the photographers snapped a black and white record.

Verlen was famous. He arrived at the Long Beach dock with 21,000 miles of the Ultimate Canoe Challenge route behind him. Paddling around the Baja Peninsula would be only a small portion of his incredible 3½-year journey. I was a rookie, and my reputation was nonexistent. The reporters politely asked my name and passed me by, figuring I was unlikely to log any victorious finish on this adventure. My attempt was not news.

The reporters were asking Verlen lots of questions. They didn't seem as interested in where he was going as how far he had come. Verlen's story hadn't changed since I had heard his answers in Seattle, except for the miles of adventure that had brought him down the West Coast.

"It seems like the most natural thing to do," Verlen explained. "The contentment I feel while paddling tells me I am where I want to be. I'm following a dream."

The reporters were taking notes as fast as they could write. I felt as if this were a dream and I might wake up any moment. I kept busy packing. Behind my seat the stern of the boat was sealed by a bulkhead for dry storage and flotation in case I capsized. The rear portion of the deck had a 14- by 16-inch hinged access door to the rear compartment. I unlatched the clips on the hatch and began filling the stern. In went my tent, clothing bag, extra maps, books, toilet articles, and 100 pounds of dehydrated food and snacks. I also stored batteries, epoxy, sea soap, a kerosene stove, water purifiers, extra toggles, surveyor's tape, and sponges in the back compartment.

I strapped my life jacket on the rear deck of the canoe, bungied bedroll fashion behind the rear hatch. My compass fit on the forward deck alongside maps in a plastic cover. I tied a spare paddle under the lip of the forward deck.

My brand new camera, my most valuable piece of equipment, went in last. Testing the waterproof lock on the carrying case, I opened the package and closed it once more, just to make sure I had followed the directions and no water would seep in. Then I tucked away all my film, lenses, and the precious camera body.

A reporter was still questioning Verlen, trying to understand what would make anyone paddle a canoe more than the distance around the globe. I shifted impatiently from one foot to another. Here I was on a dock many miles from home. There was no racing bib to pull over my head, yet I knew that the biggest event of my life was about to begin.

I wondered what I would say if one of the reporters asked me a question. The last time I had discussed the journey with someone I had prompted a dramatic reaction.

A week earlier, in the rush of organizing equipment and settling my affairs, I had managed a last minute appointment at the beauty shop. A stranger armed with scissors greeted me in the plush salon and started asking questions. Where I had been didn't seem important at all to this woman. She was only interested in where I was going.

After a brisk soaping, I sank dripping and vulnerable into her swivel chair. I looked up into the mirror to explain my case.

"Cut my hair so it will be easy to care for, I'm going on a canoe trip."

"Yes, 2,411 miles beginning at Long Beach, California, paddling south on the Pacific Ocean."

The woman's eyes were getting larger.

"I'm going to circumnavigate the entire Baja Peninsula in a solo canoe."

She hadn't started cutting yet.

"When I arrive at the southern tip of the Baja at Cabo San Lucas, I'll be turning north and paddling up the Sea of Cortez. Then I'll follow a salinity canal to Yuma, Arizona."

It helped to go over things in my mind.

"How long will this take?" she asked the crucial question.

"Three and a half months of paddling. I don't need a permanent. The sun will be hot and my hair may frizz. Just give me an easy-care style. I have some special sea soap that makes suds in salt water, but I don't expect I'll be washing my hair very often."

Inspired and immediately claiming an involvement in the trip, she seemed to know more about the upcoming adventure than I did. In fact, she didn't ask anymore questions. In charge of an expedition coiffeur, her decision was simple—a pixie cut.

Change, I hated it. Meeting myself as a pixie was a shock. The long-haired woman I had known was gone.

A reporter moved away from Verlen and walked over to shake my hand, asking how to spell my name. I repeated each letter slowly, wondering what his next question would be. But there wasn't one. I had dressed carefully, wanting to appear capable and professional. My safari shirt and expedition pants seemed to me an official uniform, but I had ruined the effect by pinning a dark red rose to my lapel. Verlen sensed my discomfort.

"They didn't take any notice of me either when I first started," he whispered with a smile. "Let's put the canoes in the water."

Mine went in first, over the edge of the wooden dock, 17 feet of seaworthy curves looking showroom new. Though both boats were white, and similar in design and construction, it was easy to tell the two boats apart. Verlen's canoe was scuffed and worn, marked by its miles of accomplishment. A monarch butterfly, the only migrating species, was pressed on the deck under a layer of fiberglass and transparent resin. Verlen's name and hometown of Lansing, Michigan, were tagged on each side in plastic letters. The boat also bore an official bumper sticker of intent: The Ultimate Canoe Challenge, a 28,000-mile Odyssey by Paddle and Portage, Exploring the North American Continent, April, 1980 to November, 1983.

My canoe was personalized by bright hopes. I had bought red plastic lettering and inscribed my own goal on the deck: Long Beach to Yuma, 2,411 miles via the Baja. I added *Abundanta Vida*, meaning abundant life, on the left side of my canoe. The words Mariposa de Amarilla, yellow butterfly, just below the cockpit rim referred to the yellow enamel butterfly I wore around my neck and matched the distinctly feminine yellow cockpit rim on my canoe. My name and the logo of my sponsoring company were printed on the boat, and the words *Baja Viaje*, Baja journey, christened another surface. The boat looked like a circus wagon stamped with graffiti. It looked like mine.

Verlen pushed the stern end of his loaded canoe off the dock and held the bow rope to ease the front end into the water ahead of mine. Then he pointed his craft toward the open bay. I knelt on the landing and crawled over the side into my canoe, shoving aside gear with my feet. Just as I settled into my seat, I looked up and saw Verlen tucking himself into his cockpit. I honked a toy bicycle horn that was bolted onto the deck of my canoe. We waved and called good-bye. When I had 10 strokes to my credit, the photographers requested that we come back to the dock and pretend we were going off again, so they could get more pictures. I needed all the practice I could get, so we went back.

As we pulled away from the landing for the second time, I was grinning broadly, paddling with innocent delight in the sheltered inner harbor. I looked back over my shoulder and saw the reporters walking back to their cars. The dock gradually disappeared as we paddled farther toward open sea.

"Hold it a minute, Verlen," I called, stopping to take off my parka. A light windbreaker seemed more appropriate as we got underway and the exertion of paddling was heating up my body. After paddling a few more strokes, I stopped again.

"Verlen, I need a drink of water." I reached behind the seat and pulled out my plastic jug for a quenching glug.

A large cabin cruiser motoring into the harbor set up a rolling wake that was headed our way. I quickly picked up my paddle and turned my canoe toward the wave. My bow went into the air, then fell with a splash over the curve of the wave as it washed under me. The cabin cruiser cut its engines and slowed to the five-mile-an-hour harbor speed. There was quite a contrast between the several-hundred-horse-power engine on the cruiser and our muscle-powered canoes. We had no throttle, no sonar, no automatic pilot, not even a radio. We each had two arms, a paddle, and a canoe. For all the gear we had crammed into our vessels, the total suddenly seemed insignificant.

After a few more strokes, I set my paddle down again and rifled through a blue stuff sack looking for my hat. As I pulled the canvas topper over my head, my palms nudged the bare skin under my ears. I winced, reminded of my most visible sacrifice to the adventure. I pulled the hat farther down over my naked ears and picked up my paddle again. Our canoes were in line with the concrete breakwater, and following this entrance ramp we were being funneled toward open sea.

Verlen was several canoe lengths in front of me, paddling strongly and surely under his load. The stern of his craft was totally underwater from the weight of his gear. He even had canned goods and tent stakes strapped on his rear deck to accommodate the expedition overload. Twisting back in his seat, Verlen faced me and smiled, waiting as I caught up.

"Teammate," he said as he laid his paddle on the deck of his canoe. "We need to start this journey together."

I had been busy gauging my own reactions to my new surroundings, and hadn't given my partner a thought. What was he up to now?

"Let's take a moment to pray," he said.

We bowed our heads and closed our eyes to the distance ahead. For several moments we bobbed on the water in quiet meditation. I had a simple request—the Lord's presence on our journey. When I opened my eyes, the moment of peace vanished. We had reached the end of the breakwater, and each ocean swell was hitting the blunt dam and shattering in spray against the concrete.

Outside the protection of the harbor, the waves were uneven and choppy. Walls of unfriendly clouds foreshortened the horizon. I was afloat in my solo canoe, bow pointed south, paddling on the Pacific Ocean. The expanse of water around me was awesome. Rolling and breathing in irrational rhythm, the sea had a wild animal personality that was oblivious to my small canoe.

The beautiful boat that I had admired so much in my garage now seemed to have shrunk. The length of my control extended a mere 17 feet. My boat was a torpedo-shaped skirt formed from a cockpit waist. I sat at the waterline, a few inches off the floor. From my seat in the middle, a sleek white Kevlar nose created my new "body" with a tapered stern and aluminum rudder trailing like a tail. Within a few days it would be Halloween, and it seemed that I was going dressed as a boat. Why should I be scared? I was scaring others in my new costume. In fact, my family and friends were terrified. Marianne had telephoned from her Iowa farm kitchen as soon as she had heard the news. The traditional white curtains and blue tiles had spoken even more clearly over the wire than my sister-in-law's worried voice.

"Canoeing on the ocean is crazy. You simply can't go. Why are you doing this?" She became even more worried when she realized I was determined to go.

My seven-year-old niece took over the phone line. Unimpressed by my imminent journey, she talked about a movie she had just seen.

"You mean the one about a little boy making friends with a creature from outer space?" I asked.

"Yes," she replied. "That's the one."

"Well, Hannah, I've found my own extraterrestrial. He's on a long canoe journey and I'm going with him."

"Into space?" she asked with wonder.

"Into the biggest space on earth. I'm going to the ocean."

"I understand, Aunt Valerie. You're going where the raindrops go."

"Thanks, Hannah. Maybe you can explain that to your mother for me?"

I thought again about the conversation with my niece and realized that the movie we had been talking about did resemble my situation, but my own script was slightly different. Instead of waving good-bye, I had resolutely accepted my place and was prepared to become a teammate with a creature from another world. I was climbing into a solo canoe rather than a spaceship, headed toward adventure on the ocean. For the short time we had known each other, Verlen Kruger was still an alien. At that moment, he was paddling his own canoe a few feet in front of my bow and we were headed for Baja.

I glanced down at my navigation chart, folded inside a plastic map case and secured by a bungie cord on the forward deck. The map confirmed that the shadowy land mass in the distance was Santa Catalina Island. Twenty-six miles across San Pedro Channel, the island stood as a barrier against the full force of the Pacific. I buried my paddle blade in the water as far forward as I could reach. Sweeping with half-circle motion, I began turning the canoe south to follow the coast.

Small-craft storm warnings had been issued for the day, but we had barely considered the poor report. The momentum of our departure plan had cut us off from any second thoughts. The waves were jumping now, nipping at my canoe. Looking at the horizon, I saw a jagged row of waves like armored points along a stegosaurus spine. A conspiracy of wind had reshaped the smooth line into a turmoil.

My partner was picking up the pace as if he were briskly strolling down Fifth Avenue. In the past five months he had paddled over 3,000 miles of salt water as he canoed south from Skagway, Alaska, down the Pacific Coast. As the understudy, I wanted rave reviews. Instead, my nervousness overtook me. With the hectic weeks of preparation suddenly over, the 2,411 miles blocked my way like a brick wall. A dizziness began to grow within my ears. I had never been seasick before and didn't know what was coming.

Plunging my paddle blade into the water, I looked down at the waves. The water was swirling and bouncing. Each wave jostled my canoe, pushing up and then pausing to slide me back into the lower level of the trough. Up and back, as my bow climbed a hill of water and then fell on the other side, the waves curved and grabbed against the belly of my craft. My palms were clammy, my body was not my own. The sea had captured me.

Everything was going wrong. I decided to quit the trip. I could return the equipment and go back, telling people it had been a joke. Before I had time to complete my plans, I was heaving over the side. My nausea surprised me, as if a big kid on the playground had come up from behind, knocking the wind out of me and pushing my face in the dirt. But there was no dirt: the base was fluid and moving. Verlen was concerned.

"Poor kid, this is really a hard way to start out." He reached out to steady my canoe.

"Don't worry, Verlen, probably something I ate for breakfast upset me." I did feel better, as if clearing out my stomach relieved the queasiness. I didn't want my partner to know my dedication could waver so easily. Verlen set down his paddle and began looking through his personal bag for a remedy.

"Here, take this pill," he said, handing a tablet toward me.

"I don't take pills," I reported. The first wave of illness had passed, but another came tumbling over the false optimism. The bully struck again, pulling my head down and twisting my stomach until I cried in protest, spitting up into the sea.

"You're going to have to take this pill," he said more forcefully. But it was too late. My head and stomach were spinning. The waves were getting bigger and a rain had started. Wind was blowing and turning the water white. Verlen took command.

"Let's connect the boats. We've got to get you horizontal, you'll feel much better." Verlen clucked like a worried nurse. "Getting you down as near the pivot point of the canoe as possible will reduce the effect of the motion," he predicted.

"I don't want to stop paddling," I said weakly, struggling to find some relief. "I feel much better when I'm moving forward."

"Stop working and save your energy. The best thing you can do for the team is lie down. I can paddle these two canoes. Your turn will come later," Verlen promised.

Using two poles, Verlen had devised a system for connecting the canoes in a catamaran for rough-water stability. The waves were less a threat at this moment than my physical condition. To assemble the connection my canoe had to be on the left side of Verlen's, so he pushed my canoe forward and maneuvered along the proper side.

Verlen untied two 7½-foot poles strapped on the outside of his canoe. Holding onto my cockpit rim, he moved my canoe backward several feet so he could place one of the connector poles into the horizontal sleeve hollowed through the front of my deck. Pressing down a spring-loaded stopper button, he pushed the pole through the sleeve and out the opposite side of my canoe. He then pushed my canoe forward so he could reach the rear sleeve. Once the second connector pole slid into place, my canoe was skewered by two bright yellow spears.

"Hold my boat." Verlen gave the order and I held the rim of his cockpit tightly as the waves and motion tossed us up and down, banging our canoes against each other. I could see that this hook-up procedure would be tricky if the sea got rough: we were a midocean balancing act. And being seasick didn't help.

Verlen leaned forward over his deck. Coming off his seat he grabbed the front pole from my boat and slid it into the corresponding sleeve on his canoe. There was a moment of uncertainty while I held his stability in my grip. But with one pole secured, I could relax. He turned around in his cockpit and reached to connect the rear pole. The boats needed to be perfectly parallel for each pole to fit into its matching sleeve, so it was necessary to hold the canoes at equal distance, bow and stern, and steady the balance so the second pole would not bind as it found its place. Once in position, the boats gained instant stability—one canoe served as an outrigger for the other.

We were now connected side by side, with the ends of the poles sticking out from the sleeves. For effective paddling, the canoes would have to be pushed apart on the poles and locked at the ends of each one. Taking his paddle, Verlen pushed hard against my deck, shoving our boats apart until we were at opposite ends of the poles and I could no longer reach out and touch his canoe. When the canoes were in the correct position, springloaded buttons on the poles would pop out from either side of the sleeve to hold the boats securely four feet apart. The stern of my canoe was still sliding on the pole, so I knew the button had not popped out. As I turned around and tapped the depressed button with my finger, a wave caught my canoe and pushed the stern hard along the pole. My finger went into the sleeve with the flattened button. I howled and yanked my finger back: a circular bite of skin had been removed. I looked at my mangled, bleeding fingertip and began to wonder about sharks. I picked up my paddle and looked through the surf toward shore.

"This is it, Verlen. I'm going in."

"Put the paddle down, Valerie. You can't paddle through the surf."

"I'm feeling better," I lied, wanting to help paddle us to shore as soon as possible. The surf didn't look all that menacing.

"You'll be feeling worse when you crash into those breakers. We're committed until the next harbor. Newport Beach is about 14 miles ahead. Just relax," Verlen cautioned.

"I'll stop paddling when I feel sick again," I said, just as I heaved over the side another time.

"Put the paddle down or I'm going to take it away from you," he vowed. I could have saved myself a lot of trouble if I had just listened to Verlen from the beginning. He grabbed the paddle out of my hand.

I sat back weakly in my seat, scrunching down until my head rested against the back of my cockpit. Verlen had to use a stronger stroke to paddle with the extra weight of my canoe. My boat weighed 75 pounds empty, and Verlen's was 60. With food, water, gear, and ourselves, the catamaraned canoes totaled over 1,000 pounds. Our normal three-mile-per-hour pace was slowed to two.

Verlen was quiet and busy working. He had been right: lying down made my dizziness bearable, but the slightest movement to sit up irritated my system. I wanted out of the boat. I knew I couldn't make it to Newport Bay, 12 miles away. Luckily, I wouldn't have to—there was a ladder up ahead.

Artist Georgia O'Keefe once did a painting of a ladder suspended in a

23

star-filled sky. I never understood that painting until I saw my ladder at Huntington Beach: up ahead a long pier edged out into the ocean, and from it a metal ladder was hanging to the water.

Verlen steered the canoes to the piling and I grabbed onto the ladder, eased my way out of the canoe, and pulled myself up to the solid platform. When I reached the flat surface of the elevated dock I got down on all fours and crawled into a corner. Then I noticed that a small crowd of people fishing on the other side of the pier had turned to watch. The ladder had led me into a fenced area at the end of the dock complete with a guard who was approaching to shoo me away. But he immediately realized I wasn't in any condition to damage the private compound, and without a word he turned and left me lying there undisturbed.

Verlen had a tougher time getting settled. He was working with the catamaraned canoes, tying them off, paddling his boat to the ladder so he could climb aboard. I watched him through the space between the planking before I fell asleep.

When I came to I was covered by a tarp and my partner was sitting patiently beside me, looking out over the ocean. He had a jar of banana bread opened and a jug of water ready to revive me.

"Here, take this pill," he said softly, as he handed me the tiny pink tablet. "It's going to take you a while. You can't put a person in the middle of the ocean and expect anyone to function top notch the first day. You'll be all right. There are just a lot of adjustments you'll need to get through. But we have to go on." He seemed to know how things would work. It sounded as if he had already been here. I suppose he had—21,000 miles worth.

I took the pill, nibbled at the bread, and slowly sucked at the water jug. Looking through the crack in the planking I could see the two canoes, parked together down below. Verlen was right, this was no permanent stopping place. The canoes were hitting the pylon and bouncing against the barnacles. I pulled myself to a wobbling stand and slowly descended each ladder rung to the waiting canoes.

By then it was midafternoon. The wind died down and the ocean began to settle. The sun broke through the clouds as Verlen paddled the canoes south. I lay back and made myself comfortable, accepting a weak beginning. Verlen paddled our boats 14 miles that first day. The sun was just setting as we turned into Newport Beach Harbor. With the last light we began looking for a place to put up our tents. The prospect of going ashore made me feel much better—I sat up and began pointing out possible landing spots. The harbor was lined with homes and private docks, so there was no open ground—everything was landscaped and fenced. We negotiated a maze of piers bordered with galvanized wire and security gates.

"Verlen, how about over there?" I asked, seeing a large building on the south side of the harbor. The structure was dark and had a wide open patio on the water side. "It looks like a swim club or museum." We paddled up to the dock and tied the canoes before climbing over the bolted gate.

"Looks good to me. I usually go for a Coast Guard station in a harbor as developed as this one, but I guess we'll settle here tonight," he said.

By then it was dark. Verlen began unpacking his boat and handing gear over the fence for me to place next to the building. Cook kit, stove, sleeping bags, tents, each piece was carried to the cement step of the building by flashlight and deposited on a wide porch. We were working to make camp, when suddenly the sky was full of light. A helicopter with a bright floodlight was circling. I began to cheer.

"Great, that light is just what I needed," I said, snapping off my flashlight. Now I could use both hands to organize our belongings. Then a patrol boat roared up to the dock and a police car careened into the drive. By land, by sea, and by air, they were attacking.

"This is private property," the megaphone blasted, pinning us against the wall of the building.

"Explain yourselves." An officer from the patrol boat jumped over the wire fence and came toward us with a menacing hand held beam.

"I'm Verlen Kruger and I'm exploring the North American continent by canoe." Verlen pulled one of his fact sheets out of a fabric briefcase full of papers. "Here is my calling card," he offered.

"Hold it right there, buddy," the officer responded, reaching for the sheet of information but cautioning us to remain at attention. The policeman began to read the paper, comparing the photo of Verlen on the page to the man standing by my side. They seemed to match.

"Says here you've got 9 children and 21 grandchildren. That's quite a family to leave behind on a canoe adventure."

"This is my dream," Verlen said positively.

"Well, this is private property," the officer snapped. "Who is this other guy on the sheet?"

"That's my son-in-law, Steve Landick. He's my usual partner but some personal problems have come up, so he's not with me right now."

"Then who is this?" the policeman demanded, shining his flashlight beam into my face.

"This is Valerie Fons, my new partner for the next several thousand miles of the journey."

Barely satisfied, the officer told us to pack up. The canoes wouldn't fit into the patrol car, so we paddled our boats, escorted by the official United States chase boat, to the Coast Guard dock. In the lights of the office we were questioned again. I could tell they had never heard a story like ours.

THREE

Sea Legs

At six A.M. I woke and stared at the tent ceiling, then closed my eyes and remembered my bedroom at home. It was painted a soft white, and I had stenciled an art nouveau border around the top of the walls with colored pencils. There were photos of my family on the dresser, along with antique perfume bottles I had collected in out-of-the-way shops. A stack of books sat by the bed and a cedar chest full of handmade quilts added to the homey atmosphere.

I opened my eyes again. The nest I found myself in on the Coast Guard dock at Newport Beach was quite different. My living space was reduced to a four-by-seven-foot tent. As early light came through the thin walls of fabric, I lay on the floor, surrounded by a clothes bag, snack-food sack, water jug, and notebook. The space was personalized by my dirty socks hanging from a cord strung across the ceiling.

If Verlen was still asleep I could lie there a little longer. The inflated foam pad and sleeping bag had fulfilled all the claims of their advertising, and I was comfortable. The only disappointing surprise was that morning had arrived.

I unzipped a small corner of the tent flap and looked out. Verlen's tent was gone, and he was nowhere in sight. Maybe he had left without me. Then I saw a dot of blue denim bobbing on the dock about 300 feet away. Verlen's trademark, his blue fisherman's cap, was already in place as he worked on the dock next to the canoes.

At that early hour the Coast Guard buildings were quiet. We had been told that a phone call from a frightened harbor resident had alerted officials to our presence the night before. Luckily, the Coast Guard had accepted

26

our story, and instead of putting us in jail for trespassing had offered us hospitality and told us to put our tents on a small corner of dry ground above the dock to the right of the Coast Guard compound.

I was surveying the scene from my peephole when Verlen came into view. His chest, covered by a cheerful red T-shirt, was a compact muscle machine. People said he looked like Popeye with his bulging arms. A white beard and moustache outlined his smile and made it even wider. His blue eyes were almost hidden by the fisherman's cap. I decided he looked like Popeye and Santa Claus combined. The energy apparent in his style denied the fact of his 61 years. As I studied my new partner, I realized he was heading straight for my tent. I quickly closed the small flap and held my breath in silence. I wasn't ready to get up yet.

"How did you sleep?" he boomed, knowing full well I was awake.

"I feel great today. It must have been my nerves yesterday. I'm going to be fine." I spoke convincingly through the tent wall.

"Come down to the dock as soon as you can. We've got to get moving," he instructed. "I'll meet you by the canoes."

I looked out the flap again. As he walked to the dock, I realized that from the back he didn't look like Popeye or Santa Claus, but just a person with calloused elbows and pants that bagged at the seat.

I began packing my gear, then pulled on the same clothing I had worn the day before. There was not enough room in the small tent to stand up, so I balanced on my knees to zip my pants. I smiled as I put on a bright yellow canvas belt: now I matched the cockpit rim on the canoe. This small sense of coordinated fashion gave me a moment of confidence.

Piece by piece I set my gear outside the tent, then got out to stretch. The sky was blue and the weather clear. The tent was still damp with dew as I dismantled and packed it. On the dock, my partner was busy mixing cereal for breakfast. Opening a plastic jug of cornflakes, he poured almost half the contents into one of his blackened nesting pots. His cereal dish was a medium-size pot from his cook set. The char from countless cooking fires rubbed off on everything the pot touched. Verlen was intent upon adding powdered milk and powdered cocoa to his bowl. Then he ladled giant spoonfuls of honey into the mixture. Opening his cookie box, he pulled out and crumbled four or five sweet wafers into the concoction. The last ingredient was a sloosh of warm water from his canteen. He began stirring, breaking down the powdered lumps with the back of his spoon. I was eager to learn, so I dished myself a serving equal to his and sipped the new breakfast goop.

Verlen chewed this delicacy bite by bite in a mechanical refueling process.

"Eat it up," he hurried me, realizing my cautious progress was far behind his near empty bowl.

"And did you take your seasickness pill this morning?" he asked.

"No. The pills you had me take yesterday didn't do any good anyway. I'll be all right today," I promised. Verlen looked surprised.

"The directions say to take the pill *before* you get sick. That was your problem yesterday," Verlen reminded me.

"Verlen, yesterday was a bad day for me. But I'm ready to paddle today," I assured him.

Verlen bent over the dock to wash out his makeshift bowl, using his fingers as a dishrag. He stacked the cook kit with a blackened wisp of well-used paper toweling between each layer of pots. He studied the spoon carefully for bits of debris, ran his fingernail into the curve of the design, inspected the utensil, and stuck the tool back into his personal bag. Then he packed the rest of his gear and began muscling his canoe off the dock.

There is an art to getting a heavily loaded canoe into the water over the edge of a dock. Pushing from the midsection is useless. The most effective procedure is to work from both ends, suspending the stern off the edge of the dock, pulling up on the bow rope, and coaxing the boat, stern first, into the water. The lifting portion of the task requires less strength with the water acting as a support for the stern. Imitating my partner, I managed to launch my own heavy canoe.

We were off to San Juan Capistrano, another seaside town 16 miles away. As we paddled out of Newport Bay I could clearly see the neighborhood in the bright morning sun. When we had arrived the night before the houses and docks had been veiled in shadow, but that morning I could see lovely homes and wide expanses of well-kept yards. I realized that Newport Beach, an elite seaside community, had no room for campers.

Expensive-looking boats were parked along sturdy docks. The sailboaters anchored in the harbor were just waking up as we headed toward the open ocean.

"Look sharp, Verlen," I joked, ordering him to attention when I noticed several people leaning curiously over railings. Playing along, he sat up straighter and paddled with an exaggerated dip into the water, saluting onlookers with his swaggering strokes. The entertainment was lost on the spectators but I was learning that my partner had a hambone sense of humor.

Even at such an early hour we needed our sunglasses, as the water surface began to glare from the reflection of the new day. We paddled off the morning chill in a matter of minutes and were soon stripping off our jackets.

What a different world a few feet of breakwater could make! As we paddled out of the harbor, the swells came to greet me. The ocean was populated by endless thousands of waves, and my canoe responded to each rise and fall like the pumping of aggressive handshakes in an overzealous receiving line.

Waves have been cataloged in scientific terms, studied in tanks and controlled chambers. Volumes have been written about their nature, and I had read many of the texts. Driven by wind from miles away and affected by tides, this natural phenomenon was usually described by formulas. But paddling in their midst was like riding a washboard of ripples on a rutted country road. Except my canoe had no springs to absorb the shock. I rode the swells, counting them like sheep. One, two, three . . . oh, no, it was going to happen again. Why hadn't I been looking at the horizon? My smile soon disappeared as I realized that once again I would be sick. I should have taken the pill.

"Don't worry, Valerie, just relax," Verlen said. Though it would have been a perfect opportunity for "I told you so," Verlen was again sympathetic. We catamaraned the canoes for the second day—I was resorting to training wheels. The only relief I found was to squash down under the cockpit, a stuff sack behind my head and my feet pushing forward. I snuggled down into the spray skirt and squeezed my shoulders below the sides of the deck. I lay there inside my canoe with the seat jabbing at my spine, watching the light filter through the sides of the boat. I could see the outline of water as it ran past. I was at rest in a floating coffin, looking down at my hands and forearms. Every so often a wave would go over the top of my cover and come in the hole at the top, drenching my head and filling my nostrils with salt water.

I stuck my finger out of the spray cover just to watch the sun on it and feel the warmth. Finally, I stuck my head out of the cover to report on my condition and tell Verlen that I was trying.

"You look like a little seal popping out of there," he said cheerfully. I wished he would drop me off somewhere. A wave of depression and failure hit me, and I thought about quitting. The details were unimportant—the main thing was to save myself. I knew I wasn't going to make it.

"Take it easy, Valerie, just lie back," Verlen said as he continued paddling. "These first few days we'll be flexible, but I can't tow you all the way around the Baja. Tomorrow you've got to take a pill before we get started." I nodded weakly. Only Verlen's confidence that it would get better and his paddling our boats allowed me to continue. I felt completely inadequate as a partner, and lost in the new ocean world.

My basic problem those first few days was shock: I was simply not prepared. Verlen had spent five years planning for his Ultimate Canoe Challenge. For him, the journey had become a lifestyle and turning back was never an option. The trip was his dream and he was where he belonged. I had cooperated with circumstance and jumped at an opportunity. Verlen's time schedule had given me three weeks to get ready. In that short time I had quit my job, sold my car, sold my Newfoundland dog, rented my house, stored a life's collection of belongings, found a sponsor, assembled gear, settled my affairs, and had my hair cut off. My good-byes were said, the bad buys were sold at a hectic garage sale. When the cyclone of activity blew itself out, I found myself set down on the ocean, in an environment of undiluted force and traumatic distractions.

I had made some drastic changes to get to the ocean, but compared to Verlen's detailed approach, mine was a silly whim of excitement. When I saw the 2,411 miles ahead as a barricade rather than a path, my enthusiasm evaporated. I lacked the deep-seated motivation necessary for success. I also lacked experience.

Verlen maintained that he liked my spirit—and to him, spirit was the most essential ingredient of all. When Steve had suggested that Verlen go on without him, Verlen had made a list of possible candidates to accompany him around the Baja Peninsula. There were two other women among the names on the list. Of all those considered, I was the only one who could rally a sponsor and be ready in the short time. Most important, I was the one who most wanted to go. Though I didn't understand how the expedition worked or what the price was, I could feel the excitement and importance of the men's commitment. I had already told Verlen and Steve that if anything happened to either of them I would go with the other. Of course, that was silly. I didn't have the experience to justify my declaration. I didn't take into account that I was a woman or the fact that I might not be wanted. I could feel the magic of the Ultimate Canoe Challenge, and it had overwhelmed me.

But the quality of spirit that Verlen was counting on was susceptible to motion sickness. All I could think about those first few days was abandoning ship. To my surprise, no matter what I said, Verlen steadfastly insisted that what I really wanted was to go on.

Verlen faithfully paddled us toward San Juan Capistrano. Arrival time is relative when traveling on the ocean in a canoe. Touching toe to sand would normally constitute arrival, but I would say we arrived at Capistrano at one in the afternoon our second day, since that was the hour I first saw the harbor wall. When we finally approached the public dock over an hour later, two elderly ladies strolling on the pier stopped to stare. I tried to appear at ease riding in my attached sidecar canoe.

"This is the life," I called to them—but oh, how I would have liked to paddle my own canoe proudly into the harbor.

Verlen tied off the catamaraned canoes at the dock and I climbed out to civilization at San Juan Capistrano, a fashionable southern California beach town. There were many small shops, restaurants, and a park within walking distance of the public dock. I found a remedy for the seasickness that had been plaguing me for the past two days—a walk on dry land and a soothing peach ice cream cone bought from a dockside counter.

We stopped at a restaurant where, displaying no queasiness, Verlen gobbled fish, chips, and soda, then asked for more. When he was finished, he pushed aside the plates and pulled out his map to make calculations. Counting under his breath he began to mark the inches from our position at Capistrano to San Diego. The map was a navigation chart with depths, soundings, buoys, and lights spotted on the drawing. One inch on the map equaled 234,270 inches of actual distance. Figuring with a pencil, he converted the inches to feet, then the feet into miles, and concluded that one inch on the map equaled approximately 3.7 miles of actual distance. Verlen figured the distance from Long Beach to San Diego at 29 inches, or 108 miles.

"Lucky for you we started in the United States," he said. "Gives you a chance to adjust before we cross the border into Baja." I knew what he meant. There are no peach ice cream cones in Baja. The navigation charts clearly showed the differences ahead. The maps were similar, but the United States charts were crowded with symbols: lights, towers, tanks, smokestacks, and developed facilities clustered at each landing. The map of the Baja coastline was nearly bare, with only an occasional detail line reading "fishing village."

"By the time we get to San Diego you should be feeling better," Verlen said, tracing his finger along the outlined coast. "We'll be there about four days. We'll get you a pair of sea legs," he promised. Verlen was thinking ahead. Surveying the charts with him appealed to my curiosity, but I was still concerned with the dizziness of there and then. I needed some comfort, so I found a phone booth and called my parents in Houston.

"Mom, I'm seasick." The confession came out in a cry for help.

"Oh, dear," she exclaimed. My father got on the extension. Dad had been a P T boat captain in World War II, and I thought he would be able to prescribe a treatment.

"I never got over it," he said, which was far from comforting.

"We're thinking of you, hon," my mother sympathized.

Reaching out in another direction for a remedy of love, I dialed my brother's Iowa home number.

"Nothing is perfect," he said encouragingly. "Everything has a price. Just think of the climbers who make it to Everest. I've read that when they reach the top their bodies are exhausted and many of them suffer from amoebic dysentery. You've got to forget yourself and focus on the goal. I know you can make it. You'll get your sea legs," he promised. I hung up the lifeline and surveyed the situation: We had come 38 miles; 2,373 remained.

"Focus on the goal," I repeated to myself.

Walking back to where Verlen was unpacking the boats, I looked down at my legs and wondered when they would be transformed.

Having learned a valuable lesson from the Newport Beach arrest, the second night we abided procedure and asked permission at the Coast Guard office to camp on the public dock. Word of our journey had been radioed ahead and the officer at the desk invited us to make camp on the dock.

The third morning, I did not rely on any store of personal strength, I simply took a seasickness tablet and began to pack. Once everything was stowed, I carried my small travel bag to the public washroom. Balancing my case on the edge of the sink, I arranged my hairbrush, lotions, and soap around the rim and looked at myself sternly in the mirror. Before I could arrive at any conclusions, a young woman about my age came into the washroom and began combing her long brown hair in front of the stainless steel mirror above the sink next to mine. She looked more friendly than the ruffian staring back at me from my mirror, so I decided to talk.

"You ever been seasick?" I asked her hopefully.

"Sure, the first few days on our sailboat I was miserable, and it's my job to cook," she answered.

"I've been seasick for two days," I confessed. "I took pills this morning."

"If your medicine doesn't work, try this," she said, pulling a small sticker patch from a pocket inside her bag. "It fits behind your ear and steadies equilibrium. I don't like taking pills, so this is what I'm using," she instructed, handing me the cellophane package.

"Thanks," I said, slipping the remedy into my travel bag. "What boat are you on?"

"The one tied off the dock named Morning Star. Four guys are aboard along with me," she continued.

"How do you get along traveling with men?" I asked.

"They treat me just fine. No problem. They've been gentlemen," she confided. "Who are you with?"

"I'm traveling with Verlen Kruger. He's a famous canoer."

"Are you in those little boats I saw tied at the dock?"

"Yep, that's us."

"I saw that guy. He's the one with the captain's hat on?" I nodded.

"He's built like a brick." I nodded again.

"I don't know him very well," I explained. "But he sure does know how to paddle a canoe. He's taking good care of me since I've been seasick. He won't let me quit," I laughed.

"Don't worry. You'll get your sea legs," she promised. I thanked her for the seasickness remedy, but I was even more grateful for her encouragement as another woman at sea. When she rinsed her face and wiped it dry on her shirt, I felt an instant kinship. Most of the other women I knew were home putting a teakettle on the stove and waking up their children. This friendly vagabond secured her long hair with a colorful ribbon and walked back to her floating galley to make breakfast for the crew. When she left, I stared back in the mirror, thinking about my womanself and my commitment to the trip.

Verlen had made clear that he considered spirit and determination more important than gender. But I felt that being a female on the Ultimate Canoe Challenge was an added pressure. To make matters more complicated, Steve had contacted us through our food sponsor the day before Verlen and I left Los Angeles. Calling from Michigan, he had announced his decision to come back to the Challenge. He suggested that I drop out and let the two men continue together; he felt a woman would mean slow progress. Verlen was in a spot, but he insisted that I stay. He reminded me that I had totally dismantled my life to paddle on the ocean, so he couldn't very well send me home. In fact, I didn't have a home anymore.

Verlen's and Steve's decision to go on the Ultimate Canoe Challenge was based on intense commitment and obsession. Paddling 28,000 miles meant leaving behind home and family for a long period of time. Verlen has said that people change in three years no matter what they are doing, even if they are staying home. Steve had said that if Sarah asked him to quit he would. But their wives never did ask them to quit because they knew the Ultimate Canoe Challenge was life to both men.

When Columbus discovered America, history never asked what happened to his family. I never asked Steve why he wanted to come back on the trip after his child died. But I did ask Verlen why he had left home in the first place.

"I had to go," he had said.

The magnitude of what Columbus was doing made it essential that he continue. Neither Verlen nor Steve was Columbus, but they were on a journey of discovery that covered as much territory as Columbus had in discovering America.

I brushed my teeth and ran a comb through my cropped hair. Then I zipped shut my small travel bag, took one last look at myself in the mirror, and walked back to the canoes, resolved to do my best.

Our destination for the day was Oceanside, California, where we would be picked up by Wayne Marsula and his wife, Loie, both sea kayak paddlers and fans of Verlen's. They had promised us a night's lodging and home-cooked food in exchange for the story of our adventures. Wayne also wanted to discuss the staging of our arrival in San Diego.

Anxious for another chance, I paddled expectantly out of the harbor.

The pills I had taken performed their magic—I hadn't needed the seasickness patch—and I was finally paddling my own canoe. That was how it should be—the ocean blue and tranquil, the shore brown, speckled with buildings, Verlen and I riding the waves in two sleek white canoes.

That day we were paddling to the distant mounds of haze 27 miles away, farther than the horizon, to the point where the land disappeared over the curve of the earth. Ahead I could see gigantic lumps of hills and mountains squeezing up from a thick atmospheric smoke, staggered like stairs to the sky. We were at the waterline, following the straight grain of the coast as it gently curved to the south. The land directly to our left was a long, beautiful beach backed by a sand ridge scattered with brush. We could see spray lifting as the surf pounded the shore, but I didn't spend much time staring. We were a half-mile away from land, and my world was the ocean.

With each stroke the water parted slightly for our canoes to pass. I pushed forward in a magic of motion created by my own power. I wondered what the fish must think of us, gliding by on top, close to their own speed, our white, almond-shaped canoe bodies passing above their heads. I hadn't seen any fish yet—it was impossible to see anything through the dark salt water. I was paddling on a thick carpet with no conception of depth. When I did think "down," the thought was so startling that I vowed to stay on top of the water with Verlen, and tried to look "up" into the clearer blue of the sky.

This was different from any trip I'd ever taken. There were no tourists here. I felt more like an explorer. I took out my camera to record the occasion. With Verlen as my first subject, I discovered how tricky it was to take pictures with the sea reflecting enormous amounts of light from the bright sun. Shadows from Verlen's cap covered his face and his sunglasses glared like signal mirrors.

I turned my camera toward the seascape and fiddled with the adjustment ring on the lens. Framed in the viewfinder was a very simple scene: two colors of blue with a line in between. I lowered the eyepiece and stared. With no trees or houses to lend scale, the expanse was limitless. But the significance I wanted to capture was not the sense of infinity, but the unique perspective of my exploration, so I focused on the forward deck of my canoe, including my two feet and soggy map case at the bottom of the frame. The sea blurred in the background.

As I turned to put the camera away in its waterproof pouch, I pushed and fumbled with the gear crowding in the bottom of my boat. Housekeeping was going to be a problem. Finding anything the first few days was nearly impossible. Upon arrival in Los Angeles before the journey started, I had spent two days resorting my gear. Even though I had tried to think ahead, determining which items I would need and where they would best fit was a real challenge.

"You'll never use that," Verlen had assured me, voting to throw out the nesting tea kettle in my cook kit. "It's too small," he said. "You'll be boiling water in one of your larger pots." Then he picked up a pair of my new socks and rubbed his fingers against the fabric. "You don't need those heavy socks. No matter what the label says, they'll never dry. Here, take some of my polypropylene ones. This synthetic fabric doesn't absorb water. You'll stay dryer." He handed me two thin, stretchy tubes of navy blue.

I listened to his advice, but I wanted to be left alone to sort through my packing. Staring at the assembled gear I saw each piece as a part of me to be chosen almost symbolically for my limited space. Besides paring down the essentials of living, my identity had to be packed in the small canoe. I added a bright swimsuit and stylish top to the bag of practical outdoor clothing provided by my sponsor. I hoped the mental lift of finding a colorful blouse deep in my pack might trick me into paddling a few more miles one day. I wrapped the clothes in a plastic waterproof bag and stored them in the stern compartment where they would stay dry.

Since we would be paddling through Halloween, Thanksgiving, Christmas, and New Year's Eve, I had stowed several holiday surprises in the stern of my canoe. One unusual addition to my cargo was a quilted Christmas banner. I had hand-stitched the red and green patchwork myself and it now fit, with a little tugging and folding, into a small waterproof bag stuffed far back in the stern. I had sorted through my gear and the impractical nature of this package continued to bother me.

It had taken hours to group and pack my belongings. As I finished, I took out the holiday bundle again and sat down on the concrete floor alongside my canoe. For several minutes I questioned the value of this piece of handwork compared to the weight and space it was taking up in my canoe. I knew taking it was silly, but when I remembered how much of myself I was leaving behind, I decided the Christmas banner was going to sea with me.

I had made many practical decisions—leaving the heavy socks, throwing out a third pair of shoes, paring down my supply of long underwear. Once out on the ocean and paddling I was pleased to find there was nothing I wished I had brought that I didn't have. The only problem was knowing where everything was and positioning it so a dozen other items didn't have to be moved to retrieve a necessity. Riveted to the sides of the canoe was a line that suspended several handy bags around my seat. This system worked fine but I had to unzip each bag to find my sun lotion or candy bars. The compartments should have been color coded. I spent 15 minutes looking for a can of peaches before Verlen discovered he had carried it all along.

And he had unpacked half the contents of his stern compartment before he found the can. I had to move my personal bag from the space behind my seat, which was continually soaked by spray and splash no matter how careful I was. At the end of each day I would find an inch of water behind my seat, even though no leaks were apparent. Many of my belongings were soaked.

I was also experimenting with floating bathroom techniques. Verlen had it all worked out. I noticed him picking up the pace and paddling ahead of me at various times. After a pause, he would empty a sawed-off top of a plastic bleach bottle into the ocean. The screw cap was in place and the handle held the bottle upside down for use as a combination urinal and bailer.

I had prepared a similar container. But when the time came to use it, I found it nearly impossible to get my pants off in my tippy craft. I tried to scrunch down and slip them off while seated, but my bench seat was mounted four inches off the floor, and by the time I wiggled and wobbled my partner would be nearly a mile ahead. My antics also jeopardized the stability of the canoe.

"Verlen, would you hold my boat?" As he stabilized my canoe by holding the cockpit rim, I leaned forward, grabbed the forward deck, and stood precariously balanced as I quickly let down my trousers, then knelt back into the safety of my cockpit.

"Hey, you can't stand up in a canoe on the ocean." Verlen was dutifully hanging on but becoming alarmed. Day by day he was finding his new partner was not the same species as Steve.

"Verlen, just hold my boat, and please look the other way," I instructed. Fitting the bleach can between my legs and balancing the canoe upright in the water, I went about this business as if nothing out of the ordinary was happening. Nothing at all happened.

"Verlen, you're going to have to talk." He looked surprised. I couldn't concentrate on my task with him in such close proximity.

"Verlen, tell me about your vacation," I prompted him. "What did you do with your family while you were waiting for me to get to Los Angeles?"

"Well, we drove to Yuma, went to the movies and saw the San Diego Zoo."

"That's great Verlen, tell me about the zoo." He wasn't catching on, so I chose a subject for him.

He began to tell me about the zoo, each animal and environment in detail. I did not listen but learned to make the most of the time that Verlen would occupy himself with his story. This soon became our standard procedure and I had only to ask my partner to "tell me about the zoo" and he would paddle over to my canoe, hold on to form a brace, and begin a story of monkeys, lions, or tigers.

By just after noontime we were halfway to Oceanside. We had paddled steadily for almost an hour when I noticed an unusual object on the water ahead.

"What's that?" I questioned, squinting into the distance.

"I'm not sure, looks like a boat, couple of fishermen inside I'll bet. They sure are moving around a lot. Maybe the fishing is good," Verlen decided.

I kept staring at the distant silhouettes, reasoning out the shapes. We were paddling only about three miles an hour, so there was plenty of time to discuss the possibilities. As we got closer I announced the mystery object in my best lookout voice.

"The fishermen are sea lions," I reported, delighted to identify a dozen animals sunning themselves on the crowded buoy perch. They looked friendly, with their whiskered clown faces.

"This is no zoo," I reminded myself as we got closer, wondering if the animals would bite. They looked smooth and velvety, and honked at us as we got out our cameras for a photo session. The buoy was alive with swaying heads, fat bellies, and slapping flippers. We spent almost an hour playing hide-and-seek with the animals. Our first close-up company on the ocean seemed a little shy. The sea lions skidded off the buoy and slid under the water when we paddled too close to their territory. A head would pop out of the water near my canoe, then disappear into the sea. Soon the buoy was vacant.

We paddled on, estimating our position at approximately 75 miles north of the Mexican border. By three in the afternoon we were still five miles from Oceanside, and the heat of the day had begun to wear us down. Verlen took an umbrella and projected the handle from a loop behind his seat, so that the bright red and white parasol shaded his head and shoulders from the afternoon sun. The ocean was still, with kelp beds hanging in the water like parsley floating on a thick soup. Examining the vegetation, I discovered small clams clinging to the stalks.

"These kelp beds are handy," my partner said. "Steve and I have tied up to a clump a few times and slept during the night when we couldn't get ashore. I remember one night in Oregon in particular. You've got to find a kelp attached firmly to the bottom to sleep peacefully," he warned.

How many nights would we be stuck at sea? When I reached down and tugged at a dangling kelp strand, it came up in my hand—not a very stable anchor. I watched carefully as the swells hit the patch of kelp. The seaweed seemed to soothe the ocean like a tranquilizer, dissipating its energy as if a blanket had settled over the waves.

"A kelp bed is a safe place to be," Verlen went on. "No waves break in a line of kelp." He continued to educate me: "No wind or clouds today makes it hot. Must be close to 90 degrees. The swells aren't as big as usual—this hot weather is settling the ocean down."

When Verlen turned around in his canoe to glance my way, I saw only the dark shadow of his body against the glare of the sun. The sea looked almost white and the sky was bleached with heat, which beat down like a weight on the back of my neck. The two days of seasickness had depleted valuable salts and fluids from my system, and by midafternoon I was flattened by dehydration. Scrunching down in my canoe, dizzy and light-headed, I lost my power to focus. My mind went blank: there was no energy to think of quitting and no energy to think of continuing. I was ready to surrender. Verlen's diagnosis was that I was suffering from a mild heat stroke. He hooked the canoes together and I lay back, taking frequent sips of water from my canteen to recover.

When we finally reached Oceanside, Verlen paddled directly to the Coast Guard station designated by a flying American flag, then hurried inside to phone Wayne Marsula. I crawled out of the canoe and slumped under a tree, resting my head on my life jacket.

When Verlen returned, he began unpacking and organizing a small pile of belongings by the curb in preparation for Wayne's arrival. The prospect of spending a night in a bed got me on my feet and sorting out the few things I would need to take with me.

"Do you think the boats will be all right just left here?" I asked my partner.

"I've never had any trouble leaving my canoe and gear anyplace in the last 23,000 miles, probably won't tonight either," he said complacently.

We covered the open cockpits with elasticized fitted covers and sat down next to our bundles on the curb. Within half an hour Wayne and Loie drove up in a van. I had never met them, but I put myself into their care and stumbled into a seat at the back of their bus. I fell asleep immediately, and didn't wake up until we stopped in their driveway.

"Verlen filled us in on your first three days. You've had a rough time," Loie said as she helped the men unload the gear. "Maybe we can talk tomorrow morning."

I was exhausted and could only think of lying down and sleeping. Loie completed a short guided tour of the house and deposited me before the collapse.

"This is your room for the night," she said, pulling back the covers on a large, comfortable looking bed.

When I stepped closer I discovered the bed was moving. After three days of seasickness on the ocean, my hostess was offering me a waterbed. The irony of the situation reduced my last hold on reason, and I began to laugh and cry at the same time. I leaned against a wall and slid down to the floor. The entire room was spinning. Verlen leaned over me.

"Get it together, Valerie." I could hear the worry in his voice.

"Verlen, it's a waterbed. They are giving me a waterbed." The whole house was rolling, and dry land was no longer a relief from the constant swells in my inner ear. I stayed right where I was, collapsed on the swaying floor. Verlen covered me with a blanket and turned out the light. As I was falling asleep I could hear the trio in the living room talking about our grand entrance into San Diego. I figured I would be lucky if I made it through the night. My dreams just about finished me off: seal monsters popped out of the water, but instead of showing their heads and disappearing like the ones earlier in the day, these visions lifted their distorted creature bodies out of the water and came after me, one by one.

FOUR

Vaya con Dios

On Halloween Sunday, Verlen and I paddled into San Diego Bay surrounded by more than 20 local paddlers in different shapes and sizes of kayaks and canoes. We were escorted the 17 miles from Mission Bay to Shelter Island in the midst of the festive flotilla. The parade had been organized by kayak enthusiasts and our friend Wayne Marsula. As we headed toward the San Diego harbor, the paddlers asked questions about our Baja journey and looked closely at our specially outfitted ocean canoes. The most popular query was, "Can I try your boat?"

"Sure," said Verlen, assuming that they meant to wait until after we had landed to make a tradeoff. But within minutes Verlen's canoe had been stabilized by a human catamaran as several paddlers sprinted to his side and firmly grasped his cockpit. The natives were overpowering us in a midocean take-over. Verlen climbed out of his appropriated vessel and swapped with a man in a skinny kayak. Two men were already holding onto each side of my rim, so I obliged by cautiously climbing out of my canoe and into an open two-person boat. The young man who crawled past me and took control of my *Monarch* soon scooted away in it, exclaiming that the unique canoe was "top class."

The warm welcome made me forget the difficult adjustments of the past week as our new friends reduced the ocean to a playground. Most of these paddlers were not experienced ocean travelers—the group was primarily a white-water bunch for whom ocean paddling was rare. The unusually calm weather conditions cooperated with our carefree attitude and supported San Diego's reputation as a water wonderland. The collection of open ca-

40

noes, down-river kayaks, and surfboats all floated without mishap. Joining this group was a relief after my discouraging ocean experience of the past six days.

I had never been good at remembering names. But since I had been paddling on the ocean I was developing a special concentration. And I was experiencing a heightened awareness of the people around me. Paddling on the ocean was a solitary task that made me appreciate the group even more. My attention was riveted on each person as I carefully tried to greet them and memorize their names.

The bright sunshine and encouraging camaraderie were the antithesis of a spooky Halloween. Instead of a witch buzzing by on a broomstick, a sailboat blew past our group flying a large banner with the message: "San Diego Welcomes the Ultimate Canoe Challenge." But the holiday traditions were not forgotten. Our parade into San Diego Bay included a masked green monster in a yellow kayak and other assorted creature disguises. We created a seascape of canoe-paddling goblins.

The ocean experience was requiring me to stretch beyond my limits, and the effort was provoking unfamiliar responses in me. For one thing, I knew that I was more tense than usual. In my 20s I had sorted through the question of "who" I was. Now, at 31 years old, I had to ask the "who" question again, and add the "what" was I doing on the Pacific Ocean. A small thing like observing the ritual of Halloween became a comfort within the upheaval. I stuck a bright orange inflated jack-o'-lantern on my rear hatch cover, and when the crowd finished trying out my boat I settled back into the familiar seat and pulled out a Lone Ranger mask from my gear. Hiding behind the disguise, I cruised up to the other boats and demanded booty. My request forced a plundering of lunch boxes as I collected a sack full of banana chips and cookies.

Since it was a Sunday morning, Verlen called the paddlers together and like a round-up of covered wagons, we circled with the bows of our canoes touching and the sterns fanning out like a star-shaped water ballet. Verlen led the assembled group in prayer before we continued paddling past Ballast Point and into the inner harbor of San Diego Bay.

The beach held a line of spectators and several cameras rolling video tape. The head of the welcoming committee, a city councilman Wayne had invited, awarded Verlen and me San Diego T-shirts and chamber of commerce buttons as we stepped ashore.

The gifts were a small token for the many new friends standing on the beach smiling at Verlen and me. The night before, Wayne had picked us up from the route and driven us to Mission Bay Aquatic Center. Many of the people on the beach had been in the crowd of over a hundred that had gathered to listen to Verlen's lecture on the Ultimate Canoe Challenge progress from its beginning to the latest months on the Pacific. During the intermission, Verlen had introduced me to the audience as his partner for the Baja portion ahead. I had stood in front of the crowd not knowing quite what to say.

"Why?" a lady in the audience had asked. A gentleman in the back row stood up and answered for me.

"If you know the reason why you are doing something, it may not be worth doing. Let the adventure happen to you," he had advised. The crowd had burst into a round of applause, and I sat down. I felt authorized by their acceptance. They were right to claim me as their own—I had not graduated to Verlen's caliber.

The newspapers had heartily agreed. When they recorded the Mission Bay lecture in the paper on Sunday morning, the announcement of the Ultimate Canoe Challenge arrival in town named Steve Landick, even though he wasn't present, and failed to mention me at all. According to the article, "several local paddlers accompanied the men into town." Maybe they had been confused by my pixie cut!

But the encouragement from the crowd gathered on the sunny beach compensated for all the newspaper inaccuracies. One woman offered a jar of homemade orange marmalade for us to take on the journey. Another kind soul clipped a small stuffed koala bear onto my seat brace. Glancing down at the stowaway, I could see the toy animal was hanging on for dear life.

"We can put you up at our house," one of the paddlers invited.

"Thanks, but we've got lodging arranged," Verlen replied. He pointed to a young couple standing arm-in-arm near the waterline.

"You're riding mightly low with that load," another paddler observed. "Why don't you send some of your gear ahead?"

"I figure the mails aren't reliable into Baja," Verlen answered.

"You're right about the mail, a package might never reach you in Mexico. But November is just the start of cruising season for hundreds of sailboaters going your way. Someone will carry your extra gear down the line," he said.

This particular paddler, with a sandy red mat of hair topping off his sunburned face and blistered lips, seemed to know what he was talking about. He explained that he had been down the coast many times in sailing vessels and had completed a 1,000-mile kayak trip down Alaska's Inside Passage. His name was Ed Gillet. Though Ed gave us some good tips, no one person was an authority and no one answer or piece of advice could prepare us for what lay ahead. We assembled each piece of information as if it were part of a puzzle, compared it with our printed maps, and calculated it with logic.

Verlen had investigated the route we were attempting. He had decided several years earlier during the planning stages of the Ultimate Canoe Challenge that winter months would be safest for paddling south on the Pacific Ocean. He also had in mind the eventual conclusion of his trip and arrival home in Michigan before another winter freeze-up. When Steve had vacillated about the journey, Verlen knew he had to continue while the weather was favorable. Though the surf is usually wilder in the winter, the prevailing northwesterly winds lend a helpful push to any craft traveling south. High winds and tropical storms are more characteristic of summer in the equatorial regions. We would be paddling beyond the Tropic of Cancer at a latitude of 23 degrees and 27 minutes north near Cabo San Lucas. Verlen knew the conditions would be to our advantage during those winter months, but we hadn't realized that an armada of sailors was also going our way, so this news from Ed was favorable.

One man in the crowd told us that finding water would be a big problem. Another person suggested we carry a pressure cooker and plastic tarps to collect rainwater and morning condensation. A woman joined in the discussion and said that if we ran low we could use a portion of sea water for cooking. The woman assured us we wouldn't get sick using a ratio of one to four and no additional salt. We didn't take a pressure cooker, but we did pack a plastic tarp for collecting rainwater.

"One of the marine stores is having a kick-off for cruising season tonight," another paddler said. "You should go and introduce yourselves. Tell the sailboaters where you're going. They'll keep an eye on your progress. The sailboaters are a source for water and your best bet for weather information," he explained. "Most of them are equipped with shortwave radios that have special weather channels. You also picked the beginning of the whale cruising season—they migrate to Scammons and other lagoons for their mating and calving season each winter."

"Looks like we're going to have lots of company on the ocean," I said, beginning to wonder what a whale would think of my tiny canoe. The afternoon went by quickly, and the crowd moved to a local restaurant near the beach, where we occupied every table in the place, consuming hamburgers and trading canoe tales. One experienced paddler felt the muscle in my upper arm and declared I had "some toughening up to do." I suspected he was right, but determinedly set my jaw and prepared to defend myself. He surprised me by chuckling and saying, "you'll make it, I'll bet."

It was dark when we cleared out of the restaurant. Jean and Ken Unitt, the couple who were going to host our stay in San Diego, waited patiently until everyone else had said good-bye. Then Ken led the way to their car and helped Verlen load our canoes on top and cram our gear in the trunk. As Jean and I sat in the back seat, with our heads touching the ceiling because of the bundles under and around us, I learned that Jean was a ranger trainee at the visitor center near San Diego Bay. She was just the right person to tell me about the marine life I would encounter on the Pacific. She began to describe urchins, sea cucumbers, turtles, and whales as we motored away from the ocean world and merged into the San Diego freeway.

Our plan was to spend several days in San Diego. Not only was the hospitality persuasive, but we also had a list of chores to be done before we crossed into Mexico. Early Monday morning Ken dropped Verlen and me off at the Mexican consulate so we could apply for tourist permits to journey south of the border.

Verlen and I tried to concentrate on the standard tourist permit form presented to us at the front desk. A few of the questions on the form were a little difficult to answer.

"Media de Transporte" looked like an easy one—there were even pictures to help the English-speaking tourist. "Just circle one of the drawings: car, boat, plane, train, motorcycle," the permit requested. There were no canoes pictured, so we put a big circle around the line drawing of a boat. The woman behind the counter smiled, and told us we needed a crew list.

"But, you see, they are canoes, one-person canoes. There is no crew other than ourselves," I explained.

The lady frowned and her gold earrings began to twitch. "Uno momento," she intoned, and began speaking rapid-fire Spanish into the telephone. We were sent to the fishing branch of the consulate and began our stories again.

"Uno momento." A crescendo of alarm went through the offices as we told our story.

"Impossible." That word I could understand. It was the same negative pronouncement as our English version. I looked at Verlen for a sign of hope.

"What will we do if we don't get our permits?" I asked.

"We will become invisible and go on." He wasn't joking.

The director of the consulate called the Navy in Ensenada. After a lengthy conversation, he turned to us and shook his head. "There is no way, señor, señorita." He tipped his head toward each of us in turn. "We cannot be responsible. The threat to your personal safety could create an international incident. We would prefer you do not enter our country in your canoes."

Verlen had come 21,000 miles at that point. Tangling with the Mexican government was certainly no bigger obstacle than paddling upstream on the entire Mississippi River or portaging the Chilkoot Trail. Having survived a week of ocean paddling myself, my determination echoed Verlen's. There was no way a man behind a desk could stop me now. We had to make the man understand. At first he would not waver, but we were persistent, stack-

44

ing news clippings and letters of introduction on the desk in front of him.

"We can issue you a tourist visa, but no further sanction. If the Navy in Ensenada or anywhere along the coast catches sight of you," he said finally, "they will pick you up from our waters. It is too dangerous, what you are attempting, and we cannot be responsible by granting permission."

After this startling conversation, we marched to the front office and obtained a fishing permit and boat permit. We had no intention of fishing and were taking no gear for the sport, but collecting these pieces of official authorization increased our confidence. At least we would not be deported over a legal technicality. We armed ourselves with as many permits as possible, hoping to avoid conflict with the local government officials in Baja.

While we were in San Diego Verlen wrote another installment of the Ultimate Canoe Challenge newsletter that was regularly sent out to a mailing list of fans who were following the journey. I used the time to put together an information sheet describing my journey. I outlined the route, equipment, and sponsor, including a short biography of myself. A woman at the consulate translated the text into Spanish and I typed the page, placing a copy of a Baja map and a photo of myself on the opposite side. This simple handout would be a way to communicate with the Mexican people, since neither Verlen nor I could speak Spanish. Verlen had a small library of dictionaries stashed in his canoe. He had been studying Spanish phrases and words for months, with the books propped on the deck of his canoe, reading even as he paddled, memorizing the Spanish translations. I began with the basics of communication: "buenas días" as a greeting and "adios" for use as I paddled away. One of the first phrases I committed to memory was "tengo hambre," I am hungry.

My brother had suggested that we fly a Mexican flag as a courtesy, so I bought the smallest one I could find and screwed one end onto half of a broom handle. Verlen installed a small loop at the base of my rear bulkhead so the flagpole could stand upright as a friendly gesture when we were at sea.

We spent many hours in a shakedown of our gear. Jettisoning numerous packages of dehydrated food into a large knapsack, we carried a 100-pound bundle to the San Diego docks and looked around for a likely sailboat candidate to play postman. Ed Gillet had given us the name of the *Vagabunda*, and we found the 30-foot sloop tied to a slip at the end of the harbor. We shouted a friendly "hello" from the pier, and a man soon appeared on deck of the boat.

"Come aboard," he said, extending his hand and introducing himself as Richard Bower.

Grabbing onto a deck rail, I pulled myself onto the sailboat. Verlen was right behind me with a helpful push over the top, then he came aboard lugging the heavy food bag.

We followed our host down a narrow four-step tunnel to the inside of the ship. Below the deck was a compact cabin lined in wood and accented with nautical print curtains hung at small portholes. The space was dark, lighted only by an oil lantern swinging on a hook at the ceiling. Braided ropes creaked outside as the ship strained at the mooring. I imagined for a moment that the cabin was a secretive rendezvous spot and we were the pirates. We sat with a map spread out on the center table, talking of adventure and places yet unknown. Within a few minutes Richard's wife Betty joined us as she emerged from a forward cabin, and her presence brought me back to the twentieth century. She smiled and welcomed us to their floating home.

"We're looking for a sailboat to carry this bag of provisions south for us," Verlen began. "The weight problem in our canoes has become a dilemma. In the past two years on my route I've picked up supplies as I've gone along, but this system won't work in the Baja."

"We're pretty cramped ourselves," Richard responded, eyeing our large parcel. "From what I read and hear from the other sailors, supplies in the Baja are sparse. American made goods are expensive and almost nonexistent. The quality of the food is questionable. We were told there would be no fresh fruit south of Ensenada other than limes and tomatoes, so we're taking potatoes, apples, oranges, lemons, and other fruits along with us in the hold." He opened a cabinet and displayed a supermarket of supplies. I was envious of their assortment, remembering the small stuff sack of plastic bottles crammed into the bow of my own canoe. Overweight baggage problems were shared by all travelers.

"We can take your parcel if it will fit into my upper deck storage. We'll be at Tortuga Bay around the middle of November. The charts note a fuel dock there, and I'll leave your bag with the port captain in the harbor if we don't see you there ourselves."

Richard and Verlen went up on deck. When they returned, I could tell by the way they were smiling that the negotiations were complete. The Bowers did us a great favor by agreeing to haul our extra weight and make a commitment to arrive on a certain date at a specific spot. Any deadline is a burden when leaving civilization and departing on an adventure. On the other hand, it was difficult for us too, giving over half our food to people we didn't know.

As we continued to talk, the Bowers began to share the excitement of our journey and we began to better understand theirs. The Bowers, like many of the sailboaters we were to meet, were a special breed. This couple had sold their home and put their savings into their oceangoing residence.

Nomadic and adventurous, these sailboaters would soon be our only link to the familiar United States.

Betty poured coffee for us and reached for a book from the top shelf. "I've been studying the history of our route," she said, handing me a volume entitled *Enchanted Vagabonds*. "This book tells of an adventure in 1933. Dana and Ginger Lamb sailed down the coast in a small dinghy, leaving San Diego Bay with $4.20 in their pockets."

Opening the book, I saw a photo of Ginger and Dana in what was labeled their "typical traveling costume." With red bandanas on their heads, cutoff shorts, and gunbelts, they were sitting posed and smiling in their 16-foot canvas vessel that looked like a combination sailboat, kayak, surfboat, and canoe. As I leafed through the story I came across the pair falling into a volcano and surviving when a boulder inexplicably rolled across the top of their escape route. In the next chapter Dana was bitten by a coyote. Dana and Ginger paddled and sailed to Cabo San Lucas and into the Sea of Cortez before crossing to the mainland and traveling into Panama. I realized I was no longer an armchair reader of adventure stories, but a full participant. Already I was comparing my first week at sea with this wild and historic version of a similar route.

Richard and Betty stood arm in arm on deck as Verlen and I prepared to paddle away.

"Vaya con Dios," Richard called out. I didn't have to ask him what that phrase meant. Verlen had the saying printed in large black letters on his paddle blade. It was a popular salutation meaning "go with God." One hundred pounds lighter, Verlen and I headed down the pier with visions of a future rendezvous with our new friends and necessary food bag in a place called Tortuga Bay, 570 miles down the coast.

Jean and Ken drove us to the San Diego harbor early on the morning of November 5th. We were going to put our canoes back into the water exactly where we had interrupted our journey six days before, so it was my chance for a fresh start. I was well prepared and mentally adjusted compared to the Long Beach departure a week before. The seasickness pill I had swallowed was working, the load in my canoe was lighter, and once we were on the water I found the paddling rhythmic and satisfying. Our friends stood on the dock, waving and hollering like cheerleaders as we paddled away.

"See you in Ensenada!" Jean called out, reminding us of their plan to drive across the border with Wayne and Loie on the following Sunday.

All morning we paddled steadily toward the international boundary, 16 miles from our starting point. Our last view of the United States was a large Navy ship anchored south of San Diego. Dozens of men crowded to the railings and waved. Looking up at the floating steel skyscraper, I waved back and clicked off photos of Verlen's canoe beside the giant ship.

"A little bit more to the left Verlen," I directed. "I want to catch both ends of your canoe in this photo. Now, put your canoe bow toward the Navy ship." Verlen was a patient subject, turning one way and then the other for my camera.

"Where are you headed?" a sailor shouted down to us.

"Baja," I said proudly, as we waved and paddled off.

By early afternoon we spotted a high, white marble obelisk set inland about 200 yards from the beach. We knew from our books and maps that this monument marked the division between the United States and Mexico. A wire fence was set in the ground perpendicular to the beach and clearly marked the line of separation. These official divisions did not impress me as much as a conspicuous bullfight ring built beside the border landmark. This structure seemed to embody the new culture we were now entering.

We stopped paddling at the border crossing and pulled a snack from our packs. Neither of us was especially anxious to make the break from the United States. Putting down our paddles, we floated just outside the surf-line. A westerly crosswind picked up, increasing the size of the breakers.

Verlen and I were spared a border inspection. No one came out to the beach ordering us to halt; we were in an ocean world of no nation. We saw no sign of the promised sailboaters either. Their course at this junction would be a straight southwest route to the Coronado Islands seven miles from the mainland. Verlen and I would be following the concave shore staying a quarter of a mile from the beach to avoid the surf.

The sea began to roll, and each swell lifted our canoes up and over the wave humps headed toward break-up on the beach. As the wind picked up, the waves collapsed in powerful bands farther from shore. The wind blew us toward the beach, and soon we were alarmingly close to the breakers. We paddled back out to where the waves remained safely curved in swells. I watched with fascination as the waves collapsed and shattered closer to the shore. The crest would mount and then pause high in the air before the face would drop away, an avalanche of water breaking from the wave as if half a mountainside were falling. To compensate for the wind blowing shoreward, we paddled with the bows of our canoes pointed a few degrees toward open sea while remaining parallel to the beach.

We counted on stopping for the night 14½ miles south of the border obelisk at El Rosarito. Several of the paddlers in San Diego had told us that the harbor there had a rock jetty projecting seaward in a giant U-shape, and had assured us we could get ashore. Though our progress had been steady, we arrived at El Rosarito well after dark and watched the lights of town blinking at us between the waves. Following a white flashing light, we located the jetty and began to work our way along the stone wall.

High swells hit the jetty and broke in thunderous claps. Spray from the explosive water covered the wall. We expected to turn into calm water when we rounded the bell buoy light at the end of the jetty, but the tide was out and the mouth was closed by breakers. We continued paddling down the shore, hoping to see another place to land, but the low sand beach went on for miles and the surf was impassable.

"Verlen, the people back in San Diego said we could land here," I said incredulously.

"You'll learn," he answered. "Most information received about conditions on waterways is unreliable. Most people can tell you the exact distance and number of stop signs to the nearest fast-food restaurant, but there are more variables when it comes to water. The people who had told us we could land were probably here at a different tide level. You can see for yourself we'll be paddling tonight."

Verlen pulled the brim of his cap farther down on his forehead. "Night travel isn't so bad. Steve and I paddled lots of nights. There are times when I don't want to be out after dark, but we've got no choice this evening. The weather looks stable enough. The wind is settling. Head your canoe further out to sea," he instructed. "We don't want to hit any surprises near the shore."

I didn't say much. We had paddled 32 miles since morning, and I figured we deserved a place to stop for the night, but the reality of the situation was apparent: there was no place to land.

"Can you manage cooking in the canoe?" Verlen asked. "We'll hook up and I'll paddle if you'll take the galley," he suggested.

My arms were tired from paddling, so I accepted the proposal eagerly. I was sure Verlen had delegated the better end of the deal to me, but soon I was faced with a string of unfamiliar problems. For one thing, it was dark. I found my small flashlight and put it between my teeth so my hands would be free to work. I pulled out bundles to look for supplies, unwrapping and organizing inside my moving canoe. The boats were hooked together, so stability was not a problem, but I had no outrigger for my stove, which teetered unsteadily when I put it on my rear hatch cover. I filled a pot from our drinking water supply and emptied a food packet of rice and seasoning into the container. Fiddling with matches and pocket lighters, I tried to start the flame on the stove.

Choosing a stove for the journey had been a difficult decision. Thinking ahead to the barren coast of Baja, I had reasoned that white gas or butane might be hard to find, so I chose a traditional model kerosene burner. The trick was to prime the fuel with enough heat from packaged burning paste to ignite the burner. The paste flamed repeatedly, but the kerosene never reached a temperature high enough to ignite. I used half the tube of burning paste before I remembered it was the only one I had brought.

Verlen was paddling steadily, not saying anything, so I was on my own. After I had used a whole box of matches, the kerosene finally caught fire and began to give heat. My stove was finally functioning, but the wind buffeted the flame in erratic bursts and I was forced to move my kitchen to the floor of my canoe between my feet, a space eight inches square. I kept my hand on the cook pot for fear a wave would disturb the contraption and pour the warming water on my feet.

After an hour of stirring and fussing, my efforts produced a burned, unpalatable pot of crunchy rice, a sorry substitute for dinner. Even in the dark the mess tasted so awful that I decided I wasn't hungry. Verlen resorted to a soda pop and a handful of crackers. We were floating a mile offshore, but there was no moon, and only a few lights were visible from the land. Dinner had been a terrible idea—it wore me out and frustrated my intentions. And I had gotten a chill from the break in paddling.

"We'll leave the canoes together and paddle in shifts," Verlen suggested. "Lie down and sleep, I'll wake you up to paddle your turn in a few hours."

Sleeping in the boat was a familiar procedure by then, but that time it was more pleasant because I wasn't seasick. Pulling out my sleeping bag from the waterproof pouch, I snuggled in my cockpit cocoon and wrapped for a nap. Looking up at the black sky I braced against the cold and hugged myself to sleep. Verlen woke me up just after midnight.

"Doesn't look like a big surf here. Nice beach up ahead, we'll try to land." His voice sounded groggy. The news came as a surprise. I was just sitting up when the first wave broke over the stern of our canoes, and we didn't have time to react. I couldn't even get my paddle out from under the deck. Though the ocean had settled to a deceptive calm, in the darkness of the early morning hour Verlen misjudged the height of the shore break where the waves collided with the beach. We were caught riding a wave bigger than we could handle. Sped forward on top of a breaker, the catamaraned canoes spun sideways in a line of crashing water. My canoe smashed into shore.

Verlen's attached craft lifted several feet above me on the next oncoming roller, and the second wave pounded in on top of my canoe, covering me under its force. I was buried in water and wrapped in a drowned sleeping bag. After the impact on the beach, the sea could not decide what to do with us. We were knocked against the shore with each wave, then pulled out again in the undertow. I was confused in the darkness, but I managed to swim out of the cockpit and untangle myself from my covers.

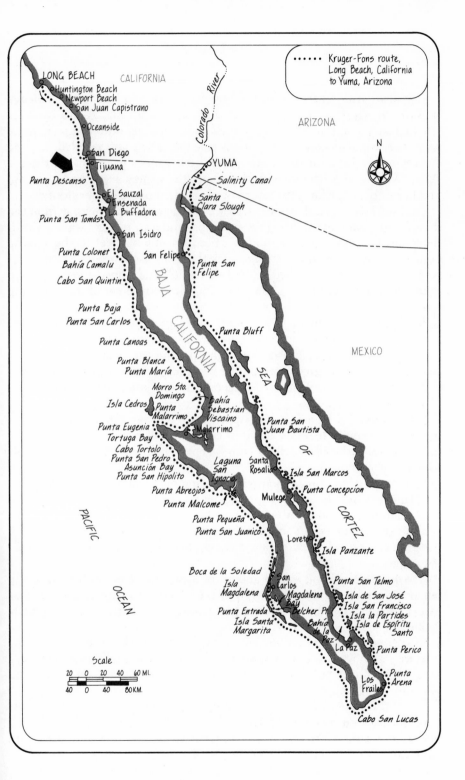

Kruger-Fons route,
Long Beach, California
to Yuma, Arizona

LONG BEACH   CALIFORNIA
Huntington Beach
Newport Beach
San Juan Capistrano

ARIZONA

Oceanside

San Diego
Tijuana   YUMA

N

Punta Descanso   Salinity Canal

El Sauzal   Santa
Ensenada   Clara Slough
La Buffadora
Punta San Tomás
San Isidro

Punta Colonet   San Felipe
Bahía Camalu   Punta San
Cabo San Quintin   Felipe

Punta Baja
Punta San Carlos   Punta Bluff

Punta Canoas   MEXICO

BAJA

Punta Blanca
Punta María

Morro Sto.
Domingo   Bahía
Isla Cedros   Sebastian
Punta   Viscaino
Malarrimo
Punta Eugenia   Malarrimo   Punta San
Tortuga Bay   Juan Bautista
Cabo Tortolo
Punta San Pedro
Asunción Bay   Laguna   Santa
Punta San Hipolito San   Rosalia
Ignacio   Isla San Marcos
Punta Abreojos
Punta Malcome   Mulege   Punta Concepción

CALIFORNIA

SEA

OF

CORTEZ

Punta Pequeña
Punta San Juanico   Loreto

PACIFIC   Isla Panzante

Boca de la Soledad   Punta San Telmo
Isla   San
Magdalena   Carlos   Isla de San José
OCEAN   Magdalena   Isla San Francisco
Bay   Isla la Partides
Punta Entrada   Belcher Pt. Isla de Espíritu
Isla Santa   Bahía   Santo
Margarita   de la
Paz   Punta Perico
La Paz

Punta
Los   Arena
Frailes

Scale
20   0   20   40 60 MI.
40   0   40   80 KM.

Cabo San Lucas

The boats had become potential bone crushers, and I dodged the heavy craft as the sea shoved the water-filled vessels toward me. Again I felt for solid ground, and that time stood in the sand holding onto the bowline of my canoe. Miraculously, Verlen was beside me. The water receded, digging out the area where we stood and pulling our canoes back toward the sea again. We had to cooperate with the ocean: the same sea that had swamped us was the only hope for getting our waterlogged canoes to higher ground.

Our boats were so full of water that we could not pull them away from the shore break. We stood holding the bowropes and waiting for a wave to wash the swamped vessels farther inland. Then, bracing our feet in the sinking sand, we hung on as the sea tried to suck the boats back into its power. Tugging on the ropes, we pulled toward the beach and hoped the next wave would float the canoes and allow us to drag the boats clear of the pounding waves.

"Bail!" Verlen shouted, trying to set me in motion. But I was in shock. The force of the impact had made me feel completely helpless. Verlen was bailing the water from the cockpits and pulling the boats toward higher ground. When the boats were safe, he began chasing gear in the water and organizing the debris. When I did respond, it was only to call off the names of the dead and missing.

"My camera!" The waves had ripped open my waterproof bag.

"My headlamp!" It was floating in corrosive salt brine.

"My food!" The plastic food storage boxes had been broken and their contents scattered.

Verlen assembled his sodden tent, leaving me to mourn the losses.

"You are going to have to move, or you'll get too cold," Verlen instructed. "You're shaking already."

The temperature was cool and my wet clothes stuck to my body like a chilly second skin. I knew Verlen was right but his advice irritated me and I got angry.

"It's your fault. I was asleep and all of a sudden we're crashing into the surf. How could you do this?" My words hit Verlen as hard as the surf that had thrown us ashore. I could feel him withdrawing but I couldn't stop attacking.

"You're supposed to be so experienced," I accused. For the first time my trust in Verlen was shaken. Finding out that Verlen was fallible scared me. I suddenly realized that I had no magic protection from the ocean, that even my hero could fail.

The surf crash had demonstrated the power of the ocean and our own insignificance. A fear was now born inside me and that fear immobilized me. I couldn't force myself to take Verlen's advice to bed down next to the ocean roar. At the moment, I couldn't forgive the ocean and I couldn't forgive my partner's mistake.

I also couldn't get warm and couldn't stop shaking. Verlen put me inside his own tent and piled every piece of dry clothing he could find on top of me. I knew that Verlen needed comfort, too. He realized that his misjudgment had caused our near disaster, but I had nothing to give my partner except a blank stare. We spent a rough night, sleeping little, listening to the ocean pound the beach, and reliving our crash with every incoming wave.

The next morning Verlen expected me to begin again. We spread out our gear to dry on the beach, but I moved in slow motion. Verlen made a concoction of macaroni, powdered cheese, and powdered eggs as a peace offering, but I was cranky and uncooperative. I looked at my brand new camera and zoom lenses: their journey was already over.

"We're bigger than these losses," Verlen claimed. "What we are experiencing is part of the risk of exploring a continent by canoe. I've lost seven cameras on this trip. I'd rather have a photo and risk losing a camera than take such good care of the machine that it is always put away and inaccessible." He kept talking, but I wasn't interested.

"Are you hurting anywhere?" Verlen finally asked. Slowly it dawned on me that if I was hurting, Verlen must be hurting too. My negative reactions were only making the hurt worse.

"Just my soul," I answered.

"Your soul isn't wet," Verlen answered logically.

"Don't you understand that I've lost my camera?" I asked. Verlen looked at me blankly. Years before, I had seen a "Twilight Zone" show where the world was destroyed by a bomb. There was one lone survivor who looked for sanity and found it in the rubble of a library, where thousands of books were scattered on the ground. The survivor seized that motivation to live and began to stack and sort the books in anticipation of reading. Finally, after days of assembling neat piles, he leaned over to open his first book and read. At that moment, his glasses fell from his face and shattered. The vision on the screen suddenly became blurred and the audience realized that his opportunity had been lost.

I had valued my camera in the same way the survivor coveted his library. The camera was my access to art and expression in this vast environment of water. I had planned to record and capture the journey through my lenses. Now I had lost my cherished tools and gained doubts about my partner's judgment. Surely Verlen had doubts about my judgment, but my limitations were no secret. The spot where we crashed was named Punta Descanso. I renamed it Desconsolar, which means "to grieve" in Spanish—and I was grieving. Verlen offered the full use of his camera for the rest of the journey, but at the time I was still too shaken to be interested.

There was no more time for regrets, though—we already had new challenges to face. Behind us was a sheer cliff, so the only way off our small portion of beachfront was back through the surf. It was midday by then, and the ocean surf had built up along the shore. As I sat on the beach and looked at the barrier between myself and the highway of sea, I lost what was left of my nerve.

Verlen methodically turned the boats, repacking gear and sponging out the remains of sand and water from our canoes. He had been watching the surf all morning, studying the sets of waves and recording the patterns. It was obvious even from my inexperienced observations that the waves were hitting the beach in sets of different sizes. Large rollers were followed by a series of smaller waves, and our strategy was to make our exit during the appearance of the smaller sets.

"You first," Verlen offered, knowing I was going to need some help. My boat was loaded and sat in the sand with the reach of the oncoming waves barely lapping at my bow. We pushed my canoe forward several feet and I jumped inside, settling into the cockpit. I drew and zippered the spray skirt tightly around my waist, held my breath, and steadied my paddle.

Verlen held the stern of my boat and waited, watching and counting the waves. The big waves crashed and continued onto the beach toward my boat. Verlen stood knee-deep in the water, still holding my canoe. He waited until the next wave broke on the beach, then pushed, and I went out between the waves. I had only seconds to paddle far enough from shore to escape the next collision of water and land.

"Paddle! Paddle!" I could hear Verlen yelling, then his voice was muffled by the surf. I could see the next wave cresting in front of me. The wave began to break, bubbling at the top, poised for explosion. I paddled as if my life depended on it—and I believed that it did. The wave broke over my bow and came toward me across the deck. I kept my boat pointed into the wave and did not hesitate for an instant. I hardly noticed the salt water that washed over me, I just kept paddling. The next wave was forming just ahead, and I dug my paddle frantically into the sea.

As I paddled through each oncoming wave the terror decreased. I was on my way out to sea. The waves no longer threatened, but were merely swells. Then I discovered inches of water in my cockpit—my spray skirt had buckled under the surf force and let gallons of salt water into my boat. Pulling the spray cover off I began to bail.

By the time I had emptied the water out of my boat Verlen still had not come and I began to worry that he would not be able to get away from the shore without assistance. I felt very much alone and all I could see was the swell of the waves racing toward the beach. After what seemed like a long time, I finally saw the familiar blue captain's hat and red-shirted shoulders coming toward me.

Verlen stopped paddling next to my canoe, bailed water from his boat, took off his shoes, and wrung out his socks, smiling and sighing with relief.

"There is good stuff in you Valerie," he said. His look was one of sincere admiration.

"Verlen, I think you must be part saint. Forget about my camera. I have."

We had learned our lesson—no unscheduled stops from now on. The harbors were our only hope of a safe landing.

It cheered us both that the afternoon was sunny and beautiful. We began paddling south, headed—18 hours away—to a harbor just outside Ensenada called El Sauzal, where our friends were to meet us the next morning. To arrive on time, we would have to paddle all night. I was just barely hanging on. I took one paddle stroke after another, but the motion was not smooth. I felt handicapped by my fear and the turmoil that had surfaced within me.

We paddled past Sugarloaf Rock as the sun set. The island, only 13 feet high, is about 2 miles offshore and 5 miles southeast of Punta Descanso. Dozens of sea lions were crowded on the rock, pointing their noses in the air and expressing themselves in loud honks and snorts. It looked as if the sea lions were having a party and fanning themselves with their tails. Birds could find no place to land between the sea lion bodies and chose to dive into the sea. Somehow the abundance of life on the rock made me begin to feel it once again in myself.

The sea lions were coughing and sputtering in the water around my canoe, and I stopped paddling to enjoy the commotion.

"I need this Verlen. Slow down," I yelled cheerfully.

Verlen continued paddling and looked over his shoulder.

"Isn't paddling enough?"

"No, not enough for me."

"It will be," he said. He kept going, but he did slow down.

I let him go and floated beside the lively rock. The company of the marine animals and birds worked on me like therapy. Their hullabaloo was a welcome disturbance. I let my worries slip away and filled my emptiness with the energy of life I saw at the congested rock. The animals weren't afraid of the ocean—they dove into the crashing waves and popped up again like corks. The enthusiasm and simplicity of the water-loving creatures consoled my losses. I finally paddled on.

"Wait for me," I yelled loudly. "I'm coming."

Paddling that night was tough. When I looked over at Verlen about midnight his eyes were closed, but he was swaying his body in the rocking-horse motions of paddling. When I asked him questions to see if he was awake he jerked to attention, but his answers were never in response to the questions. Then I asked him for a candy bar, and he fell asleep while he leaned to reach for it. I knew it was time to put the boats together. There were only a few lights on shore, and the swells rolled and blotted out the occasional twinkling. There was no discerning the shore from the water in the darkness. We kept moving, but since we took turns sleeping, we didn't make any great speed. When Verlen slept I could barely paddle the catamaraned canoes with forward speed, and I kept falling asleep myself.

Nodding off was a frightening problem, because of the possibility of drifting too close to shore or too far away. In the early morning hours I was so tired I hallucinated: I saw birds flying toward me and lights changing into houses and cars in front of me on the water. We tried to find a kelp bed to tie to so we could both sleep safely, but that stretch of ocean contained no such hitching post. So we continued through the night, paddling each other south. Though I understood how we had gotten into this predicament, I still saw no sense in it. I could see nothing in the darkness, and felt nothing but my own fatigue.

As the sun rose the next morning, I felt I could paddle no farther. We were rounding Punta San Miguel and had seven more miles before we reached Sauzal, a small harbor just north of Ensenada. The waves and wind picked up as if the sunrise had started a motion, and the dawn revived my partner.

"Why don't you sing?" he said. "Greet the new day. We'll be landing in two hours." I began to sing, songs of the ocean, hymns from my church back home. From inside of me came another bit of energy that I didn't know I had—just enough to get me to Sauzal.

We finally docked behind a rock jetty next to town. I climbed out of the canoe with my sleeping bag sack and lay right down on the cement dock. Verlen was not so desperate and his habits did not fail him. Like a cowboy tending the horses before himself, he secured the boats and fired up his stove. Soon he was setting a cup of hot chocolate next to my nose. That was Verlen's last attempt at communication. Then he lay down too, his head next to my head, and we slept.

About two hours later, Wayne Marsula's van rolled to a stop beside our bodies. Our four friends jumped out of the vehicle to survey the damage. They could tell something was wrong: our gear was littered on the ground, and the boats were 10 feet below us, floating inside the jetty. The tide had dropped and left them almost strangled at their ropes. Verlen and I had left San Diego bright and hopeful; our friends now saw us miserable and exhausted. As I woke up and untangled myself from the sleeping bag, Jean hugged me in an embrace that pressed life into my body.

Verlen began recounting the past three days of adventure, trying to make the story sound matter-of-fact, but the strain showed on his face. It was a great relief to have friends there to take over. Wayne dissected my camera and confirmed that it was dead.

"If you had just plunged the camera into some fresh water you might have saved it, but the salt water has already started to corrode the body and parts," he declared, showing me where the fittings and chrome were being eaten away.

"Let's talk about something positive," Verlen advised, looking in my direction.

"Let's eat, I'm positively hungry," said Ken.

"Tengo hambre," I confirmed.

We abandoned our gear on the dock and Wayne drove us to "the best Mexican food in Ensenada." Our destination turned out to be Cueva de los Tigros, a restaurant on the beach with a large picture window looking out on the surf. I chose a chair that didn't face the scenery. After the past few days, I considered the view menacing. While the others studied the menus, I headed for the ladies' room. When I caught sight of myself in the mirror, I began to cry. I was relieved just to see myself in the glass. Sitting on a bench in the powder room, I looked at the salt-stained, blistered hands in my lap. They seemed to belong to someone else. I was so glad to be alive and safe that I raised one hand and kissed it.

Loie followed me into the washroom and sat down beside me on the bench.

"You don't have to go on," she comforted. "I'll help in anyway I can if you decide to stop this madness. It isn't worth destroying yourself. Verlen is driven, but this trip doesn't have to become your obsession, too."

"But it already is," I said calmly. I was worn down, my clothes salt stained and stiff, my hair dirty and matted. I looked at the woman in the mirror: she had already changed. Emptying the sand from my pockets and the sorrows from my soul, I walked back to the table, subdued but resolute.

My partner was used to routine exhaustion, but that day he was still berating himself for the muffed calculation that led to the surf crash. His usually efficient body was drained of energy, but he had his map out and was calculating our mileage.

"We've come 183 miles," Verlen said. Obviously comforted, he seemed to relax. As he sat in the restaurant, the warm glow of good food in his stomach and the comfortable spell of supporting company put him to sleep in his chair. We walked him out to the van and covered him with a blanket.

Wayne drove us through the streets of Ensenada looking for a grocery, bakery, and laundry. We made stops that healed the exhaustion of the past few days, putting us back together with clean clothes and fresh Mexican pastries. Verlen remained prone in the back of the van, occasionally talking jibberish and making paddling motions in the air before falling asleep again.

Too soon our errands were done, and the afternoon was over. Our friends deposited us back on the El Sauzal dock. Verlen was awake by then and took charge of making camp on the cement. With one last good-bye, our friends left for San Diego—we would not see them again for 3½ months. As they drove away, Jean waved from the back window of the van and Loie stuck her head out of the front passenger window and called, "vaya con Dios."

FIVE

Yellow Brick Road

Verlen and I sat cross legged on the cement pier at El Sauzal eating Mexican pastries from a grease-stained paper bag. The only color on that gray day was a bouquet of yellow floats hanging on a fishing trawler out in the harbor and the yellow rain jacket snapped around my body. I washed down the fried cakes with bottled water, gulping several vitamins and a seasickness tablet.

The western sky looked dark and the eastern half was beginning to fume. Between the cloud banks, one clear path of blue sky was open in a southern line to our destination. The outlined hump of Cabo Punta Banda nine miles across the Bahía Todos Santos was barely visible on the horizon. We used the map like a giant napkin, dropping crumbs onto the wrinkled chart as we studied the route. Our next landing would be La Buffadora, several miles past the distant point and 14 miles from our current location.

"Bays can cause rough water," Verlen explained. "Bays make their own wind. Semicircular forms of land can incite stronger winds than the blow along a linear coast." Verlen searched the ocean before us, squinting as he tried to estimate the conditions.

"The ocean looks calm to me," I reported, glaring at the squared-off cloud opponents in the sky.

"We're not out there yet," Verlen cautioned. "The roughest spot will be around that point." He placed his finger on the map at Punta Banda. "Wind can zoom around a headland and mix with a tide coming into the bay to create some wild waves. The swells we've seen on the ocean have

59

been directional, but in a bay almost anything can happen when the currents and wind start acting together."

If we paddled from El Sauzal across the mouth of Bahía Todos Santos, our route would bypass Ensenada and lead us five miles from land at the halfway point. The safer route would be paddling around the inside curve of the bay, but the distance would double—and if the menacing clouds did collide in a squall, the resulting surf would make it difficult to land. Remembering the lecture we had received at the consulate, we definitely wanted to avoid the Mexican navy stationed at Ensenada, so we chose the vulnerable shortcut. Counting on the weather to hold, we decided to make the nine-mile dash across the mouth of the bay.

A Mexican dock worker beckoned to us from a cinderblock building at the end of the pier. Verlen and I started toward him, dodging the rusty machinery populating the work yard.

"Cafe?" he offered, bringing his hand to his lips in a pantomime of drink.

"Sí," we nodded, and followed him inside the building.

Seated on the floor were three men who looked up as we entered. Between them on the cement was a coffeepot plugged into an open wall socket and a scattering of paper cups. One spoon rested in a brown puddle on the floor, and a crusty jar of instant coffee was open and waiting. The place was devoid of furniture. This sheltered coffee headquarters of the harbor welcomed all seamen. The men's attitude was one of polite acknowledgement: we had joined the workers of the sea. Nobody spoke to us, though they were talking among themselves—I assumed about the work that was to begin.

We drank the hot liquid gratefully and hurried outside to pack our gear. I climbed down a five-rung ladder to our canoes, balanced on the reinforced deck, and reached for bundles as Verlen handed down our equipment. An oil slick on the industrial harbor had fouled the ropes tying off our boats, and the white hulls were stained with scum from the backwater. But a wash-off was in sight. As I pushed the last package into place I looked again at the sky.

"Let's get going. Those clouds aren't getting any brighter," I said, committing myself to the route across the bay.

Paddling out of the harbor, we steered around fishing boats and industrial tugs. When we had reached the halfway point of our crossing, the rain began. We pulled on our spray skirts to cover the open cockpits and braced for the storm.

The sky hurled pellets of rain down on us. Giant drops splashed and bounced until the ocean was a sparkling carpet of jumping bugle beads. There was no point in turning back, since we had already come halfway, so we pushed on toward the rocky headland of Punta Banda, which slowly loomed larger as we continued paddling. I bent my chin farther into the collar of my rain jacket. The weight of the downpour flattened the waves, but no wind accompanied the squall. I was surprised to find that the temperature remained warm, and paddling was not unpleasant once I adjusted the brim of my hat to protect my face from the stinging drops. The rain gradually let up after about an hour, then stopped.

"Hey, Verlen, you can come out now," I yelled to my partner. He had withdrawn his neck so far into his jacket that he looked like a hat sitting on a collar. His protruding nose acted like a ski slope for the rain drops still falling from his saturated cap brim. I took off my own hat and shook the rain puddles off my spray skirt. The sky remained gray and swollen, as if bruised from the force of the afternoon deluge.

As we neared the point, we discovered a ragged ledge of rocks extending into the sea northwest of the headland. I voted to paddle around the obstructions, but Verlen headed straight for the maze and threaded his way through it.

I cautiously followed Verlen, paddling my canoe so closely behind his boat that I bumped his stern. The ocean rocks unnerved me—as the waves sucked and knocked against the shiny black surfaces, the humps looked as if they were moving toward me faster than I could paddle away. It was only a partial help to remind myself that the rocks were stationary. As Verlen navigated the rocks, I dubbed him "point captain." The maneuver was perfectly suited for his disposition—he calmly led us around the point and into the unknown.

Several miles past Punta Banda's rock garden, we paddled into the harbor of La Buffadora. Here, too, the land was jagged and rocky. La Buffadora was sheltered in a quiet web at the base of the finger projections of rock outcroppings. The town was built on a hillside ringing the sea, with small shacks and trailers clustered together on the rock ledges. On the north side of the village we saw the blowhole that gives the town its name. As each wave hit the shore it was blasted straight up out of the top of a natural rock tunnel, then showered back on itself. Mexicans named the spot La Buffadora, which means "buffalo snort," because of the loud exhaling clap accompanying each blast of water.

Verlen hesitated as we approached the shore break. Ever since the surf crash at Descanso, he had been extra cautious when it came time to land. Getting through the surf was risky, but it contained a sure reward and wasn't nearly as frightening as navigating a rocky point, so I took the lead. Timing the waves, I rode in on the swells, back-paddled when the wave did not suit me, then came ashore right behind a tumbling breaker. I quickly jumped out of the boat and held onto the bowrope, ready for the next wave to float my canoe so I could pull the craft farther up on the sand. Verlen came in then, traveling on the back of a wave, following the foam onto the

61

beach. I hurried over to his canoe and grabbed the bowline as he climbed out of the boat.

"Okay," he said. "I may be the point captain, but you're the surf queen."

Verlen slipped his paddle through the loop in the bowrope several feet from the nose of his canoe. With one of us on each side of the rope, we walked ahead with our thighs pressing against the paddle shaft, pushing forward like plow ponies dragging the heavily loaded canoe to higher ground.

As I sat back on the rock ledge to rest a moment, feeling a sense of belonging that came from the physical effort of getting there, I looked at my canoe. There had been a time for preparation, a time for organizing, but now we were on the trip. My boat was in use. The gear would be repeatedly reshuffled and unpacked, but my boat was a constant: the red and black letters stood out on the sleek body, the yellow-rimmed cockpit was mine. This special canoe was becoming an extension of me.

I suspected Verlen had the same thought about his own boat, but he didn't stop to mull over the implications. He was busy working, wiping off his canoe and unpacking supplies. Verlen didn't need adjustment time—he was already part canoe.

On the hillside above the sea, a menagerie greeted us. Tame deer with faded red tags around their necks nosed us with curiosity. Kittens and small dogs with sores sat staring, their heads swaying with an unhealthy dizziness.

The town appeared to hang onto economic life as precariously as it clung to the cliffs above the sea. La Buffadora was close enough to the American border to attract some tourists, but was located too far from the main highway to attract much traffic. There were no stores and there was no electricity. I saw an abandoned restaurant on a hill at the edge of town, but that was the only sign of commerce. The place looked as if it had been deserted for some time, and only a handful of houses showed signs of life.

An old stake-bed truck rumbled down to the beach with what I thought was a bird riding on the roof. The "bird" turned out to be hound dog standing in the truck bed and looking over the roof of the cab, rocking with the motion of the vehicle that was bouncing toward us, his ears flapping wildly in the wind.

Stepping down from the wheel of the cab, the driver of the truck introduced himself as Bernardino. Several small children ran out from the house closest to the road and gathered around him, pulling at his pantlegs and beginning to drag the big man toward the house. His arms around the children, Bernardino stooped to enter the narrow doorway with his enthusiastic crowd and motioned for us to follow.

Verlen and I came closer and stationed ourselves at the door, looking in. Bernardino spoke to a woman inside, who nodded and dutifully moved toward the stove. She lit the stove and placed a tortilla directly on the heating element to warm. Verlen flipped through his Spanish-English dictionary looking for the word "camp." When he couldn't find one, he began making hand motions in the shape of a tent, then closed his eyes in a pantomime of sleep. We played a game of charades until Bernardino's puzzled face turned to understanding.

"Campanmento, sí, carpa," he exclaimed gesturing to the ledge above the sea outside his home. His wife gave each of us a warm tortilla. We said thank you and walked back to the canoes.

As we put up our tents on the hill above the sea, I watched the ocean change color, turning a deep, enchanted green. For one moment the sun came out from behind the clouds, spreading a glittering path toward us across the sea. It had been quite a day: we had survived the rainstorm, the rocks of Punta Banda, and the landing at La Buffadora, but now I was exhausted.

While making camp, I backed into a cactus, which poked me unmercifully. When I turned to rebuke the plant, I was surprised to see initials and a heart carved in the thick stalk. That sentiment cheered me up until I crushed my toes under my boat as I was dragging my canoe farther up the beach away from the tideline. Then, as I sat in my tent, I discovered my cook kit was corroding from the salt water—even my stainless steel knife was rusting. As I cleaned the blade, I sliced a layer off my finger with the sharp edge. So this was expedition life? It was like being shipwrecked by choice.

When I was back home, my habits testified to my secure routines. At night I would call my dog into the laundry room, lock the house, wash the supper dishes, turn out the lights, and feel a reasonable assurance that when I awoke the scene would be as I had left it. But there in the Baja the environment was in control. Nature's constant changes required monitoring and adjustment—we lived by the dictates of sky, ocean, and wind.

Before zipping my tent closed, I took another look outside. As the ocean pressed toward the beach, a dory anchored in the bay was tugging at its rope, pushed by a gentle offshore breeze. The light was fading fast, the tide came high on the beach. The next day it would all be different.

When I took off my shoes and a scattering of sand fell into the nylon folds of my sleeping bag, I didn't bother to brush it away, but wiggled into the softness of the bag and stretched out on the inch-thick pad that protected my body from the uneven ground. Before I fell asleep I wondered again why I was there. There was no denying that I was reaching for something beyond myself. But it was exactly myself—the programming of 31 years and a normal lifestyle—that was constantly coming to mind and standing in the way. Everything was so new that at times I clung desperately to familiar parts of who I was, even when they weren't effective in my new situation. If I wanted to grow, I would have to change. I would have to let go and become one with the Baja. I had been willing to tear my life apart, so I must have known the experience would be worth it.

The next morning we made plans to paddle 14 miles to Santo Tomás. There was no hurry for that short distance—by our calculations we could enjoy a slow morning start and still arrive well before dark.

The pet deer from the town rubbed at my elbow as I dismantled my tent. There was a slight wind from the southwest and cooler temperatures were blowing in, but the changes were so slight that I didn't pay much attention to the weather. I should have known there was trouble brewing when I unhooked the tent fly and set the fabric on the sand—the wind puffed and scooted it across the dirt road. I chased after it and brought it back, folding it securely under my arm. When I removed the ground pegs, my tent swooped airborne like a balloon. So intent was I on packing that I still didn't comprehend the consequences of the gradually increasing wind. As I freed the fabric from the poles, I pinned the flapping material with my elbows, knees, feet, and chest, tackling, folding, and stuffing my collapsible house into its bag.

Verlen had turned the canoes around in the sand and pulled them closer to the water by the time I arrived with my parcels. He walked back up the hill to check the campsite for anything we might have left behind, then stood a long moment looking at the sea.

"Do you see that?" He pointed toward the dory anchored in the harbor, which swung like a weather vane on a tether, its stern blown toward the beach. The sun had lifted to a 10 o'clock position in the sky. A wedge of black followed, rising from the south. A storm was blowing in, and the wind was not settling but beginning to gust.

Though we had just broken camp, we immediately looked around for shelter away from the exposed hillside. Sighting a palm palapa about 300 yards from the beach, we grabbed our water bag, food sack, personal items, and the larger of our two tents. Dragging our awkward load, we hurried toward the gazebo-shaped structure on the patio of an abandoned restaurant. We put up our tent, tying all four corners to the pillars of the palm shelter, and climbed inside just before the rain began. Though lashed in four directions and weighted with our bodies and gear, the tent continued to billow. The edges hovered above the ground and the cap fly collected wind and threatened to flap and tear apart. Rain trickled down the sides and the noise of the fly slapped and resounded as if the tent would any moment burst from the stress.

Despite the racket, sitting out a storm on dry land was a blessing. I didn't care how big or ugly the weather got, I was just glad to be ashore. Verlen and I could laugh at the clouds and wind. We were safe. The wind blew a regular gale, picking up the seas and throwing water in our direction. We saw no sign of life in the small village—even the deer were in hiding. The wind whipped the high ocean swells into white-capped foam. The waves grew in size and rolled violently onto the beach.

The day was given over to the storm. Verlen unscrewed the top from his gorp jar and busied himself popping candies into his mouth and looking out a small peephole at the top of the zippered doorway. Through the few opened inches of our tent, the rain and wind blasted in, washing Verlen's face.

I fired up Verlen's stove and began heating a pot of reconstituted spaghetti. After five minutes of service the fuel bottle gave out, and I realized the spare was back on the beach with the canoes. Neither one of us wanted to run through the rain to fetch the extra bottle, so we made do and nibbled the cold, crunchy spaghetti.

Even after the first few hours of pleasant security were gone, Verlen seemed content with our imprisoned safety, and began cutting his fingernails with his pocket knife. But I felt trapped as the afternoon dragged on and the storm continued to blow in gusts. Tinted by the fabric, a ghoulish green light came in the sides of the tent. My sister's telephone number crowded into my mind, and I repeated the numerals out loud. They sounded foreign and bleak. There were no phones in La Buffadora and no entertainment in our cramped space. Zipped inside the tent, I felt a tinge of homesickness in an unwelcoming world.

"Verlen," I said, wishing for a bit of sympathy.

"Huh?" he responded, absentmindedly. He was busy with his knife, flicking mud from his shoes onto the tent floor.

"Verlen," I began again. "Do you ever get restless?"

"No." He looked at me strangely. "Is there somewhere else you'd rather be? I wouldn't go outside if I were you."

"Guess you're right," I said quietly. He didn't seem to understand.

By late afternoon the storm settled, and Verlen was starting to talk about making a run to the boats for the extra fuel bottle when I heard the noise of a vehicle pulling to a stop outside the tent. Six magic words ended our isolation:

"Do you guys want a shower?" I looked out of the tent to see a blue and gold van and a gray-haired American leaning from the driver's window.

"Yes, we girls sure do." I nearly stepped on Verlen as I clambered out of the tent, dragging my personal bag and boarding the back of the wagon with no questions asked.

Verlen was more dignified. He picked up his briefcase of papers, zipped the tent, and checked the tent pole ties before climbing into the passenger seat next to our host.

65

"I've been watching you guys through my binoculars." He never did decide to call us girls. "I'm Walter. What do you think you're doing sitting here all day?" He didn't seem to need an answer. He had already accepted us and was busy driving toward his trailer.

I noticed hand-painted signs on the road saying "Walt's House" and pointing with an arrow to a trailer and patio on a high cliff. I wondered if the signs were for Walter should he forget the way home, or were just an expression of his hospitable nature. He looked about Verlen's age, but Walter didn't seem to have the same spark of life as my partner. His eyes were dull and his shoulders stooped. As we pulled into his driveway I saw a white flag flying from the roof of his lean-to, as if he were admitting surrender.

As soon as we were parked and unloaded, Walter handed me a towel for the shower. I didn't argue—I looked forward to a complete transformation. As I shut the door on the bathroom latrine, a pair of pink plastic breasts greeted me, stuck to the back of the divider. A stack of girlie magazines sat on a shelf with other essentials of the toilet. I forced my attentions to the gravity flow of lukewarm water. Paying respects to the plastic female parts taking a shower with me, I wiped a splash from the synthetic nipples as I toweled my own body dry.

I could hear Verlen and Walter talking on the patio while I got dressed. I stepped from the shower room grinning and tugging at my soaked, squeaky hair. I wondered what Verlen would think of the pink bathroom companions when he went in next.

"Mi casa es su casa. My home is your home," Walter said with genuine friendliness.

The three of us sat on the patio looking out over the ocean, watching the weather and passing Walter's binoculars back and forth. Verlen and I recounted our canoe adventure and our host began talking about himself. This man was no adventurer, but a victim.

Twice his heart had attacked him. The first time the assault was physical and put him in the hospital. The second time it was an emotional attack when his wife ran away with the doctor. Walter had retreated to the Baja with his dog and a bottle.

The storm continued, so Walter offered Verlen and me his house trailer for the night. Our host said he would sleep on a cot in the kitchen shed. When we glanced down on the palapa through the binoculars to see how the tent was faring without human ballast, it looked all right. Verlen checked our boats, which were resting quietly in the sand. We accepted the offer. Walter proceeded to cook a big supper for us, and we sat talking until long after dark. Even when the conversation wore out, we sat together watching the sea.

After eleven o'clock, just as I climbed into my bunk, a knock came at the door of the trailer. Walter was outside, offering a glass of milk and cookies served on a paper napkin printed with the name of an American hotel. I rated Walter's accommodations five stars.

When I woke up the next morning I didn't want to move. Before leaving Seattle a friend had given me a carved wooden needle case. The small treasure held my needle, thread, and thimble. Chiseled on the bottom were the words "carpe diem." This Latin phrase instructed me to "seize the day." I could hear the roar of the ocean outside. I didn't want to seize the day—I wanted to burrow under the covers. But, applying the aggressive directive, I sat up and began to get dressed.

"No paddling today." Verlen stuck his head into the trailer to announce a reprieve. "More clouds are forming. The storm is still with us." I settled back into the covers to relax a few more minutes, and pulled the special needle case out of my personal bag and held onto it.

The townspeople of La Buffadora must have seen our white canoes, which stood out against the beach like spaceships, and must also have known where we were staying, because soon after breakfast Walter's Mexican neighbor, Arthur Vasquez, trudged up the lane for a visit. His roundish wife was close behind. Arthur wore a flap of cloth across his throat, and when he talked he sounded like a squeaking robot. His larynx had been removed, but he was able to talk through a device implanted in his throat. He leaned close for me to look, raising the fabric swatch so I could examine the inner workings of his mechanical voice box. Arthur spoke good English. He asked me to feel the muscles of his upper arms, saying he could have canoed with us in his younger days. I didn't know whether to giggle or scream. Arthur's wife was staring at us without saying a word. I decided that the need to check our gear was a good excuse to get away, hastily said goodbye, pulled on my rain clothes, and walked down the hill. I also wanted to explore La Buffadora. Verlen came running behind me, and between rain squalls we hiked around the village.

A winding footpath led to the blowhole, where a series of concrete steps approached a balcony that overlooked the ocean. Every few moments a wave would hit the rocks at an angle and shoot a rocket of salt water into the air. As I looked down at the jagged rocks I thought gratefully of the small strip of sand where we had landed.

When we walked back to check the canoes, I discovered that my paddle had disappeared and the tennis shoes I had tied on the back of the boat were missing. The theft of the shoes didn't bother me—I realized the thief probably needed them more than I did. But the loss of my paddle was more serious, since it was an essential piece of equipment and that particular blade had been custom-made for me. We looked up and down the beach, then walked back up the hill toward Bernardino's house. Our knock brought his wife to the door, but as we explained our problem she shook her head.

"No comprende, señor, no comprende." I was dejected, as we walked back to the canoes. I untied my spare paddle and carried it back to Walt's trailer for safekeeping. When I told Walter of the loss, he was as discouraged as we were—he couldn't recall any past problems with theft in his small village. There was nothing we could do. I didn't want to knock on anymore doors and have the residents tell me we could not communicate, so I spent the afternoon sitting at Walter's writing letters.

I wrote a letter to my friend Chris, who had made the sewing tube, and imagined how comfortable it would feel to be at home. I had met Chris in Seattle right after making my commitment to the Baja journey, and even though he encouraged my adventure, his good looks had made me wonder why I was going at all. To my surprise, when I began to address the envelope I realized I could not remember his last name. I felt another loss. Accepting this journey was like stepping through a door: I feared that I was changing irreversibly. When I described my problem to Verlen, he picked up my address book and went through the pages, calling off names until I recognized Chris's surname. That turned out to be the last letter I wrote to my Seattle friend. I imagined Chris sliding off the back of my canoe and disappearing into the wake. If I found him up ahead I would be joyous, but I knew now I wasn't going back.

The next morning my first waking sense was of departure. Two days of sitting on the sidelines had revived my energy, and I was anxious to move on. Pulling aside the curtain, I looked out the window above my bunk. The dory tied in the harbor was rocking gently, bow pointed toward land as a normal offshore wind propelled it. The sky looked clear and bright.

I had slept in my clothes, so I simply rolled out of the bunk and began setting gear outside the trailer. Walter and Verlen were already busy in the kitchen concocting a traveler's fortification: powdered eggs mixed with a dose of cornmeal, bread fried in butter, and strong coffee. After breakfast Walter offered a shower as a going-away gift, and I knew by then how valuable a gift it was. The desert land we were traveling in didn't have abundant fresh water supplies, and a water wagon had traveled from Ensenada to fill his holding tank. We were dependent on others even for our drinking water, so a fresh-water bath was real luxury. I accepted the offer, realizing it might be weeks before I got another chance. The men did the dishes while I stepped under the piped-in stream, hooting and hollering in delight.

Walt filled our drinking jugs, then handed us a bag of cookies to include in our packing. When it was time to leave, we piled our bundles into Walt's van and he drove us to the canoes. We were stowing our gear and saying good-bye when one of Bernardino's children ran toward us carrying my paddle and presented it like a gift. I reached out my hand to claim the special blade, and the child turned and raced back home before I could say muchas gracias. With tears of gratitude, I gave Walter one last hug and climbed into my boat.

It was 10 o'clock when we pushed off from the shore, paddled through the surf, and worked our way past the rocks of the harbor into open sea. Walter stood on the hillside and waved, then got into his van and followed us as far as the road would allow. I realized our visit had been as much a treat for him as for us.

"Did you take your seasick pill today?" Verlen's question interrupted my daydreaming and focused my attention on the 15 miles ahead. I had forgotten to take the pill, and though the weather was clear I could already feel a storm gathering in my stomach.

"Look out over the horizon," my partner suggested, sympathizing with my pained expression. I tried my best, staring in the direction of Punta Santo Tomás, a bullseye target 15 miles ahead. I fought as long as I could, then lost my breakfast over the side. I slumped down into the canoe, embarrassed by my forgetfulness and my continuing seasickness. Once again, we catamaraned the canoes. After an hour I thought I heard Verlen saying something.

"Are you singing?" I asked, after listening for several moments.

"No, not singing. I'm praying for you and hoping that you will learn to take your pills next time." I lay back in my canoe, somewhat comforted but still seasick.

"I won't forget next time," I promised. I had been off the water only two days, but I felt like I was starting over.

Verlen paddled our canoes for five hours before we arrived in the harbor at Santo Tomás. The beach was a small patch of sand deposited between rock cliffs, and the village fishing fleet was tied in the bay because the landing was too small. The point so sheltered the area that the surf was nonexistent, and we had no difficulty bringing the canoes ashore. When we pulled them onto the sand they took up all the space on the postage-stamp beach, and the sterns were still precariously close to the waterline.

"The tide seems to be going out. Don't worry about the canoes," Verlen said, as we scrambled up the rocks toward the townsite.

The chart book said Santo Tomás had a store, which turned out to be the front room of a small house. The owners introduced themselves as Frank and Silva. Dogs congregated on the door stoop and chickens walked in and out through the open door. On the floor near the front door, a small child was playing with three dolls covered by a blanket. As Frank walked by them, he put his finger to his lips, indicating playfully that we should be quiet as we entered. He directed us to several rows of nearly empty shelves.

The inventory was sparse: several bags of candy, one brand of canned meat, and a dozen cans of spaghetti sauce. A refrigerator with no electricity to plug into stored warm pop. I left the choice to Verlen, who began gesturing and trying to communicate in Spanish with Frank.

I walked outside into the afternoon sun and saw a building crowned by a white cross high on the hill behind the village. I hiked up a rocky path and pushed open the creaking door on a small one-room chapel. There were melted candles on the floor, plastic flowers stuck into a slab of cement, and an altar picture of Jesus on the cross and Mary beneath it. This graphic version of Catholic faith made me hesitate at the door before I moved inside. Momentarily forgetting all my blessings, I knelt in discouragement. Verlen's having had to paddle us into Santo Tomás was a blow to my pride—my enthusiasm seemed to vanish when the going got rough. I felt ashamed, and prayed for a change.

When I got up and walked outside, the sun startled me with its light and life. Walking down the hill from the chapel, I looked out to sea and spotted two sailboats gliding into the harbor. Verlen was walking back to our boats with an armload of softdrinks.

"Come on, we're going visiting," I shouted to Verlen as I ran toward the canoes.

"Wait for me," he said. Beginning to trot, he handed me several of the bottles as I passed him on the run. Together we made a happy race to greet our new neighbors. We jumped into the canoes and sprinted across the water, stopping our paddling to wave as the sailboaters appeared on deck when we neared. We didn't need to introduce ourselves—the captain on one of the sailboats recognized our canoes.

"Of course we've heard of you. In fact, I've got an article from San Diego with your photos," the man declared. He ducked into the cabin to pull out the evidence.

"Wow," I said, grabbing at the paper handed down over the side of the larger boat. "It's me!" On closer inspection I realized the paper had spelled my name wrong, noted an improper mileage figure for my portion of the trip, and concentrated the story on my partner. Even so, I was glad to see the report of our adventure.

We bobbed on the water beside the sailboat, trying not to scratch the hull with our canoes. Verlen bent his head back and looked up, talking with the skipper about the weather.

"Looks clear for the next few days," the man told us. "We sat out that last blow at Ensenada." The woman on board shook her head as if it had been rough. "What kind of mileage are you guys making?"

"We're making over 20 miles a day so far," Verlen answered.

"We're lucky if we make that ourselves," the captain replied. "Our sailboat depends on the wind. We don't like using our motor."

"We're hoping for as little wind as possible to keep the seas calm for paddling," I said, noting our conflicting needs. "The only motor I've got is me!" We chatted for about 20 minutes, then headed back for camp, waving at the other schooner as we paddled to shore. The sailboaters would not be coming to the beach—most of the boats were equipped with dinghies for landings, but the sailors usually slept aboard.

The sun was just disappearing when we got back to land. Verlen took a critical look at the beach: our tiny inlet of sand was surrounded by rocks, and a mass of debris mashed against the back wall of the canyon landing gave us a clue to the tideline. We couldn't pull the canoes to higher ground because of the rocks. Verlen anticipated our boats riding the surf during the night as the water came up, so he parked them and hog-tied them together, bow to bow and stern to stern, then lashed them from four points to jutted rocks protruding from the rocky bank.

We camped above the beach, climbing the rocks like kids headed for a top bunk bed, leaving the boats far below. The tents were slanted and braced against the wind, and I huddled in my sleeping bag and went to sleep with the newspaper article stuffed inside my shirt.

At dawn we made several trips down the cliff with gear to prepare our take-off. A fisherman stopped on his way to work and helped me get my packages down the hillside. I accepted his aid, thinking it was a courtesy due my female gender, but once my gear was in the boat he helped Verlen load his.

The two sailboats anchored in the harbor bobbed quietly. We assumed the crews were still asleep, so we didn't disturb them as we paddled past and out to sea. The night before we had paddled into the bay tightly around the point, so I hadn't gotten a clear picture of the town. I turned in my seat and looked as the first light of morning brightened the landscape. Santo Tomás was only a few houses clustered above the sea and seemed to be sliding off the hillside. A dirt road wound into the distance along the shore, then disappeared over a crest. The land was bare and almost shapeless as it mounded and blurred into one sandy desert clump.

I turned around in my seat and looked ahead: the sea was calm, the weather didn't threaten. There seemed to be no barriers, just limitless space. This day was going to be different. I gulped a seasickness pill and started to sing.

The ocean, sky, and wind were the undisputed rulers of the environment, but I could be in charge of myself. If the conditions could change, so could I. The first thing I did was get out my own map and locate myself. I charted the course of the day ahead, watching the compass and reading the coastline. I began a new game of looking at my watch, noting the time and then not missing a paddle stroke for an hour. The reward was a drink or a cookie. The remaining 2,203 miles was an unmanageable distance to think of all in one day, so I decided to make it to Yuma in 60-minute intervals.

I wanted to claim the trip as my own, but so far, with Verlen paddling me, I wasn't making it. I wanted to be a full participant and not feel that I was just along for the ride. Negative thinking would have to go overboard. To get down the coast I needed dreams and plans of my own.

In relation to Verlen's experience, the record of his usual partner, and the distance of a 28,000-mile canoe trip, I felt lost. So I began to search for my own motivation. I had signed on for 2,411 miles: Yuma was my goal and my purpose was to make it to the finish. My mind received fuel from my spirit: we had come 208 miles so far, and keeping track of our progress made a surprising difference. I would keep moving one paddle stroke at a time, one day at a time. The struggle of the beginning days was finally justified as I saw the possibility of success and made a commitment to it. I watched the water, paddled hard, and patiently played my 60-minute game. I was never seasick again.

As we skimmed the water, the sun sparkled on the horizon and reflected a path on the waves as if a yellow brick road were spread in the distance ahead.

"We're off to see the wizard," I announced, as if this explained it all. Verlen looked at me as if I were nuts.

"Why am I going to the wizard?" I asked, trying to help him see the point. "I'm not the lion. I don't need any more courage. I'm not the tin man, I have a heart already. The scarecrow, why did he go to the wizard? Do you remember Verlen?"

"What are you talking about?"

"The *Wizard of Oz*. Haven't you seen that movie?" I asked in amazement. Verlen shook his head no.

"You're deprived," I said adamantly. "Everyone has seen the *Wizard of Oz*." It is an awful feeling to forget something and be out at sea with no one to ask. I remembered being at a party one New Year's Eve when no one could remember the name of a certain street in Chicago. We finally called a friend in the midwest to put an end to our frustrations. But there were no telephones on the ocean, the blue water gave no clue, and my partner didn't know what I was talking about. I paddled forward a while, looking at the map and calculating when I might find sailboaters who had seen the *Wizard of Oz* and would remember what the scarecrow needed.

Verlen and I paddled for hours. Then it hit me.

"A brain, Verlen, the scarecrow needed a brain." I was jubilant. Verlen shook his head in disbelief.

"He isn't the only one who needs a brain," he quipped.

"You mean you're looking for one, too?" I asked.
"Well, anyone with any brain wouldn't be out here," he laughed.
"That's it Verlen. I've come to the ocean for a brain." I followed the yellow brick road until the afternoon heat wiped it off the sea. I was off to see the wizard, 60 minutes at a time.

SIX

Expedition in Swing

Twenty miles north of Punta Colonet the ocean erupted as a school of dolphins jumped above the surface. Their sleek bodies arched as they nose-dived through a series of imaginary hoops, then dove below to swim under our canoes. A few miles farther on, sea lions popped up like jack-in-the-boxes between floating kelp beds. A flock of pelicans zoomed skyward after a low formation reconnaissance of our boats, and small flying fish skimmed the tops of the waves as our bows disturbed the open water. I heard a snort close to the stern of my canoe, and turned just in time to see a shiny-eyed seal disappear into the deep. Verlen and I kept paddling. After 254 miles, I was feeling as much a part of the seascape as the creatures around us.

"I want to pet a sea lion before this trip is over," I commented. Verlen shook his head in mock consternation. I could see by the smile on his face that he was getting used to me.

I was getting used to him. Verlen was a quiet man—he didn't say much except what needed to be said. The day before he'd told me that he didn't even have a high school education, which had surprised me. Verlen wasn't polished, but he had an uncluttered perception of the world and when he talked he spoke with the simple eloquence of truth. I never understood how Verlen could be so strong and forceful with his paddling and yet remain such a gentle character. The ocean was like that too—both calm and powerful. But the ocean was unpredictable, and Verlen was consistent, balanced, steady. He was the most stable man I'd ever known.

It was about noon when we spotted a motorboat heading for us. All we could see was a wide expanse of bow lifted out of the water and a cascade wake discharging from each side of the stern. As the boat came nearer and slowed, the bow began to lower and the boat leveled as it glided to a stop beside our canoes. Wooden lobster traps took up half the space in the work boat. Straddling the centerboard was a young boy dressed in a rain slicker twice his size, with both sleeves rolled up from his small hands. I guessed the man standing by the outboard motor in the stern must be his father. An extra-wide-brimmed hat shaded the older man's eyes, and his belly bulged through his shirt.

Within a few moments their wake rolled toward us, gently bobbing our canoes as the waves passed under our hulls. The fisherman and his son stared at us. I was sure that in all his mornings of going to sea, the older fisherman had never seen the likes of Verlen and me. I waved.

"Buenas días," Verlen shouted.

To explain our journey, I mentioned Cabo San Lucas and made paddling motions in the air. The fisherman looked startled.

"Muy lejos," he said with feeling.

"Yes, many miles." I was glad we had established communication.

"Mucho trabaja," the fisherman said, shaking his head in sympathy.

"Sí, much work," I repeated.

The boy had not said a word, but his brown eyes were wide and staring toward Verlen and me. The man reached into one of the wooden crates and held up a lobster, dripping and clawing at the air.

"Langosta?" he offered, handing the monster over the edge of his boat toward us.

"No, gracias," Verlen responded.

"Verlen, that's a lobster he is offering us," I said, incredulous that my teammate would turn down such a delicacy.

"I don't trust any seafood other than fish," my partner declared. "These blobs and strange shapes are unfit to eat."

"What gave you that idea?" I argued.

"I was born on a sandhill in Indiana and we ate simple food," Verlen insisted.

"Verlen, what could be simpler than lobster from the sea?" I asked.

"The bread and milk my mother put on the table," Verlen insisted. The fisherman remained poised leaning against the gunwale of his boat, holding the lobster over the sea as we squabbled.

"Where will you put the thing?" Verlen asked rationally. "How do you think you are going to cook it?"

He stumped me with these questions. My desire had a lot to do with knowing how much the lobster would cost back in the United States. I couldn't think of anywhere to store it, and I certainly didn't want the animal crawling around inside my canoe. For one brief moment I envi-

75

sioned lashing the beast alongside my boat to dog-paddle and await the dinner pot, but I realized Verlen was probably right.

My only other experience with lobsters had been one special Christmas Eve when I had driven 20 miles to the Pike Place Market in Seattle to buy a live one. I had carried the thing home wrapped in newspaper, put it in the bathtub, and turned on the tap, adding a cupful of table salt so it would feel at home. I flipped on the light and checked it five times during the night, even snapping the tape binding its pincers so it could relax.

By morning the lobster had become a pet, and my dog and I sat on the floor beside the tub looking in. Cooking the lobster for lunch was out of the question. Besides, the directions had said to cook him alive and by one o'clock the lobster was dead. I didn't know what to do once it was motionless in the bottom of the enamel basin. I sure couldn't eat the poor thing, and my dog wasn't interested either. I threw the dead lobster away in a casket of holiday wrapping paper, never realizing I would come face to face with his relatives in the Baja.

Remembering this bit of history helped make my decision—I joined Verlen in declining the squirming seafood. We both waved and called, "Vaya con Dios," as we resumed our paddling. I wondered how the fisherman would describe to his village the strange American sea creatures who had refused his gift of a lobster.

Verlen and I paddled toward Punta Colonet, a 55-mile haul southeastward from Punta Santo Tomás. We had shortened the stretch by stopping the night before at Punta San Isidro, but the miles still seemed endless. I took one paddle stroke after another, staring at the horizon and the bow of my canoe: that slim triangle of white was always eager to slice through more water. The nose of my boat created a wave of parting water that pressed up a few inches against the body of the boat, then fell like petals opening for me to pass.

Keeping us company most of the day was a great bulk of mesa on the shore, its brown sides dotted with green. Silhouettes of more mesas continued in the distant haze. As we neared the closest headland, a spectacular cliff of stratified rocks and sand rose from the sea. We rounded the corner of the snub-nosed point, but couldn't see any landing spot. The daylight was almost gone as we continued paddling into the bay, searching for a landing site. The ocean swells wrapped around the curve of the cape and seemed to be breaking with as much force inside the bay as the surf we had observed on the exposed outside coast before making the turn.

The cliffs finally tapered off to a beach about half a mile farther inside the bay. A row of fishing boats high on the beach seemed to indicate the best landing—surely the local fishermen had chosen the safest spot. But we could see wild breakers in front of their parking strip. A little scouting revealed the reason. Our charts noted an arroyo just south of the fishing fleet, and when we looked toward land we saw the scar of a dried riverbed cutting a channel to the beach. The effects of the early evening tide were intensified by a sandspit deposited at the mouth of the arroyo. The resulting large surf would be reduced at other times of the day, and probably never interfered with the comings and goings of the fishermen, who adjusted their schedule to the tide.

After studying the possibilities, we chose a gravel shoal about a quarter of a mile north of the arroyo, where the surf looked more manageable. Even there we waited 20 minutes, floating, watching, and counting the breakers, before we dared to paddle ashore between the waves.

We had paddled 28 miles, our bodies were weary and our imaginations quick to inflate the danger. Even Verlen's confidence in my talent as surf queen failed to boost me forward through the menacing surf. Our final approach was a decision made of necessity. We would have stayed outside the surf, continuing to hesitate, if the darkness hadn't hurried us along. The actual landing was not as bad as we had expected, though we did take on water getting to the beach. We carried our gear along the bottom of the cliff line, stumbling over the rocks in our wet tennis shoes. As we walked along the ledge, a light rain began to fall. Just as darkness came, we reached an abandoned building on the north edge of the arroyo.

We dropped our gear and Verlen went back to the canoes for the last load. I watched his flashlight grow dim as he walked down the rocky shore under the cliffs. The rain soon stopped and the night turned clear and bright with stars. Relying on my own flashlight, I put up my tent. When Verlen came back, he stopped to say goodnight.

"I sure hope I tied our boats well enough," he said, as he knotted several leftover pieces of rope. "When the tide comes in those boats will be floating." My mind was on other things.

"This is going to make a beautiful photo tomorrow morning," I said. "The bows of the fishing boats will be silhouetted at dawn. Wake me up so I can borrow your camera."

When we woke the next morning and saw our canoes, I forgot about the photo of the fishing boats. Our boats were completely stranded on the highest spot of rocky shore. Between us and them a section of the shore was completely underwater, and the rising tide was pounding against the cliff in a powerful surf, so there was no way we could get to the canoes. I hoped Verlen's ropes would hold. The bigger waves crashed over the white hulls, knocking them together and against the rock face of the cliff.

We cooked breakfast, packed up camp, and sat on our luggage waiting for the tide to change. My watch said it was Sunday morning, so we assumed the beach would remain deserted for the weekend. To our surprise, several

77

beat-up cars and a pickup truck arrived midmorning. The drivers looked first at us sitting on our packs and then at our canoes being beaten on the ledge. One man described our situation in a word—"loco." The fisherman all laughed as they went about their work.

That was the first time I had had a chance to sit and watch Baja fishermen at work. These men were not daredevils, but cautious workmen. Their timing was so carefully calculated, they made going out through the surf look like a snap. They would row the wide, deep bows of the boats through the breakers until their motors could be lowered on the transom and started. Coming back to shore was a problem they anticipated and handled with team effort. They came in bow first. Then the bowman would jump out with a lead rope, run up the beach, and fasten the rope to a truck bumper, jump inside, slam the machine into reverse, and haul the boat out of the tumbling breakers. The catch of the day was deposited in the car trunks—I looked inside one and saw an octopus slithering around the spare tire well, and a lobster pinching a tire iron.

By noon the tide was abating and we were able to hike to the canoes. Our well-constructed boats had survived the pounding, and the elasticized oval weather covers Verlen had put over the cockpits the night before had kept the waves from filling the insides. But water had saturated the coated cloth and dripped into the boats, so we spent 15 minutes mopping with our sponges. Then I hopped into my canoe and Verlen shoved me off the beach.

We were soon paddling down the coast, and from our position a little over a quarter of a mile from shore, I could see the hills sloping into the sea with predictable regularity. I scanned the landscape for signs of human habitation, but the peninsula looked bleak and empty. Yawning chasms of rock widening in some places made me wonder what might be deep inside the dark shadows, but the more I saw the more I realized that the Baja was barren desert. From our vantage, though, it was beautiful, as the colors of the landscape wove from brown to green to deep burgundy. As the clouds moved overhead, the colors shifted with the light and shadow.

The water scenery directly in front of my bow was livelier. Not only did the swells heave with life, but at any moment some sea creature might pop up from below and gasp. I let the land blur into the periphery and concentrated on staring into the water ahead. I was mesmerized by my paddling task: each stroke carried me farther into a timeless blue suspension. The horizon line wavered as I continued to stare. Maybe it was the heat that caused the line to shimmer, then dissolve into a smudge. I felt as if I were paddling in space. A dolphin rose out of the water, making a smooth bridge between sea and air. Instead of breaking my trance, the appearance seemed to lull me deeper into the watery world.

A brisk wind came from the north to push us southward. After half an hour of paddling, I sat back in my canoe, laid my paddle across the cockpit, and relaxed. The sky seemed to sparkle, the ocean twinkled in unison, and my boat bobbed happily between the two hues of blue. I felt as if I could really get used to this.

"Keep it moving," Verlen said when he saw me resting. "We've lost a lot of time to storms and we're behind schedule." Even though his tone was matter-of-fact, not accusatory, I took offense.

"Each night we've reached our goal for the day," I said defensively. "What do you mean?"

"Steve and I would be making about twice the distance," Verlen explained. "You and I have stopped at every available harbor since we started. We should be passing some of them and pushing farther." That news bothered me. I was doing the best I could, and had thought we were right on schedule.

"I have to be in Yuma, Arizona, by February 9th to catch a plane. At this pace we won't make the finish of our trip before I have to head to the National Sporting Goods Show in Chicago," Verlen said.

"Verlen, I'm just getting used to being here," I explained. "How can you look that far ahead?"

"It's all a matter of time and distance. A schedule is very important."

"I thought you told me we would live by the conditions," I reminded him.

"One of the conditions is getting to Chicago," he responded. "But we'll make it if you keep it moving. Camalu is 10 miles ahead. We'll stop there for the night."

"Verlen, let's go on. I'll show you I can make more distance," I said enthusiastically.

"Not this time," Verlen said. "We're low on water and snacks, and the map shows a town several miles inland on the main highway. If we can get to shore, it would probably be a good idea to walk into town and resupply."

By 3:30 in the afternoon we had paddled around Punta Camalu. The beach was low and sandy with no rise, so landing would be easy. A local fisherman was walking on the beach with a lobster trap slung over his shoulder. He put down his burden and stood ankle-deep in the water, waiting for us to nose our canoes into the sand so he could help. Pulling ashore a fully loaded canoe was not a one-person job. Verlen and I usually emptied most of the heavy gear and the water bags and then helped each other tug the boat to high ground. The waiting stranger needed no instruction: his pantlegs were already rolled up as he prepared to shove, drag, and haul to make our task easier.

"Muchas gracias," Verlen said as the man reached for our bowline.

Working together we soon had our boats on the beach. When we asked directions, the fisherman pointed the way to the town of Camalu as directly east from the water. We helped lift the lobster traps back onto his shoulders and watched as he walked away across the sand and continued around the point.

We decided to reorganize our gear in the several hours of daylight remaining. When I unpacked, I found that everything in my boat was wet, even the articles in the rear compartment. Several of my waterproof bags were leaking. We spread our gear on the rocks above the beach to dry in the late afternoon breeze.

It was early evening by the time we started our two-mile hike to Camalu. For a path we had several dirt ruts to choose from. Walking across the desert, we struck a course toward the lights of town. In the still evening, Camalu looked like a miniature runway as we approached through the darkness. We could easily make out the main highway, where car headlights roamed across the invisible landscape. After 10 days of paddling on the sea, I felt like an amphibian: our land instincts were aroused. Carrying our depleted water jugs and traveling on empty stomachs, we made our way toward town, sniffing civilization.

The road took us to a gas station on Baja Highway 1, where vehicles of all descriptions were filling their tanks. Trucks and roadsters, animal-drawn wagons, and family sedans congregated at the pumps. Lights from the station and the headlamps made us squint from the glare. We crossed the main highway and strolled among the booths of an open-air market. It was late and the merchants were just packing up their merchandise—the blankets, used clothing, paintings, and sombreros that filled the tables and covered the curtains of the stalls.

We watched closely for people carrying packaged goods and backtracked their steps to locate the one grocery store in town. There were lights on in the store, and a small crowd of people gathered around the cash register, visiting with the storekeeper. In this store there were no grocery carts, and of the people buying, no one left with a full sack of provisions.

Though Verlen and I had nearly 100 pounds of dehydrated food back at the canoes, our eyes popped at the packaged goods. Shopping purely on impulse, we gathered an armload of crackers, sweet potato candies, and large sugared cookies. We filled our packs with pop, jugs of filtered water, pastas, and tortillas sold in bulk. I looked at the rows of chilies hanging from the ceiling and walked past cans of jalapeños and beans. Just looking at the assortment was a treat. There were times out on the ocean when the paddling and the distance ahead consumed me so totally that I forgot there were stores with shelves full of goodies and routines as quiet and peaceful as shopping down the aisles. The ocean world had no packages labeled by ingredients. The ocean was one giant cauldron of simmering stock.

I felt conspicuous as we paid at the counter, handing over 700 pesos to the storekeeper. The normal chatter in the store had stopped, and everyone seemed to be looking at us. I wanted to tell them that we had come by the sea, but I could not speak their language and they said nothing to me.

Using our Spanish-English dictionary, we pieced together the words to ask if there was a telephone. That was our one link with home, and I knew my family would be wondering how we were. Since Camalu was on the main highway and had electricity, we were surprised to be told the town had no phone. We did get directions to the one restaurant in town. As we entered, a blinking jukebox was spinning a mariachi polka. We chose a table by the window looking out on the main highway. My chair faced the kitchen: while Verlen ordered steak, I watched the flies keeping the meat company on the counter slab by the stove. I chose an enchilada with a filling I couldn't translate and remembered that friends back home had warned me not to eat the lettuce in Mexico. A picture of the Last Supper hung over the cash register.

Verlen and I didn't say much as we ate. I had been excited about getting away from our campstove routine and eating out at a restaurant but I was already eager to get back to the sea. It was another world out there, and I hoped that coming into town had not broken the spell that was settling over me as an ocean paddler.

Belching our meal, we began the dark walk back to the canoes.

There were no lights ahead to lead us to the sea. Though we had no reason to believe the place was dangerous, we felt vulnerable walking back to the boats; every so often we looked back to make sure no one was following these strange gringos into the night. For most of the two miles we walked in the blackness, not even able to see the dirt beneath our feet. I reached out to hold Verlen's hand, and every 15 minutes we shifted and exchanged our loaded packs with each other to momentarily relieve our aching muscles. Eventually we heard the surf encouraging our direction, and as we neared the ocean, a warm onshore breeze greeted us. Our tents and canoes were just as we had left them. We would repack and store our new supplies the next morning—first it was time to sleep. The sound of the ocean came to me like a constant friend, humming and rumbling with low comforting vibrations like the churning washing machines in the laundromat back home.

When I climbed out of my tent the next morning, I discovered Verlen sitting on his map case by the edge of the sea. For breakfast he was pulling out jam, shortcake, cookies, and potato chips from our Camalu shopping trip.

"Verlen, you can't live on junk food," I admonished.

"This is fuel," my partner attested. "Think of your stomach as a furnace.

81

When the fire is raging you can throw anything in and it will be consumed. Only a sputtering fire has to be babied and primed."

My mother had repeatedly advised the merits of a good breakfast. For a nutritious morning start I was accustomed to oatmeal, eggs, toast, and juice. Verlen had thrown out the rule book: he not only didn't eat properly, he ate all the time. His secret for paddling 15 hours a day was "keep eating." A cookie, a piece of candy, a soda pop—each was good for another 40 minutes of paddling. Then, when the sugar began to let him down, he would swallow another candy bar as if it were simply fuel for his body's engine. My body couldn't accept the sugar as well as Verlen's high-octane system did—candy bars made me irritable, but Verlen cheerfully pushed his canoe through the water fueled by junk food.

But that morning I sat down beside Verlen and ate a handful of cookies to fuel my tank. There were 38 miles, probably 15 hours of paddling, between us and San Quintin. Before I had time to cook anything wholesome, Verlen was shoving his canoe off the beach.

It was a long afternoon. The scenery didn't look very special, just more brown desert hills, and even the ocean was sullen. I hadn't seen a dolphin in hours, and I was getting lonely. My canoe and I were trying to make friends with the sea, but for all the movement and life the ocean displayed, we had not achieved communication. I was learning more about the ocean day by day, but I craved dialogue, and Verlen was the only one who could give it to me.

"Verlen, how you doing?"

"Fine." I kept paddling. One stroke after another. I glanced over at my partner.

"Hey, Verlen. Do you want to talk?"

"Sure. What do you want to talk about?" He kept paddling, one stroke after another.

"I don't know."

"Why don't you tell me about yourself," he said. "You've got a captive audience." He was right. There was only the rhythm of the paddle strokes, the endless distance ahead, and my partner. I paddled another 10 minutes more before I turned my paddle strokes on automatic pilot and began to talk.

Starting with my childhood and working up through the school years, I related every detail I could remember. I told Verlen about roller skating on the driveway when I was in fifth grade and the fall that broke my front tooth. I confessed the embarrassment of the silver cap the dentist had applied and the reason I didn't smile for years, until I had a porcelain cap fitted. I described the many moves our family had experienced, and the feelings of always being a new kid on the block. I told him about the kitten

I had when I was 9 and the time I'd tap danced on television when I was 10.

When I came to recent history, I had lots of questions. How did the pieces fit? There were parts of my life I didn't understand—a broken relationship had been a burden for years. Verlen didn't have an answer, but he listened with genuine concern.

The sun set as we paddled past Punta Azufre, but the sky held the light for almost an hour before it faded into twilight and all we could see was the outline of the coastal hills against the dark sky.

"How are we going to land?" I asked.

"By compass," Verlen said. "And by the navigation lights." Every few minutes we would snap on our flashlights to check the map and compass, then paddle blindly as we waited for our eyes to readjust to the night.

We came around Cabo San Quintin navigating purely by sound, compass, and timing, staying a safe distance from the crashing shore break. A solid cloud covering made it even darker than usual. We checked our position on the compass: directly east was a flashing red light and northeast was a flashing white light, so we headed north toward a supposed channel to Punta Azufre. Punta Entrada should have been north and west, but we never found it, and after 40 minutes of paddling we were near more breakers.

"How are we going to know when we're around the point?" I began to fret.

"There is a navigation light at Punta Azufre, the inside point of the bay. We head for the light after we clear the rocks on shore," Verlen explained.

When we rounded the cape the light was where it should have been, but it seemed to be leading us straight for the sound of crashing water.

"I hear breakers between us and that light," Verlen warned.

"We're too close to shore," I howled.

"No, there is something else going on—shallows, some kind of shoals. We'll have to figure out a way around," Verlen said, altering our strategy as we paddled. We headed back and paddled farther into the bay, then circled cautiously back toward the light, feeling our way forward. We searched the maps, but none of them printed the shoal locations or extensions into the bay. There were breakers to the left of us, crashing on the right and noise from waves straight ahead. In the blackness, my depth perception was gone. A wave pushing from the right had me zigging and zagging for balance.

"It's impossible to paddle in this blackness!" I exclaimed. "I can't see. I feel so tippy in my boat!" It was like entering a dark room and bumping into all the furniture. "No wonder I'm cranky, Verlen, I've paddled 38 miles today on cookie fuel, and now I'm blindfolded."

We were human pinballs, hitting dead ends, banging against a maze of obstructions. We had now figured there were shallows to the left and shoal to the right. If we headed toward the light we might make it to a landing, but there was a set of breakers ahead. When we saw the white foam crash in the darkness just a couple of canoe lengths away, we backed up and headed off to the right. Even then we were going toward yet another noise, hoping to thread our way behind the breakers and wind our way back to the light.

"Just keep paddling," Verlen instructed. "The light should be on solid ground and if we can get there we can camp."

"Are we going to get through this maze?" I asked, frustrated and scared. Verlen stopped paddling. He pulled out his copy of Vern Jones's *Cruising Notes* and read past the map section with his flashlight: "There is a navigation light on Punta Azufre. It is placed in such a way that, no matter where you are, if you see it and can head for it, you and your vessel (no matter what size) will be aground long before you reach the point. Disregard this light and its white tower when entering and leaving the lagoon." Verlen snapped off his flashlight and we were once again in the blackness. We had heard that all navigation lights in the Baja were unreliable. The white light ahead was an indicator, but we could not navigate from its position. As we strained our eyes and ears, suddenly I heard a break different from all the rest, a break that sounded as if it responded to shore, as if a hammer had suddenly hit a stud. A lapping sound came from our right, and when I turned my flashlight in that direction, I could see land right next to our canoes.

We had reached a sandy landing and beached the canoes. We seemed to be on a low peninsula that would be submerged at high tide, and there was hardly a suitable spot for the tents. The wet sand sucked at our feet, and bugs were everywhere, flying and jumping around us. Verlen and I walked all over the dune, testing the ground and looking for a high, flat spot. When we failed to find one, we decided to put up our tents near the water, next to the boats, and tie a long line from them to a tent pole.

"If the water comes up while we're still asleep, it will float the canoes," Verlen explained. "As the tide current flows by this peninsula, the boats will go with it and tug on the tents. We'll wake up by feeling the tug and we'll have a line to retrieve the boats. All this area will probably go under water, so when the tug comes we'll have to be ready to move quickly."

"How long have we got to rest?" I wondered.

"A few hours at the most," Verlen answered.

I hurried to put up my tent. Once inside the awning I could hear bugs splattering like raindrops on the outside walls. We had to keep our flashlights on during dinner to recognize and repel the critters that fought their way inside our tents and nose dived into the cook pot.

We slept, then sometime later awoke with a start. The canoes were floating—one was tugging at the corner of my tent. I heard the waves lapping on the sand. When I looked at my watch I discovered we had slept only three hours, but it was time to pack up and move before the incoming tide covered our campsite. It was a strange feeling to have arrived and be leaving in the dark.

Verlen seemed to remember how we had arrived, so I followed the stern of his boat as he threaded his way back out through the breakers. He aimed his canoe without saying a word, and when he paddled even a few feet ahead and his canoe was lost in the darkness, I would yell out.

"Verlen, Verlen."

Finally he would answer, "What?"

"Nothing, I just wanted to know where you were."

We paddled for an hour before dawn began to lighten the sky. When I looked back, I couldn't see any sign of where we had been. A light bulb suddenly went on inside my head.

"Verlen, this is just like the parts of life I was telling you about. Maybe there are some things we're not meant to understand, but just have to get through. We had been able to enter and leave San Quintin without an understanding or glimpse of the area. Wasn't that a lesson for me? I can enter and leave portions of my life without total understanding, just as I did the harbor. I never saw San Quintin, but I can go on. It isn't necessary to stand and wonder about circumstances or a place that I've never understood. We're free, Verlen, paddling into a new day. We're going on, and I can do that in my life, too," I said triumphantly.

"You do have to understand your goal," Verlen added. "That's what makes a difference."

"I've got a goal," I said, holding up the map. "This is my direction. I can't get lost."

"Daniel Boone used to say that he never got lost, only terribly confused for a few days," Verlen said with a chuckle.

"Now, that's possible!" We both laughed. Paddling away from the mystery of San Quintin, I felt a new freedom.

"Verlen, I'm going to write a book about this Baja experience." The light inside my head was getting brighter.

"Yes, I think you should write, you write better than you talk." My buddy was trying to be helpful. He seemed to have an unusual amount of confidence in me, even when my train of thought was hard to follow. "*In Search of the Perfect Enchilada*, how's that for a title?" he asked. "How about, *She Met Her Match in the Baja?*"

"Verlen, don't laugh at me." I stopped in midpaddle stroke to see if he was teasing.

"Just keep it moving, Valerie, that's the secret."

SEVEN

Captain for the Day

All morning we paddled at a comfortable speed. The swells rolled gently in a series of deep, heaving breaths. Verlen's stroke was as consistent as the rhythm of the sea, and his canoe continued to edge ahead of mine as he shoveled water toward his stern. His body swayed forward with each bite of his paddle beneath the surface. It was comforting to paddle uninterrupted, each stroke a measure of our purpose.

We made steady progress, but by late afternoon the safety of Bahía del Rosario was still eight miles ahead and the sun was moving toward the horizon at an alarming rate. Our charts warned of a reef and had advised caution while navigating Punta Baja, so we were counting on daylight to find a landing.

Each day we calculated the mileage to the next harbor, divided by our three-mile-an-hour pace, then counted backward from sunset to find what time we had to start each morning. But this time we must have miscalculated, because the point ahead was still a hazy shape on the horizon, teasing me in the distance. For all my paddling, the land mass was not growing but seemed to get farther away the longer I stared.

"Will we make it to the point before dark?" I asked.

"Not unless we race for it," Verlen said. "Even then our chances are slim."

"Let's go for it, Verlen," I said tensely. We increased our paddling speed and neither of us spoke. Out of the corner of my eye I could see the shaft of Verlen's paddle actually bend from the pressure as he shoveled water along the sides of his canoe, pushing his boat faster. His movements communicated urgency and his breathing increased to panting.

My own momentum built more slowly as my muscles rallied for the sprint. The fear of negotiating Punta Baja in the dark called forth a surge of power from my body. We were racing the sun. I remembered my race instructions from Seattle: "Never look at the other team during a race," the coach said. "Breaks your concentration and sets up an inefficient anxiety. Run your own race and pace yourself," he had warned.

Though my head was bent and my body hunched to reach and pull with the paddle, I couldn't help glancing at the sun dropping lower, sinking into the ocean, yielding to the approach of night. I paddled faster, almost in a panic, digging my blade into the water and pulling harder. My heart was pounding, and every bit of my energy was dedicated to making landfall while we could still see the hazards barring our way.

In the frenzy that accompanies any good fight, the cliffs seemed to stare. The ocean churned and heaved like a passionate crowd pressing against the ropes of a ring. Along a high ridge onshore we saw the shapes of people running toward the point. The reef was ahead, and we quickly discovered that predicting the pattern of the wild, foaming breakers was impossible. We chose to round the headland, steering a wide course to avoid the reef. Luckily, we discovered a line of kelp beds and a trail of lobster pot floats, the best indicators of safe passage. Small spots of light on shore waved erratically as we continued our frantic pace.

Clearing the reef, we cut in behind the turbulence, approaching the landing just as the darkness closed in.

We wouldn't have been sure where to land, but the spectators from the ridge were now on the beach signaling to us.

"Donde? Donde?" we yelled.

"Aqui! Aqui!" they shouted in reply. We timed the waves, backpaddled, and gave full-arm throttle for a perfect landing. Then we jumped out of our canoes and quickly pulled them to higher ground.

The observers who had become so involved in our landing with their lights and encouragement stood awkward and shy, wondering how to approach us now that we were ashore. Shaking hands and grinning, we drew them into our celebration of success.

Not only had we landed safely, Verlen and I had raced together as a team in a crucial situation. Neither of us had let up. I felt like a bigshot, as if I had just flattened Muhammad Ali with a knockout, though my knees were shaking and I steadied myself with the paddle buried in the sand. On a wave of exhilaration, I carried my gear up a steep rocky wall at the back of the landing.

But I had not bargained for the consequences of our success. Holding the flashlight in my teeth, I set up my tent on the high ground above the beach. As my body cooled down from the race, I began to realize something was wrong. I had paddled furiously for eight miles with the tremendous weight of the canoe and strain of the already long distance, and my shoulders now stung with pain. The sockets holding arms to body felt stripped and raw. No matter what position I took, I could not find relief.

The villagers wanted to know where we had come from and what we were doing, but suddenly the language barrier was insurmountable. I had no energy left to explain. I felt as if I were going to be sick.

After setting up camp, I crawled into my tent like a wounded animal and eased down on my sleeping pad. I wanted to be left alone, but Verlen came in after me. Switching on my flashlight I saw him dragging several bundles into my shelter as if he were moving in.

"The reason we brought these pills is to use them," he said. Holding out a capsuled Percogesic and aspirin, he requested that I open my mouth wide. I opened my mouth and said no.

"I don't take pills." I stubbornly eyed the tablets. Verlen opened his first-aid kit on the tarp, exposing a sinister looking array of gauzes and ointments, needles and scissors.

"Talk to your body," he proposed.

"I listen to my body, and right now both arms are screaming," I cried, rubbing my shoulders.

"Do you realize your refusal to help yourself with medicine is not only hurting you but our journey?" Verlen browbeat me with logic as he recalled the seasickness pill controversy. "A fair-weather traveler you are," he continued. "Explorers push through the hardships to accomplish what they set out to do. You'll never get past the threshold of pain unless you take these," he said, offering the white pill and capsule impatiently.

I had only a thin margin of confidence—refusing to ingest the pills was my last stand. I had always had an aversion to pills, even as a child. Verlen couldn't have all the answers. What if he were some Pied Piper of the canoe world? My motivation was blocked by a temporary bout of confusion.

"Can't I complain about discomfort without having you pester me with tablets?" I argued.

"Suit yourself," he concluded, popping the pills into his own mouth, swigging from his canteen, and drenching the front of his shirt with the overflow. He smiled as if to prove the medicine harmless, then wiped his beard with the cuff of his windbreaker before screwing the top back on the canteen. Pulling out his map and pencil, he retreated from our argument. Then he fit on a headlamp, banding his cap with the elasticized strap. Studying the chart, he looked like an accomplished doctor. Still miffed with his uncooperative patient, he examined the chart, apparently totally absorbed in calculating time and distance. He walked his ruled compass over the ocean portion of the graph and scribbled with his pencil as he figured the distance to the next harbor. When the operation was complete, he described the plan: "We'll be leaving here at three o'clock tomorrow morning so that we can be sure of reaching San Carlos before dark." Putting away his tools, he pulled his captain's hat over his eyes and leaned against a pack.

Rocking my body, I held my elbows and tried to relax my knotted shoulders. Several minutes later Verlen opened one eye and looked out from beneath the bill of his cap.

"You did a good job out there," he comforted. "Always remember to leave a little energy. Save a reserve for settling into camp and for the next day." Then he lay back with his arms folded over his chest, lounging like a night nurse. Soon he was snoring peacefully.

Within what seemed like minutes, Verlen was shaking my arms, the ones that still hurt, telling me to wake up. I looked in the direction I thought was up and wondered why it was so dark.

"Time to go," Verlen said firmly. The pain in my shoulders had awakened with me, and the rest of my body felt stiff and wooden. When I pressed the light button on my watch, the small bulb punched at my eyes with its brightness. I squinted to read three o'clock: Verlen was right on schedule. He snapped on a small flashlight and I saw him, squatted in my tent, dressed and bundled in a jacket. I refused to move.

Verlen must have reconsidered his plan, because the next time I opened my eyes dawn was coming in through the fabric walls of the tent. Then I heard rain pelting against the nylon and realized why Verlen had let me sleep. Looking out my window flap I stared at the ocean. It moved, but I had lost all momentum. Maybe I was taking on the characteristics of the sea and a tide cycle had invaded my body. For the moment I was depleted and drained, my fragile ecosystem exposed and vulnerable, waiting to be replenished by an incoming flood of energy.

Without knocking, Verlen crawled inside my tent. He sat cross-legged and dripping, his coat wet from the rain. After handing me a pot of cooked grain cereal, he pulled out a stained handkerchief and blew his nose. I wasn't hungry, so I set the breakfast offering by the screen flap at the door of the tent. Verlen took off his glasses and rubbed the lenses with another corner of the handkerchief. Noticing that the right hinge of his glasses had lost its pin, he fished into his personal bag for a pair of pliers. I watched him pinching and twisting until he mangled a safety pin into place and set the black-rimmed spectacles back on his face.

I looked at the charred cook pot by the door, with the cold cereal gummed to the bottom. A drop of rain came in the zippered doorway and splattered with a plop into the mush.

"Verlen, I'm miserable," I stated weakly. "I think I should quit."

"You said there was no way you were going back," Verlen said evenly.

"But, Verlen, my body hurts terribly." He didn't seem at all surprised.

"The other guy is hurting just as bad as you," he reasoned, narrowing his eyes and pulling out half of a toothpick from his frontpocket to poke between his teeth.

"You're the other guy, and you don't look like you're hurting half as much as I am. Besides, I'm a girl," I countered, retreating to the false assumption of female weakness. Verlen wouldn't let me get away with it.

"I go by your actions. You're here aren't you? I don't want to hear you talk about quitting. You wouldn't be satisfied if you quit," he challenged.

"I'm not satisfied now," I said defiantly. His perpetual stability made me mad—my spirit hadn't been totally destroyed. I knew my rights: I could quit if I wanted to. He tried a different tack.

"How do you think it makes me feel? Put yourself in my shoes. What about my feelings? My partner wants to walk out." His tone combined accusation and a plea for sympathy. I felt as if Verlen's hand were on my forehead, holding me at arm's length as I punched and swung my feeble excuses into midair. But he was right. Wanting to quit would pass.

"Use your energy to paddle. I've been looking at the map—we can cross from here to San Geronimo Island. We won't need to paddle straight through to San Carlos. We'll settle for an easy day," he offered.

San Geronimo Island was 10 miles southward from Punta Baja, which sounded like a manageable distance. I picked up the pot of cereal and began to eat small bites, willing life back into my body.

"Take your time," Verlen said as he backed out of my tent. "The tide is turning around and we'll wait until it stops raining before going on."

Sitting with my sleeping bag tucked around me, I pulled out my memory pack from a waterproof bag. Inside were my birth certificate, my tourist papers, and several photographs. The pictures of my three nieces grinned at me—one so small she was toothless. What a nice family to think of, all warm and cosy in an Iowa farmhouse.

I decided to write a letter home. But what could I tell them? There at Punta Baja I itched all over from the dirt and sweat of days without a bath, and the tent was full of sand that was wet and mushy from the early morning rain. I started the letter by telling my family how hard it was to paddle on the ocean and how much I had to learn. Then I stopped writing and cried. The salty drops stung the sunburn on my cheeks, but the tears were just what I needed. Acknowledging the hurt allowed me to move away from it.

Where were the joys and excitement that had brought me there in the first place? My whims had evaporated. The responsibility of piloting my own canoe on the Pacific Ocean was hard work, and the adjustments necessary for success threatened to swamp me. At times it was hard to see the joys for all the hardships, but I knew they were there.

The ocean experience was mine and I wanted to accept it, but the ocean was so much bigger than I was. Try as I might, I could not produce a lasting effect on the ocean. Each cut I made with my paddle healed immediately. Even the impression of my canoe was smoothed within a few moments of my passing. The sea could swallow us without a trace.

The significance of my position was the opportunity for my growth. As I accepted the challenge, I tried to concentrate on my goal. I did have a purpose: every morning when I got up there was no question in my mind what we had to do—paddle to the next harbor. Maybe the key to discovering the value was the Baja itself. I went back to my letter and tried to describe the environment around us.

Our world was made of land, sea, and sky, and our perspective from the seat of a canoe gave us an unusual view of a majestic balance of power. Here was a paradox of abundance and famine: this desert peninsula was surrounded by water, but struggling precisely for lack of water. Day by day, Verlen and I witnessed a co-existence of contrasts. The land stood fierce and steady, spouting tall mountains and rugged terrain. This rocky, barren desert seemed always ready to welcome Verlen and me. Even though we chose to travel on the sea, the land forgave us and beckoned to us. The coast opened itself in sheltered harbor landing pads, and when our energy was spent, we came washing ashore to collapse on rocks or sun-warmed sand.

Verlen and I were privileged to know the land in every changing mood. At times it formed a low, dark lump spreading on the horizon. Hills crowded and blocked each other from view until their mass became one intriguing shadow against the sky. Only when we paddled close to shore did the wrinkles show—the terrain folded like overlapping skin on a pachyderm's knees. Eroded and simmering in waves of heat, the desert cracked and stretched with dryness.

I had known that four-fifths of the earth's surface is water, but I had never known what that meant when my view extended only from the house I lived in to the one across the street. Once afloat, I struggled to describe the ocean world that extended farther than my eyes could see and farther than my imagination could reach. I realized that the ocean is the life force of the planet. The sea in front of me gathered all the water the land seemed so in need of. It replenished itself from myriad rivulets and streams injected far from the Baja. Built up from daily transfusions, the sea teased and taunted the desert shore.

The land stood firm against the sea, extending its rocky edges into the

91

surf. The sea chewed at the land, leaving steep ridges and new cliff faces. Where the water could not destroy, a wainscoting of barnacles defined the narrow measure of confrontation. Some of the cliffs swept back from the water, as if in an effort to retreat, and triangular landslides opened the rock, cascading small pebbles and sand from great tears in the earth.

The sky watched over all. Each morning it changed from pink to gold, mauve, lavender, then white. The ocean responded to the different hues and melted from dark slate to clear liquid glass. Sometimes the ocean was so translucent that I believed we were paddling suspended in space, as the clouds rolled over and under us. At other times the ocean turned dark and brooding.

There was no post office at Punta Baja and I didn't know where I could find one, but I signed the letter and added the postscript "wish you were here."

When I stepped outside the tent I saw that the tide had devoured most of the beach, and our canoes were floating in foamy salt water. Rocks skidded under my shoes as I shuttled gear down to the beach, where Verlen was already loading. He bent to pack the stern and pointed out an empty carrying spot on his rear deck where our canned goods had formerly ridden. The ropes and shock cords had loosened and the tide had carried away our precious store. I continued to pack my canoe, barely registering any regret. I was learning to live with the losses.

The sky was a mass of gray clouds, but the rain had stopped. As we cleared the Punta Baja reef I looked at the breakers evident around the point. Our victorious arrival had been costly, but I shuddered to think of the price we would have paid if the darkness had cornered us near the turbulence. As we paddled side-by-side toward Isla San Geronimo, I took out my chart and studied the dot we were headed for. The chart indicated occasional submerged reefs between us and the island. The map was drawn with squiggles of kelp and undersea pinnacles. We paddled due south, bypassing the curve of Bahía del Rosario and staying clear of the suspicious three- and four-fathom shoal areas highlighted on our charts. Playing dot-to-dot I took the map from its plastic cover and marked a line from Punta Baja to the island, noting the date as November 17. Then I looked up—and there it was! The island looked just like its mapped picture.

"Let's hook up the canoes before we get any surprises," Verlen suggested. "I don't know if the rain has totally passed." I nodded in agreement, thankful my arms could rest for a moment. Verlen crouched in his cockpit and began the gyrations necessary to catamaran our canoes. I was relaxing and looking around when I saw his wallet floating several feet from my bow.

"Hey, what's going on?" I yelled, grabbing at my paddle and pulling us toward the runaway. Verlen was as startled as I was. He frisked his pockets and realized his glasses had also gone overboard. He worked the half-connected boats like a hobbled forklift, reversing and then charging toward the still-floating wallet. I scooped the billfold out of the water and looked at the soggy pesos inside. Verlen laughed a little sheepishly as he reached out to receive his possession.

"I always did want to design some canoe pants," he said as he crammed the dripping wallet deep into his pants pocket, patting it confidently. "I'd make a lot of changes." I smiled at the thought of special Verlen Kruger pants. He had already customized the ones he was wearing: the cuffs were rolled up and the belt remained loosened for comfort while paddling.

"I'd cut these pockets deeper and tack in the corners for safety," he continued. As he talked he was probing into his personal bag for his spare pair of glasses. They were just like the pair that had gone overboard—even to the rusted safety pin holding the bow to the frame.

"Verlen, I can't imagine you at a sewing machine," I remarked.

"Why, I sewed the tent for my first big trip. Nobody made one the way I wanted, so I did it myself. I've made cockpit covers and packs too," he said simply. "The pants—well, I guess I'm getting lazy." My partner had not one ounce of fashion sense, but his perception of efficient design was top quality. Verlen went on rhapsodizing about the perfect canoe pants. Most of the paddlers I knew spent their spare time dreaming of hot fudge sundaes, not inseams.

The waves were boisterous, but not threatening. We paddled for several hours with Isla San Geronimo growing in size just ahead. As we neared, the island appeared gray and sandy, with no visible greenery. It was a barren place, with a high, rocky spine bisecting a humped back. As we approached the outpost, I realized that the spot of land was totally isolated, merely a large rock cut off from the mainland, with miles of ocean all around.

We landed on a small shingled beach wedged at the foot of a slight indentation on the southeastern side of the island. Once again the smooth sand of our landing was backed by high rock walls, but these were cut in flat stepping-stone ledges. A navigation lighthouse sat farther up the hill.

Verlen immediately set to the business of securing the boats and dragging gear up the hillside to make camp. I wanted to help, so I picked up several bundles and followed the leader like a pup. Verlen ignored me and began his ritual of smoothing the sand, tossing rocks out of the way, and walking over every square inch where his sleeping pad would lie.

I don't know what came over me. Maybe it was the isolation of the island or just the fact that I was tired. Whatever it was, all of a sudden I lost perspective. Instead of focusing on the goal, I had a momentary flash of doubt. I realized that I was on a rock in the middle of the Pacific with a white-bearded *voyageur* who was hunched over on his knees, smoothing out the sand with his palms and flinging stones over his shoulder. I was a long way from anything familiar, and the thought toppled my reason. When I felt the panic rising, I tried to push it down, but as I stood watching Verlen's precautions, my emotions spilled over.

"That isn't necessary, Verlen," I said. My procedure was to eyeball a flat spot and set up my tent. The only figuring I did was to position the door so my head was on the uphill plane.

"A good night's sleep is essential," he countered. "I made my own pad for my early trips. Four inches of foam." He had a smile of remembered bliss on his face. "Comfort is efficiency," he decreed. "Taking a little extra time to make sure the lumps are out is well worth the effort."

I picked up my towel and personal bag, leaving Verlen to his housekeeping. I had spotted a tidal pool and recognized it immediately as a Baja bathtub. The pool was a hollowed-out formation of rock surrounded by a four-foot ledge. I took off my clothes but left on my canvas shoes and eased myself down into the shallow cave. The action of the waves surged into the rocky tub and filled the scooped dish area. Lathering in the salt water with my special sea soap, I braced at the entrance to catch the chilly blast of ocean water coming into the opening. I was pleased with my unique hydrant shower system. The tension I had felt began to disappear.

I had been given a bottle of green shampoo by a friend back in Seattle, who had claimed that this brand was the only shampoo that would lather in salt water. She had been wrong—the bath left me polka-dotted with emerald globs of soap that would not rinse off.

I carefully touched the sores on my bottom that had developed from sitting in the dampness of my canoe seat, and scratched the saltwater rash that had started on the back of my legs. My hands, thankfully, were not blistered or sore. Racing had toughened me up before I started the Baja journey, and the salt air and sunshine kept my hands fairly dry. I had brought a pair of gloves, but Verlen had warned me that these would only soften my hands and make them more susceptible to abrasion and blistering.

Looking over the ledge as I toweled off, I saw two young men bent over and punching at the sand several hundred yards down the beach. They each had a bucket and hand tool and were gathering clams, tromping over the tide line in black rubber boots. Verlen had seen them too, and walked over to talk with them. I saw him gesturing with his pocket dictionary and pointing out our route on the map of his fact sheet. I got dressed and hurried to join the conversation.

The men spoke a little English. They motioned to the other side of the island, saying they had come from a fishing camp. They also confirmed that no water was available on the island, but our jugs were still half full from

Camalu, so that wasn't a problem for us. We walked back with them to the ridge above their homes. The camp below was a handful of shacks and three boats pulled up on a tiny crescent beach.

We exchanged best wishes all around, and then Verlen and I shook hands with the men and turned north to explore the rest of the island. We headed first for the lighthouse, which seemed as aged as the land itself. As we approached, I could see that the stucco coating had fallen away from the tower, exposing dark, weather-pitted bricks. The beam wasn't working, but the structure looked solid enough, almost as if it were a part of the rocks.

The earth at the top of the island was full of burrows, which we kept falling into as we walked along. But we never saw the animals that had tunneled and claimed the summit.

When we returned to camp, Verlen started dinner. He methodically set down his salt and pepper pouch, cook kit sack, and water jug. Pumping the stove he lit the burner, then backed down the fuel switch. I could see he was busy and withdrawn into his task. I sat next to a bulky pack, leaning against my makeshift chair and writing in my journal.

After a few minutes I began to feel the same irritation I had when we landed. It was an overwhelming feeling that things weren't right. Maybe it was because Verlen was so preoccupied and I was so restless. I was envious of his perpetual calm. Maybe Verlen didn't have anything to do with it at all, but he was in the line of fire.

"Add some more barley," I said. Without saying a word, Verlen dutifully emptied another handful into the bubbling pot. As he began to pour in pancake mix I interrupted again.

"That's too much," I cautioned. I knew I was being bossy, but couldn't seem to stop myself. Verlen leaned closer to his work. The pot innocently blurped as it cooked. Carefully, Verlen set his spoon down, balancing it on the pot lid. He would taste from the spoon, sipping in a small mouthful to test the concoction while kneeling in front of the cook pot, stirring and tasting. Leaning back on his heels he sat for several moments, then leaned forward again to stir and taste. For some reason Verlen's devotion to the cooking chore irritated me.

"That's not necessary," I snapped. My own technique was to put the pot on the fire and attend to other chores, coming back periodically to sit, gambling that I wouldn't wind up with scorched food at the bottom. Stiff from sitting, I walked over to his tent.

"Verlen, you've got to close this screen, a scorpion could crawl into your tent. And your sleeping bag and mat are turned all wrong. Your head will be pointing down. That's not good for the blood." I listened to my voice as if it were a stranger's—and I didn't like what I heard.

I walked away from camp in a huff and sat on a rock. The sun disappeared into the ocean, the sea seemed to breathe in a calming rise and flow. I snuggled against the rock as if it were a friend while I tried to reason out my problems. I needed some control. The ocean didn't give me any confidence —the weather and the surf did not even acknowledge my existence. I had been anxious to prove myself qualified, yet my habits had settled into complaints while Verlen handled most of the chores. Much of the time I was orchestrating, telling Verlen how to cook and how to put up his tent. When I did participate, I charged ahead rather than asking what was best for the team. Since I had so much to learn, Verlen had discovered that the greater part of efficiency was doing things himself. When we were hungry, it didn't seem like the best time to teach me to cook. This routine was turning me into a spectator. I needed to make a change.

When I walked back to camp, Verlen was still sitting and stirring and sipping from the stew pot. My foot spit a spray of sand into the pot as I sat down next to the fire, but when I apologized, Verlen didn't say a word, just dipped with his spoon and tossed out the top layer of gritty sauce. I expected him to snap at me, but he didn't.

"You got your spoon?" he questioned.

"Right here," I said, digging the spoon out of my pocket and looking at the pot.

"It's ready," he declared. I watched Verlen carefully divide the stew between the cooking pot and his next size kettle. He dipped a spoon into the portion to test the depth.

"Now you choose," he said. If the cook divided the portions the guest could choose the pot, so there was no misunderstanding as to who was getting more. Verlen prayed before we dug into the feast. Appealing to a higher authority seemed to clear the air. Dinner was a treat—a mixture of colors, flavor, and crunch that included chicken stew, rice, barley, and pancake mix dumplings. As my stomach began to fill I decided to talk.

"Verlen, your persistence has seen you through a lot of canoe travel."

"Yep."

"Verlen, do you know anything about teaching?" I asked.

"Sure," he grinned. "I was a flight instructor during the war. None of my students ever failed." He looked at me, probably wondering if I would be the first. I plunged right in.

"Verlen, you're the team and I'm not yet. You've got to teach me. Don't shut me out. It may be easier for you to do things by yourself, but please help me to be a part of the team so I can feel some value." Verlen's shoulders were relaxing, but I didn't know if he understood.

"I would be delighted to teach you all I know, but you will have to be willing to learn."

96

"I'll try," I said gratefully. I was ready for the first lesson. "Verlen, you never seem to get ruffled. What gives?"

"No point in reacting," he said. "Besides, you're doing plenty for both of us. I don't want to fan the flames." He looked down into his supper pot and took another bite. "The biggest hazard we have out here is the disintegration of our team." I looked at him, surprised.

"Sure, the ocean can crush us, but we can ruin the journey just as quickly. It doesn't pay to be hotheaded," he said calmly. "You're really doing better than most. One man I was traveling with almost insisted on how I should part my hair," Verlen chuckled. "It's the pressure. There's a lot of tension that builds up when you're out on that ocean. You may not even realize it, but that's what's got you." It sounded almost like a spook story, and I pulled my jacket closer around my shoulders.

"Whatever it is," I said, "I'm not very happy with the way I've been acting."

"Don't be too hard on yourself," he said. "I know what's in you. I've seen it out there." Verlen pointed toward the sea. "You're paddling your heart out. You've just got to learn to fight the circumstances instead of yourself or me. The bossiness is just veneer. You'll get over it."

"I bet you're hoping I will!" I said ruefully.

"Tension may be the culprit, but excuses are a luxury," he said seriously. "Involvement is one of the important facts of expedition life. It is essential to prevent disinterest."

"I learned that with my paddling and map reading. But I didn't know it was important in our camplife and partnership," I said.

"It isn't easy to get involved when the other guy has it all figured out. That's where the tension comes in. I think I know something that might help," he said, slowly chewing on another bite of dinner. "We'll go into the 'captain-for-the-day' system. On odd-numbered days I'll be captain. On even-numbered days, you can rule the team. Now, when you're captain you get the executive power over the minor decisions about what to eat and where to camp. These harbors pretty much dictate where we're going to stop at night, but there are a lot of fine points of business that can be chosen. When you're captain, you're in charge. But don't get cocky," he warned. "I'll be captain the next day and I may get back at you."

I didn't know what to say. It sounded as if I was getting more than I had bargained for.

"As captain, you'll be outlining our travel plans and cooking our meals," he continued.

"Well, thanks, Verlen." I continued eating and there was a silence for a good long while, until I looked at the date on my watch.

"Hey, Verlen. It's an even-numbered day. I'm captain! I'll do the dishes," I offered.

"You're learning already," he said proudly.

"Yeah, well you'd better enjoy it. Tomorrow's my day off," I reminded him. He laughed.

"Verlen?"

"Yep."

"Did you listen to him?"

"What do you mean?"

"Well, how do you part your hair, I can't remember and I can't see in the dark."

"Well, he was a funny type of guy. No, I didn't listen to him, but I was in a race once, a real long 240-mile race and that guy was in another boat and the pressure got so bad for him that I came around a bend and there he was out on the river bank duking it out with his partner."

"You mean they were actually coming to blows?" I was astonished.

"Yep, probably trying to part the other guy's hair." Verlen chuckled and then trailed off as if he were remembering.

We woke early, packed and loaded the canoes, and surveyed the beach. Verlen was captain for the day, but I still had plenty to do. Fighting the circumstances took all my energy. There was no time to struggle with my partner. Our easy landing of the evening before was buried in 10 feet of water and the surf of an incoming tide. Water charged the flat rock ledges, leaving only a few feet of sand to turn our boats around for the launch.

Every morning at that point I would get scared. The fear began when I first woke and heard the surf pounding and snarling at the edge of the beach. I would snuggle deeper into my sleeping bag, wishing the surf would go away. While I packed and arranged my gear I stayed busy, shutting out the roar. Then, when Verlen began to turn the boats, the sheer terror of fighting through the shore break would overwhelm me. I had heard of standing ground at the approach of a fearsome dragon, but rarely did a heroine actually charge the open mouth of a beast, ducking into the jaws and hacking through the foam at the throat of an excited monster. Each morning it was the same. My fear worked as a laxative. I would hunch on a ledge, making cat holes in the sand, staring at the adversary, and preparing myself for battle. Verlen knew no such problems. In fact, no matter how bad the surf looked, he usually was standing by my boat, holding the cockpit steady so he could assist, then pushing me into the fray.

As soon as I paddled out through the surf, I relaxed. The rhythm of my strokes settled my nerves. It didn't take much thought to pull one stroke after another, and the paddling soothed me like a mantra.

Our charts showed the Sacramento Reef ahead. It was named for a steamship that had struck an unmapped pinnacle in 1872. Since then many famous wrecks had piled up on the ominmous landmark. Using a compass for direction we headed east toward Punta San Antonio, leaving the reef many miles to our southwest.

A flock of birds flew by, strung together in formation like a kite tail. The ocean seemed almost friendly, and we enjoyed a spanking tail wind hitting our sterns and scooting us toward San Carlos. As we neared the mainland, the coast turned brown and welcoming. The hills looked like oversized russet potatoes stacked together in a grocery bin.

Verlen was a spectacle. He had his spray skirt on and no shirt. The black rubberized skirt form-fit over his chest, and a knotted bow of suspender straps decorated one shoulder. He looked like a mermaid fan dancer, but the captain's hat gave him away.

We nearly flew past Punta San Fernando, and completed the 19 miles to Punta San Carlos ahead of schedule. The headland loomed straight up a few feet from our boats, and the water rippled as it shifted against the rocks. When we rounded the point into Bahía San Carlos, the land fell back and curved into the prettiest bay I'd seen. The beach was a strip of white sand surrounded by hills gathering height as they stacked to the east.

A fishing boat zoomed past our canoes. It didn't bother to stop, but every head on board was turned in our direction as the boat sped toward the middle of the bay curve. I watched it go and saw that it was headed toward a small group of dwellings close to the beach. From the distance the buildings blurred together like an overgrown cactus patch, but I could see white shapes on the beach and knew it was a fishing village and a line of boats.

The beach was dwarfed by sandhills and a towering mesa sloping inland. As we paddled closer we could see Mexicans standing on shore waving us in—the fishing boat must have announced our approach, and it seemed as if the entire village was waiting and watching curiously. There were four lines of breakers ahead of our entry, but we weren't in a hurry, so we sat and watched.

The boat that had zoomed past us had landed and was parked with a dozen other fishing boats onshore. At first glance we might have chosen the beach in front of the boats to land but we paddled slowly, looking over our shoulders, watching the swells rise up from behind and back-paddling cautiously, letting the waves roll under the canoes while we looked for the best landing.

Verlen watched a flock of birds. The group would fly and land, scampering on the beach before the incoming waves. Finally they settled on an area of beach about 200 yards from the fishing boats. As each wave hit that section of the beach, the birds remained content and continued to feed close to the water's edge.

"The birds know better than the fishermen," Verlen said. "That's where we'll land." We paddled toward the birds. I let one more wave roll under my boat and then chased the curl to shore, carefully staying just behind the crest. The secret was to ride behind the break and not be pushed forward into the turbulence. Verlen had figured the landing precisely, and he was right: the birds had chosen the calmest spot on the beach. We came ashore without shipping a drop.

The crowd of fishermen stood back watching, motionless. I jumped from my canoe and pulled it far enough ashore so that I could run over and help Verlen with his boat. We began our usual procedure: Verlen put his paddle through the bow loop, then we stood on either side of the rope and began to pull the canoe to higher ground.

As soon as we began hauling the canoes, the fishermen drew near and soon were motioning me away as they surrounded the boat and prepared to pick it up. Rolling up their sleeves, they tried to find a handhold on the rounded surface, but finally reached underneath. They struggled with the weight and laughed in disbelief as they discovered that the canoe and its load were much heavier than they had expected.

Verlen suggested by pantomime that someone help him by pulling on the paddle harness, as he and I had demonstrated. Others grasped the cockpit to assist. Verlen soon had trained the group, and the canoe was skidding toward higher ground beside the work boats. The newly formed team then went back to the water's edge to retrieve my canoe. The men pointed to where the high-tide range was on their familiar shore and persuaded Verlen to continue pulling the boats past any harm of the evening high water.

I stood back watching. I liked the village right away. The fishing boats had names—*Vanesa*, *Jedy*, *Patti*, and *Marna*—a bevy of sturdy maidens outfitted with motors and stacked in the sand for a rest break.

As I looked up the hill toward the village shacks, I saw the women of the village standing and staring. Their legs were wrapped by children as if the babies clutching their hems were helping to support their stance. Verlen was busy with the men, showing off our equipment and passing out maps of our route. The women and I looked at each other. I would have liked to follow the discussion on the beach, but I was already segregated to visit with the women. I walked up the hill wondering how I must look. I remembered I wasn't wearing a bra, and felt self-conscious as I walked toward them. All the women wore cotton dresses and had their hair neatly combed or braided, which made me even more aware of my dirty, salt-stained slacks. I smiled at one woman, but the group continued to stare. I couldn't tell if they were frightened or offended at my unkempt appearance.

The woman I had smiled at put her hand to her mouth and asked "Comidas?" Always the question of food.

"Sí, muchas gracias," I answered.

The woman, who told me her name was Tila, led me to a paper shack no wider than my tent. She walked into the doorway and stood in front of a gas stove burner. When I looked around, the other women and children had disappeared, and there was no door to close after I walked in. I brushed the flies aside and cleared a space to sit, crammed into a corner so that I was eye level with the wooden counter. It seemed as if all the flies in the Baja were alive in that small kitchen, none of them lying dead, but all buzzing in excitement around the food.

Tila lit the burner on the stove and pulled a link of sausage off a rope on the ceiling. She began to warm a frying pan filled with beans that sat on the stove. There was no sink, so dishes were stacked on a crate. A pail of water with a scum of soap on top sat outside the door.

Tila and I did not speak the same language, but her actions were a language I understood. As she worked at the stove she smiled at me gently. Her role as wife and mother spoke to me as one alternative to my lifestyle. What was I doing paddling on the ocean, she seemed to ask. She was comfortable in her space. She cared for her children and her eyes lit at the sight of her husband. She was feeding the hungry—her hand was outstretched not as a pilgrim but to share the fruits of her domestic labors.

While she worked, I carried on a conversation in my mind with Verlen, thinking of things I might tell him about Tila. Several little children stood outside the doorway looking in. A woman came and shooed the children away, sneaking in a look herself before she disappeared.

I looked again at the food: it sat on unrefrigerated shelves, with flies covering the spoilage like plastic wrap. Everything in me wanted to refuse the welcome Tila was preparing, but how could I? I was hoping Verlen would come and save me, but instead he came and joined me.

Verlen could not fit into the cook shack, but stood in the doorway and gratefully accepted the plate Tila handed out to him. The feast was refried beans with chorizo sausage, rice, and fresh fish in lime juice. Within a few moments I knew I could wait for the health department to close the place before I would complain. The food tasted wonderful.

The people of the fishing village shared everything they had with us and would not accept any payment. Tila's husband even filled our water jugs from their precious supply that had been trucked in from the main highway and sat in large drum containers outside the door.

As we walked back to the beach after our welcome dinner, I noticed a man in a wide-brimmed hat standing amid a confusion of fishing lines strung between two clothes poles, working diligently mending the village nets. A stack of lobster cages awaiting repair littered the ground. Dogs played tug-of-war with fish carcasses on the beach. The homes in the little village were discarded truck boxes and tarpaper. I remembered that one of the San Diego paddlers had told us these were seasonal fishing camps, and I wondered where the people lived during the rest of the year.

I slowly unpacked my gear from the boat and set my tent in a hollow between two sand dunes, poking the tent poles through their channels and propping up the structure of my own seasonal home, stepping on the pegs to hold the shelter down.

I flopped onto the mat inside the tent, spreading out my sleeping pad and fluffing the synthetic bag. I thought of my sheets and quilts stored in Seattle, and remembered the homey smell of cedar. Taking out a mirror, I used the last bit of daylight to stare at my face. My skin was burned and stretched from exposure, and I had a stain of salt across my cheek. My hair was growing and the bangs, matted by my cap, were crowding my forehead. My eyes were the worst—they looked wild.

EIGHT

In Case of Death

I heard voices and poked my head out of the tent. The morning sun was just beginning to crack the horizon, but already the men of San Carlos Bay were preparing their boats for a day of fishing. Each village we visited had adapted its surf entries and exits to its specific beach characteristics. At San Carlos the beach was a long, shallow reach ending in a low-cut bank that formed a shelf where the village had been built. The work boats were parked tightly against the bank at the back of the beach. The tide had gone out, exposing a wide margin of sand and leaving the boats far from the water.

The villagers used a rusty American-made pickup to tow each boat to the sea, unhooking at the waterline. Several fishermen waded into the water, coaxing the boats to the surf. Two men stood on either side of each boat, holding the gunwales to steady the craft as it tilted and bucked when the shore waves rolled under its belly. When the boat was floating, another man loaded crates and lobster pots into the center section. He climbed aboard and pulled at the starter cord until the engine was running, then the other men jumped aboard and the captain steered the boat into deeper water before the surf could push them back on the sand. Verlen was standing on the beach watching the precision team at work.

"Bring the powdered milk when you come," I called to my partner. Our own launching procedure would not begin until after breakfast. I had found that Verlen wasn't as crazy about junk food as I had thought. He had told me that it wasn't that he really liked candy bars, but that they were handy. It wasn't good food that he minded, Verlen begrudged the time it took to cook and eat it. He liked to roll out of his sleeping bag and get right in the canoe before he had time to change his mind.

As soon as Verlen let me know that he was susceptible to lolling in bed of a morning, I was much more likely to jump up when I woke. Much of my behavior had been in response to Verlen's relentless moderation. Once he explained that it was a matter of will, and that even he had difficulties, I began to pick up on the discipline game and got to be a much better traveler.

I preferred a big breakfast: thinking about food helped start my morning. I was captain, so I lit the camp stove to heat a pot of four-grain cereal that had been soaking overnight and threw in a handful of dried apples for flavor. The goop was bubbling by the time Verlen arrived at my tent with his plastic pouch of powdered milk. He sat down and pulled a tin cup and spoon from his personal bag. Noticing a small cardboard package beside the stove, he began to study the Spanish words written on the front and back.

"That's the pudding I bought at Camalu," I explained. "I'm going to cook it this morning and take it with us for lunch. Today we'll have a change from peanut butter and tortillas."

"Sounds good to me, but let's get going," Verlen said. He handed me the pudding package and reached for his portion of breakfast. "It's a beautiful day with a little breeze starting up." Busy decoding the foreign language directions on the box, I didn't pay much attention to his weather reporting. We ate a hardy breakfast and the breakfast ate our time. We were late getting on the water—it was after seven o'clock when I was finally ready and standing on the beach staring at the surf.

"Verlen, I'm going to do this all by myself. I don't want any help today," I said positively, dragging the nose of my canoe around to face the sea and loading my gear. "Just stand back and take care of yourself," I instructed.

Removing my shoes, I waded knee-deep in the water, held onto my canoe and waited for the right wave. A roller broke and curled under my canoe in a turmoil of bubbles. Hopping into the cockpit, I grabbed my paddle and worked my way through the surf. Verlen was right behind me, and within a few minutes he had his canoe next to mine. I was already putting on my shoes, drawing my leg out from under the cockpit and tying the laces. I would have liked to wiggle my toes for a while, but paddling barefoot was uncomfortable because of the metal bar rudder control. While I waited for Verlen to get organized, I bent my head down to straighten my gear. Something was missing.

"Have you got the pudding pot?" I asked, shoving my packs aside and folding my head between my knees to look under the seat.

"I haven't got it," Verlen said, as he wiped a splash off his glasses.

"Are you sure?" I asked. "I haven't got it either."

We both looked at the beach. Verlen didn't say a word, but I detected a sigh as he turned his canoe around and paddled again toward shore. I lost sight of him as he entered the surf and the humped back of the waves blocked my view.

Forgetting the pot was a silly mistake. If I hadn't been so anxious about launching solo, I probably would have rechecked the campsite. Expeditions are an exercise in procedure: when I packed, I was supposed to follow habits. Pudding cooked at breakfast to eat for lunch was a departure from routine, and breaking camp had wiped the pudding from my mind.

I remembered that whenever our family left on vacation, by the time we had reached the first corner my mother would be worried that she had left the coffeepot on. No problem—my father had only to drive back around the block and open up the house again to make sure. Here on the ocean, every move was crucial. I needed to stay alert and be thinking all the time.

Twenty minutes later the pudding-pot hero was back, handing over a dripping saucepan and sponging the bottom of his canoe. He had spilled half the mixture during the rescue, and as he squeezed water from his clean-up sponge, globs of butterscotch custard plopped into the water and hung suspended a few inches under the ocean surface before breaking apart in the brine. I adjusted the lid and stuck the pot under my seat.

By the time we finally were ready to paddle, it was close to eight o'clock. My watch also told me it was November 19th. Looking at the horizon line, I plunged my paddle into the ocean, forcing an entry as far forward as I could reach and pulling back like the drive arm on a locomotive. The paddle blade shoved a section of water against my stern and the canoe moved forward. I lifted the blade from the water and began again with step one—reaching, entry, power, return, and again; reaching, entry, power, and return.

I had heard that when a paddler is doing it right, the flat of the blade is stuck in the water and the canoe is actually pulled up to the paddle, rather than the water being pushed back. I spent hours experimenting with this theory and found that I produced much more power when I had the image in mind of pulling my canoe forward to meet the paddle.

Typical of his extensive planning and preparation, Verlen had calculated that 24,300,000 paddle strokes would be necessary to complete his 28,000-mile Ultimate Canoe Challenge. I could look forward to an assembly line of 2,090,337 paddle strokes for my 2,411-mile portion of the trip. Verlen would swear each moment was exciting and precious. I will attest that many moments were dull.

"There is no necessity for boredom," Verlen claimed. "Just look around, there is always something going on. The joy of discovery is endless. Think about the wave pattern or the chain of life out here, the little fishes being eaten by the big fishes." He looked at me suspiciously. "You were excited when we first started this journey. The ocean hasn't changed, you are just getting lazy."

I agreed with him. My curiosity had been satisfied the first few days, so after three weeks my contentment required imagination. Pulling the boat forward depleted my physical energy but left my mind free to roam. At the end of each day I could total the number of miles we had paddled and record the progress on the map, but during the day I could only account for doodles inside my head. Sometimes I would lose myself for hours, talking to Verlen, or just staring at the bow of my canoe. Most days I escaped the expanse of endless water by taking off in a capsule of thought, sifting through the past or visiting the future. As we paddled toward Punta Canoas, I looked down at the pudding pot and anticipated some variety in our lunch menu. The tedium of the miles ahead began to lull me into a mechanical, monotonous pace.

We had the benefit of a mild tail wind, and a light breeze dallied on the surface of the sea, sending a stir of ripples southward. I didn't notice the gradual increase in the wind speed because the canoes were moving forward and my back was receiving only a gentle push. By eleven o'clock my hair was blowing past my face. I laid my paddle across the cockpit and reached up to hook the windblown strands behind my ears. Soon the wind was forcing my paddle forward toward the next stroke as I pulled the blade from the water. At noon Verlen consulted his map and looked closely at his watch.

"Twenty-five miles in the last five hours. Great guns, Valerie, we're flying," he said incredulously. It was obvious our success was due not to improved paddling skills but to the wind pushing us south. When I turned around in my seat to pull a bag from the rear compartment, the wind slapped at my face, startling me as it rudely entered my unzipped jacket and billowed the fabric into a berserk balloon.

The ocean, too, was violated by the steady increase of wind. The strong gusts were inciting large following seas. The wind built the swells into waves, rolling them so big that the tops broke in white bubbles. Then the wind blew even harder, lopping off the tops of the waves and shooting spray into the air. The sea rose in newly formed mountains. We could tell when a wave had reached its maximum height—the build-up would pause before breaking at the top. Then it would send an avalanche of water down the slope and our canoes would slide down the foaming rubble. It was a sparkling blue sunny day; all the usual trappings of a storm were absent. The wind had blown all the clouds from the sky until the dome above us was perfectly clear and bright. The paradox was unsettling.

"Verlen, I don't like this at all. Put on your life jacket," I advised, even as I fastened on my own. We had hooked up an hour before, but even the catamaran felt tippy and insecure. As each wave came under us it would lift and turn the canoes, rotating the boats like a pitcher grinding a baseball in his mitt before the send-off. We were riding a continuous surf, our paddle rhythm interrupted by the rollers. My instinct was to slow down. I back-paddled to stay out of the dancing water in the break and ruddered to keep the boat straight on each mountainous slope.

I was soaked in spray. The water riding over the stern of my canoe swirled and grabbed at my waist before dropping back over the sides of the deck. Water pooled around my spray skirt and dripped into the cockpit from the zipper. The cold, uncomfortable wetness began to saturate my pants and soak in on my legs.

When I looked over at Verlen, I could see he was having the same problems. The neoprene created a miniature trampoline over the cockpit. Verlen opened the zipper a few inches, stuck his fist under the spray skirt, and thumped the rubberized fabric to bounce the water off the cover.

"Verlen, tie yourself into the boat," I said, for fear of losing him. I knew that with our boats catamaraned together I could never turn the unwieldy craft around to save my partner if he washed overboard. I took a piece of rope from my parts bag and tied a secure loop, pulled the lasso over my head, and passed it under my arms to my waist. Then I reached inside my boat and knotted the loose end around the lower right seat bracket.

The sea was fuming—the waves by then were breaking over the tops of our canoes. I turned around and looked over my shoulder to see what was going to climb over us next.

"Here comes a big one," I shouted. But the warnings were useless since all the waves were big. We paddled and ruddered, trying to keep the boats pointed straight into the waves.

"Are we in danger of flipping over?" I asked, not sure I wanted to hear the answer.

"It will take bigger waves than these to flip us. These are steep seas, but as long as our bows are perpendicular to the waves we can ride some pretty big stuff. But I'll be as glad as you are when we can get around the next point. Conditions are getting worse. Put on an extra jacket if you can reach it. You'll need one if you're getting wet." I knew he was right and reached for my synthetic fleece. We needed all our energy for paddling, so we couldn't afford to give any away.

Punta Canoas was ahead—a sharp cliff surrounded by high hills. The point intensified the turbulence as the air currents fought to wrap around the corner and the waves bounced in confusion around the base of the land mass. The water around the point was a transparent aqua green. The waves reflected off the headland and stacked in columns, jerking up and plunging down like glistening pistons. A wave larger than the rest caught us sideways. Verlen's boat was lifted high above my head as my own canoe swung down to bury in the trough. The canoes shifted, rubbing and protesting on the poles holding us together, as the wave tilted our catamaran on the slope. I leaned back in the cockpit, a terrified passenger rushing downhill on the water slide. My first reaction was to grab the gunwales, but I kept paddling. I could not hope to conquer the sea, but fought to control my fear. The water was noisy—loud and consuming. I had been humming to myself, trying to stay calm, but then I could feel myself shaking.

As we turned the corner into the bay the protection of land began to save us from the wind. We did not pause, but sped our paddling in anticipation of getting ashore. There was no beach to welcome us, only rock cliffs rising out of the surf. Verlen spotted the mouth of an arroyo that had opened a fissure in the rocks, and we pointed the catamaran toward the narrow landing. The back of a wave pulled our boats into the landing and the next wave shoved us forward, lifting the sterns and snubbing the noses of our canoes into the sand. I jumped out of the boat and grabbed the bowline, but my lifeline was still attached and I tripped over the cord. Verlen hurried over to untie the line and helped me to my feet.

As we pulled the canoes forward, they floated and twirled in the few inches of water spreading up the dried riverbed. As my body relaxed from the tension of the wind, a trickle of urine ran down my leg. With a cold reckoning, I realized the danger of the situation we had been in. I sat down beside my boat, still holding the bowline. When I set it down I felt the warmth of the stones that covered the ground. I picked up several of the larger ones and held them close to my cheeks. Verlen stood by the canoes holding his cap in one hand, his white head bowed for several moments of silence. Beyond the point I saw the ocean still churning white tops, but we had escaped the wind.

Looking around our new camp we spotted a noisy sea lion colony roosted on a postage-stamp sandhill a few hundred yards away. The bulls were clumped together and didn't look as if they had spotted us yet. The daily cycle of tide and surf pressed against the cliffs and had flooded the narrow beach. Pebbles and dirt cascaded down the cliff walls in miniature landslides. The landing was a remote spot, with no sign of human beings past or present. Our campsite was barely distinguishable among the rocks.

The boats were so full of water we had to bail before pulling them into the cleft of the arroyo, so I went to work scooping water with my sawed-off bleach bottle. The pudding pot was swamped and floating upside down. As we began spreading gear on the outcroppings of rocks to dry, the routine of organizing camp brought us back to normal, and on dry land our fear was transformed into euphoria. We laughed like children.

"Don't bother those sea lions," Verlen warned. But it was too late. I was already stalking the animals, moving toward them as I clutched Verlen's camera. My intention was not to spook them but to celebrate our landing with the creatures. They honked madly and flopped into the water, then sat in the surf bawling at my intrusion.

When I crouched under an overhang to study some shells, a football-sized rock fell and crashed only a few feet from me. Counting the dangers, I figured if the sea lions didn't attack, if the rocks didn't fall on the tents, if the tide didn't come up and drown us during the night, we might survive.

I had learned the dangers of surf when we crashed at Descanso, but this was the first time on the journey I had experienced the terrifying ocean of force beyond the beach. Verlen already knew the power of the sea from his capsizing off the Oregon coast. I wanted to talk about the dangers of what we were doing. Settling in after supper we began the serious discussion of "what if."

We talked about our fears rationally, discussing the alternatives and measures we would take in emergency situations. We outlined all possible catastrophes and mentally walked through them together as we sat in the tent on dry land. I began by reading the label on my life jacket.

"Buoyancy aid, supports 15½ pounds," it said. "I weigh 140 pounds!" The life jacket suddenly appeared inadequate.

"That means your head above water," my partner tried to comfort me. "Your best flotation is the watertight rear compartment of the canoe," he advised.

"But my watertight compartment is leaking from the rear of my seat," I said, remembering the tiny hole in the bulkhead.

"That's no problem," Verlen assured. "My canoe floated offshore in Oregon for two weeks before it was recovered. The water seepage was minimal and the boat continued to float. At all costs, stay with the canoe if you go over."

"But what about the surf?" I wanted to know. "What if we had to crash in the surf? I wouldn't want my canoe to ram on top of me."

"Let the boat go in first through the surf," Verlen instructed. "Hang onto the stern and let go only when a breaker dumps on you. The canoe could certainly crush you if your body turned into the sand before it did."

"Verlen, what if we're catamaraned and the poles break, or one of the boats is flipped in the air? What if one of us is thrown out?" I asked, trying to think of all possibilities.

"The poles won't break. I had them made to my specifications and they're strong enough, but I have wondered at what point it would be safer to be tied into the boat or better to be free. We will want a long enough rope attached to us so that the guy thrown out doesn't get clunked on the head with the airborne canoe." I was glad he didn't say "girl."

"I don't think the catamaran will flip," he continued. "The two boats would flip only if the low-end canoe buried in the water. These boats are built with a smooth shape, so the water hasn't got a surface to grab and hang onto. Our boats slide on the water."

"Maybe we should carry a small jug of fresh water in our life vests in case we're washed ashore. How could we get through the desert without a survival kit?" I wondered. "I could sew some supplies into our jackets."

We knew enough to tie in our bailers and reminded one another about wearing proper clothing and pulling on our wetsuits if time permitted and we were stabilized in the catamaran. Hypothermia was a real possibility if we should capsize—the water was far from icy, but was still cold enough to lower the core temperature of our fatigued bodies.

"It sure is morbid talking about how we're going to be killed by the sea," I said, looking to Verlen for support as we prepared our defense.

"The idea is how not to get killed by your favorite ocean or your favorite boat," he grinned. "But that is something we should talk about." I looked at him blankly.

"What should you do in case of death?" he asked.

"Mine or yours?"

"In case it's me," he paused. "Tell my family it was the way I wanted to go." We didn't say another word.

We had seen no sailboaters since Santo Tomás. Punta Canoas was totally isolated, like a planet all its own. The beach was ours, with no one but a few sea lions to dispute ownership. Cut off from land with the cliffs behind us and the water built up into a white foam on the seaside, we had a spot just big enough for us to stand and erect our tents for the night—one small area of hope.

That evening Verlen and I were closer than we had ever been. Sharing resources and experience was a comfort, and combatting the problems of survival drew us together.

"The mistake most people make," Verlen told me, "is they fight themselves and each other. If we fight anything, it's got to be the circumstances. We're in the business of staying alive." It was a cozy scene. As a flashlight hung from the top of Verlen's tent, he sat inside fixing a piece of gear and I was beside him, writing in my journal. I looked at my partner. If I had been mending socks and he reading a newspaper, we could have passed for any couple, but I knew we were partners on an expedition sitting in a tent in the Baja.

Verlen was obsessed with exploring a continent by canoe. In 1971 he had traversed 7,000 miles of Canadian and Alaskan waters, following a historic fur trade route from Montreal to the Bering Sea. He had named his first trip "Never Before, Never Again." Yet here he was paddling 28,000 miles farther. He had told me many times that he was an explorer at heart, a traveling man, and I believed him. He had told me adventures from dozens of shorter trips. The dangers didn't ruffle him—he considered even the long, boring stretches a part of the experience.

When I asked Verlen why he had left home in the first place, he said something in him had to go. From what I understood, he was headed home now with every paddle stroke he took. I wondered if he had planned another adventure to follow the Ultimate Canoe Challenge, if he would ever be able to stay home.

It was hard to know who this man was to me. He was my father, brother, mentor, and friend. In a way we were married—both of us mated to our goal. Verlen was an explorer, that was sure. Developing the pride of an explorer myself, I finished the entry in my notes, said good-night, and walked the few steps back to my tent.

For a long time I sat looking at the point and wondering about Steve Landick. Had he resumed the journey? Would he have the foresight to take a partner down the coast? I knew how much Verlen and I were needing one another and hoped Steve was not alone. As the sun went down I kept looking out to sea. Then I zipped my door flap shut and snuggled into my sleeping bag. Off and on during the night rocks skittered down the cliff and lightly showered my tent.

When we woke the next morning the ocean around the point was calm, so we launched as soon as we could pack. Leaving Punta Canoas, we headed for the next harbor, Punta Blanca, 42 miles away. After punching through the surf I continued to paddle steadily, and soon pulled into the lead. For days Verlen had been paddling in front of me, assuming that I would follow. Now he was the one trailing. I soon discovered that being in the lead offered a different perspective. The ocean ahead was mine. When I looked over my shoulder and saw the small dot of Verlen's canoe about a quarter of a mile behind me, I was reminded of a Morris Louis painting I had seen at the Art Institute in Chicago, a giant canvas with one small speck of color in one corner.

I wished that I hadn't looked back, because I suddenly felt afraid. I scolded myself for getting separated from Verlen. The ocean rolled and heaved around my small boat, and I looked toward the shore trying to find a stable reference point. But the shore was no comfort. I saw not even one dot of color, only a barrier of rocks and desert hills and a distracting variety of texture. Thin riverbeds broadened into deep valleys, and as I looked farther inland I saw the earth scarred by sandy landslides that fell into the sea.

The morning had begun peacefully enough—the irrational wind was absent, but high swells were in evidence even at dawn. The new day had encouraged me forward, but now I stopped paddling and floated, wanting

Verlen to catch up. As his boat came closer I began to relax. The security of our team made a big difference and seemed to push back the immensity of the ocean. Reunited, we shared a pot of macaroni left over from our evening meal.

"There has got to be a storm system somewhere," Verlen said as he searched the sky. "The swells are reaching us first. The distance between the swells indicates how far the weather system is traveling. The amount of stored energy is transferred over distance and increases the length of the swells. I hope that wind doesn't build up again today."

"Eat this stuff before it gets cold," I ordered. The cook pot had been off the burner since the night before, and I made the joke to mask my nervousness. I didn't want to paddle ahead again, so I stayed right next to Verlen, hoping he would suggest that we hook up.

The swells responded to a morning wind, and soon the waves next to us were so tall that we could hardly see over them. We hooked up the canoes.

I had thought that being better prepared—tying ourselves into the boats, putting on life jackets and extra clothing—would make me feel better. But when the time came to tie in I did it not with an attitude of responsible caution, but with a feeling of resignation to our fate. By the middle of the afternoon the waves were breaking so heavily I realized nothing we did made any difference. Only by the grace of God and the design of the boats were we surviving.

Verlen's ironman nature remained stable, and looking at him inspired me. His muscled arms did not stop working. I never thought of Verlen dying, he is so much alive. But the waves seemed bigger than life, and the constant sound of surf beating the shore roared in my ears like a buzz saw. Paddling in each trough was like entering a cave. I watched the waves, losing my concentration and parts of my sanity as the day continued. We wanted to get off the water, but each projection of land proved useless as the surf ripped into the indented bays along the coast. We were still looking for an inlet when the sun went down, and the security of Punta Blanca was miles ahead.

"Don't worry," Verlen said pointing to a thin sliver of moon. "We've got enough light to get where we're going."

"I don't like this," I said, paddling blindly. I looked at the moon for hope and realized that a bank of clouds was beginning to smother the crescent.

"Now we're done for sure, the clouds are coming over the moon!" I wailed.

"Well, why don't you stop 'em?" my partner said simply. One of us had to panic, and since Verlen never did I habitually responded to the danger of our situation. I saw us as a couple again, this time watching television. A knock comes at the door. Verlen pays no attention, mesmerized by the

112

tube. Why can't he answer the door? Someone has to answer the knock, so I get up to let the caller in. But now I realize there is a choice. I don't have to answer the door, especially if I know fear is waiting to get in.

As the waves climbed around us, Verlen's attitude took root in me and I decided to think positively—a technique of survival we had failed to discuss at Punta Canoas, but one that was just as important as the life jacket around my body and even better than the rope tied around my waist. Clouds covered the sky and blocked the moon. The swells had still not settled. I formed a three-point plan of resistance.

"Verlen, if I shout doom and nothing happens, then I'm either a fool, a liar, or both, and I don't want to be either. Number two—if we do capsize, why not go cheerfully? Number three—what I believe usually does happen: we get what we want. Why not look forward to success? Failure out here is bleak." Smiling, I began to sing in the turmoil of the sea. I might not be able to stop the clouds from swallowing the moon, but I could keep paddling and remain a contender for the finish. With those thoughts in mind, I sang as loudly as I could.

"I must go to the ocean, to the ocean wide and blue. I must go to the ocean, to paddle there with you."

"Valerie, your moods go up and down like the swells we're riding," Verlen complained. "But you're on the right track now. Stay with it."

"I'm learning the secrets, Verlen. One of them is song. No wonder songs and ballads are tuned in harmony with the ocean. The surf roars and song is the appropriate response."

"I'm not convinced," he replied.

"Why don't you join me?"

"I think you might lose some of the magic if one of us is off key," he explained.

We arrived at Punta Blanca around midnight. The point was so low we lost sight of it in the darkness and swung too far south, missing the natural harbor. We turned around and paddled back, following along the edge of the dark shadows of land until we had aligned our canoes with the sheltering curve of a landing. The swells raced under us and we knew the waves were breaking against the beach, but we couldn't see anything. Our flashlights were as useless as fireflies and only dimmed our vision.

"Verlen, you got us around the point," I said. "Let me take us through the surf." We approached slowly, back-paddling cautiously. We could only feel the rise and fall of our boats in the swells. Then I saw the white flash of shore break in the dark.

"This is it Verlen! Go for it!" Paddling madly, we rode a high crest without mishap and were deposited on an uninhabited beach.

Within an hour we had set up our tents and I was nursing the stove that burped from the cheap Mexican gas we were burning. I couldn't breathe and my eyes smarted from the smoke, so I turned the thing off and forgot about cooking dinner. Biting into a cold tortilla, I walked down to the water's edge and looked up to see the thin moon shining bravely above our camp. The clouds had been pushed away.

The next morning the surf was mean, dumping hard as it broke over rock fingers. At first I couldn't understand how we had managed to land the evening before, but the difference was the tide. We couldn't wait for the tide to change, though—the weather was good, so we would have to pass through the surf and keep moving.

Our plan for departure was to wade and wait for the smaller sets. My canoe sat in the sand like a reluctant mule, and tugging at the bowline did no good, so Verlen had to help get the boat into the water. I was standing knee-deep in the ocean, trying to hold my jacket above the splash and time the intervals for jumping into my canoe and paddling out, when a wave came for shore that was larger than the rest. I gripped the cockpit rim to hold on tight as it passed, but it grabbed my boat sideways. Though I still held the bowrope, the canoe was forced out of my grasp. The next wave turned the boat even farther sideways, until the following wave picked up the boat and threw it like a battering ram into my groin. I doubled over in pain and hobbled back onto the beach, pulling the canoe to shore. Handing Verlen the bowline, I waded to dry ground and fell down. My groin was bruised and an egg-shaped lump appeared. Verlen sat beside me stroking my head.

"If you're all right, we'd just as well keep moving, Valerie. I'll help you with your canoe. The surf is getting bigger as the tide comes in. Do you think you can paddle?" I made some experimental motions in the air and nodded weakly. I moved my legs. Nothing seemed to be broken. Once I was in my boat, Verlen stretched the spray cover from my waist to the cockpit, then held my deck and waited for a settling in the waves. When the ocean paused, he pushed me into a set of oncoming foam. I could hear him yelling.

"Paddle! Paddle!" My adrenaline was pumping and my muscles straining near panic as the swells began to crash around me. I was punching through the breakers, but just when I thought it was over, another swell neared the breaking point as it rose from the sea. My canoe punched through the roller just before it heaved a curl of water down upon itself, and I came through soaked and shivering on the open-water side. My nose was running and I was talking to myself.

Verlen was out of sight behind the surf wall, and there was no one to help him. Finally I saw him coming.

"Punch through! Punch through!" I shouted. He did—his boat grew larger as it came toward me, his arms paddling quick strokes, chomping at the sea.

Once we were both outside the surfline, I realized how cold I was.

"Save your energy Valerie, bundle up," my partner instructed. "Let's eat a bite. That will make you feel better." I dug into my pack and pulled out a jar of peanut butter. Carefully scraping the last particles of food from the glass, I said good-bye to my last bite of San Diego.

We had paddled for four hours when I looked at my watch calendar: it was Sunday morning and almost 11 o'clock. Thoughts of home filled me—back home, church services would just be starting. We connected the boats and had our own service. Afterwards I was able to return to my paddling with a renewed energy and sense of purpose. The ocean shrank in size when I thought about God.

After church in Woodinville, I would drive home, change clothes, enjoy Sunday dinner, and relax. At sea, in the Baja tradition, Verlen and I paddled around Punta Maria and came through the surf, riding a quiet crest onto the beach. We had come 22 miles since morning and landed in the Baja I had always imagined: there were no rocks, but a desert of cactus and sand. We spent the rest of the day drying out, removing everything from the boats and hanging gear and clothes on bushes with lines strung from one cactus to the next.

Our days were busy—there was hardly time for everything. Mammoth paddling jobs, unpacking and packing, judging the surf, and cooking by flashlight had become a way of life. That afternoon we sat relaxed, watching the surf as it danced like rows of white petticoats on a blue party dress ruffling along the shore.

Verlen made a fire and took out a griddle from the back of his canoe—what all did he carry in there, anyway? He made huge, hard cookie pancakes filled with cornmeal, granola, powdered eggs, and pancake mix. They were not like the pancakes my mother used to make, and the powdered butter didn't add to any resemblance. But it didn't matter much—they were loaded with calories that would burn as energy.

While Verlen patched the bulkhead with tape where my rear compartment was leaking, I sat in the sand, propped against a pack. Enjoying our quiet moments, I scribbled in my journal until long after dark.

NINE

Thanksgiving

"Wake up!" my partner was urging from outside the tent. "It's a beautiful day, and there are lots of questions to be answered about those lagoons ahead." Mention of the lagoons roused me, but I was suspicious of his beautiful day report.

"Sounds like bribery to me," I countered. There was no sign of daylight—not surprising, since it was four in the morning—and Verlen was beginning to dismantle my tent poles.

"I'm captain today, and we're going to cook breakfast. I don't care what kind of a hurry you're in. I'll be out in a minute," I yelled, preparing a stall. Using precious moments of privacy I propped myself on the air-filled sleeping pad. Balancing a pocket mirror on my knee and holding a flashlight between my teeth, I poured cleaning solution and saline juice to wash the sand from my contact lenses before I popped them in place.

The tour poster picture of perpetual sun and warmth in the Baja is all wrong. At Morro Santo Domingo, for example, my tent was stuck on a cold sandhill in what felt like an arctic chill. I finally forced myself out of my sleeping bag. As I sat up, my head was trapped in a cloud cover of damp trousers, shirt, and underwear hanging from a ceiling guy wire. There hadn't been a laundry in the last month or enough fresh water to rinse the salt and sweat from our garments. My pillow was a stuff sack of extra clothing, but I didn't want to use dry clothes each morning—whatever we had on was soon splashed by our launching in the surf. Wet clothes never dried rolled in a ball and stored in a corner of the canoes. The week before, at Punta Colonet, I had cleaned and emptied my boat only to find a soggy

116

shirt that had floated forward and lodged in the bow. Verlen sensibly taught me to "wear 'em dry." The discomfort lasted only a moment, he reminded me. My jaw set as I slowly pulled on cold, dampish clothes, unzipped the tent, and stepped out under the stars to face the man who was harassing me.

"Good morning, Verlen," I said. He had already moved to the water's edge and was busy with the canoes, turning them around in the sand toward another day at sea. The bow of his canoe lay at the farthest reach of the surfline, the nose of the boat lifting slightly with each wave, the stern end firmly planted in the sand. Verlen snapped the weather cover off the cockpit of the canoe and began stuffing his boat with gear. His tent was down, his bags were packed, his mind was on only one thing.

I began setting up a camper breakfast on the beach by starlight, placing the stove beside a cobble of rocks and spreading cooking gear on flat stone tabletops, trying to avoid the sand. The morning before, when Verlen had been captain, we had eaten cold tortillas with powdered cheese filling as we floated—a miserly reward for paddling for an hour and making four miles before dawn.

When the weather was good, we had to take advantage of it. Every daylight hour meant travel time and it was especially important that day because we had only a sketchy idea of what we would find ahead in the Bahía de Sebastian Viscaino, but at least we could set off into the unknown with full stomachs. Studying the charts by flashlight, we ate reconstituted spaghetti and soy protein in the dark. I wasn't sure how much improvement this was over tortillas and powdered cheese, but at least it was hot.

The Baja Peninsula juts southward into the ocean like a sturdy leg, complete with heavy upper thigh at the north end, a knee joint 500 miles south, and toes dangling below the Tropic of Cancer at Cabo San Lucas. About halfway down the coast on the west side a large pocket bay cuts into the land. From there the sailboaters took a direct 59-mile open water route to Cedros Island, but our canoe route would be much longer because we followed the coast. Along our path, three lagoons extended inland into the deep pocket. Laguna Manuela, four miles south of our camp at Morro Santo Domingo, was small and relatively unused. Laguna Guerrero Negro, considerably larger, had been of commercial importance some years ago, serving as an export outlet for sodium chloride from the village base of Puerto Venustiano Carranza. This facility was reportedly abandoned, and the entrance channel was no longer dredged for barge traffic. The village was within six miles of Guerrero Negro, a town settled on the major transportation link of Baja Highway 1. The third and largest lagoon, Ojo de Liebre, better known as Scammons, is famed for the seasonal migration of California gray whales to the calm inland breeding waters, and for a traffic of salt production important to the economy of Baja. Those lagoons were our only hope for protected landings. Sixty-three miles farther south and around the cup of the bay, a small dot of a village with the name of Malarrimo was noted on our charts. The words "boat landing" were printed in dark letters.

Verlen and I sat in the sand, finishing our breakfast and watching the dawn arrive. My pants were beginning to soak through from the damp ground. I glanced over at my partner—he was wisely crouched on his plastic map case. He held the grimy cook pot in his rough, sea-cracked hands. While he chewed, he spat out balls of soy protein that hadn't cooked properly. He never complained and I never corrected my impatience to get the food off the stove and into my stomach. A few more minutes of cooking time could have made the dried food more palatable. Verlen fished into his pot, scooped out the undesirables with his spoon, and flipped the tough chunks into the sand. The mechanics of the trip were by now second nature to him. Verlen was an explorer who had adjusted to the wilderness environment: he fit there. The night before I had caught him staring off into space with a strange look on his face.

"Verlen, you seem sad, are you thinking of your family?" He looked at me rather surprised. "Sad? When I think of my family, I'm never sad."

"Well, do you miss your home?" I continued to probe.

"This is my home." His simple optimism was profound. I envied his stability, but it frustrated me because I couldn't match it.

We had a standing disagreement about pot-scrubbing technique. Verlen insisted we clean up and pack immediately after eating, which meant going down to the surfline and jumping back and forth between the waves while scraping the pots in wet sand. My method was to carry the dirty pots out through the surf on our take-off, and when I needed a break from paddling, dunk them over the side. Since I was captain that day, I loaded the dirty dishes into my canoe. Verlen took his pan down to the water, and without getting even one toe wet, he cleaned the pot and packed it neatly in his boat.

I packed my own boat, setting the dirty dishes on the floor, and pushed my bow into the sea. The surf was minimal. I stood in knee-deep water, my pantlegs rolled, one leg in the canoe and the other stuck in the moving water to steady the boat. Once I achieved a balance and figured out that the waves were cooperating, I drew the other leg on board. Raising my paddle, I reached out with a first stroke and escaped from the surfline before the waves could push me back on shore. That morning my exit was clean—only a bit of water sloshed into the canoe. I stopped paddling outside the shore break, sponged out the bottom of my boat, and worked on cleaning the blackened cook pot. Verlen paddled out next, commenting on the even temper of the swells. His habit was to wipe the water from his glasses after he came through the surf. We would paddle 10 minutes more and then remove our jackets as our body temperatures increased from our efforts. Weather conditions were stable: no wind, and consequently, no need to hook up the boats. I appreciated Verlen's careful planning. He had designed boats that could be hooked together for safety but that could also be paddled separately so each person felt independent. For days we had been attached in straitjacket stability because of the uncertain weather. What a relief it was that morning to cavort around in my own boat, free from my partner's assistance. I felt like a happy seal. The canoes were also moving faster without the drag of the catamaran system.

That day Verlen and I shared an exciting expectancy but I also felt a tinge of fear. The lagoons ahead were new to us. We had heard that the entrances of these exotic inland ponds were flanked, crossed, and sided by humping swells, breakers of tide going in and out over shifting sandbars, stiff currents, and wild reef systems. All advice warned that entering a lagoon was a job for a local pilot of considerable experience. Our charts were almost worthless as guidance—they lacked detail and made no provision for the storms and tidal currents that continually altered the openings.

By midmorning we arrived at Laguna Manuela. Our introduction was a white line of breakers stretching out into the sea as far as we could squint our eyes. Sitting at the water line in our small craft we lost the advantage of an elevated view. We were accustomed to surf on the shore side, but at the lagoon mouth ahead white breakers extended for over a mile in a perpendicular line from the beach.

"Don't worry, Verlen, we'll just squeeze close to the shore and paddle into the mouth," I declared. I was willing to paddle into the apex of the angle ahead, hoping to find passage through the turmoil in the narrow area where the shore formed a T with the bar. We floated close to the shore surf looking for a way into the lagoon, but lines of white breakers criss-crossed in a series of overlapping baffles. The only way into the lagoon was out and around the bar, which extended as a multiple ridge into the sea. The open-water breaks were deceptive and appeared to move as I paddled toward them. Without the land line for reference, it seemed that I was paddling past a snoring white-water giant.

Which was the last breaker? I strained to understand this new territory. When could we safely make the turn around the breakers and head again toward shore? I gave the turbulence lots of room, paddling out a quarter of a mile farther than Verlen's observation point. His reconnaissance was a calm hundred feet from the foaming violence. I stared at the white breakers, trying to memorize the rhythmic disorder of destruction. As the breakers melted into the sea, the ocean lay calm for a moment, then another swell broke and surfaced over the submerged bar. The entire area was erupting in white water. After watching for a while longer, we realized it was impossible to make an entrance there. We paddled past the roar of Laguna Manuela and set sights for Laguna Guerrero Negro. Both of us were optimistic and began to plan our entrance to the second lagoon.

"Hey, Verlen, the map swears there's a town inside this lagoon, and that it's on the highway. Maybe there's a telephone! I can call my folks."

"A town is a good sign that this lagoon mouth is navigable," Verlen replied.

"Enchiladas, Verlen." I could already envision the evening's celebration. But at the second lagoon, Guerrero Negro, we encountered the same un-friendly barricade of breakers obscuring the lagoon entrance. The guidebook had said the entrance was impassable, but we had thought the warning was only for sailboaters with keels and depth limits—surely a canoe could slip in anywhere. We were surprised at the wild turmoil of waves, scrambling and pushing themselves at each doorway ahead of us, dis-courteously shoving their way before us like an impatient concert crowd.

By then it was two o'clock and Scammons Lagoon was 15 miles farther south. That meant five hours of steady paddling, if we were to land before dark. We dug into the water with strong, even strokes.

The coastline was low and sandy, with enormous waves rolling toward the beach. Our boats rode up and down on each swell. The weather was hot and the ocean surface glared back at us from the reflected afternoon sun. My hat and colored glasses protected my face as I stared at the pencil-line horizon looking for any sign of another boat. But the ocean seemed empty except for the two of us.

I was tired—the lagoon attempts had used more of my adrenaline than I realized and my arms were rebelling—that familiar ache from paddling too hard and too fast. We paddled on silently, but the tension buzzed in my ears. It was getting dark.

When we finally neared Scammons, its entrance didn't look any more promising than the others had. The entire area was shoals and sea-bottom gradations. Our sea guide noted that the entrance buoy was a black can, but in the mountains of swells I could not see a can, black or otherwise. There were several lights stationed on the shore and floating at sea, none of them diagramed on our charts. Again, we saw no entrance. A rolling surf was breaking on the beach to the north, and combers broke on the bar to the south. The entrance course would have to be threaded between a maze of breakers. My only thought was to go out, way out, and avoid the imminent possibility of crashing close to shore. The swells seemed to be gathering mo-mentum, as if any moment their building and heaving force would break apart even as we floated on top.

"We can't make it, Verlen. There's no understanding this entrance, and there's no more daylight to try." My nerves were on edge, and with the evening coming I was looking for some way to quit. I spotted a tall three-legged dolphin navigation light, the first free-standing navigation post I'd seen for 500 miles of Baja coast.

"Let's tie to the light and wait for dawn," I suggested.

"It's not going to be fun." Verlen was skeptical. As we paddled to the light over the swells, I questioned my decision. The lamp offered a beacon of security, but as we got closer I saw three bare poles stuck in the water, a small platform 25 feet above the waves, and nothing around for miles.

"This is really bleak," my partner said, looking at our temporary hitching post. "You sure wouldn't want to be tied here in a storm—we'd be yanked like yo-yos. It would be better to float free."

"Looks safe to me. Look at that lightning over there." I directed his attention to the northern sky. "If it gets really rough, I can shinny up on the platform and hang on." Besides, what was the alternative? We could be paddling all night in a storm if the lightning was an indicator, and we were still 32 miles from "boat landing." I couldn't see any way into Scammons Lagoon through the scanty directions and uncharted navigation lights. Reviewing the situation, we accepted our three-legged host and rafted the canoes together in a catamaran.

Verlen removed the long end of his bowline from the starboard hook on his canoe and paddled close enough to one leg of the light to begin tying a seaman's knot. The swells were pushing us up and into the encrusted metal leg. I back-paddled to keep the canoes from bruising themselves against the poles, but each swell shoved us into the pipe again and the barnacles scraped layers of white gelcoat from our hulls. The navigation light, which had at first been our hope, was now abusing us, taunting us, as if saying, "so you want to get close? Well, get real close," and shoving our noses into its crusted leg. Verlen took an extra length of rope from his bag and soon had the canoes secured with two lines. A tremendous current coursed under us heading into the lagoon mouth. Our canoes reminded me of a dog rushing out of his house and choking himself at the end of his chain as the ropes yanked us in a continuous metrical reprimand. Each swell buoyed us toward the light in a margin of ease. Then, as the boats dropped into the trough of each wave, the ropes tightened and caught our motion, defining our boundary with a jerk.

We layered on every piece of clothing we had to protect our bodies from the evening chill. Verlen took off his captain's hat and pulled his hood over his ears as the night settled in on us. Then he reached down and unscrewed the top of his gorp jar and sat nibbling, like a kid eating popcorn at the movies. The show was the lightning that sprayed technicolor sparks in the northern sky.

I cooked supper in the bottom of my canoe. Pushing gear aside with my toes, I cleared a space to set our stove, and between my feet a cook pot full of water balanced on top of the burner. I steadied the bubbling tower and shifted my legs beyond the increasing heat.

"There's not much of a selection tonight, Verlen," I said sadly. The main food sack was buried deep in the stern, and I wasn't going to dig for it. We would make do with noodles and powdered milk. When the noodles were cooked, Verlen ate with unquestioning patience. I tossed most of my portion overboard. Giving up on supper, I took out my contacts, stowed my gear, punched at stuff sacks, and removed my seat, making a nest in my boat for my body to sink into.

To ride out the night I pulled the spray skirt around the cockpit above me. An opening about the size of a dinner plate in the skirt served as a breathing space, and through it I could see the stars in the sky and the one intense star we had tied to. Occasionally a wave would cover the deck and drip in on my face.

"Valerie, look at this—visitors!" Verlen reported. As I peeked out of my makeshift tent my eyes searched the darkness and focused on a salt barge lumbering toward the lagoon. We had spent a month paddling on the ocean without seeing any commercial traffic.

"They'll send someone out to us. Maybe the authorities will come and arrest us." I knew it was against the law to tie to a navigation light, and I envisioned the night spent in a jail after a midsea arrest—what a comfort. "Verlen, remember the consulate in San Diego?"

"Sure, they promised to pick us up if they caught us on the water," he said. The thought gave us hope. The barge traveled past us toward the entrance of the lagoon. In addition to the required running lights, a bright spotlight beam flashed from the barge in our direction and centered on our predicament. An observant pilot had discovered us hitched to the post.

"I figure the Navy has already been radioed. Even now they're planning to come and arrest us—let's follow them. I'll gladly turn myself in."

"They're moving too fast," Verlen pointed out. We watched as the barge threaded through the lights and was lost as it entered the lagoon.

Hours passed. The barge crew was probably home, warm and comfortable on dry land. I myself was cramped in a narrow sleeping berth, and different parts of my body slept better than I did. My foot, leg, then arm went to sleep, and I would wake up to readjust and relieve the pinpricked sensation of my sluggish parts. Suddenly I became aware of Verlen reaching and thrashing about, digging frantically through his cockpit. I struggled to sit up through my spray skirt opening.

"I've lost my personal bag," he announced. Verlen had used his personal bag as a headrest, and woke up realizing it had fallen overboard. His precious bundle, a bulging masculine purse with knife, mirror, film, pills, candy, address book, toolkit, diary, and dozens more small items had fallen into the sea.

"Verlen, I can't believe it. How did you do that?" I knew how important the bag was to him. He was stunned but stoic about the loss. I told him how sorry I was, then burrowed down again in my canoe, adjusting my spray skirt, positioning my head rest. . . .

"Verlen," I screeched. Now my headrest had fallen in the water. A small stuff-sack pillow of clothes floated away as fast as the tide could carry it toward the lagoon mouth. Verlen lunged for the bag with his paddle, climbing over the stern of his canoe and giving the reach all of his length. He lost his grip, and the paddle he had used for 20,000 miles fell into the sea. The current carried it away and out of sight in the darkness.

"Quick, untie the boats," I hollered. With several fierce strokes I pushed our catamaran toward the navigation light to give Verlen access to the tied connection. The constant tug of the waves had tightened the knots, and Verlen's cold fingers could not loosen the glued nest of fibers. He seemed to be in shock.

"Cut the line, Verlen," I ordered, reminding him of a sure procedure. He pulled out his pocketknife and cut the tether, freeing us to pursue his missing paddle, and retrieve it from the water thief. He slit the cord that held his spare paddle beneath his deck. His first strokes tore holes in the water as he fumbled with the unfamiliar stick.

We searched, criss-crossing the wide area of sea within the reflected navigation light, but there was no sign of the paddle. I strained to see the yellow handle or a portion of the green blade floating in the darkness. I looked over at Verlen on the right side of the catamaran and saw his intent face. The farther we reached into the blackness, the larger the ocean grew. Our search was futile. Verlen finally gave up and moaned in dejection. This was the first complaint I had ever heard from him.

"I would have rather broken my arm than lost that paddle," he said in a small, almost unrecognizable voice. He had taken the first stroke of the Ultimate Canoe Challenge more than two years before with that same green and yellow paddle. When I met him in Seattle he had logged 20,000,000 paddle strokes and pushed aside more than 18,000 miles of water with the same blade. Even away from the water it was an important part of Verlen's equipment—he would pick up his paddle to lean on and hold during press interviews. A butterfly decal decorated the blade and testified to its handmade quality. Its salutation, "Vaya con Dios," flashed at me with every dip.

Even though I was just a rookie with barely a month of ocean travel, I could understand how Verlen felt. My own paddle had become an essential tool. It was an extension of my arms that not only transferred the stretch of motion into the water, but waved like a grand baton as I exchanged from the right side to the left. I could forgive my paddle for anything—the patter of water droplets that showered down from an upraised blade, the occasional clatter of handle to gunwale during a careless forward swing. My paddle helped push me offshore in the mornings and at night steadied my leap onto dry land.

"Maybe some fisherman will find it one day," I encouraged, trying to cheer Verlen. But his face remained silent with grief. This was only the second time I had seen Verlen sad—the first had been a few days earlier, when he had told me of a far more serious loss, one that brought tears to his eyes as he recounted it.

Verlen had joined Clint Waddell on a Cross Continent Canoe Safari in 1973. Paddling upstream on the Ottawa River, they saw a man on a highway bridge waving and yelling. As they paddled closer they made out the words: "Your father has died."

"Clint, is he talking to you?" Verlen squinted over his shoulder, asking his partner.

"It can't be mine, my dad died 10 years ago," Clint answered. Paddling closer to the bridge, Verlen realized the message was for him.

"Hey, your name Kruger?" the messenger asked. "Your father died. That's all I know, just got a telegram at the station house. Lucky I found you guys." Verlen and Clint had pulled their canoe out of the water, and then Verlen had left the two men to walk by himself along the empty road, grieving and praying.

"Verlen, it's gone," I said. "The paddle is gone, what do you want to do?"

"It's late, no point heading south at this hour. Let's go back to the light," he said. He was back to his usual self again—I could tell by the tone of his voice that he was recovering.

Slowly we returned to the navigation light and retied the canoes. The night's pace had slowed from excitement and fear to a depressing quiet. I made myself as comfortable as I could in my canoe. Grasping the cockpit rim, I eased my body onto the floor of the boat, using my seat as a pillow. I pulled my life jacket under my shoulders to absorb the angle and soften the flat plane. How could I sleep? Cold and cramped, my body was Cinderella's ugly sister trying to fit into the glass slipper. If I could just dismantle my frame, store my torso in a stuff sack in the rear compartment, and detach my arms and legs like folding tent poles. My body was scrunched between the two foot braces and rudder pedals, colliding with equipment jammed in the nose of my boat. I adjusted my buttocks and legs to the space and tried to welcome the miserable sleep.

Hours later I was jolted awake with a direct hit. Confused, I found myself inside a cage of steel legs that was banging and jostling our canoes. As I gained sense I realized the navigation light was still stationary and had not attacked us. But the tide had changed. After sweeping into the lagoon for the prescribed 12 hours, the tide had now begun its race back to the open ocean, pulling us with it. Our canoes had shifted their direction of drift and were now wedged under the navigation posts, where each swell smacked us against the pipes. We paddled and pushed to untangle ourselves. Could we trust our position to sleep again?

I was grateful that the dreadful night was finally nearing dawn. I looked up at the inhospitable beacon light, wondering why we were still hanging on. I was too tired to move, but not secure enough to sleep. By five A.M. the moon was gone and the heat lightning in the sky had cooled and settled. Our bodies were stiff. A new day had begun.

Verlen was captain, and he chose to leave the canoes catamaraned and direct us toward another beacon light farther west and out of the bay. We paddled for an hour before the sky began to brighten. The pinpoint of light we headed for enlarged into a large, bouncing orange buoy. As we paddled closer, we studied the new monster waiting to greet us. This one didn't have three legs, but was a strange, thick stalk rising from the sea, dancing up and down and clanging in the swells.

"I'm going to have to stop for breakfast," I cautioned in a dizzy fatigue.

"There's no place to tie here," Verlen decided. "Can you cook while we're moving?"

"Sure, hand me the stove," I said. I had done it before, and began to make room in the small cockpit space to cook breakfast on the floor of my canoe.

"Here you go, kid, make mine a cheese omelet," Verlen said jokingly, as he transferred the stove across the open water and into my outstretched palm. I opened the release valve of the stove and lit the burner. Verlen had pumped the pressure too far, and fuel began to spill over the floor of my canoe in a lava flow of burning liquid. Between my legs, in just inches of space, I had a runaway fire.

"Verlen!" I shouted.

"Well, put it out," my partner instructed as he continued paddling our rig.

I pulled my spray skirt from beneath my seat and swatted at the blaze. My feet were feeling hot, and I was getting panicky. The space was so small that I was able to overpower the flames, but I kept beating at them to make sure they were all out. Luckily, the boat material was fireproof, and the fire left behind only a smudge of black smoke on the insides of my craft and a distinct smell of melting rubber as my neoprene spray skirt began to cool.

"Burritos."

"What did you say?" Verlen looked quizically in my direction.

"Burritos, tacos, enchiladas, guacamole, too. Oh, I'm so blue." I had a new sea song about a Mexican-food dream. Funny how we both reacted so differently to exhaustion. Verlen became unresponsive and quiet, while I swung from irritability and jagged nerves to simple-minded hallucinations.

"Just hand me a candy bar, Verlen." I was finally giving in. A candy bar for breakfast, but what did it matter? I couldn't remember dinner, or even a regular sleep. Sipping tepid powdered milk, I nibbled a damp tortilla, taking small bites so my stomach would not reject the offering. Then my good humor was gone, and I paddled on, nodding off in exhaustion as the day began. My energy store was depleted; the night had not renewed us.

We were forgotten convicts. The Navy was not even interested in arresting us. I could hear them say, "Let the sea take care of the intruders." We had been in the canoes for 25 hours.

Having paddled clear of the tidal influence at the entrance of Scammons Lagoon, we were within the south basin of Bahia de Sebastian Viscaino, where the coast encircled the ocean like a great hook. The low, sandy land that baked into the Viscaino desert looked desolate. Nothing seemed to be moving except the water under us. I could think of a hundred reasons to stop paddling. My glasses were sliding down my nose—I would have to stop and readjust. My pants were riding up—set that paddle down and pause. The canoe deck needed a cleansing sponge, my hat needed a tug over my ears, I needed more suntan lotion, a dab of lip balm. Put on a windbreaker, take it off, reach for a snack, stop to chew a snack. And every time I put my paddle down, I looked over to see if Verlen noticed my interruptions. My partner was fairly tolerant, but occasionally I could see disapproval. I tried to discipline myself, but soon began to wonder what time it was. I would take ten more strokes, and then look at my watch. Just five more strokes and I can look at my watch. One more stroke and I can break long enough to look at my watch. I put the paddle down and cocked my wrist toward line of sight.

"Verlen, it's Thanksgiving." I noted the time and date in surprise. I had never had a Thanksgiving like this before. The ocean seemed to spread out to forever. I looked at Verlen. "Tell me about your holidays at home." I asked. Conversation always made paddling easier. Verlen had 9 children and 21 grandchildren, so my energy revived in anticipation of a story from the memories of his warm family getherings. I was not disappointed.

"Our holidays were important times. Lots of food was eaten when my family got together. There was always someone new popping in, a birthday or marriage announcement." As he talked I could envision his tribe assembling for the celebration, with Verlen officiating and adding a blessing for the occasion.

"I always did get restless," he admitted. Paddling more forcefully for a moment, he stopped talking.

"My family would eat until we couldn't move," I reminisced. "My mother was a great cook, and she outdid herself on Thanksgiving."

"Don't you have some cookies tucked someplace?" Verlen asked. "Talking about Thanksgiving is making me hungry."

From a waterproof bag I pulled out two pounds of animal crackers, a treasure found at the Mexican store in Camalu. We began to devour hippopotami shapes dipped in the orange marmalade rationed from San Diego. We dined on hippos rather than turkey, our canoe decks serving as our table. I had to smile seeing those animals climb onto my deck so far from shore.

"When you built these canoe-arks did you ever envision animals two-by-two?" I asked the designer.

"The animals were your idea, Valerie, and I sure am glad I didn't bring two of you," he said with a grin.

"A few unwanted guests." Verlen motioned to the horizon, where the sky was filling with mountain-size cloud billows. Within minutes the formations had been rearranged by high altitude wind gusts. Who has seen the wind? We saw the wind, ripping and tearing at the clouds above. I saw a gust that shoved a cloud clear out of line and ripped off its head, sending it shredded and streaked across the sky. But the water around us was calm.

"Those clouds are telling us what it's like up on top," said Verlen. "Let's hope that wind doesn't come down to our level."

All afternoon the clouds were batted around in the sky. Crossing the Bay of Sebastian Viscaino, we were almost six miles from land, the farthest we had been from shore. A thin sliver of earth was squeezed between the sky and waterline, and the swells of the ocean bounced and blocked our view every few minutes. Verlen was steering by compass, heading for the village marked Malarrimo on our maps. He had a homing instinct I never understood. He conscientiously consulted his compass, wristwatch, and charts, his face hidden beneath his captain's hat. By late afternoon we had spotted a different color of land and continued toward the estimated target of Malarrimo.

"Verlen, that's it," I shouted, and pointed to a small fishing village far ahead on the shore.

"No, it can't be," he reported.

"It's a village," I insisted.

"But not Malarrimo. Not the "boat landing" shown on the charts. According to the map, the landing will appear further west." The precious daylight was disappearing. Heat or distant storms made the corners of the sky crack again with electricity, as if the show from the night before would be running again for our amusement. Winds generally settle at night, but that holiday evening they were descending from the sky to ravage the water. Though we had not been ashore in the past 30 hours, our fatigue was now compounded by the wind.

"It's going to be rough, but we'll try to land," Verlen declared. We paddled with all our effort toward the little village I had spotted, but as we approached, it was evident that the small outcropping of land did not protect the harbor from the growing westerly swells. Breakers came around the point with full ocean force. A scattering of shacks hung on the hillside, but no safe boat landing was visible.

We headed back to sea and west along the shore, hoping Verlen's calculations were right and that Malarrimo would be ahead. As the sun went down, the wind increased. Verlen wasn't saying much. Scrunching and twisting in my cockpit, I took off my clothing and pulled on my wetsuit for warmth. Then I tied myself into the canoe and put on my life jacket.

"Drink some water, eat more cookies," Verlen broke the silence in a command. The diminishing bag of animal crackers was passed back and forth between the boats as we ate handfuls of critters in preparation for defense.

"Are you sure about a boat landing up ahead?" I asked. There were three small lights on the horizon, but the pattern looked to be an outline of a ship rather than a town. I squinted to search the distance ahead as the waves grew and thrashed around our canoes. If we followed the lights and they were a ship, we would be paddling out to sea. Our only safeguard was keeping a close eye on the compass. The night had gone black.

"The lights aren't moving. I think that's Malarrimo ahead. Right rudder." Verlen was paddling hard, trying to head us into the waves. We worked our way west along the coast following the curve of the large bay, making scarcely one-mile-an-hour progress against the intense head wind that had developed.

"Pray those lights don't go out before we land," Verlen said. I reached down into my side emergency pocket and brought out a strobe light I had never used before. My sponsor had given it to me, and I had brought it along because it was a neat little piece of machinery.

"That's not going to help," Verlen warned. Ignoring him, I stuck the flasher into the rim of my hat and set the light pulsing as a beacon. It lit the deck of my canoe and the foaming sea around me, pulsing into the darkness.

Verlen was fighting with the storm, and I had never seen him so serious.

I was detached, tired and numb, forfeiting any resistance, merely paddling on in a stupor of fatigue. Then I began to see more lights—a runway of lights—fogged and blurred through the salt spray on my glasses. It was Malarrimo. The boat landing.

We continued to paddle against the wind, directing the canoes toward the magic welcome of the brilliance ahead. We stared at the spots and lost our night vision, blinded by a glare of safety. Immediately around us the ocean was boiling. A reef roared on our right, a shore break wailed on the left. We approached on a narrow avenue through the crashing sea, paddling into another world where the reef was not an enemy but a friend, protecting the boat landing from the sea. As we made our way deeper into the harbor, we were drawn into a sheltered calm.

And people—we could make them out now, standing and calling to us, reaching out their arms toward us. Our canoes finally touched the shore after 36 hours afloat. Someone was lifting me out of my canoe. As I tried to straighten my body, I stumbled and couldn't understand what was holding me back. Then I realized that the safety line was still fastened. A man in the crowd cut my safety line as several people supported me. A woman was standing on the ridge, the lights silhouetting her against the night. Her arms were tightly drawn around her body, holding a bathrobe to her chest, and her skirt was blowing and flapping in the wind. The townspeople had seen the strobe light on my hat band and had come to help. The lights of the landing were half a dozen trucks and autos parked on the beach, pointing their headlights toward the sea.

I became part of the village crowd moving up the dirt landing toward a lighted shack. The arch of the firm doorway welcomed us as we moved inside. Papa Hernandez greeted us and introduced his family. Mama Hernandez stood at a propane stove, busy with her daughters preparing food. Papa motioned Verlen to a wooden chair at the central table.

I was ushered into a small back room crowded with sleeping children and beds stacked side-by-side. A worn blanket hung in the doorway, separating me from the rest of the household and the villagers who were standing in the kitchen staring at Verlen. I pulled dry clothes from my waterproof bag and stripped off the rubber wetsuit. In the dim light from the bare light bulb, I saw a worn reflection of myself in an old splotched mirror. My hair was wet and my face stained with salt. A young girl seated on one of the beds was nursing a baby and looking at me silently.

I dressed quickly and returned to the table, where laughter and warmth were a universal language. Food was brought—tortillas, beans, and dried beef. A frayed dish towel was carefully wrapped over the sugarbowl and dish of peppers to keep out the flies. Verlen and I were served heaping plates of food. The other guests propped their elbows on the space in front of them at the table. When I looked at Verlen I saw that his eyes were bugged out from fatigue.

Anibal, who was probably in his twenties, began talking in wild gestures and pantomime as he tried to explain the lobster fishing career of the village. His zany body picture of a frozen lobster had us perplexed until he flexed his finger pincers. Papa looked wise and nodded his head as we talked. Laura was her mother's best helper. Her T-shirt advertised an American auto company, and her eyes were wide with dark mascara. Verlen and I didn't argue about the extra portions mama forced on us. Once the elation of the food passed and my stomach filled, I realized that I could hardly move.

Papa Hernandez put us to bed. Walking down the landing to our boats, broom in hand, he pointed to where our tents should be, then swept the area of dirt. Verlen and I unloaded our gear and set up camp. Once we had zippered in, the lights of the landing were turned off and all was dark. I sat a long time there in the darkness, welcoming the silence and the stable moment of calm until, thankfully, I slept.

TEN

With Open Arms

November 26th was a regular work day for the villagers of Malarrimo. Outside our tents the fishermen were loading lobster traps into their boats and setting out for the sea. I didn't feel like going anywhere. Sore and exhausted from 36 hours of marathon paddling past the lagoons, I was slow motion. Verlen tried to talk me out of the slump.

"The secret is circulation," he said. "Get your body moving and you'll feel lots better. The tiredness is all in your mind. Remember what I told you yesterday." Gesturing like an optimistic camp counselor, he demonstrated by taking vigorous paddle strokes in the air. By then I had heard every one of my partner's pet theories. The day before, late in the afternoon, when each paddle stroke felt like pulling a broom through molasses, I had listened to Verlen's advice. He had explained that relief would come when I increased my stroke rate—it was Verlen's opinion that revving the heart rate flushed the system.

"Tiredness is a residue in the muscle system. Increasing the pumping action of the heart rejuvenates the body," he claimed.

Even though I thought the idea was silly, I'd learned enough from my partner's experience to give his theory a try. I picked up my paddle and sprinted for 60 seconds. Verlen was right—I immediately felt refreshed, as if I had rolled down a car window and gulped a breath of fresh air. Sprinting began to remove the lactic acid from my muscles. Continuing the experiment, I found that the more slowly I paddled trying to conserve energy, the more lethargic I became. But I was not convinced this technique would work on dry land. That day at Malarrimo my momentum was zero.

131

Laura was the first to visit our tents, bringing steaming mugs of coffee from the Hernandez kitchen. She sympathized with my condition and made it clear we would remain the honored guests of the village until I recovered. I felt guilty calling a rest day. I wasn't sick: my ailment was anemic ambition.

Sipping hot coffee, I lounged against my pack and dutifully looked at the map. It was no puddle-jump to the next harbor—the water route curved north and west around a peninsula of land marked Punta Eugenia. By our calculations Tortugas Bay was 50 miles away.

"We're headed for the best all-weather port between San Diego and Magdalena Bay," Verlen pointed out as he looked over my shoulder.

The map showed a clam-shaped bay sheltered by two pincers of land forming a three-quarter-mile entrance.

"I'll bet we find some good burritos in the harbor town of Tortugas. It's a popular sailboat stop. Maybe the *Vagabunda* will still be there," Verlen mused.

"In any case, our food drop should be waiting at the fuel dock," I remembered. "If the Bowers were able to make it." I scanned the ocean and saw that outside the reef, swells from the previous night's blow continued. A line of white was evident where the waves crashed into the rock barrier. If the water there at Malarrimo was unsettled, it would be even rougher around the point of land at Punta Eugenia. I studied the map—a road connected Malarrimo to Tortugas Bay in a direct southerly line. The distance looked to be about 20 miles.

"Verlen, I've got an idea. Maybe someone from Malarrimo is going to town this morning and we can catch a ride. We could both use a break from paddling, and it might be smart to locate our food bag and get our errands done before the weekend closes down the shops. Tomorrow, when we do paddle around Punta Eugenia, we won't have to stop in port for anything other than a second helping of burritos." I was energized by the prospect of an alternative to paddling.

"Boy, that's a great idea," Verlen said positively, thumping me on the back.

" 'Girl,' Verlen, I'm a girl," I reminded. "And if we do make it to town, I'll share with you my secret of rejuvenation."

"What's that?" he asked.

"I'm going shopping!" Pretending a miraculous cure, I jumped to my feet, picked up the paddle, and pantomimed a frenzied sprint. "I need a new hat," I explained.

Between Verlen and me and the Spanish-English dictionary, we conveyed to Laura our intention of hitching a ride to Tortugas Bay. She nodded her head and went in search of a driver. I began to look around my tent and get organized for a trip to town. It seemed as if every piece of my clothing were either wet or dirty. I was still sorting clothes when a pickup truck rattled to a halt beside the tents. Laura got out of the passenger side and introduced her friend, Placido. The driver looked about 30 years old, and he wasn't dressed like one of the fishermen but had on a pair of wash-worn slacks and a snap-front shirt. Instead of thongs, he was wearing cowboy boots. Verlen pointed on the map to Tortugas Bay and Placido nodded his head in agreement. He then walked to the front of his truck and lifted the hood to consult the machinery.

Opening the dictionary again, I asked Laura if we could expect a laundry at Tortugas Bay. She was sure there was no such service available and reached out her hands to take my bundle upon herself. Leaving the clothes with Laura, we climbed into the truck. I didn't know when we would get back to Malarrimo and wasn't sure if Placido had a clear notion of our plan, but I figured we would get back one way or another. I had to—I was leaving behind my boat and my underwear.

Crowded in the front seat of the pickup, Placido, Verlen, and I began our overland adventure. The vehicle was decorated with gold fringe over the front windshield and a picture of Jesus pasted on the dash. As we drove across the desert, I realized that the fringe was not a decoration, but served as a visor against the glare of the sun. Placido didn't speak any English and he didn't seem interested in talking, but the picture of Jesus was a clue to the heart of our silent driver and his expression of faith was a comfort to me. I hung onto the door handle as we knocked along—the ride was one bump after another in a sea of dry holes. The countryside was flat and sandy, and the road was bare except for an occasional beer bottle lying along the side. There was no shoulder, curbing, or center stripe. We followed a two-track ribbon of sand through the desert toward Tortugas Bay.

We arrived by midmorning. Curved around a sparkling waterfront, the town grew from the beach in a series of narrow dirt streets. The houses looked broken and fatigued, and many were without windows or doors. There were no front yards—pink, orange, and green sunbleached walls bordered on the street. Placido steered the truck through town, avoiding dogs and children playing in the dirt. Adults stood in the open doorways looking out. I didn't see any addresses or house numbers. Instead, each family proclaimed its identity by flying flags of multicolored wash from clotheslines hung between the buildings.

Our driver made his way precariously close to a ditch down the center of the road. Looking out the truck window, Verlen pointed to the pipes laid together in an uneven bed of crumbling dirt. Before beginning his canoe odyssey, Verlen had been a master plumber and he recognized the midstreet canal system as a Mexican attempt to install water and sewer disposal in town. He looked skeptical, and didn't seem surprised when we rounded a corner and came to a street full of water bubbling up and flooding the intersection. Placido drove the truck through the water and stopped in front of a small restaurant on higher ground.

"Persona ingles?" Verlen questioned, piecing together the words from our dictionary.

"Sí, sí, señor," Placido nodded.

When we got out of the truck, Placido motioned toward the restaurant and drove away.

"Do you think he understood?" I asked Verlen.

"Whether he knows a person who speaks English or not, he seems to understand our needs. Being abandoned in front of a restaurant can't be all bad." We entered the establishment. Taking a table by the door I looked out at a woman we had passed on the way in. She was sweeping the dirt with a rake, making neat furrows in front of the restaurant. I thought of my mother with her vacuum cleaner.

Verlen and I sat expectantly, our elbows on the table. We were the only customers. Reading the menu was easy, since I am a Mexican food fan from way back. I ordered burritos, quesadillas, papas, frijoles, and rice. Verlen added a request for enchiladas and soda pop. The waitress was stunned when we insisted on double portions of all our choices.

We had cleaned our plates and ordered a second round of pop when Placido returned. Walking in front of him with an air of assurance was a compact, efficient looking Mexican man. He came purposefully toward us.

"Buenas días. My name is Fernando. Placido asked me to speak with you." The man spoke perfect English. I knew he looked different—Mexican and yet foreign to his own country, a rare breed straddling two cultures. His sportshirt was new and his moustache trimmed and neat.

"I've been a skipper for many years and know your language well," Fernando said as he pulled up a chair. "I'll show you the town and help in any way I can." Verlen and I were delighted. Thoughts and questions stored from three weeks without English-speaking friends could now be raised. Gratefully accepting his offer, we spent nearly an hour sharing the story of our canoe adventure. All the while Fernando translated our conversation to Placido.

"Could you thank Placido for the ride and ask when we will return to Malarrimo?" I requested. With our timing arranged, Placido smiled broadly and walked outside to climb into his truck. Pulling his hat over his eyes, he began an afternoon siesta.

We had many errands, the first of which was to see if our food bag had made its way to the fuel dock. Fernando led the way. Our guide assured us that there was no way to get lost, even though there were no street signs, since all roads led to the sea.

The life of Tortugas centered around the harbor. Dozens of sailboats dotted the blue water and a substantial 400-foot pier jutted into the sea—a welcoming platform for cargo and sailboaters. The fuel dock was at the base of the pier. Fernando knocked on the door of a metal shed and asked for the boss. Not knowing the language, Verlen and I stood by as spectators. The dock worker mentioned a name and pointed north. This was like no other scavenger hunt I'd ever been on. We shook hands and walked several blocks to knock on another door. A large, muscular man came to the doorway, greeting Fernando with enthusiasm. Yes, he had the bag for Señor Kruger and Señorita Fons. He set the bag on his front step and produced a letter from the Bowers. I tore into the note: the Vagabunda had left the harbor three days before. The Bowers wished us well and hoped to meet us in Cabo San Lucas by Christmas.

Fernando tried to lift the food bag on his shoulder, but the look of surprise on his face showed he wasn't ready for the load. Verlen easily hefted the 100-pound weight onto his own shoulders. We must have made an unusual trio: one gringo looking like Santa shouldering a bag, one gringa holding the fluttering note, and Fernando gesturing and reciting town history as we made our way through the streets.

"There were once great sea turtles here. That is why our town is known as Tortugas. It means 'Turtle Bay,' " Fernando explained. "You won't see any turtles here today, they have long since disappeared from this area from overfishing."

"I remember a photo from the book Enchanted Vagabonds," I said to Verlen. "The author was riding a turtle the size of a stove." The heavy food bag looked as if it were riding him, and Verlen bent under the weight.

"The plumbing is a government project," Fernando continued. "And the church, it is our finest building." He pointed proudly toward a large stucco structure with a high steeple and iron bell.

We stopped at the correo and bought stamps for eight pesos each (approximately five cents). The telegrafo office was open, so I sent a telegram to my parents—the first word they would receive from me in nearly a month. At each stop Verlen set down the food bag beside the door. There was no phone in town, and Laura had been right—no laundry. We bought lip balm at the farmacia. The tienda sold cans of juice and crackers. We visited a candy store to buy pop and snacks.

I left the men and walked to a corner stand that sold tortillas, then waited while the women fried a stack of four dozen corn rounds. As I was packing the tortillas into my carrying bag, Verlen came around the corner and tugged at my arm.

"I've found your hat," he said, pointing toward an open-air shop. He led me to a column of hats and triumphantly handed over a flat straw bonnet with a shallow crown. The word "Mexico" was printed on the brim in pink yarn. I knew it wasn't me, so I began trying on the other hats in stock, saying I'd just like to see what else the store had to offer. Holding up my favorite I asked Verlen's opinion.

"Can't you see the character of this one?" I asked, holding up a hat that reminded me of Mabel Dodge Luhan on the range in New Mexico. The straw hat closed over my forehead and was so big that it covered my eyes and cozied around my ears. "This is it Verlen, this is the type of hat the Little Prince drew when he tried to visualize a boa constrictor swallowing an elephant. This is the new me."

"How are you going to keep that hat dry?" Verlen said, looking on in disbelief.

"I'll never take it off," I said simply. "Just watch, Verlen, I like it."

Fernando had produced everything on our list except one thing: I hadn't seen a public toilet on the route of our sight-seeing tour.

"No problem," he said, knocking on the next doorway we came to. I was invited into a private home and directed to their facilities. When I came back to the living room, Verlen and Fernando were sitting on a wooden bench looking at family photos. From what Fernando said, it seemed as if everyone in town was related.

Weighted down with loot, we returned to Placido's truck. He was sitting at the steering wheel with the engine running. Fernando held out his arms to hug us both. We thanked him for all his help, climbed into the truck, and headed across the desert.

My rejuvenating techniques hadn't worked for Verlen. Exhausted from shopping and lugging the food bag, he fell asleep with his head on my shoulder as we drove to Malarrimo. Only on rare occasions had I seen him tired on the water. Apparently on dry land he became human.

Halfway to Malarrimo the truck came to an unscheduled stop when the engine choked and failed. Verlen woke with a start. All was quiet, the most comforting silence I'd heard in weeks. No surf was roaring, and a vast, clear emptiness of desert surrounded us.

Placido held one finger in the air as if to signal we would wait. There was only one road to Malarrimo, so eventually someone would find us. I stepped out of the truck and sat against a sand mound. Next to me was a gray thorn branch with orange-red flowers and green nodules. I studied the desert plant and wrote in my journal, hoping the truck would never be fixed.

Before half an hour had passed, a carload of villagers came by and stopped to help. Soon there were six Mexicans and Verlen peering under the hood of the truck, removing bolts and thumping hoses. I looked on from the sandhill, shading my eyes from the sun with my new hat. A different kind of ocean stretched as far as I could see—the low swells of sand. Too soon the engine came alive.

We arrived in Malarrimo by early evening, and Verlen and I went right to work sorting and storing our new food supplies. As we packed the canoes a crowd gathered, some of the villagers sitting on crates and others standing against the fishing boats. One woman even brought a chair. Verlen and I passed out packages of banana chips and trail mix to the spectators and laughed at our wide-eyed, silent supervisors. I understood their curiosity—I had experienced the same wonderment many years before when my brother was packing for a trip abroad. I had sat on the edge of his bed, out of the way yet close enough to watch each item he stuffed inside the duffel. Would he find something that didn't fit in his bag and leave it with me? I was drawn to watch the preparations of adventure, totally involved in the excitement of seeing him packing for the unknown. Now the crowd watched us.

Laura waited until we had finished our work, then made it clear that we were expected for supper at the Hernandez household. After snapping shut the lid on my rear hatch, we followed her up the hill, smiling at our good fortune.

We ducked into the familiar doorway and entered the kitchen. Papa Hernandez extended his hand and motioned me to his chair—the one at the head of the table with the matted cushion. I sat instead on a stool beside his chair and left his place reserved. I thought papa would be pleased to be directed to his rightful place of honor in the household, but he was embarrassed at my refusal to accept his hospitality. I had not yet learned that in Mexico the host is in charge—acknowledging his authority would have been the highest compliment I could have paid him. In my well-meaning way, I had insulted him by playing the role of a generous guest, when all generosity rightfully belonged to our host.

Mama held a squirming lobster, and I watched as she pulled the tail and body apart and popped the meat into boiling water. The women stood at the stove and waited their turn at the table: guests and men were first to eat. I enjoyed a feast of lobster, mayonnaise, and tortillas with dashes of tabasco. Verlen ate beans and rice, picking at his lobster, still convinced the crustacean was junk food. We enjoyed the friendship of the Hernandez family even more than the pleasures of the food: these people had adopted us as family.

The next morning the weather was clear and we were rested. Laura had done our laundry and would take no payment for it. She stood in front of me trying to say something as I finished loading the boat.

"How old am I?" Is that what Laura was asking?

"What is my name?" I thought I had already answered these questions. I couldn't understand what she was trying to communicate. Laura reached for my Spanish-English dictionary and pieced together her question.

"When, will, you, return?" She reached out to me with open arms and I hugged her, not knowing what to answer. Though it was time to be back on the water, I was sad to say good-bye.

As I launched my canoe into the sea, a crowd of village people stood on the beach watching. Mama Hernandez smiled and hung onto Laura's arm, her pink quilted bathrobe looking like a bright flower on the beach. Every few strokes I set down my paddle and turned in the seat to wave good-bye. The people of Malarrimo had been generous and kind—thoughts of their hospitality warmed my heart as I picked up my paddle and began pushing the ocean back, boosting the canoe south toward Punta Eugenia.

That day was our best-ever paddling day. Knowing where we were going made a difference—the 50 miles to Tortugas Bay shortened to a trip around the block because we had visited the town the day before. I could see the Tortugas harbor in my mind and the vision helped to pull me forward. I could see Fernando and the beach, the houses and the church on the hill. Using my arms and working my body, I felt the joy of paddling, moving in response to the sea and gliding on a cushion of friendship from Malarrimo.

We paddled, one stroke after another. Verlen was a few canoe lengths in front of me and the swells lifted his boat up, tilting the plane of water so that he was paddling uphill. Water was all around us, rolling up into the sky.

It was about two o'clock when I saw water spouting ahead. At first I thought it was spray from a breaker in the middle of the ocean, but then I looked closer.

"Whale ahead," I yelled, straightening to attention.

A huge black body propelled itself into the air, defying the laws of gravity, curving up and nosediving into the ocean. I strained my eyes.

"Did you see that?" I shouted, not believing it myself. Verlen didn't say a word, but put down his paddle and waited. He must have seen it. After 10 minutes more, the water again flew like sparks and the huge body and triangular tail surfaced, then disappeared into the sea. I had gotten used to things that were big: the sky, desert, and ocean were all limitlessly "big." But the whale was enormous, and out of scale with anything familiar.

When I had first started the journey I had been afraid to think of down, but after sighting the whale I let my imagination freely roam beneath the surface. Seeing the whale was not a frightening experience, but a privilege. We waited a long time, floating there on the surface, letting the waves lift and buoy our canoes, before paddling on.

The wind came up when we rounded Punta Eugenia in the late afternoon, but it gave us no difficulty. The sunset was a sky-filled Rothko painting, a transition of pink mauve tones in the west melting into dark blues in the east. A full moon presided over the color show.

We would paddle all night to reach Tortugas. Night paddling was like no other experience. In the bright light of day the sun moves imperceptibly across the sky, but night was more intimate and allowed a look behind the scenes. Watching the night move toward morning was like being in on a great secret. Each paddle stroke was a push into the shadows of darkness. The distant sounds of the surf were amplified, and even my own breathing sounded loud in the surrounding stillness. We followed the stars in a world we had all to ourselves. Verlen and I kept nudging each other and nibbling candy bars to stay awake.

At three A.M. the navigation lights of Punta Sargazo came into view, and by four we spotted twinkling lights inside the bay of Tortugas. As we paddled farther into the harbor, the lights grew brighter. We were soon paddling around silent, anchored sailboats, their lights bobbing at the tops of their masts. At five we reached the dock inside the bay. I came through the slight shore break beside the pier, and as my bow touched the sand I remained seated, savoring the relief of landing after 20 hours of paddling. I would have known better if I hadn't been so tired: a wave came over my boat and swamped the cockpit, sloshing around my legs. Sputtering, I crawled out of the canoe.

Two fishermen walking by on their way to work helped pull our boats onto the beach and asked many questions about our journey. I set up my tent in a daze—all I wanted was sleep. The last thing I remember is taking off my hat and checking to make sure it was still dry.

I woke hearing bells and wondered if an alarm was going off. But I didn't have an alarm. Church bells—that's what was ringing. So it was Sunday. The tent was hot—my fabric house had turned into a sauna from the mid-morning sun. I crawled out to the fresh air.

"Verlen, I'm going to church," I said, lifting the door flap of his tent. My partner was spread-eagled on his sleeping pad, passed out after our long night of paddling.

"Wait for me," he mumbled.

"Let's go," I said, shaking the sand from his shoes. Still groggy, we climbed the dirt path to church. Entering the sanctuary we sat in the back row. Not understanding the Spanish service, Verlen and I watched for signals to join in. Following the movements of the congregation, we stood and sat on cue. Women walked the aisles nursing babies, and nuns scolded the rambunctious children who played between the pews. There were several sailboaters in the crowd, and when the service was over we went up to them.

"Good morning. I'm Verlen."

"Pleased to meet you, Merlin. This is Becky and I'm Al." The young man leaned forward and extended his hand.

139

"Verlen," I corrected, laughing at the thought of my partner as King Arthur's magician. The image wasn't totally inaccurate. The four of us walked outside, passing a woman in the arched doorway who was selling sugared treats from a basket on her arm. Al told us of seas pushing seven knots with rigging stripped to bare poles. Becky confided that the best restaurant in town was the Bahía Cafe.

"We've been here all week. There's no problem with the vegetables—eat all the lettuce and tomatoes you want," Becky assured us.

By midafternoon we were waddling back to the tents. Becky had been right: the Bahía Cafe was great. My stomach was now zoned high density, with a total of 16 burritos straining my belt. Lunch at the Bahía had been our first real chance to sit and visit with the sailboat crowd, and we found them to be a unique group. Like the whales swimming each year to Scammons, the sailboaters migrated down the Baja Coast—over 300 sailboats had left San Diego during that year's cruising season. Many of the people had sold their homes to buy boats, and theirs was not a cautious investment. An element of risk was present, but the sailboaters we met were not reckless—they were cruising a dream. For some the sea was an extended vacation, for others it had become a lifestyle.

We shared their motivation and respect for the sea. Still, Verlen and I were oddities. We were answering the same spirit, but pushing ourselves with an expedition purpose. The "yates," as the Mexicans called them, waited for the wind to blow south and turned on their engines to maneuver into port. In canoes, Verlen and I traveled under our own power: the next day we would paddle 25 miles to San Pedro. Though we were part of the camaraderie, we were also separate.

When we returned to the beach, our campsite was the center of attention. All afternoon the townspeople walked by, and children climbed on the canoes and poked at the weather covers, staring at Verlen and me as if we were a display. It was obvious that Verlen and I weren't going to paddle that day. Our bellies were full and our energy was busy recuperating and digesting. I perched on a wooden dinghy half-buried in the sand and decided to write some letters home. I was ready to describe the positive parts of our journey, having swapped white-knuckle tales with sailboaters at the cafe. While I stacked my letters in a neat bundle, Verlen handed out maps and "talked" to the people, his head bent into the dictionary, wetting his fingers with his tongue so he could flip the pages faster.

One small, barefoot boy, Carlos, kept hanging around. There was nothing shy about him—he walked over to Verlen, grinned, and pulled at his sleeve. His energy appointed him a natural ringleader. Carlos wanted to take us around town.

His tour needed no translation. The first stop was the candy store, where he pointed out his favorites. Then he took us home to meet his parents, barging in on his mother, Jesús, and proudly showing us the bathroom. The fixtures were installed but nothing worked: all was in readiness for the town's new water project. When I complimented their facilities, Jesús suggested that perhaps I would like to wash and handed me a towel. Five-year-old Carlos staggered toward me with a bucket of water. I pulled closed a flowered curtain on the doorway and stripped for a bucket bath in cold water. What a luxury! With the salt washed off my skin, I felt as if it could breathe again.

When I rejoined the family, Verlen was sitting among a crowd of neighbors tracing the line of our journey on the map. I took over the interpreting while Verlen had his turn in the bathroom.

Clean and happy, we returned to our camp at sunset. Loud music had started on the other side of the pier.

"Sounds like a wild party," I said, looking across the sand at the group of figures dancing and shouting to guitar music.

"We won't be joining them. It's going to be an early morning for us," Verlen warned, as he zipped into his tent.

"Fine with me," I yawned, crawling into my sleeping bag and gratefully surrendering to dreamland. We had slept only three hours in the past 36.

A sound woke me, and I realized that someone was outside the tent. My body tensed as I listened.

"Amigo," a drunken voice echoed and jeered. I clutched the sleeping bag and hoped Verlen was close next door. The music from the party had stopped. I stayed quiet, not wanting the man to hear my female voice. But I knew the entire town was aware of our boats and the paddle journey. When I peered out a corner of the window flap, I could see a dark figure prowling in the sand. I wanted to be aggressive and firm, but I waited, keeping still while the man paced outside. Silhouetted by the light on the pier, the figure flashed the glint of a knife. Sharpening the blade on the dory beside the tent, he rubbed the weapon back and forth, splintering the wood.

Bellowing in loud, angry Spanish he began to circle the tent, pawing at the door. Already his shadow was inside, a hulk of darkness blotting the fabric. My tent trembled as he scratched at the door, mumbling outside the thin wall. I had to act. He was coming in and I prepared to meet him, gathering my pocketknife and flashlight, touching my Bible, and pulling on a jacket. I untangled the sleeping bag from my legs.

My friends had told me this would happen. When I announced I was traveling in Baja I had heard about beatings and rape and murder and people who never returned. All the scary stories pointed to this moment. Then other voices came, and more shadows overtook the tent. I gave up and burrowed deep into my covers, hoping to disappear. The voices grew loud. There was a scuffle in the sand and an argument I could not understand. When I dared to look, the shadows were gone and I heard the voices moving away in the darkness.

Instantly, Verlen was outside my tent directing.

"Come on, we've got to get out of here," he said, unzipping my door.

"It sure is good to hear your voice," I said, crawling out of the tent. "Where have you been?"

"I was here, just didn't want to encourage the guy. Best thing was to ignore him."

"I couldn't very well ignore him. In another moment you would have heard me scream." Pulling on my pants I stood to face my partner. Verlen had armed himself with the seven-foot connector poles from our canoes.

"They may be back, let's go." Never had I been so anxious to follow my partner's advice. As we hurried toward Carlos's house, Verlen took out his dictionary and by flashlight searched for the words "knife" and "drunk."

Still straightening a robe around her body, Jesús opened the door. Realizing something was wrong, she quickly let us in, listening and shaking her head sympathetically as we tried to explain. She brought blankets and made it clear we should sleep in Carlos's room. We spread the blankets on the floor. Carlos was in bed, hugging his teddy bear. I put my arm around one of the connector poles and fell asleep.

The next morning our first thought was getting back to our gear. The boats were still in the sand, our tents were as we had left them. But someone had come back during the night: both life jackets were missing. The thief could not have known what he was taking. The jackets had been stowed in a stuff sack bedroll fashion on the back of the canoes. Looped under a shock cord, they had been easy to swipe. As I reached down to open the rear compartment, I saw that the hinges had been bent and the hatch cover tampered with. Some of the lettering on the side of my canoe had been peeled off.

"This isn't usual," Fernando said as he walked over to our canoes. Word had gotten around and our friend had come to help. "Will you come to the navy and make a report?"

"I think we should get going," said Verlen. "We've spent enough time here."

"I'm not going anywhere without two life jackets," I vowed.

Fernando led the way to the white barracks of the Mexican navy. Cadets were walking guard duty as we approached, and the commander was busy listening to a frantic sailboater who had left his ship's papers at Cedros Island. The navy radio was a blare of static as the man tried to communicate the problem to the port captain in Cedros. The sailboater was trying to be heard and we were standing by explaining our problems while Fernando translated. Three guards finally accompanied us back to the beach. They walked around our canoes and nodded their heads, accepting the fact that a theft had occurred. They looked so official in their boots and uniforms, carrying polished rifles and knives, but there was nothing they could do.

"Follow me," Fernando requested. He took us to the one gas station in town and knocked on the side door.

"This is the Mexican FBI," he explained. A Mexican Lois Lane, wearing a two-piece suit, fingernail polish, lipstick and shoes all the same color red, opened the door and invited us in. The space was cramped. We stood at attention in a room the size of a walk-in closet. There was one desk. A man in shirtsleeves looked up as we crowded in the door.

"Buenas días," he said, looking at us.

We looked back, and Fernando began to recite our story. The agent listened like a sympathetic neighbor. I had been so anxious to come to town, but by standing there I could think of nothing but paddling again. Verlen and I longed to be back on the ocean.

The formality of reporting the incident took most of the day, and by the time we finally returned to the canoes, it was too late in the afternoon to paddle any distance. Word circulated among the sailboaters and two orange kapok life vests were soon delivered to us. Then a sailboater named Don Homan rescued us from spending another night on the beach. He arrived on the beach in his dinghy and invited us aboard his boat, Gone with the Wind. Verlen and I thanked him profusely, and it didn't take us long to pack and paddle toward his vessel. Tying our canoes to the stern ladder of the sailboat, we climbed aboard. Don added us to his crew of girlfriend Franki, son Mark and pet lizard, Herman.

"I just happen to have some beef canned from before the trip," Franki said, busy in the galley. She was a whirlwind in the small space. The cushion we sat on was also a bed, and the living room merged with the galley which gave space to the stairway leading outside. There were no margins—the entire boat was a marvel of efficient space. Don spread out his charts and asked where we were headed next. It was a treat to go over our route with a full-fledged skipper and find weather news on the radio.

"Anyone you want to talk to?" Don asked.

"Sure, I haven't talked to my parents in a month," I said excitedly.

"We can try a phone patch," Don offered as we ate dinner. Turning the dials of his radio, he explained that the system connected with a San Francisco radio station to place long distance calls from sea. But the station returned static, nothing was getting through.

"Must be a storm somewhere," Don reasoned, though he continued fiddling with the set, trying to clear a channel.

Don was still working with the radio when Verlen and I climbed into the front berth. The sailboat rocked gently in the bay. Cradled for sleep, I felt cozy and safe.

Franki was already cooking in the galley when we woke, and as soon as I sat down at the table, she handed me a plate of pancakes. My eyes widened with delight: her pancakes looked like French pastries. I confessed Verlen's recipe for pancakes—powdered eggs, wheat germ, cornmeal, and cracker crumbs—better known as rock cookies. They were not my favorites.

"Eat all you want," Franki said, busy pouring more batter on her griddle.

Don emerged from the back cabin and sat down by the radio, working with the dials to try to find a clear channel. We had finished eating and were almost ready to leave when he handed me the mike.

"Here's a clear channel. Press the button when you want to talk." The wire rang my parents' home in Houston.

"Would you accept a collect call from *Gone with the Wind?*" I heard the operator say.

"What?" My father's voice came loud and clear.

"*Gone with the Wind,* sir. Will you accept charges?"

"Sure," he said, after thinking for a moment.

"Dad."

"Valerie?"

"Hey, Dad."

"Let me get your mother."

"I love you."

"Are you still seasick?"

"Not anymore. I'm doing better!"

"Where are you?" I started to cry with joy and hung onto the radio mike. Their voices crackled over space as I pressed the button to bring them close. What was the news? They loved me. I loved them and I was alive.

"What about the people there?" my mother asked.

"We've heard so many stories since you left. Whenever we tell someone you're in Baja, they're concerned. We've heard Baja is a lawless place," my father said. For a brief moment I thought about the vandalism and the frightening man on the beach. But there was no point in worrying my parents.

"They've greeted us with open arms," I assured them. This was the truth—the beach incident was small compared to the generosity and kindness we had been met with.

Franki, Verlen and Don had gone up on deck to give me privacy, but as I talked they were drawn back into the cabin. When the good-byes were said I opened my eyes and saw them sitting across from me, smiling. Feeling the emotion and life being communicated by the call, they had wanted to be a part of it.

"It was beautiful," Franki said, as she hugged me.

I moved aside as Don took over the mike and called for the latest weather report. The radio connected with a sailboater 20 miles away; 20-knot winds were reported coming from the west. The sailboater also said that a big storm from Hawaii had hit the California coast, that 500 miles north power was out in the States. But there in Tortugas Bay the water was tranquil.

Don placed a call to San Diego so that Verlen could talk with Wayne Marsula and bring him up-to-date on our progress. Wayne told us that Steve had left November 19th with a new partner, Ed Gillet, the sandy-haired kayaker we had met earlier in San Diego. We were glad Steve had not tried to set out alone. And now we were not alone: two other people were paddling on the ocean along our route.

When the phone call was over Verlen and I finished packing the canoes. It was time to get moving. Climbing over the side of the sailboat, I lowered into my canoe. We waved to our new friends on *Gone with the Wind.* I looked over my shoulder as we left the bay: maybe one day we would see Steve and Ed coming around a point. They had started out two weeks behind us, but it was possible that they might catch up with us, depending on their speed and our delays. I imagined them pulling into our campsite one night for a fine celebration.

ELEVEN

Lightening the Load

Crossing Tortugas Bay, we paddled out the mouth past Cabo Tortolo. Several large outlying rocks rose from the sea at the south boundary of the bay opening, and we gave them a wide berth before turning back toward shore and following the headland. With the shelter of Tortugas Bay behind us, we paddled alongside a rough rock cliff of exposed coast that swept upward to form Mount Belcher about a mile inland. We were headed toward a point of land called Thurloe Head, four miles away.

After we had paddled two miles farther, the wind picked up. The ocean responded immediately—waves crashed on the rocky shore, sending spray high into the air. Soon the ocean was rolling, with whitecaps dancing on the tops of each wave.

We had just set down our paddles and were preparing to catamaran when we saw a fisherman motoring toward us. He was a big bear of a man standing braced at the stern of his boat, one hand on the throttle, his other hand waving in the air, signaling us to shore.

"Mucho mal tiempo," he shouted in alarm. Pointing to the sky he repeated the warning.

The sailboaters had given us a clear report earlier in the morning, but the present conditions confirmed the fisherman's forecast. He circled our canoes, herding us to shore. Looking over his shoulder to make sure we were following, he guided us to a landing tucked around the point, where we beached the canoes between two rocky hills in a narrow gully. Landing beside us, the fisherman came ashore, and we helped one another drag the canoes and his fishing boat away from the surf.

The area where we landed looked devastated, as though it had been bombed. There were portions of dilapidated buildings standing on the hill-side, old cook pots and trash littered among the rocks. A brown shack stood at the head of the ravine and a muddy pickup truck was parked on a slant, its bed stacked with wooden lobster traps.

Verlen took out his dictionary and tried to begin a weather discussion with the Mexican fisherman. The man stared at the book. Verlen pointed to the Spanish word for wind. The man stood mute. Verlen pointed to the Spanish word for rain. The man did not respond. Verlen offered him the dictionary. The man turned the book over in his hands looking at the printed pages upside down.

"What's your name?" I asked in Spanish, reaching out to touch his sleeve.

"Fernando," he said smiling, relieved he had been asked a question he could answer.

"I guess we'll stop here to see what the weather is going to do," Verlen decided. "We might as well eat a bite and get settled. It doesn't look good," he said, gazing at the overcast sky. We put our tents on the edge of a cliff between the posts of a crumbling shed overlooking the great expanse of sea, which gave us an unusual view of the workings of the wind: the waves and surf below. It also put us on a level with sea gulls and other marine birds riding the air currents off the face of the cliff.

Making lunch with our cook kit and packed supplies, we gratefully returned to our familiar habits. Tortugas had been a break from routine, but I remembered the shadowy night visitor, and the robbery in Tortugas still haunted me. At Thurloe there would be no such problems.

The tide receded from the beach, exposing several hundred feet of sea-weed-covered rocks. When we had landed earlier, the area was being pounded by white surf. Now Fernando and another Mexican fisherman were pacing the green carpet, armed with buckets and pick, leaning over to chip between the rocks, gathering sea urchins for lobster bait. Just before sunset a rainbow colored the horizon. The wind blew fiercely and the tents flapped and sagged in what became a nightlong storm.

When I woke, the wind was still blowing and the sea was pitched in whitecaps. I walked over to Verlen's tent.

"Good morning. How're you doing?" I called out. When he didn't answer, I poked my head into his tent.

"Hey. How're you doing?" I repeated.

"Not good," Verlen responded. He was feverish and he lay flat on his sleeping pad. "I must have eaten something that didn't agree with me."

"In town?" I asked, bending over him to put my hand on his forehead.

"No, I think it was those peas in the camper's stew last night. My stom-

ach can't take split peas if they're not altogether cooked. I had an ulcer condition several years ago and it acts up every once in a while."
This was news to me. Verlen had complained of stomach cramps one evening when we camped at Isidro but it hadn't amounted to anything. Now he looked pale. I picked up his map and traced a line to the next harbor: San Pablo was 42 miles away.

"I guess we're sitting this one out," I said, putting the map aside. "Maybe you'll be feeling better tomorrow. The wind is too strong to travel anyway."
When I went outside to boil some water for cocoa, Fernando was walking up the hill to our camp.

"Buenas días," I said. "Señor Verlen mucho mal enfermo," I explained, rubbing my stomach and grimacing in pantomime. Fernando said something I did not understand and hurried back to his cabin. He returned with a medicine capsule. Rubbing his stomach and grimacing to match my diagnosis, he handed me the pill. No dictionary was needed. I took the pill and a cup of cocoa to Verlen's tent and met him coming out.

"Let's take some photos from the top of that high ridge on Mount Belcher," he said cheerfully.

"I can't be hearing you right. You're sick and now you want to go mountain climbing?"

"Circulation is the key," he said as he accepted the cocoa and pill. "Come on." This man was obsessed with positive thinking—his standard procedure was to push himself against all limits. I was no mountain climber, but I felt compelled to follow, if only to be there when he collapsed. We scrambled through the scrub and cactus over a surface of loose rock and shell. After an hour of climbing we got to the top of a ridge, where we discovered a small white cross stuck in the dirt. The ocean was a deep blue from our vantage point. I looked back at our camp: the tiny boats and Fernando's shack stood out like toys against the brown, scaly earth. I could see the pickup and a small house farther up the dirt road winding away from the beach. Tortugas Bay was visible in the distance, a blot of activity against the desert surroundings. I could make out the fuel dock and small buildings clearly dotted the townsite. One road followed the curve of the bay toward Thurloe and another wound off into the distance toward Punta Eugenia.

Verlen took many pictures, then passed the camera to me. It dangled from a strap around my neck, knocking against my body as we started down the incline. Verlen was ahead. I followed cautiously, using my bottom as a brake, sitting down when the momentum of descent threatened to roll me down the hill like a snowball.

When we reached camp, Verlen admitted to fatigue and lay down for a nap. I sat against a post reading a water-wrinkled paperback, but I didn't feel like losing myself in a fictional story. I soon put down the book and

Loading gear at the Long Beach dock.

Valerie engages sea lions in lively dialogue.

The San Diego welcoming committee.

Making friends at the Malarrimo fish camp.

Final check before hitting the surf.

Ominous clouds over Laguna San Ignacio.

The waiting place,
Laguna San Ignacio.

San Carlos fishermen
set their nets.

Paddling the inland
waterway.

Leaving San Carlos.

The catamaran system in action.

Verlen heads south near Isla Santa Margarita.

Cooking class.

Valerie navigates the
arch at Cabo San
Lucas.

Birds are
abundant in the
Sea of Cortez.

*Overlooking camp on
the Isla de Espíritu
Santo.*

*Wind-blown camp along the
Sea of Cortez.*

Rough water in the Sea of Cortez.

*Undercut cliffs of the
Isla de Espíritu
Santo.*

*Houses at Buena Vista,
near Punta Arena.*

Snoozing sea lion off Loreto.

The long haul toward Yuma.

Keep it moving on the Santa Clara slough.

looked at the ocean. The wind blew huge patches of goose bumps on the ocean surface. The sky was a vivid blue—even with sunglasses on, I had to squint. Fernando stood sewing nets at the base of the ravine. Life was simple. I sat like a cat in the sun, shaded under by big-brimmed hat. My world was the here-and-now.

An hour later I picked up one of our empty water jugs, and leaving Verlen to sleep, I walked on down the road to the house we had seen from the mountain. Over the first hill more than a hundred birds roosted on a flat area beside the road: pelicans stretched their wings, black cormorants preened and ducked their bills. Half of the birds flew away when I approached. The others raised slightly on their legs, preparing to escape if I turned out to be dangerous. The road was dusty and looked as if no one used it. I remembered that Fernando's truck hadn't moved since we arrived.

Approaching the shack, I saw a wash flapping on a heavy rope line. The door of the cabin was open, and inside a woman about my age sat on a chair watching a baby play. The room was bare, and since it had no windows, was much darker than the bright outside. It took my eyes a moment to become accustomed to the dim light, but when they did I could see a bottled-gas stove and a drum of water against the back wall. Several chairs were pulled around the central table. Seeing me in the doorway the woman stood, smoothing her skirt and squinting against the glare.

"Agua, por favor?" I said, lifting my empty jug into the air.

"Sí," she replied. Taking the container from my hand, she removed the lid from her water barrel and dipped my entire jug into the basin. I heard the bubbles escaping as the bottle filled. Her home didn't feel separated from the outdoors, merely shaded, since the door was wide open to welcome the fresh breezes. When she handed me the bottle I offered to pay, but she waved my money away. Not knowing what to say or even how to say it, I flipped the pages of my pocket dictionary. As I did, the woman picked up a plastic bowl from the table and lifted off a worn dish towel covering to reveal a stack of tortillas.

"Comidas?" she offered.

I accepted eagerly, still looking in my dictionary.

"Ensenor," I said. Teach me. "Tortillas," I said, patting my hands to shape imaginary flour cakes. She smiled and nodded. The lesson began. Taking a sack from a cupboard beneath the stove, she scooped several cups of flour onto her kitchen table. Holding a large tin canister against her waist, she opened the lid and reached in for a handful of lard. Working with her fingers she blended the two ingredients, then with a few sure strokes mixed water into the substance and formed a dough. Then, after separating the dough into small rounds, she flattened each ball. Lighting the stove with a match, she heated an iron griddle and fried the tortillas one by one. I was an appreciative student, sampling the tortillas as fast as she produced them. The remainder were stacked in the plastic bowl and covered with the dish towel.

I wondered how often this woman got to the store in Tortugas. Thurloe Head was a lonely place. My grandmother had experienced a similar isolation 50 years before, working for a Wisconsin logging camp. Grandma told stories of making 10 loaves of bread each morning for the loggers. This Mexican woman had her chores too. Keeping the plastic dish full of tortillas would be a full-time job if she had many visitors like me.

When her husband came to the door with a bucket of abalone and clams, I recognized him as Fernando's partner. He handed the bucket to the woman and reached down to pat the baby. The woman dutifully washed the seafood in a pot of fresh water drawn from the large drum while the fisherman sat at the table with a big knife, cutting the abalone muscles and exposing the still-moving flesh. He pried open the clams, then rinsed his fingers in the bucket and pulled his chair to the table, waiting to be fed. Using gestures, the couple invited me to stay, but I left the tiny house and walked back to camp with the brimming water jug and several more tortillas rolled into my pocket.

Over the past ten days our progress had slowed dramatically. We had spent four days at Tortugas and waited what turned into four days at Thurloe Head while Verlen rested. The wind continued to blow and the ocean stayed rough.

We had come only 682 miles and were falling behind schedule. I should have been restless, but my pace had slowed. It was comfortable sitting on the hill: creating my own version of Mexican village life, I kept house inside my tent. I spent hours watching the tide cycles and staring at Fernando while he gathered bait and repaired his nets. But my reverie lasted only as long as the wind blew.

The afternoon of December 2nd the wind settled, and Verlen declared he was ready for travel, that we would leave the next morning.

When we woke at three A.M. to pack the boats, there was a beautiful moon and the air was still. We didn't make a lot of noise, but a light came on in Fernando's cabin. When I walked over to say good-bye Fernando came out on the porch and we stood for a moment in the moonlight, hands touching. The dictionary had been useless—this man couldn't even read. But I had shared his beach for four days, and he followed me in the dark back to the canoes and helped pull my boat down to the surf. Pushing rocks out of the way, he stood knee-deep in the water, steadying my boat as I prepared to launch.

No matter how ceremoniously I was given to the sea that morning, I rebelled. Moments before I had been warm in my sleeping bag, and suddenly I was cold and wet, straining to see the breakers in the dark. Most of what I saw was my own hand and the paddle shaft obscuring my vision with every stroke.

The day before, we had met four Americans on the beach as we hiked around Thurloe Bay. They had driven down from San Diego for a fishing vacation, and as I paddled I remembered their trucks and realized they could have driven me and my boat back to the States. At the time I hadn't been interested, but paddling in the dark I saw I had missed an opportunity to escape.

The waves tipped my boat precariously, and I could tell I wasn't ready for the struggle of survival. During the four days at Thurloe, I had let down my guard. I didn't want to fight the ocean—its movement made me dizzy and I was out of practice. My nerves took over.

"Verlen, could we raft the boats? I'm not feeling well."

"Sure," he said. "Take it easy, we've got over 40 miles to paddle today."

"Maybe I'm just hungry, Verlen." I lay down in my canoe and looked at the stars. I pulled out the bag of animal crackers and ate them one by one. As I was passing a handful to Verlen, several dropped into the water.

"Oops, rhinoceros overboard," I said, watching the cookies sink. "Verlen, what type of animal would you be?"

"A monkey," he said. I started to laugh. "Monkeys are flexible. I've always wanted to be a quadruped." I remembered Verlen climbing the mountain at Thurloe Head. He was part monkey already.

Within an hour the sun appeared on the horizon. As the day brightened, the scenery became visible on shore and I felt better. I picked up my paddle and went to work. Cutting across the gentle curve of Bahía San Cristobal, we traveled a mile from shore, passing fishing villages set in miniature against the barren rocks.

It was a long day. I took steady strokes with my paddle and slowly submitted to the fact that Thurloe Head was gone. We were paddling on. I forced myself to make the transition between the calm of our hillside camp and the aggression needed to become an ocean paddling machine. A mild tail wind developed, pushing us south. Paddling steadily, we took advantage of this extra boost and arrived at San Pablo point at dusk. I saw a sailboat ahead of us ducking for shelter inside the bay, and as we turned the corner, we spotted a fishing camp east of the point. It was settled on a ridge against dark, slate-colored bluffs. Our charts showed deep water close to the rocky shore, but while we searched for a landing the last rays of light left the sky. The high, close hills of the bay seemed to soak all light from the scene and the sounds of surf pounding the shore increased in volume. The bluffs echoed the blast into the darkness.

"Let's try the sailboat," I said. Fearful of colliding with the surf in the dark, I hoped for an invitation to come aboard. We paddled toward the mast light on the anchored craft and knocked on the hull. Within a few moments five people were looking over the side and insisting we come aboard. Their arms reached out to welcome us as we climbed over the rail.

The boat was named the *Illusie*. Adrian, Ingrid, and their three sons— Mark, Doug, and Drake—had sailed from Vancouver, British Columbia, and were on their way to Holland in the spacious homemade craft. Ingrid led me into the forward cabin and in her words "sized up my bum" to see if I would fit in a pair of her pants. She offered me dry clothes so I wouldn't have to climb back over the rail and unpack my canoe. Meanwhile, Adrian proudly gave Verlen a tour. When we met back on deck, I could see that Adrian and Verlen had reached an understanding. The two men shared the joys of building their own boats and they admired each other's crafts-manship.

When Ingrid heard we had paddled 42 miles since morning, she went straight to work in the galley.

"What'll you have?" she asked. "Tell me your favorite."

"Macaroni and cheese," Verlen piped up. I could have hit him. Why did he have to be so honest? We had macaroni and cheese every other night. Ingrid stooped to reach a round of Dutch cheese in a deep storage bin, but Verlen stopped her.

"I've got some great powdered cheese I want you to sample," he said. I edged closer to Verlen so I could step on his toe. I would have much pre-ferred a surprise to macaroni and powdered cheese. But I need not have worried—dinner turned out to be wonderful.

The first course was raw bonita, caught that day from a trolling line be-hind their boat, and the meat was firm and delicious. The boys ate with chopsticks, dipping the fish in a special soy sauce. Besides the pot of macaroni for Verlen, tortillas, beans, and beef began to simmer on the stove.

Adrian talked philosophy. He applauded when he heard I didn't know what I was going to do after the trip. "What's the point of going on a trip if you know where you are ending up afterward?" he asked.

Verlen had it figured out. His plans included buying a travel trailer to conduct a slide tour of the country.

"Let the adventure happen to you, my friend," our host suggested. "You have no idea what may be in store."

Ingrid told about their 19-year-old daughter, who was not on board. Two days before she had jumped ship at Tortugas Bay, climbing aboard a cata-maran with her duffel bag. Adrian had been glad to see her go.

"Headstrong lass," he lamented. "She found a tall, blond Seattle man who had sailed around the world single-handed."

"I'm not worried," Ingrid replied stoically. "They each have their separate pontoons."

Silently I wondered about the mating possibilities on the center trampoline. At 19 I had hardly been allowed on dates. We talked until midnight, then climbed into our assigned bunks and slept comfortably on the rolling schooner.

The next morning we ate a hearty breakfast, then Verlen offered our hosts a small package of powdered cheese and we said good-bye. As we climbed over the side of the 45-foot *Illusie*, I remembered the day before and how reluctantly I had launched. But that morning, after rolling gently in the swells all night on the sailboat, I felt refreshed and anxious to be paddling again. Our canoes bobbed on the water surface, straining at the ropes as if they too felt keen anticipation.

As we crossed San Pablo Bay my body responded to the familiar motions of paddling. In fact, that morning I felt as if paddling were what I had been made to do. We had covered 736 miles by then, and each stroke worked from my back and through my well-trained shoulders to take another bite out of the ocean and then another and another. The swells picked up our canoes and I lost sight of Verlen as he paddled down into a trough. I looked over my shoulder and saw the *Illusie* coming from behind, its rainbow spinnaker filled to capacity in the morning breeze.

"I thought you might like some color," Adrian shouted, leaning over the rail. With the sail unfurled to its maximum, the sailboat shot past us toward the horizon, flying with the wind.

Verlen and I stayed close to shore, and soon lost sight of the *Illusie*. But there was plenty of activity to pique our interest: dozens of fishermen motored about their work, grabbing the foam marker buoys and hauling in line. Leaning over the gunwales, they dragged lobster traps on board spewing water like sieves. We watched the fishermen transfer the pinching lobsters into gunny sacks and sink the cage for another catch. Always the men stopped their work to gawk at our canoes. Verlen and I were usually the first to speak.

"Buenas días," we called across the water. "Cabo San Lucas. Remar." I made paddle motions in the air. The fishermen waved and shook their heads. They understood perfectly well *what* we were doing, but I wondered if they would ever figure out why.

When we crossed between San Roque Island and the peninsula, we saw a small village nestled in a flat spot above the sea north of us. With the hills closed in around the fringe of houses, it looked as if the village had grown into its boundaries. I saw a lone dirt trail—the lifeline to the main highway—winding in curls, then disappearing over the hills. A tall steeple and cross were the most prominent structures in sight. The other buildings were small shacks connected by a criss-cross of dirt paths etched into the gradually sloping hillside. Against the background of sandy emptiness, the little village was an oasis of life.

Asunción Bay, where we planned to stop for the night, was 14 miles ahead. The weather was beautiful, and the ocean cooperated with our plans. The only thing in the way that morning was my vision of a burrito—the sailboaters as far back as Tortugas Bay had recommended the cafe in Asunción. I began to dream of a restaurant meal: I could see one gigantic tortilla, rolled and stuffed, lying on my plate with fried potatoes and frijoles crowding from all sides. In my mind I was already in town and sitting down to a feast, and we weren't getting there fast enough.

The canoes were hooked together, and I foolishly blamed Verlen for our slow progress because he was steering. Both of us had rudder and foot controls, but when the canoes were rafted together one of us pulled our flip-up rudder out of the water so the boats would not fight one another. As we paddled around the point, my rudder was pulled out of the water and Verlen was calling the course. I found fault: Verlen was not pointing our boats toward the land, but had us angled toward open sea.

"Verlen, you're not even going in the direction of land," I said, impatiently striking the water.

"Have you studied your chart?" Verlen asked. "There is an island off the point and I'm not sure we can go between it and the mainland. The passage is foul with rocks, and obstructions are shown sticking out from the point. The wind is blowing us toward land," he said. Taking off his hat, he held it in the air and watched it sway toward shore. "To compensate we have to angle to sea. By the time we get to the point, we'll have a perfect entry into the harbor. Just wait and see."

"All I see is you are taking us out of the way. I feel powerless with you shifting the rudder. I've never had this problem steering my own boat," I said, thinking he must be exaggerating.

"Maybe we should talk about something else. Those burritos are going to wait," Verlen said gently.

"Okay. How about racing? I've been thinking about canoe racing when this trip is over," I confided.

"You'll make a good racer—you've got lots of power on your stroke. But you'll soon find that on the water, the fastest way to a point is sometimes not what it seems. Wind, current, and speed all have to be considered when you navigate." All the time we talked, we were paddling closer to the point, yet our bows were still pointed toward open sea. Ahead I saw rows of breakers not only near the land, but between the point and an offshore island.

"Verlen, do you see that?" I said.

"Yes. I've been watching those breakers for quite a while. We'll miss them."

"How can we miss the breakers?" I asked. "We're headed straight for them."

"We'll make it," Verlen said. He raised his paddle into the air and pointed out a channel right of center between the mainland and the island. Verlen's experience won again. I was glad he was steering—I wouldn't have known how to make our way through the passage. I would have chosen the route outside the island and clear of the turbulence. Verlen had discovered a shortcut that saved us several miles. There was no end to the lessons I needed to learn.

By midafternoon we landed in Asunción, a village sheltered behind the point. As we beached the boats in the quiet harbor, we were surrounded by a crowd of children. They climbed on the canoes, straddling the decks and thumping the hollow bodies. They snapped the elastic shock cords on the decks and talked excitedly with one another. Verlen and I handed out several maps and traced our journey for the spectators. When the excitement settled, we stuffed our valuables into our personal bags, pulled the weather covers over our cockpits, and walked into town.

Asunción has one dusty main street. At the north end we found the restaurant, home of the now infamous burritos. Inside, a plastic Christmas tree sat on a formica table with rusted legs. One woman was cook, waitress, and hostess. With a smile she set steaming plates of burritos in front of us, then sat at another table and sorted piles of dried beans. Working from a paper sack, she mounded the legumes, culling rocks and withered pieces from the lot.

On the wall by our table was a mirror, and Verlen and I looked into it. After 40 days of travel the sunburned faces staring back were hardly recognizable. I saw my mouth opening to accommodate a giant forkful of burritos. Then I quit watching so I could devote my full attention to eating. The sailboaters had been right—the food was great!

When our stomachs were stuffed full, we slowly walked back toward the boats. Exploring the south end of town, we came upon a large multicolored circus tent braced with ropes and supported by pillar-size poles. Flags were flying from each peak on the big top.

"I sure wouldn't want to assemble this canopy on the beach every night," I said, thinking about my compact nylon house. When we looked around, we saw a large chimpanzee restrained by a leash tied to a truck bumper. When I walked over to the animal, he held out his foot. Raising my own foot, I touched his. He held out his hand and I reached one finger to touch his leathery palm.

"How 'bout a date tonight?" Verlen teased.

"Not with this monkey!" I said.

"No, with this one," Verlen claimed, pointing at himself. "Let's you and me come to the circus." It sounded great to me. We asked four people and received four different answers as to what time the show started. We came back at eight and took our place on wood benches. Drinking orange pop and eating popcorn, we joined the people of Asunción to watch the show. Every seat was full. To begin, a strutting ringmaster introduced a clown dressed in oversized shoes, billowing pants, and a tie reaching down to his knees. The skit was in Spanish, but Verlen and I laughed anyway. The appeal of a bulbous red nose and ear-to-ear grin is universal.

My favorite part was the man on the flying trapeze, whose legs glittered with silver sequins sewn on each side of his skintight costume. Somersaulting through the air, he twisted and stretched, reaching out to catch the bar and escape from earth. With each leap he demonstrated a wild and wonderful risk. I had been to the circus before, but this time I really identified with the man on the flying trapeze. I admired his discipline, and instead of being dazzled by his tricks, I thought of his commitment. He had worked to gain the necessary skills to fly through the air.

Verlen and I had also escaped from the earth. Though we did not have sequins sewn on our pants, we practiced the same commitment and knew the movements of studied risk. We had taken the leap.

Applauding wildly, we looked up until our necks ached. The show continued for hours with more clown and animal reviews, and it was past our bedtime, when we walked back to the tents. I went straight for the sleeping bag, while Verlen walked over to check the boats.

"Your shock cords are missing," he said, calling out the damage.

"Whatever else, I don't want to hear," I said, pulling a jacket over my ears. Verlen didn't say another word, but my curiosity got the better of me, so I got up and took my flashlight outside to make sure the rest of the gear was safe. The boats lay quietly in the sand as if they were resting too. I sat down on the forward deck and patted the sleek white body. Except for the missing shock cords, everything looked just fine. The ocean lapped at the beach in the sheltered harbor, and I looked up to see a sky brilliant with stars, as if millions of spotlights were shining to light the earth. When I climbed back into my tent to sleep, I dreamt that I had sequins on my legs and the fishermen applauded whenever we came ashore.

The circus had more influence over us than we thought. The next day, on our way to San Hipolito, Verlen brandished his paddle like a baton and we spent most of the morning clowning. We paddled past a series of pilings and several large barges anchored in the bay. Our charts noted an abalone cannery north of town, and there must have been a runway, because we watched a small twin-engine plane climbing from the hills and disappearing into the sky. There were quite a few buildings back of the beach that we had not seen in our tour the day before.

We had stopped at a small grocery in Asunción the day before to buy a bottle of milk and boxes of cookies and crackers. Verlen pulled the bottle of warm milk from his storage area behind the seat, and we fixed a breakfast of cereal and crumbled cookies, then sat munching while we floated past the black rock point at the south end of the bay.

My mind went back over our stay in Asunción. The plastic Christmas tree in the restaurant had started me thinking about the holidays, and by the time we finished breakfast, I had decided to give myself the gift of arriving in Cabo San Lucas by December 25th.

"Verlen, I've got an appointment," I said, setting down my bowl and announcing my intention.

"Well, that'll be some trick. We've got nearly 500 miles to go before reaching Cabo San Lucas, and it's already December 5th."

I was quiet for a long while. Then the "how" began to take shape from words I had heard Verlen use so often—efficiency and strategy. We paddled on, and by midmorning I had it figured out. In a spirit of independence I had doubled up on all sorts of unnecessary items, so my boat weighed as much as Verlen's. Many times I was huffing and puffing as I paddled, while Verlen would glance at a Spanish book between strokes. "I've been stubborn," I said. "This self-sufficient kick is over."

"Valerie, you are finally coming around. I told you the same thing when we first started this journey."

"First chance we get I'm going to slim down this barge," I declared.

"I'll carry all the water if you can get some of your gear off the load," Verlen offered.

"Partner, you've got a deal." That evening when we paddled into a fishing village north of San Hipolito Point, the local men came to the beach and helped carry our gear to a small cement building above the surfline. Inside was a large fish scale, and I sat on the weighing platform and opened my cook kit to start supper. Before I had the water boiling, a little girl came shyly toward me holding a bowl of tortillas for our dinner.

As Verlen and I ate, I wondered what I would jettison from my gear. I looked up at the scale face, and saw that my own body weight was lower than it had been when I had started the trip. My gear was overweight, but getting fat was one problem I didn't have. I could eat almost anything in sight and not gain a pound, since our exercise more than worked it off. While I jotted down a list of what might be pared from my equipment, I ate several more tortillas, then reached for a cookie dessert.

The following day we left before sunup and paddled 42 miles to Abreojos. High tablelands and hills gradually swept down in a ski slope of sand before disappearing into the surf. We were about half a mile from shore, and the ocean pitched in gentle mounds, rolling to form a dancing sea. As the day wore on, the sky turned almost gray from heat and layers of haze.

By late afternoon we saw the white eruptions of water tumbling over a shoal bank outside La Bocana and Pond Lagoon. We stayed clear of the turbulence and continued paddling for several more hours before arriving at Punta Abreojos, where the swells collided with Roca Ballena and a maze of shoals, creating huge walls of powerful white breakers that seemed to stand out even more dramatically in the fading light.

When we paddled around the corner of the point, we saw nine sailboats in the anchorage. *Gone with the Wind* was one of them, and a reunion began when we knocked on the hull of our friends' boat. Franki, Don, Mark, and even the pet lizard came on deck to welcome us.

"As long as we are afloat in this harbor you're staying with us," Franki ordered.

"Aye, aye, captain," I said, climbing over the rail. I brought aboard my clothes bag and locked myself in the tiny bathroom, washing off the salt stains and applying cream to all the sunburned areas of my body.

We didn't go ashore at Abreojos. Instead, we sat in the cozy cabin, eating lobster, fresh baked banana bread, and beef burritos. Franki outdid herself in the galley and finally stopped cooking long enough to sit down and enjoy the feast. Don had lots of news.

"We heard on the radio last night that Steve and Ed were sighted in Tortugas Bay three days ago," Don reported. Verlen got out the charts and tried to figure where they might be.

"It's hard to tell," he said, searching the map. "At least we know he's moving pretty fast. He should catch up with us before we get to Cabo San Lucas." Verlen continued to study the chart. "This area past Ignacio Lagoon will be our longest distance without a harbor."

Don looked over our shoulder checking the route.

"That's 70 miles of treacherous coast," he cautioned. "We're cutting across that area and heading to Cabo San Lazaro. Do you want a ride?" he offered.

"No, we're making this journey under our own power," Verlen answered. "It's always been a rule of the Ultimate Canoe Challenge—no outside help. It should take us about 30 hours. We'll spend tomorrow night here inside San Ignacio Lagoon," he pointed on the map. "We'll take it from there."

"The longest we've paddled in one stretch was 50 miles from Malarrimo to Tortugas, and that took us 20 hours," I remembered.

"This stretch may take us over 30 hours of paddling," Verlen explained. "There is one area where we do accept help," he smiled. "If you've got any extra snack food we'd sure like to buy it. I don't suppose we'll be cooking much during that 70-mile stretch.

"No way will you buy anything from me," Franki said, already busy opening her cupboards. She started stacking pudding tins and fruit cups on the table for us to take. "It's my pleasure. I'm just glad you found us. We wouldn't be here if our rudder hadn't broken. Don has been working with the other sailors to fix it. Once we leave here we won't be landing again until Magdalena Bay."

Franki and I got to talking about Christmas and the possibility of caroling the sailboaters from a dinghy when we got to the harbor of Cabo San Lucas. We looked 18 days and 400 miles ahead of ourselves, making plans for the holiday.

"I have a favor to ask you," I said. "My load is too heavy. I've doubled up on all sorts of unnecessary items. Have you got room for some storage?" I asked.

"We sure do," Don said. We both climbed on deck and he showed me a roomy storage compartment. "Tomorrow you just fill it up."

Our schedule was always slowed when we slept on sailboats overnight—waking people before dawn to say good-bye wasn't courteous. Besides, if I waited until Franki woke, I could hope for more tasty pancakes and Don could get us an up-to-date weather report.

It wasn't until after eight that the sailboat crew got moving. I didn't have to ask for pancakes, Franki had them all planned, and Don went to work on the radio for a weather report. We joked that the last time we got an official weather bulletin it had been all wrong and we had been beached for four days at Thurloe. The radio tuned an all-clear ahead.

Verlen climbed down the stern ladder and sat in my canoe, handing all my gear over the sailboat rail for me to sort. The deck looked like a garage sale as I unpacked. I had a good idea of what to leave, and I said good-bye to half my clothes, used maps, stove, cooking gear, spare parts, waterlogged books, and odds and ends that either hadn't been used or were used up from the past month and a half at sea. Before I was through, over 50 pounds of excess weight were safely stowed in Don's cargo hold.

Verlen agreed to carry our entire water supply. The amount of water we carried depended on our location, next destination, and availability. Because we were headed for a marathon paddling session the next few days, we had eight gallons topped up from Don's supply. That weighted down Verlen's canoe by 65 pounds.

By midmorning Verlen and I were paddling away from *Gone with the Wind*, waving and shouting our enthusiasm for snorkeling in Cabo San Lucas, and promising to help scrape barnacles off their hull for midwinter cleanup.

Free from the burden of extra gear, I felt like a new person. My canoe was manageable, sitting high in the water, and even with the head wind, I was able to speed along. I knew at last that not only would I make it to Cabo San Lucas, but that I could plan for Yuma. I even began talking about future trips. Verlen, on the other hand, no longer had time to study his Spanish book. Carrying our eight-gallon load of water, he was sweating to keep up. His heavier load now made us about equal in paddling speed. Now that I was paddling faster, Verlen started thinking ahead—he seemed preoccupied with deadlines.

"I've got to be at the Chicago Sporting Goods Show February 9th. That's probably where I'll meet Steve again if we miss him in Cabo San Lucas," Verlen said. "From there we'll paddle up the Colorado River and through the Grand Canyon together. You and I may not make it to Yuma if we have many more delays." My increased speed gave me confidence.

"Then I'll go alone," I said boldly. "You can take off anytime for your sporting show. I'll finish this trip." I patted the red letters on the side of my canoe—"Long Beach to Yuma" was becoming my heartfelt slogan.

The land was low and sandy ahead, with one large sandhill looming to the east. This landmark was noted on our maps. But all we could see on the horizon were dark, shimmering images close to the water. These apparitions finally transformed themselves into land as we paddled nearer. The land had no height, but seemed to barely escape being buried in the waves.

We paddled 22 miles in only five hours with no hookup necessary. The only problem we had was navigating the mouth of Ignacio—a submerged reef turned the entrance into a minefield. I followed Verlen and we played hide-and-seek with the random breakers until we had successfully entered our first lagoon on the coast. When we landed inside the lagoon, I jumped up and down, splashing and roaring with the newfound pleasure of movement. My lightened canoe was a delight—even pulling it to shore was easier.

Verlen thought I was nuts, but I was celebrating the cementing of the journey. My shoulders were aching, but there was no reason to complain. The day was a triumph: finally I was a partner on the water. In the beginning of our trip I had thought my own gear was necessary for independence. Once I had discarded my self-sufficient pride, I discovered the confidence of true freedom gained from paddling. Verlen and I talked about team effort as we studied the charts for the next day.

"Verlen, I want your evaluation." I was so impressed by the difference 50 pounds could make, I wanted more improvement.

"My only suggestion for you is the two-canoe length rule."

I knew what he meant, since he had recommended that procedure before we left San Diego.

"I know I can clean camp better." There had been a rebellion of letting this slide. "But Verlen, it's cold and dark when I get up to go to the bathroom in the middle of the night."

"It's two canoe lengths, Valerie, that's not unreasonable."

"I'll try," I vowed.

The sun set in royal purple with clouds sculptured against the sky. The surf was reduced to gentle lapping on the sand beach. I had never seen a place so beautiful as our lagoon. There was one old flatbed truck sitting on the sandbar, but we couldn't see any roads and wondered how the ancient machine had arrived. I realized the old truck might be wondering the same thing about us.

TWELVE

Chubasco

The deadly Pacific Ocean surf had dictated our strategy of paddling from harbor to harbor along the coast. Once we were afloat and headed south, no retreat from the sea was possible until we could duck behind a projection of land that would enable us to beach our canoes through a reduced surf-line. Studying our charts, we soon came to recognize the rounding curve of coastline nestled behind sheltering points of land that appeared as possible harbors. The distance from one harbor to the next became our goal for the day.

Most of the natural harbors along the Baja coast are populated by seasonal fishing camps, and bear little resemblance to a United States harbor. In the Baja there are no standard lights, buoys, signals, or jetties to welcome an entrance, and navigational aids are rare. Occasionally we would find a string of lobster trap floats that would guide our path into a harbor village. Flimsy tarpaper shanties clustered along the beach, and a row of work boats wedged into the sand signaled Mexican civilization. But a collection of dwellings and fishing boats along the shore did not guarantee a safe landing for Verlen and me. The surf-penetrating capabilities of native fishermen in wide-bellied, motorized craft often surpassed those of our 17-foot paddle-powered canoes. At other sites, villagers had resigned themselves to the impassable surf at their doorstep and anchored the fishing fleet in a floating sea garage outside the breakers, accessible by a manueverable sea taxi. Harbors affording the best shelter were outlined in the *Baja Sea Guide*, by Leland Lewis, and other sets of cruising notes for sailboaters.

162

Each listing usually carried its own disclaimer for weather and ocean swell conditions.

The surf could be monstrous, crashing forward in line after line to attack the shore. The ocean breathed in rhythmic swells and surges. If pushed by wind or aggravated by weather conditions, the character of this force could change drastically. Though slow and predictable in its sweep, the tide pulse could collaborate with weather, the shape of the sea bottom, the configuration of the land, even the time of month, to create violent changes in the conditions of an otherwise protected harbor. Depending on the direction of the wind, a harbor—with its possible shoal and shallow mouth—could generate even more surf than the open coast.

As we proceeded south, several stretches of our course offered no protection for many miles, requiring that we continue paddling for more than a day. That particular morning we faced a marathon distance of 70 miles without a harbor. On our charts, the coast was pictured as a smooth, straight line, extending from the lagoon where we were camped to Punta Pequeña. A slight projection of land labeled Punta Santo Domingo was 55 miles away, but with the shallow depth of the harbor noted on our charts, we suspected that even on a calm day ground swells might well begin three-quarters of a mile from the beach. So we would almost certainly need to paddle for 30 hours to arrive at a harbor where we could be assured of a safe landing.

The day began in a relatively civilized manner for Verlen and me. We were munching our cereal on the beach at San Ignacio Lagoon as the sun came up. My stainless cook kit sat on a corroded wire-frame lobster trap, and a tablecloth of sand was spread beneath our outdoor kitchen.

I wasn't particularly eager to push off into 70 miles with no escape route to shore. But the air was calm, with little wind, and the route was clear; the only unstable condition was my confidence. The prize of shelter at Punta Pequeña loomed ahead as an uneasy target. I knew I could paddle the distance, but would the weather hold? What I could control was my attitude. I decided to consider our activity with a degree of professionalism and accept the Russian roulette aspect of the distance. As I loaded myself into the canoe and shoved myself free of the beach, the quiet lagoon cooperated with my good intentions.

But not far ahead, the San Ignacio reef stood across our path to the open sea, and my resolution wavered as we paddled toward the disturbance. I closed my eyes to the threatening jaws of the reef system and began to whine excuses.

"Those clouds, I'm worried about that gray ahead."

"You worry about all clouds, those are friendly ones," my partner ex-

163

plained. Our cloud evaluation was a recurring discussion. I had only recently begun to study the white floating formations, but Verlen had been living under their presence for many outdoor years. I viewed the changing layers as warnings of possible danger and weather violence. Clouds are hard to analyze, but the longer I stared at the passing shapes the more ominous they became in my imagination. What were they doing scooting around in the sky? Up to no good, I suspected.

"Some of the strongest winds I've encountered have been in cloudless skies," Verlen reported.

"Is my caution so unrealistic?" I was nervous as we worked our way past the reef and decided to have it out with this guy. "Why does your optimism always overrule my instincts?"

"It hurts me that you don't have faith in me or trust in these boats." Verlen was trying to talk me out of fear and redirect my thinking.

"I'll be scared when I want to be scared," I countered. "It has nothing to do with my confidence in you. You aren't paddling my canoe. I need confidence in *me*. Valerie has responsibility of this ship."

As we made it out and around the reef, I began to calm down. Open water allowed strong paddling and room for dreaming. We could continue our argument some other time, I decided, and those clouds did begin to look friendly. With each stroke I reached out and buried my blade, petting the water beast with new hope. I was excited at the prospect of arriving in Cabo San Lucas, the tip of the Baja Peninsula, and the turning point of our journey. The threatening 70 miles ahead foreshortened as I looked 400 miles more to Cabo.

"When I get to Cabo San Lucas I'm going to send out telegrams that say 'I've arrived!'" I began assembling a mailing list in my mind and practicing a shout to be heard around the cape. Verlen silently let me carry on, but I could sense his excitement too. His journey had already been full of turning points. For him, reaching the tip of the Baja meant the conclusion of 6,000 miles of saltwater paddling. From Alaska to Cabo San Lucas, a record-breaking distance to be logged in his 28,000-mile adventure.

"Lunch time," I alerted my partner. We had tried eating in our separate floats, but handing cookies back and forth was inconvenient as the canoes bobbed and slid away from each other. In between bites I would grab for Verlen's cockpit rim and pull my boat close for conversation, but if I waited too long, we would drift more than an arm's length apart, and Verlen would reach out his paddle for me to grab as I pulled my canoe over. So on that day we figured it was easier to "hook'um up" with our catamaran poles and float together during the lunch break.

My earlier weather worries were forgotten, though the sky had become a blanket of gray, sticky haze. After lunch we left the boats connected and

164

resumed paddling. A wind picked up, but I hardly noticed. I was off on some tangent about an old boyfriend. Soap-opera city rode the waves as I recounted one more episode of true-life adventure to Verlen. So lost was I in my recital that I didn't notice the sky turn ghastly pale, or the layers of high cirrus and a mounting wind funnel coming from the south. I just kept paddling in dreamland until I realized that we weren't making headway and my hat was blown back from my ears. Verlen was aware of the conditions—every part of him was listening and tuned to the signs.

"Hey, what did they tell us about wind coming from the south?" I asked, yanked from my reverie.

"To get off the water, that is where the worst of them come from." His voice was steady, but I could hear the tension in it. I remembered the word "chubasco," meaning a tropical storm from the south. No matter what the wind intensity, a disturbance from the south meant a serious storm warning.

"Are you worried?" I tried to assess Verlen's view of the situation.

"Do you like to worry?" was his reply. Why couldn't he answer with a straightforward "yes"? Once again my emotions flared to a high pitch, and I was howling at my partner rather than face the fear inside. I could read the signs. They were coming in over a loud-speaker, a billboard was painted across the sky: a storm was coming, and a big one.

I aimed at Verlen and yelled. "This is no time to argue. If the wind is bad enough, we should make an alternate plan, maybe turn around or something." My face was tight against the wind, and I was paddling with everything in me to stay forward.

"We're not really in danger. As long as the breakers aren't higher than the width of the catamaran we won't flip, but it doesn't look too good," he admitted. Taking out his maps and steadying them against the wind, he viewed our options. I was gritting my teeth as he carefully studied the charts.

"No place to go but back. This isn't just an afternoon wind change." He motioned to the sky: "It's a storm. We could stay here and fight, but we can't keep this up, we'd just be spinning our wheels. It must be over 50 miles to the next harbor up ahead." Even as he decided, the wind was increasing.

"Have you ever turned around before?" I wanted him to get to the point. The water was getting rough as we bucked each wave.

"No, I don't remember going backwards because of a storm. This time I'd say it's the only wise solution. Let's do it." On a dime, the catamaran we had been struggling with into the wind turned in its tracks and swung northwest.

"Tie yourself into the boat, Verlen." I called over to him. This was the first time I didn't have to urge him—he had already begun to secure his body with a rope from his waist to the seat mount.

One at a time, we attended to rough-weather procedures. I leaned back in my seat and grabbed the yellow life jacket that rode on the stern of the canoe behind the hatch cover. The jacket felt good going on, and gave me a sense of security as well as warmth as I pulled it around my body. From beneath the seat I pulled out my spray skirt and drew the clammy rubberized material over my head. The elastic bindings of the skirt eased around the cockpit rim to form a complete circle and thin aluminum staves positioned in the molding of the cockpit rim acted as a ribbed frame for the skirt. Once the neoprene was zippered from the cockpit to my chest, the canoe was sealed against the waves, with my body acting as a plug. As each crashing wave broke over the boat, the water rolled down the tent shape and returned to the sea. I took up my paddle again and Verlen began to make the same alterations on his side of the catamaran.

At times a wave would collapse the rubber structure, and I would frantically reposition the aluminum brace to keep the canoe from swamping. In that emergency I would rely on a short, tubular plastic pump. Except for pumping air at the check-out counter of the marine supply store back home, I had never tried it. The bright red handle glared at me from its storage position beside the seat.

"We can make it to San Ignacio Lagoon," Verlen shouted in my direction. "We're about 14 miles out, maybe three hours of daylight left, with this tail wind we should just make the lagoon mouth." It was a wise choice, to turn and run with the wind. Fighting for distance southeast was foolhardy with no harbor ahead.

My sheltered upbringing in the suburbs of America had defined gale warnings as raindrops on the outside of the windowpane. Hollywood movies educated me on the blues of stormy weather with a vision of Lena Horne standing on a brightly lighted stage torching her popular song. My favorite television weatherman declared atmospheric disturbance with a wave of his hand-held map pointer. The reality of a storm was vastly different as I sat at the waterline in my small canoe. We were literally sailing northwest. Putting paddle in the water did little good, since there was no water to draw—it was all scooting under the boats from the force of the wind machine at our backs.

We were flying, but not on course. The wind was pressing us toward shore, and the coastal land there was a low, flat plain with sand shoals and breakers off the lagoon openings heading to the main channel of San Ignacio. Both of us paddled maniacally, turning the canoes sideways into the wind, quartering the force against us, trying to work our way into open water. The canoes were making no progress west in the sea of constant motion. Waves climbed like angry fists punching toward the sky. We could not judge the reef systems—the entire ocean was erupting. Pointing the bows directly away from land, we headed west against the blast that was pushing us shoreward.

"We can't turn north yet, Verlen, I see breakers over there," I cautioned. Steering judgment was now more critical than ever: we were in danger of losing control and being shoved on a northeast angle that would put us between an evident reef break and the frenzied surf beating onshore. The collision course became unavoidable. Breakers crashed fore and aft, and ahead a crest tumbled forward, falling in a mass of foaming white water. A nightmare was made real in the storm. "Keep your bow pointed straight into it," Verlen was yelling. I had never hit an explosion head-on, but the angle of direct confrontation was crucial if we were to stay upright. Light blue water and bubbles of violence cascaded over our bows, smashed our faces, and covered the sky. I was buried in a rush of water that pressed my arms and paddle flat to the deck of my canoe. In an instant I recovered my motion and kept paddling as we punched out and through.

The scene would soon repeat, and we had only a moment to clear the space before another swell arrived for its disintegration. Precisely as the jaws shut, we had slid through a space between the front incisors, and were spit clear from the force of the reef.

Terror has a limit. There on the reef, when Verlen and I escaped with our lives, my fear died in the battle. The miracle of coming through brought a humble acceptance of the work to be done: we would have to paddle without letup to avoid being swallowed in the storm.

Daylight was running out, and after struggling for hours in the wind, we had gone only a few hundred feet in the necessary direction. The proposed safety of San Ignacio Lagoon was out of the question, since it would be impossible to navigate past the reef in the darkness.

The next harbor was Abreojos, another 20 miles north of Ignacio, where we had been two days before. I remembered the mast lights of sailboaters, and our friends on *Gone with the Wind* shouting greetings and welcoming us aboard for dinner and sleep. Don's radio had reported fair weather for the next few days.

The sun setting through black storm clouds was just a tiny spot of light fast disappearing in the horizon of the storm. I could see there was nowhere to get off the ocean until morning. Once more I rummaged under the stern hatch to find my pile jacket, temporarily dismantling my spray skirt to adjust my armor for the night ahead. Already my clothing was saturated with sea water. I relied on the wet layers of polypropylene, pile, and Goretex to insulate my body.

Eating was no fun. Verlen kept paddling as I unzipped the spray skirt just enough to stick one hand down inside the canoe and pull up whatever my fingers could reach: the plastic gorp jar, the sealed cookie box, sometimes a handful of cold macaroni we had cooked in advance. The wind now produced gusts of rain, and opening the gorp jar required swift action and careful timing. Grasp-unscrew-grab-gulp-rescrew. Then a long, deliberate chewing during which I discovered what it was I had grabbed. We juggled snacks and battened down the hatches for the worst.

It was as though I were looking down at two characters, viewed from a high perspective. There were Verlen and Valerie paddling. The night was ahead, with a storm to be gotten through. I remembered a glass snowstorm I had at home, with a polar bear standing in the center. I would shake up the globe and watch the bear disappear in a swirl of flakes. Now I vowed that if I made it home alive, I would never shake him again. The snowstorm was now my chubasco and there was no stopping as it swirled around the boat.

Night descended in a torrent of black. As if the sight would have been too horrible to endure, the merciful driver above put blinders on our team of canoes struggling against the storm. Before the lightning started, I could not see the top of my boat. The only glimpses of light came from colonies of tiny, phosphorescent water creatures. I would see pools of light and believe it to be a town calling from the horizon. We would paddle, believing a sure line of sight reading Abreojos ahead. But, as we paddled toward the glow, we instead found ourselves illuminated like transparent slides, afloat on a sea of life within the storm. The canoe bottom became radiant with light, as if God had wanted to check on us, and had turned on a light bulb in the sea to locate our struggle.

Then the rain came with a force that bowed our heads. It would flood down and then pause, as if the storm were taking a breath and couldn't keep up with itself. I couldn't hear Verlen yelling the compass headings, even though he was just five feet from me in the attached catamaran system.

We were lost in the storm, with no point of reference other than the motion of the gigantic waves. Verlen held a flashlight in his teeth and continued to take readings on his compass and watch, heading us in a northwest direction. Our best indicator was a perpendicular stance of our canoes to the waves: though the wind continued to change directions in the heart of the storm, most of the force was hitting us from the northwest. In the darkness I would know we had gone off course when the swells attacked the canoe from the side and spilled over the deck. When the wind and rain let up against our faces, we would turn the boats into the blast to regain our bearings.

We were not battling the elements, but had been caught in the middle as the wind, rain, thunder, and lightning battled each other. It was as if we were in the middle of a test range. Some authority had cleared out the civilians but hadn't told Verlen and me that the bombs were due to go off. Thunder gained as absolute ruler of the war. The deafening sledge silenced the ocean, and even the roar of the wind was steadied. It reminded me of the disoriented smears of jetted black on a Jackson Pollock canvas. Blinding white flashes of lightning only startled our concentration. So bright and quick did it strike, my pupil could hardly adjust.

By 3:30 A.M. I was spent and began to sing, imagining myself a character in a musical. What would Peter Pan do at a moment like this? He would be flying way up high in the sky. "Look at me, Verlen, I'm flying." I reported. I became Eliza Doolittle wishing the rain in Spain had stayed on the plain instead of coming to the Baja. I could actually put energy into my body with the words of the songs, so the music kept me going for another hour. But, by 4:30 the songs no longer did any good. I felt as if my system were shorting out—the constant paddling had worked up some chemical imbalance in my body that had to be released from a pause in the physical action. I felt a strain, as if my body would begin to explode through my eyes, nose, and ears, and that my heart would break from the effort. I would have to stop.

"Why don't you rest?" Verlen offered in salvation. I put down my paddle, but the wind weathervaned the canoes toward shore and the unruly waves took advantage of our weakness. I had to paddle with Verlen: one person could not hold the course of our canoes in the storm.

"Verlen, look ahead!" I commanded, blinking my eyes. The lights of Abreojos appeared and then vanished beneath the waves. An entire town twinkling on the horizon disappeared and then reappeared, rising from behind the swells. We paddled up a rolling water slide and realized that this time the town was not imaginary—we were headed for the lights and dawn.

"We're making it!" I yelled. The elation carried me to reach for another stroke and continue paddling.

"It will be hours yet," Verlen said, and he was right: we paddled for another two hours before we could discern individual spots of light and not just a glow on the horizon.

Abreojos means "open your eyes" in Spanish, warning sailors to take heed of the rocks and shoals that lie to the south and east of the harbor. Two months before, I had spread out all the charts on my living room floor, unfurling the roll of fresh maps and placing together the pieces measuring the length of the Baja Peninsula. When I was making preliminary notes, I had written the translation of Abreojos on my chart. The chart was now folded and soggy in its plastic case, but the recollection came to mind.

"We've made it this far, let's hold here until dawn," I pleaded. In my exhaustion I was fighting for steering control from my partner, wanting to hold the canoes as far from the submerged mountains as possible. As we neared the relief of land I heard the increased sound of crashing sea against the rocks. I paddled with my rudder in a hard left turn to open sea. Verlen was paddling with his rudder pushed to the right, headed closer to shore. Hooked in the catamaran, we were stalemated. Both of us had the same notion that since paddling had kept us afloat through the night, it seemed a better hope than chancing an avenue through the surf and a barricade of breakers. But Verlen was more comfortable paddling a few yards outside the surf, and because I wanted a wider margin, I kept paddling toward the open sea.

Compromising with each of our instincts, we remained in a good position and continued to hold into the wind. The rain ripped at us and the waves seemed bigger than they had the entire night. But we took some comfort from the fact that night was almost over, we had come many miles and not capsized in the storm, and the town was in sight.

As the first light came I looked over at Verlen: he was drained. My partner had lost pounds of flesh during the night, and his face was hollow. But his paddling was reassuringly continuous and steady. I wanted to break down from the pain of our exertion, but I had no energy for crying; no tears would come. My mouth was cracked from salt splashes, and I licked my lips to cool the sting. The salt burned my eyes, and I shut them tight against the brine.

We could see the town clearly by then, and people were lined on the shore looking our way. A crowd had gathered and trucks were pulling up on the beach. The fishing boats were pulled up high on the sand. The surf in the harbor was enormous, and none of the spectators were yelling for us to jump. They all stood with their hands clasped at the sight of us bobbing on the crazed sea.

We attempted to land through the surf, but the waves stacked up against us, and we back-paddled to reconsider. A multiple band of surf crashed between us and the people waiting on shore. We looked for a weak spot in the surf so that we could go through, but after testing the surf from several angles, we paddled back to sea. It had been a steady battle through the night, and the surf was a new hurdle.

"We need a fishing boat to come out and show us the way through," I told Verlen. I was convinced we could not negotiate the breakers ourselves, since the harbor had a wide southern exposure to the storm swells. The fishermen knew the beach and had the opportunity of judging the surf from the shore side.

"None of those fishing boats is going out today." Verlen sounded sure.

"One has to come, we need help." When I lit a flare and held it high, the wind blew the red drippings down my arm and onto the deck. I wondered if the villagers could read my request as it lifted toward the sky.

"There is a boat coming," I said after a few minutes.

"It looks like it's swamping, they're not going to make it." Verlen tried to correct my hope. But there one came, out through the surf, the large hull smashing above the spray, slowly, painfully making its way through the crashing sea.

"It is coming!" I cried in relief. "Steve! It's Steve in the boat." I was astonished as I recognized Verlen's Ultimate Canoe Challenge partner in a tight-skinned wetsuit, riding between two fishermen in their motorized craft.

"We can get the boats ashore, I'm going to take your place," Steve called out.

"Mine or Verlen's?" I yelled back.

"Yours," he said certainly. I was being asked to leave my boat. We were jostling and dancing upon the swells, the rescuers had come and there was no time to argue. The Mexicans were mute, Verlen was exhausted, I was confused, and Steve was taking charge of the situation. Steve jumped into the water like a frogman and climbed onto my deck.

I was not happy about this unexpected takeover, but it was hardly the time or place to argue. I unzipped myself from the spray skirt, untied myself from the boat frame, and sprawled over the gunwale of the fish boat. The fishermen grabbed my arms and pulled me over the side like a gaffed seal. My poor canoe was a mess: when I looked back I saw macaroni swimming in the cockpit, wet clothes mashed in the bottom, crumbs and pudding jars floating. Steve became the captain of the ship I had struggled with throughout the stormy night. I saluted Verlen and sat down in the fishing boat between lobster traps and two very somber Mexicans, watching the Ultimate Canoe Challenge team disappearing through the breakers as they paddled for shore. The situation sank into my soul: I had been rescued, put in the fishing boat with the lobster bait. I had not taken my boat ashore like a champion. I sat a long time there on the rolling sea as the fishermen hauled in their lobster pots.

I felt beaten, but the storm had not done it. All night the storm had tried, but that morning at Abreojos, I had given my victory away. When the fishing boat finally landed me on the shore, no one was waiting for me. Instead, everyone was crowded around the canoes. What a rough landing: the surf would never have been as harsh.

THIRTEEN

Stranded

As soon as we set up camp between the parked fishing boats at Abreojos, I crawled inside my tent and burrowed into my sleeping bag, trying to shut out the memory of the storm. Outside, the ocean roared and chewed on the beach. Now that I was safe in my familiar shelter, I didn't care if the clouds burst, but the wind was beginning to settle as if it too were exhausted. Verlen stuck his head inside my tent.

"We're supposed to meet Steve and Ed at the restaurant. Are you ready?" he asked. My muscles were sore from paddling all night in the storm, and I hadn't slept, but I responded to the promise of food. As soon as I crawled out of the sleeping bag, I was cold—my body had spent its resistance. I put on several layers of dry clothes and within a few minutes was walking through the rain with Verlen to Punta Abreojos Buñelo restaurant.

When we arrived, Ed was reading a Spanish adventure novel with his feet propped on a chair and Steve was sitting at a table writing letters. Neither Steve nor Verlen smiled in greeting. Straight away I got the feeling that these two men were strangers to each other and not long-lost friends. I felt no warmth in their greeting, but tried to cover up by plunging ahead with conversation.

"How long have you been in Abreojos?" I questioned.

"We've been here for two days," Steve explained as we began to compare notes. "When the wind turned around and came from the south, we stayed ashore."

"When we left San Ignacio yesterday, Verlen described them as friendly looking clouds," I said, pulling a chair to their table.

172

"Verlen's weather reports aren't always right," Steve said with a laugh.

"I didn't make any predictions, but those friendly clouds did turn pretty mean," Verlen agreed.

"It was a freak storm," Ed explained. "I talked to a guy on the beach who had a radio. They're calling it a chubasco."

We were to learn later that the storm, which had started as a major disturbance centered 300 miles north of Cabo San Lucas and 100 miles offshore, had moved southeast at 6 knots an hour. The unseasonable storm gave little warning. At the cape there were reports of 70-knot winds and 20-foot seas. The same night that we survived in our small canoes, 27 sailboats were washed ashore and wrecked in the harbor at Cabo San Lucas.

The four of us were the only customers in the tiny restaurant. We ordered double portions of food and guzzled pop. Verlen and I told our stories, wanting to compare them with when and where Steve and Ed had arrived at various harbors and campsites, but Steve was only slightly interested in our trip and didn't offer much information. Even so, it was still clear that he and Ed were traveling faster and lighter than Verlen and I were, and that fact seemed to please him.

The subject changed to Cabo San Lucas and the deadlines ahead. As the men talked I sensed friction between Verlen and Steve. I wondered if Steve was still upset that I was along on the journey. That was part of the difficulty but something else was chafing. The two men were different characters. Though they shared the common goal of a 28,000-mile dream, their philosophies were in conflict. For two people involved in a journey as intense as the Ultimate Canoe Challenge, there was bound to be friction, but that was a different story and I didn't know the details. I tuned out the conversation and looked at Verlen, thinking of our night battling the storm. I realized I couldn't stay awake much longer so I excused myself and returned to camp.

As I lay in my tent, instead of falling asleep, my mind wandered back to the strained conversation at the restaurant and I began to wonder if I should quit the expedition, not because I was giving up, but because maybe I didn't belong. No matter what the problems, Verlen and Steve had a mutual respect for each other's abilities. Though Verlen and I had fought a chubasco and survived to tell about it, I still felt inadequate because I hadn't brought my boat ashore. All my thoughts were colored by deep fatigue. When Verlen visited my tent an hour later I told him my new plan.

"You've got to go on with Steve. He's your real partner. I'll drop out," I offered.

"No way. I won't leave without you," Verlen snorted as if I were crazy.

"But I feel like a failure since Steve paddled my boat ashore."

"How can you say that?" he asked. "Paddling in the storm was a victory.

173

You came through like a champ."

"Well, you were talking just the other day about joining Steve at the sporting goods show."

"Cutting our journey short to meet my deadlines is not the same thing as abandoning you here." Verlen looked at me seriously. "You and I made a big commitment way back at Long Beach that required major decisions and changes for both of us. I honor that. I will stick with you through thick and thin."

"But you made a big commitment to Steve at the start of your journey." I felt like an interloper.

"Steve altered that commitment when he told me to go on without him," Verlen reminded me. "I had traveled over 18,000 miles on my trip and still hadn't found someone who could really share what I was experiencing. Then I met you. You are that one person above all others who understands why I'm on this journey. You're able to feel as I do, and I value that. We share an explorer instinct."

"Thanks, Verlen," I said. "But I can't do it. I was able to fight a chubasco but I won't fight your journey. I love it too much. The Ultimate Canoe Challenge is you and Steve. After Yuma you've got a lot of miles to paddle with Steve, and I don't want to cause any friction. Also, Steve is a better paddler than I am. You'd probably be safer with him. I'm sure I should quit."

"I've always known you belonged here and you know it, too," Verlen responded. "A large portion of the trip I haven't paddled with Steve..." I cut him off.

"But, Verlen, Steve has more skill than I do. I saw his canoe. He even has it set up so he can roll upright if he capsizes. I can't do that."

"I can't Eskimo-roll either," Verlen said. "We don't need special skills to follow our dream. Rolling a canoe is essential to the showman, not the explorer. How many times do you think we could have rolled last night in the storm? I built these boats stable to resist upsets. Our safety lies in *not* tipping over. Our best safety feature is the catamaran system. This past summer when I was on the Washington coast, Steve and two other guys tried to teach me about surf entries," Verlen went on. "They played around in some spectacular surf, but all three ended up swimming to shore, and one of them even lost a canoe. Steve and his friends had taken precautions, they wore helmets and wetsuits, but the experience showed me that rolling in the surf is not the answer. I spent so much time chasing after the three of them and looking for the lost canoe that I never did get in the water to practice myself. We never found the canoe—it disappeared in the sea. What I already believed was confirmed right then and there: that strength and skill are not the secrets to survival on the ocean."

"Can we go with Steve and Ed when they leave?" I asked.

"No, I've already asked Steve and he doesn't want us along. He and Ed are going to push themselves even harder because of this questionable weather," Verlen said.

I didn't have the energy to argue any more. Verlen was still talking when I fell asleep.

The next afternoon I stood on the beach watching as Steve and Ed prepared to leave. Steve put airbags in the bow and stern of his canoe, but Verlen had said I didn't need any, that my bulkhead would be sufficient flotation. I looked at Steve's thigh braces that were set up for rolling the canoe, and remembered Verlen telling me that we didn't need those. I hoped he was right.

Steve turned his canoe toward the sea and loaded his gear without saying a word. I waved, watching as he and Ed disappeared through the surf.

"Explain to me again why we aren't going?" I asked Verlen.

"We're not rested yet. We haven't resupplied. The weather isn't settled, and besides we're not wanted. Be patient." Verlen tried to make me understand.

There was a black dog on the beach at Abreojos that played no favorites, but followed everyone around the village. He joined me as I walked alone down the beach. When I patted his head, he showed his pleasure by rolling over in the sand and handing me his paw.

As far as I was concerned, Steve was still the "official" partner, the one news media talked about, the partner people asked about even when he wasn't there. Verlen and I had often wondered where he might be, how he was coming, and when we would see him. When our paths had finally crossed, he had left without even paddling with us for a day.

As I walked to the tent, I heard the fishermen talking. They were speaking a foreign language, and I heard it as if for the first time. I was in a strange country alone with Verlen. No other canoers were coming from the rear. I patted the dog's head and crawled inside my tent.

All the worst thoughts crowded into my head. I still hadn't recovered from the physical and emotional strain of fighting for our survival in the storm. My fatigue made me wonder if I would ever make it to Yuma alive, and I realized that my parents were probably worried sick. Besides these anxieties, I worried that if I did survive I might never be able to adjust to normal life again. The black dog was lying just outside my tent, so close he indented the fabric. I stretched out my feet to touch him through the nylon, as if he were a hot-water bottle. My brother's words came to mind: "concentrate on the goal," he had said.

I had almost forgotten. Yuma was ahead and I was an explorer! Though I was overly tired and my expectations of our reunion with Steve had been disappointed, I took time to give myself a pep talk. My parents loved me, and yes, I would adapt to normal life after the expedition, probably with more serenity than before.

"No way, I won't go without you, Valerie. You belong here." I remembered what Verlen had said. His words echoed in my mind as I fell asleep.

Steve and Ed had taken advantage of what turned out to be a temporary break in the weather, and the next day was windy and rough. Verlen and I packed the tents and went through the motions of clearing camp, but the wind howled and the sea began working itself up even in the early morning hours.

We spent the morning exploring Abreojos and taking photos. Tortugas had been crowded, but in Abreojos the houses were separated by sandy yards, and most of them had plants growing in rows of rubber tires cut with scalloped edges. There was no sign of sun, yet many housewives had hung out the family wash, and the breeze filled the pants, shirts, and blouses, so that they billowed like crazed windsocks. One house had a play yard built beside it, and two shy children watched from their front doorway as Verlen and I tried their homemade teeter-totter and sat in their swing fashioned from a strip of rubber and two knotted ropes.

Built on the point like a king's scepter rising from the sand was a concrete light-house. When Verlen and I walked to the tower and looked over the flat, sandy plain to sea, we saw water breaking on the reef and a bank of detached rocks sitting out from shore. There were no sailboats in the harbor. I wondered how our sailboat friends were, and if they had survived the chubasco. Only four days earlier, we had been in the same harbor, sleeping aboard *Gone with the Wind*.

When we made our way back to the one restaurant in town, we found the place crowded with circus performers. They were waiting for the wind to die down so that they could put up the tents. I wondered briefly if this was the same troupe we had seen in Asunción, but there were no chimpanzees and no sparkling sequins. The preformers were camped in their trucks waiting for the weather to clear, and on our way in we had seen a pair of monkeys shivering in the damp as they huddled beneath the vehicles, a squealing pig tied to an axle and two lions cramped in a cage slightly larger than themselves. Tethered next to the restaurant was a scruffy burro.

Inside the restaurant, a magician from the sideshow was having breakfast, performing magic tricks with a coin to amuse the customers. I wanted to ask him to do a trick that would calm the wind, but my small amount of Spanish allowed me only to order a burrito and wait.

After five days, we were still waiting. The time had gone slowly, as we walked the streets, sat at the restaurant, and stared at the sea. The local fishermen had not ventured out to sea since the big storm and the circus tent had not been raised. On December 12th we decided we could wait no longer. I looked at the sky.

"Do you think the wind has died?" I asked Verlen.

"The wind doesn't die, it just stops blowing for a while," he said.

"Then let's go!" I hurriedly packed my canoe and pulled it toward the surf. I was ready. Pushing off into the sea I repeated an affirmation to bolster my courage: "I'll do my best," I said out loud to the waves.

What a relief it was to be paddling again and free from the shore. We had covered the same distance across Bahía Ballenas from Abreojos to San Ignacio six days earlier, but we had a new plan—to cross the bay and duck behind Punta Molcomb, entering the lagoon system and paddling in protected water to a far southern exit noted on our charts. The lagoon was fronted by a low island about eight miles long lying in the curve of the shore. We would use a shallow channel about a mile wide separating the island from the mainland to paddle on the sheltered north side of the island before cutting back to the open ocean. The maneuver would shorten the open ocean distance to Punta Pequeña by about 15 miles. The chart looked favorable and the fishermen at Abreojos had nodded in agreement as we pointed to the map and pantomimed our intentions of finding a southern lagoon exit to the sea.

By noon we reached the mouth of Ignacio and entered the lagoon. There were rows of surf past Punta Molcomb, and I got anxious.

"We've got to hook the boats together," I said.

"It's just a sandbar with the tide crossing. You'll be fine. Ride it out. Keep your canoe pointed straight ahead and stay behind the crest," Verlen instructed.

The water was shallow, but that didn't ease my fears. When the waves picked up my canoe and pushed me forward, I could see the bottom of the ocean whizzing past beneath. As the roll of surf rushed over the bar, my canoe turned sideways. Verlen was right beside me, and I could see that his boat, too, was turning on the wave. We braced, leaning into the wave with our paddles firmly planted over the top of the crest, and the incoming tide sucked us further into the lagoon.

Safe behind the island, we entered an estuary full of birds. Herons gracefully stood on shore and lifted into flight as we paddled by. Brants ducked under the water as we approached. Cormorants circled in the sky. Looking ahead, I thought I saw surf, but as we got closer the surf turned into a flock of white birds weaving in the air above the shore.

The channel between the mainland and the island was full of life. Seals popped their heads out of the water and quickly disappeared to spread the word of intruders. Beyond the island the water became shallow, and we could see a school of small fish swimming beneath the canoes.

By midafternoon the tide turned around and threatened to strand us—within a few hours our channel was reduced to less than a foot of water. The birds were good indicators of depth: when we saw them congregated ahead standing on the sandy bottom, we would bypass the area and search for deeper water farther from shore. We poled and pushed our boats forward with our sturdy paddles. Neither of us wanted to get out and pull the boats because of the stingrays we saw swirling in the sand. These monsters, flat fish with long tails and spikes on their backs, skittered ahead as we disturbed the bottom. We inched forward in barely enough water to keep moving.

As the light faded, we searched for high ground protected from the tide and mudflats, but we couldn't get close enough to shore because the retreating water created a wide expanse of mud and wet sand between us and dry land. Finally, there was no other choice but to get out of the canoes. We tugged the boats ashore, sinking to our ankles in sticky gook. The low island we came to was hardly a refuge: there was a salt pond in the center of the formation and pools of water were spotted over the marshy land. We found a reasonably dry place on a bed of shells and tied the boats to mangroves. For the first time in two months, I saw the sunset over a piece of land rather than open ocean.

A wind came up during the night—I heard the mangroves rustling and sand blowing against the shells. I got up to go to the bathroom, walked two canoe lengths away from the tent, and squatted, looking at the stars. When I turned back I discovered that the wind had persuaded my tent to hover. I ran back and flopped inside, sprawling on all fours as the tent lifted off around me.

"Come and help," I yelled, waking Verlen to the rescue. He tied down my ballooning house and we both went back to sleep, hoping the wind would blow itself out and settle by morning.

By morning everything had changed: the water was high and our boats were floating, mangroves were under water, the wind was brisk, and the weather had turned cold. Waves in the lagoon were whitecapped. Verlen lit the stove to make a pot of macaroni and powdered cheese.

"With those clouds in the south, maybe this is the chubasco moving in from Cabo," Verlen said, attempting a weather forecast. I looked at the sky, then stared at Verlen's cooking methods with equal distress.

"Hey, please don't put powdered onions in the macaroni this morning," I requested.

"The weather doesn't look stable," Verlen said. He continued to stir the macaroni soup. "If a storm came, this island wouldn't be the place to sit it out. The waves would come over this entire sand point." He poured pepper into the pot until the surface was nearly black. There wasn't much I could say since he was captain for the day. We ate in silence, knowing we would have to move.

After breakfast, we broke camp and climbed into our boats. Within two hours we had paddled to the south end of the island, where a fish camp sat on a high spot of land on the point. The camp consisted of three tarpaper shacks and half a dozen men standing in the sun. Several boats loaded with clams were tied at the shore. Looking around the end of the island, we could see breakers and surf—but no passage to sea. When we pulled ashore the fishermen gathered around us, and as we reviewed our plan they shook their heads and pointed on our charts to the opening at San Ignacio as the only passable exit.

"That's 15 miles back. The way we've come!" I said increduously. We looked around the island in disbelief. Facing the stack of waves, we realized the fishermen might be right. The waves tumbled on top of one another, crowding the water space between Isla Arena, where we were standing, and the next piece of land across the channel. One fisherman offered to tow us back to the main lagoon mouth so we could paddle through the next day.

"Is a tow backward acceptable to the integrity of the Ultimate Canoe Challenge?" I asked.

"I think we should take it," Verlen confirmed. "We'd never make it through this channel and we can't take any more delays." Neither one of us considered waiting to see what a different tide condition would do to the opening. The fishermen seemed so positive that our attempt was futile, and it certainly looked that way.

Standing knee-deep in the water, we rafted the canoes and tied our bow-ropes together in readiness for a tow. When the fisherman pushed off from shore in his boat and motioned to us, we paddled out and began tying our line to his transom. He looked nervous and waved us to hurry.

"Darse presa, darse presa," he said, looking around over our heads. We didn't understand the rush. Verlen got out of his canoe and climbed aboard the fishing boat, holding the bowrope while I maneuvered the catamaran around so my canoe came alongside the larger boat. Then I climbed aboard, but my weather cover was being stubborn—it wouldn't stretch over the cockpit. All the while the fisherman was impatiently saying "darse presa, darse presa." By now Verlen was pointing. His mouth fell open in surprise.

"Forget the cover!" Verlen shouted. My weather cover popped off again as I jumped into the launch, but there was no time to secure it. Then I saw the panic: a strong tide current was carrying us into the turbulent channel and the fishing boat was drifting around the point. The fisherman frantically pulled on the starting cord, but the motor wouldn't start.

"I think we should get back into the canoes and paddle," Verlen said tensely. He was looking at the breakers as we drifted closer. The fisherman pulled again on the cord and the engine sputtered. Verlen looked down and discovered that the gas hose to the motor was disconnected, plugged it in, and pumped the bulb. The fisherman pulled one more time, and the motor started and held. The load of the boat was heavy and the current strong, so it took many minutes to regain our position. Finally, making headway around the point, we began to move away from the disastrous surf.

Verlen and I were crammed into the fiberglass fishing boat that overflowed with cartons of clams, its bow tilted up as the motor churned at the stern. When we came to shallow places in the lagoon, the pilot motioned me forward to climb over crates of clams and weight the bow. When he called me back I would scramble over the clams again, shifting to wherever he needed ballast in the boat. For most of the ride I sat in the midsection with Verlen, our feet propped on boxes of clams. The clams were alive and moving, biting on Verlen's map case, his paddle, and anything else that got in the way.

"Como se llama usted?" I asked the pilot.

"Manuel," he replied.

After asking several simple questions, I understood his job to be a ferryer of clams from the family fishing village to the main camp inside the lagoon. I asked Manuel if he cooked the clams.

"No, no," he shook his head vigorously. "Espousa preparar." Verlen and I both grinned. Manuel was so emphatic that his wife did the cooking, it sounded funny. He was a thin stalk of a man whose brown bare feet stuck out from beneath wet knit pants. He hadn't bothered to roll the legs, but left the material soaking in the sea water collecting at the stern of the boat. Every few minutes he would lean forward and scoop water out of the stern with a plastic dipper. He wore a tattered coat, and a cap with the name of a United States football team printed on it. When Manuel wanted a cigarette, he would bring his jacket around like a vampire's cape to shield his lighter from the wind. I imagined this man to be even more of a stoic sea captain than the one at my side.

Because we were Americans, Verlen and I attracted attention wherever we went. At the same time, we also enjoyed privacy because few people could understand us. Manuel was intent on his driving while Verlen and I, surrounded by the clam cartons, talked most of the way—public yet invisible.

Instead of setting us off at San Vignacio, Manuel took us to a village deep inside the lagoon, where the clams were loaded onto a truck. He made it clear he would take us to the mouth of the lagoon mañana.

"We can't sit here all afternoon," I said. Verlen agreed. The tide was going our way, so we said good-bye to Manuel and launched our canoes. But even though we closely watched our compass and chart, Verlen and I were soon lost in the lagoon channels and stuck in low water. Stingrays be hanged—I got out of my canoe, yelling for the beasts to get out of the way. Walking, dragging, and yanking my boat, I plodded toward the ocean. Verlen followed in the same manner, but without my style of screaming announcement to the stingrays.

Finally, in the late afternoon sun, we could see the beach at the lagoon mouth straight ahead. The familiar old truck sat half-buried in the sand where we had camped six days previously, and where we had begun our 70-mile paddle toward Punta San Pequeña before the chubasco. As Verlen made camp, I set out to walk off my discouragement.

I couldn't understand our setbacks. The wide expanse of sand and ocean spread before me in the evening sunset. I began to pick up some of the shells that were all around, filling my pockets with treaures as I walked farther from camp. When I could hold no more, I walked back to camp, eager to share with Verlen.

"Look, look what I've found!" I beamed. "I traded 15 pounds of frustration for this pink shell. I bought this beauty with 30 pounds of unhappiness and 10 pounds of sorrow was all it cost for this lovely coral shape. I paid 5 pounds of confusion for this bargain," I said, holding up a colorful spiral. I decorated our camp with the shells until my tent was encircled with the beautiful seashore treasure. "Verlen," I concluded, "there is no way home but south."

We woke to a heavy wind, and since we didn't know if it was merely a lagoon breeze or a portent of bad weather, we were in no hurry to leave. As the day went on, the Mexican flag Verlen planted in the sand beside the tents continued to blow straight out to the southwest. Our journey had been halted again. Reaching for our goal and moving forward each day had sustained our morale, but it was a whole different world to be stuck.

"Surely the wind can't last too long," I said hopefully. Whenever we were stranded, the first day was welcome rest for work in our diaries, writing home, fixing broken gear. But by the second day, impatience set in. We both thought about the time we were losing. Days behind and overdue, it was painful to sit and know we would have to push even harder to catch up with our schedule.

The wind blew all day and all night. When I climbed out of my tent the following morning, I found the white body of my boat was camouflaged by a mound of sand that had drifted against its side. The wind was still blowing while I inspected my canoe, but I didn't realize how hard it was blowing until I turned around and saw that the beach was beginning to collect inside my tent. I hurried back inside and tried peeking out of the screen, but the wind blasted grit into my face and forced me to zip up the fly of my nylon shell.

At noon, unable to sit in our tents any longer, Verlen and I took shelter in the old truck which sat immobile in the sand. We tried to guess how it had arrived on the beach. There were no visible roads to this spot, so it must have been driven in during low tide and set to rest on the dune. The cab was rusted, the door handles off, the windshield cracked, and springs showed from the seat. We spent much of the day sitting in the cab, traveling nowhere, but seeming to get there with Verlen behind the wheel and me cross-legged beside him riding out the wind. The keys were in the ignition—I wondered if some strange phoenix flight could take this truck to Cabo? The wind continued all day. We ate our dinner in the truck like two customers at a drive-in.

"What's the possibility of leaving tomorrow, Verlen?"

"Don't know, wait and see," he said. Setting his plate on the dashboard, he began cutting his whiskers in the rearview mirror.

I went to bed without being tired, just for something to do. I dreamed that my sponsor and Verlen's sponsor landed in a helicopter and were yelling to us:

"It's okay, you can go home now, it's over."

When I woke, there was no end in sight: sand covered the entire tent floor and sifted everywhere. The flag whipped in the air outside, and my mind turned to home. If I were home I would be making star-shaped cookies and trimming a fir tree, writing Christmas cards and dressing up for holiday parties. These are activities a person plans and follows through with. On our journey, there was no certainty. The weather and conditions were unknown and changing.

"Are you hurting?" Verlen had asked me. "You aren't in danger are you? Are you wet, or cold?" If my answers to these questions were negative, Verlen knew I must be all right.

The wind blew steadily all the next day and I grew even more depressed until I realized that the weather didn't rule my life. The weather could keep us off the water, but for all the wind's power, I still had to maintain morale. I remembered the Christmas decorations packed in the stern of my canoe.

"Verlen, today I'm going to glue the manger scene on my deck. I'll decorate for Christmas." I collected my supplies and climbed into the truck. I epoxied the six wooden figures on the deck hatch cover, then put the freshly glued nativity scene on the dashboard of the truck to cure in the sun.

On December 15th I celebrated my sister Leesa's birthday. She was thousands of miles away but I sang happy birthday out loud and hoped the wind was listening.

The wind howled, picking up the sand and blowing up whitecaps on the lagoon. The reef at the lagoon mouth stood in high foam, and the shells I had discovered were buried in drift. My fingers were peeling from the salt water and sun, my body stank, my lips were salty, and my teeth ground sand particles. Besides these inconveniences, my tent tried to levitate each night, as the wind worsened. We had tied our tents to the canoes, and as the wind increased, the bows of our boats were lifted into the air. But I wasn't depressed any more. I sat patiently in the tent, reading candy wrappers to pass the time.

"Verlen, I heard a motor!" I jumped out of the tent. When I saw that it was a boat, I ran on the beach, waving urgently for it to stop. Two Mexicans landed and pointed inside the lagoon.

"Americano, interior," were the only two words we could understand. Were there really Americans in the interior of the lagoon? The Mexicans were ready to take us, so we climbed into the fishing boat and bumped over the waves into the belly of the lagoon. I was afraid as we left our tents and boats and the safety of our truck, but I realized I had to have faith that a rescue had come. I hung onto the bucking gunwale as Manuel and Francisco took us toward a far island point. As we got nearer I could see a tent—an American tent—and I recognized an American-made camp stove set on the beach. I jumped out of the boat as we landed, running over the rocks to grasp the hands of two people like us. How glad I was to see Americans! Petting their husky dog and looking over their gear, I wondered how they had ever arrived at the lagoon.

David and Lee introduced themselves and explained that they were two students from Oregon studying brants and their habits. They had parked their truck in Ignacio and motored in a small launch to the point, where they had spent several months watching black brants eat lagoon grass. They told us stories of whales, too, sighted from their lookout. Our burst of friendship to these strangers cut across all rules of formal communication— there was no small talk; we were mighty glad to see them.

Lee knew more Spanish than we did, and as she spoke with Manuel and Francisco she was able to identify the navigable route that would put us at the south end of the lagoon pointing toward Punta Pequeña. We plotted the course on our map, then all too soon said good-bye and accepted a return ride from the fishermen.

Finally, in the night, the wind mercifully stopped. When morning came we started off, paddling until the water gave out, then trudging the maze of lagoon channels until we found the fishing camp at Degalito.

The village looked poor: the shacks were flimsier than most we had seen, and even the fishing boats looked worn out. There was no sand, but an area of mud leading to a ragged fence line. A lone fisherman was busy anchoring his boat as we assembled our tents above the tide markings. He had come home from work and now waded through the mud with his hat in one hand and a gunnysack in the other. The sack was tied close to the base and looked as if it contained a small catch. He stopped and watched us.

"Como se llama usted?" I asked, busy with my chores.

"Armand," he answered.

Hardly looking up from the preparation of making camp, I didn't try to speak again. He continued to watch.

"Comidas?" he offered, lifting his sack into the air.

"Sí, muchas gracias," I said, thankful I wouldn't have to unpack my cook kit.

"I'm not so sure we want to eat with this man," said Verlen more cautiously.

"We've been invited," I said zipping shut my tent. "Come on, I'm starved." We followed Armand to an abandoned container truck stationed in the sand beside a pile of cans and litter. At the back end of the truck his wife María stood frying tortillas on a wood fire beneath a metal drum. Armand pointed into the truck and told us by gesturing with his hands that we should enter. His family had scavenged a home from the truck body, and five children played in the shadows of a kerosene light.

"I don't want to eat here," Verlen hesitated. "We are imposing on these people." Armand was already motioning us to the table. Verlen took out his wallet and offered it to Armand.

"No," Armand said, shaking his head positively. "Estar sentado por favor," he said pulling out a chair. María climbed into the truck holding a lobster. Attesting to life, its claws waved madly. Before our eyes, María clubbed the creature, pulled off its head, and threw the wasted portion out the door. Splitting the tail with a butcher knife, she placed the meat in a pan.

Armand handed us mugs of steaming water and María pushed a jar of instant coffee and a bowl of sugar toward us. Then Armand sat down. I noticed that a Bible was beside his place at the table. The children stood behind their papa on the edge of the lantern glow watching us and waiting their turn to be fed. While we were eating, a large cockroach walked across the back of Verlen's chair, but I didn't point it out. Verlen was still uncomfortable about our intrusion and impatient to leave, wanting to vacate our seats for the rest of the family. I followed Verlen's urgings and quickly finished dinner. We thanked them for the good food and returned to our tents.

But I was restless and drawn back to the family. Taking my Bible, I walked back to the truck and knocked on its side. Armand welcomed me and cleared a place for me at the table.

I didn't know how to say I was homesick, so I put my Bible on the table beside me. Armand cleaned the grease from his fingers by wiping his hands on his shirt, then pushed aside his plate and brought forward his own Bible. Pointing to the Christmas story in Luke, I asked him to read.

His deep voice began in Spanish and I followed along with my English version. The children gathered around their papa as I listened to a familiar story in an unfamiliar language. The words of the wonderful story came to life as Armand read, and when he finished we looked at each other and smiled. Armand pointed to the 23rd psalm and I read the verses aloud in English. When I finished, Armand read the same scripture in Spanish. In this manner we read several other passages, and the language barrier vanished.

"Muchas gracias," I said as I stood up to leave, pleased with our unique communication.

"Un momento," Papa enjoined. He turned the pages of his Bible to Numbers 6:25–27 and read: "Jehová te bendiga, y te garde. Haga resplandecer Jehová su rostro sobre ti, y haya de ti misericordia: Jehová alce a ti su rostro, y ponga en ti paz." Armand's voice was expressive. He raised his head and looked into my eyes, gesturing with the words as he read.

I found the passage in my own Bible and read: "May the Lord bless you and keep you, the Lord make his face to shine upon you and give you peace. Amen."

Armand understood my journey. The children's brown eyes were large with wonder.

"God bless your casa," I said as I left. I was overwhelmed with gratitude.

Verlen was talking with another villager when I returned to the tents. I didn't know how to tell him, but I knew that we had been blessed. I could feel it.

At dawn, when the fishermen went out the southern mouth of the lagoon, we followed their path through the breakers. With their help, we bypassed large rollers dumping over the shoals. Verlen paddled steadily beside me. The land on each side of the opening was low, sandy, and bare. The ocean spread out before us: we were once again an adventure on the move.

FOURTEEN

Flux

Several miles from shore I stopped paddling and looked over my shoulder: Punta Pequeña was shrinking in the distance. We had launched at 5:30 A.M. when the hills were still muted in the last shades of night, and we were too far from land to see the white ruff of shore break by the time the soft pinks of dawn were giving way to silver streaks of new light. The morning came in colors with a feeling of special magic, and there was a coolness and innocence to the day. Because we were up early and already paddling, I felt a certain anticipation, as if we had a part in shaping the hours of daylight, or at least in urging it on as enthusiastic spectators. I looked at my watch. It was December 16th, 7:00 A.M.

"This is far enough," I declared. "Let's eat breakfast." Verlen set his paddle down across the cockpit and looked at his watch.

"Getting hungry myself," he said. Using long, sweeping strokes and pushing his rudder control, he paddled over to my boat and grabbed my cockpit as the swells bumped our canoes together. The boats now bobbed up and down in the stillness. My energy level was low, so whenever I interrupted the task of paddling, my purpose wavered, and the ocean seemed to grow in that moment, breathing on me from all sides. To distract myself from feeling so small, I busied myself with breakfast.

"Have a banana," I said, pulling one from the food bag. Verlen reached for the fresh fruit and settled back against his cockpit to munch. Emptying the bag, I arranged our other choices on my lap. The day before we had shopped at a small grocery in San Juanico. Since it had no electricity, the

186

store looked more like a cellar full of supplies. Scouting the shelves, we bypassed canned beans and tomatoes to horde special treats for breakfast. Along with the bananas, there were two varieties of cookies to sample and a new package of dry, unbroken crackers. Verlen set cookie pieces and cracker sandwiches on the deck of his canoe to eat as he read his Spanish dictionary. He seemed to forget we were going anywhere at all—when the boats drifted sideways on the swells, he took his paddle in one hand and pulled at the water without looking up from his book. I pushed on my rudder and the canoes slowly turned back into a more comfortable position, headed into the waves.

Eating totally absorbed me, and I didn't want to share my moment of satisfaction with a book or conversation. I pulled out a sack of caramels I had stashed in the bottom of my food bag, offering a handful to Verlen and balancing half a dozen on my thigh. The wrappers were melted into the candies. Long strings of sugar spun in wisps as I pulled on the cellophane. Not wanting to lose a bite, I sucked the wrapper for the last bit of flavor. Verlen opened a small sack of Mexican confections he had tucked in his personal bag. He handed me a piece of candied sweet potato and a lump of pressed brown sugar.

When we started paddling again, the sun was brighter, and highlighted a landscape of steep-sided mesas.

"Verlen, what made those shapes?" I asked, paddling steadily.

"A giant sat on top of a mountain one day," he answered, without a trace of humor.

"Thanks, Verlen, but I don't believe you."

"Good," he replied, looking straight ahead and continuing to stroke. "It's erosion," he said more seriously. "What you are seeing is the harder rock in a plateau protecting the land between stream valleys."

"It's easier to imagine a giant flattening the top than enough rainfall in this desert land to cause a gradual wearing away," I said, staring at the squared-off hillsides.

"Wind can cause erosion too," Verlen explained.

The rest of the afternoon, I paid particular attention to the arid land. Though rainfall was scarce, dry riverbeds gouged the hillsides. Like a relief map I'd once seen of river systems, ever-smaller branches spread outward across the plains from a deep main artery where water had once flowed.

After six hours of paddling we reached Punta San Juanico, where the gentle swells we had been riding all day crashed at the base of the scalloped headland. Deceptively calm away from the shore, the ocean displayed its energy as it hurtled surf and spray upon the rocks. The beach, which created its own lagoon, was an extension of silt deposited from the Cadegomo River south of the point. It was dotted with separate pools of shallow water and strewn with dried fish heads and spines. Pieces of stiffened fish skin lay baked and curled in the sun.

A man who looked like a skeleton himself was bent over a boat gunwale knotting a bowline. He straightened when he saw Verlen and me, but his back seemed to have a permanent curve of fatigue. Introducing himself as Federico, he held out a calloused brown hand. His eyes squinted as if his cap were pulled too tightly on his forehead, and gray hair stuck out from all directions under the brim of his visor. We followed him to the fishing camp set against the hill.

Federico's place was as bleak as I've ever seen: flies were everywhere, and dishes sat in the dirt, covered with dried food and grease. Federico stopped outside a rusted trailer and poked at a small cooking fire half-buried in the sand. Verlen and I set our packs down after clearing a spot with our feet. Federico went to his trailer and returned with a half a loaf of white bread, a jar of warm mayonnaise, a can of white sugar frosting, a sack of sugar, and a bag of salt, which he set on a stump beside the fire.

Within a few minutes Verlen had his cook kit unpacked and a pot of water simmering on the fire. Federico watched intently as Verlen added macaroni and unwrapped a sack of powdered cheese. We didn't say much as the food cooked—I stayed busy brushing flies away. When the macaroni was soft, Verlen stirred in cheese and powdered milk, then passed the pot toward our host. Federico held up his hand to refuse, then pointed to his own offerings of bread and frosting to see if we wanted any. We made gestures of complete delight toward our own food and divided the macaroni between the two of us without touching Federico's supplies.

When we finished eating, Verlen took out his map and his Spanish-English dictionary—we needed information about the coastline ahead. The map showed a half-moon crescent of land jutting to a point 90 miles away at Cabo San Lazaro. Thirty miles south of us lay the beginning of an intercoastal lagoon system that bypassed Cabo San Lazaro and emptied into Bahía Magdalena. For a small boat going south, the lagoon system would be the safest and most comfortable route past the dangerous cape, which is notorious for its high surf and numerous shipwrecks.

The lagoon waterway looked inviting—the only trick was entering the system. The mouths of these lagoons, as we well knew, were marked by rolling breakers curling over shoal bars, so passage is blocked for all except small boats in calm weather. Verlen pointed at our boats and made paddling motions in the air. He took a pen and outlined our choices on the map. Then he looked to Federico for advice.

Federico watched the pantomime of our plan and leaned close, putting his frosting-smudged finger on the map and tracing a line into the channel at the third entrance, marked Boca de Soledad. Tapping the map at that point he nodded his head emphatically.

"Bueno, bueno," he said.

"Muchas gracias," Verlen responded, and folded the map into its plastic case. Sitting with Federico, we watched as the sun disappeared and an uncountable number of stars took over the sky. The weather seemed stable. We walked back to our canoes, set up camp, and watched from the beach as waves rolled into the shallow bay, slamming against the rocky point in bursts of white against the night.

The next morning we set out early for Boca de Soledad. The coast was uneven, with hills and low, rocky mesas close by the sea. Farther south, the tablelands pulled away from the coast and the land appeared level, with plains rising upward to distant mesas and interior peaks. As we suspected, the entrances at Boca de las Animas and Boca de Santo Domingo were blocked by waves and threatening swells. The third entrance, Boca de Soledad, opened like a narrow doorway and we paddled through the lagoon mouth into a world of flat water lined by dark green mangroves. It was as if we had paddled into another world. The change was remarkable. We were separated from the sea by a sandy strip of an island. In places we could hear the surf over the sand and even see spray from the breakers splashing into the air above the dunes.

After paddling for five miles beyond the entrance, we saw the loading pier and navigation light of Lopez Mateo. A large antenna rose like a skyscraper above a clutter of sloping roofs. We paddled past an airstrip and followed a border of mangroves along the mainland edge of the lagoon. We couldn't see town through the mangrove screen, but we heard an occasional car rattling and bumping on the street. Chickens squawked and children's voices mixed together. The mangroves formed such a dense barricade that there was no beach to the lagoon, but Verlen and I finally found an opening in the brush that offered us a few feet of wet mud. We pulled the boats ashore, eager to explore.

Mateo looked as if it had a firm hold on civilization. Our map showed a road connecting Mateo to Constitución and the transpeninsular highway. Because of this connection with the main highway, Mateo had electricity. Plastic Christmas trees stood in many of the windows, and strings of holiday lights twisted around splintered doorways. Our guidebook said Mateo had a population of 1,500 people—a mix of fishermen, farmers, cannery workers, merchants, and families. The book also said Mateo had a phone.

"I'll be back in a few minutes," I promised. Leaving Verlen in the street, I ran toward a small hut at the base of a tall antenna. Inside, a young woman at a switchboard gave me a small pad of paper to write the number I wanted to call. Carefully, I printed my parents' name and city. For five minutes the operator repeated the numerals into the phone, waiting for a connection. I could see she was used to delays: she had a page of doodles beside the phone, and her fingernails were bitten to the quick. Playing with her shoe and scratching her foot to pass the time, the girl looked as if she were rooted to the chair. Finally, she handed me the receiver.

"Venita, get on the other line," I heard my father say. "It's Valerie." Their voices sounded far away. "Where are you?" Dad wanted to know exactly. "I can see the channel you are describing on the map," he said excitedly. "Looks good," he encouraged.

I tried to explain the storm and delays.

"We've heard about the weather," my father interrupted. "The news calls it El Niño—some kind of warming trend in the Pacific. The equatorial current has reversed direction across the entire ocean. Surface temperatures are 14 degrees above normal. Last week a volcano in Mexico erupted and the dust misled the satellite sensors. They say this is the worst winter California has ever experienced."

The conversation transported me to Houston, and I felt as if I were sitting next to my folks in their living room. I shut out the telephone static and beamed myself home. In a tumble of news and emotion, we hugged each other over the wire.

"It'll be a quiet Christmas here," I said. "I love you both." When I handed the receiver to the operator, I was still glowing. By the look on her face, I knew she had taken part in my call. Though she didn't speak much English, she was able to translate my smile. A clear spark of interest flashed in her eyes because of the life transmitted to me through her machine.

When I walked into the street to look for Verlen, I found him sitting on a cement step with a box of doughnuts. Repeating every word, I relived my call. He shared my exuberance and seemed to brighten up himself. Verlen nodded his head when I told him the official description of our weather problems. We both knew the conditions weren't normal.

Verlen carried the box of doughnuts as we looked for a place to eat. There were several restaurants to choose from, but we were drawn to an open-air cafe where the proprietor fried pieces of beef on a countertop grill. His wife looked at us and smiled, but her hands remained busy stuffing taco shells with shredded lettuce and tomatoes. Ten tables filled the place. The customers were quiet, eating their food and staring at a television set on top of an icebox. The program was a Mexican boxing match. I picked up two tacos at the counter and reserved a table for Verlen, who had wandered closer to the small screen. The program didn't interest me—I wanted to be catching up on my journal. Two months had gone by since I had left Seattle, and when I looked at the water-stained pages of my notes I felt a certain satisfaction. I leaned over to the empty seat and pulled one of the damp maps from Verlen's plastic case. I pushed my plate to the far side of the table and unfolded the chart in front of me. San Carlos was 30 miles ahead of us through the protected lagoon, and the next day's work was clear: we would paddle south in the narrow channel and enter Magdalena Bay through the Hull Canal. What a change it was to anticipate our progress without being threatened by the ocean.

As I looked at Verlen watching the fights, and at the Christmas decorations and artificial plants hung in tin cans from the ceiling, I felt separated from the ocean by a lot more than a narrow spit of sand dunes. I missed the fish camps and lanterns that had welcomed us on other nights. Mateo was close enough to the main highway to receive many Anglo visitors, so we were just another couple in the Saturday night crowd. We were not special, and without our paddles or boats to introduce us, no one paid much attention. The town hardly noticed us as we resupplied and planned to move on. A commercial came on showing a couple on a sailboat smoking cigarettes. I knew I was getting restless when I paid no attention to the characters, but only stared at the ocean in the background.

We soon walked back to our dab of mud beach outside town. With no space to set up camp, we had cozied our tent up to a barbed wire fence that pressed against the road. There was no ocean wind to chase away the mosquitoes that buzzed around the nylon. We were safe, but strangely displaced in the quiet lagoon world.

The next morning we gulped a dozen doughnuts and left San Mateo as the sun came up. Pushing off from the mud, I felt as though we were launching in a bathtub. There were no swells on the intercoastal, and not even a ripple of wind on the water. Mangroves lined the mainland side of the lagoon like a wall and oatmeal-colored dunes barricaded the west. I could hear the ocean and smell the salt air even though I couldn't see the water. Finally my curiosity took over.

"Let's park the boats and walk to the ocean," I said, looking at the sand-hills.

"You know what the ocean looks like," Verlen answered.

"I want to walk on the dunes," I explained.

At noon Verlen gave in to my pleading, and we beached the boats and prepared for a hike. Outfitted with compass and water canteens, we stuck our paddles upright in a sandhill to mark where our canoes were parked so we wouldn't get lost. We soon realized this wasn't necessary as there were no other footprints and we could easily follow our own back.

Nearly a mile of sand dunes separated the lagoon from the ocean. We walked into hollows and marched up mountains of damp, heavy sand. The terrain was creased in wind drifts and corrugated ripples, and I hesitated to smudge the time-worn patterns with my feet. It looked as if the wind had the same effect on land as the ocean currents did on the ocean floor. As we walked closer to the ocean, the roar of the surf steadily increased until we climbed one last hill—and there was the sea.

Spray from the breakers created its own dark cloud system above the multitiered surf on a long, shallow sand beach. The dunes diminished to anthill shapes, pushed by the tide to clear a runway for the full force of ocean. It was a fearsome view: the waves did not merely roll onto the beach, they chewed and clawed on the backs of each other as they powered toward us. The biggest surf ever reported on the West Coast had been in this area just north of Cabo San Lázaro, and I could now confirm the terrifying reputation. While I cautiously followed the tideline roaming for treasure, Verlen discovered a dead dolphin, frayed and rotting on top of a dried kelp bed. When my pockets were full of shells and my ears numb from the turbine sound, we turned and followed our path of backward footprints to our canoes.

As we climbed back into the canoes I noticed how hot it had gotten. No breeze was stirring in the lagoon, and the air seemed to press down on us in the still backwater. On the ocean side my eyes had smarted from the brine of sea water splashing my face. On the lagoon side it was my own sweat that trickled down my forehead and stung my eyes.

Neither of us complained. After two months of hurrying from harbor to harbor, we were able to pull ashore whenever we wanted. Without fear of surf and no need of figuring strategy, I pushed my canoe into the sand and hopped out to squat behind a bush, joyfully abandoning my usual midocean bathroom techniques.

Verlen continued paddling. There was no need to keep up with him—I wasn't in a hurry and didn't fear being on my own. With each stroke his paddle waved at me as he pushed farther ahead and soon was reduced to a dot. Throughout the day we played leapfrog with one another, passing and then dropping back at a leisurely pace. In the late afternoon I came around a curve and saw Verlen just ahead. The low sun cut through a line of coral pink horizon haze. The sky turned to purple and changed the mountains of sand to gold. Rays of light glittered on the glassy lagoon surface and Verlen's canoe trailed a perfect triangular wake. His body and canoe seemed to be one piece of carved silhouette.

We made camp in a peaceful glade. Sitting in the sand, I leaned against my pack and toasted my feet by a snapping fire. A tiny moon lit the water and the lights of San Carlos were visible over the mangroves. Verlen's face glowed in the light of the fire. His bristly beard shadowed his jaw like a fur ruff. The familiar captain's hat covered his head. I heard mosquitoes buzzing around my ears and felt sand fleas bite my legs, but they were only a minor distraction in the tranquil lagoon. It was so quiet I could hear dolphins breathing as they swam past our beach.

Verlen stood up, brushed the sand from his pants, and walked to the water's edge. He knelt and rubbed his fingers and a handful of sand in his cook pot to scrub away the residue of dinner.

"We went too slowly today," he chided. "We should be in San Carlos by now."

"We'll get there tomorrow," I said, looking contentedly into the fire.

"Staying on schedule is important. If you could contain your whims we would make better progress," he said, referring to our sidetrip on the dunes.

"Maybe you can contain the weather," I countered, reminding him of the reasons for our past delays, I insisted on enjoying the calm. Not wanting to argue, he stopped talking and climbed into his tent. The fabric listed to one side because of two broken tent poles and the zipper had popped—I saw Verlen's fingers pinning the opening with a clothes hook. I felt a pang of guilt. He was right: the lagoon was not our life, we had a goal. One way or another, Verlen needed to be in Chicago by February 9th and we had over 1,400 miles yet to Yuma. I left the cozy fire and crawled into my own tent, accompanied by a crowd of mosquitoes.

During the night a thick fog settled over the lagoon and when I woke, the tents were soaked in moisture. Puddles formed in the low spaces of my shelter and the beach sand beneath the coated plastic floor felt cold and hard. I packed and walked to the water's edge. The lagoon water was so still by our beach that the residue from Verlen's cook pot remained where he had rinsed it the night before. Pieces of macaroni lay in the sand under a few inches of water—even the fish didn't like powdered cheese.

We paddled south following the mangrove line and reading our compass. In the water beneath us, we could see fish swimming and plants waving with the slight current. When I began counting stingrays swishing on the bottom I suddenly got dizzy. I knew I'd better stop looking down, but even when I stared straight ahead, the dizziness did not go away. Maybe I had eaten too many cookies for breakfast. I kept paddling.

A school of fish crowded beneath our boats. Startled by our paddles dipping into their territory they abandoned formation and moved in all directions. Confused about which way was up, many of the fish flopped into the air, somersaulting and gyrating above the water before falling back into anonymity below. Moments later Verlen and I saw two men in a fishing boat prowling for a catch. We pointed toward the panicked school, then felt like traitors. The men immediately snapped into action: steering the boat in a large circle, the sternsman applied full throttle, setting their bow into the air. All the while the bowman quickly let out armloads of net.

Orange floats fell over the side, bobbing from the wake and turmoil of captured fish. Around and around the boat went. The bowman poked at the floats with a gaff, widening the circle and beating an oar on the side of the boat to hustle the fish into the trap. It was a massacre: the floats were pulled half underwater by the weight of so many captured fish. The men worked intently until the floats hung like a necklace dripping pearls. We watched for half an hour, then turned our canoes for the final miles to San Carlos.

Gradually, the lagoon opened into Hull Canal and when the channel widened, we knew the bay was close. As the fog lifted we paddled past Punta Edie. Aiming for a metal warehouse and watertower visible ahead, we paddled for 45 minutes more before we saw the pier at San Carlos. Buoys marked the deep-water channel for the larger boats. Shrimpers, fishing trollers, and ocean ships congested the dock area, tied up for refueling and repairs—our canoes were dwarfed beside the tall ships. We continued paddling along the beach and landed next to a scattered fleet of fishing boats just south of town.

In the past few days we had gotten spoiled. If a village was near, we looked for a restaurant instead of taking out our cook kit and packaged supply of dehydrated food. Verlen and I went through the familiar motions of tying up the boats, covering the cockpits, and collecting our personal bags. Neither of us said anything, but I knew we would walk into town for lunch.

San Carlos was not exactly bustling. The town had a central square that served as an open-air community center and looked like an overgrown sand box, with playground equipment stuck in the loamy soil and trees lining the border. Two run-down taxis were parked on the south corner of the main intersection. One of the drivers sat leaning back on a wooden bench, his cap covering his eyes, both legs spread out and crossed at the ankles in front of him. Waiting for a fare had put him to sleep.

We found a restaurant, and when I looked in the window I liked the place right away. No customers were inside, but I could see a sink with clean towels and a bar of soap right by the door. This was just where I wanted to eat: I walked in and went right to the enamel basin and washed my hands several times. It had been weeks since I'd had the chance to wash my hands in anything other than a tidal pool. We ordered our usual double portions of food.

A woman sat sewing at one of the tables, and I imagined she might be making Christmas gifts for her family. A little girl came in and sat with Verlen and me. Plastic bracelets jangled on her chubby wrists and she cracked pecans with her teeth and smiled at us. The restaurant was also this family's living room.

"You're not eating anything," Verlen said, looking up from his lunch. A mouthful of burritos slurred his words.

194

"I think it's the heat. I haven't felt right all morning," I answered. Picking up my fork I played with the beans at the side of my plate.

"If this town has a phone, I should make some calls this afternoon," Verlen said, taking another bite. "In about an hour we'll head for Punta Belcher."

I wasn't so sure I was going anywhere, but I didn't say much. It was hard to describe how I was feeling. It was like carrying a weight inside my head and chest. Verlen ate his lunch, then traded plates and cleaned mine too.

As soon as we were finished, we walked through town looking for a phone, which we found in a small grocery stuck behind the cash register. The cashier pointed to the tall wooden phone booth and insisted that the lines to San Carlos did not open until three o'clock, so Verlen took his place in the line of people already waiting. I wasn't feeling very well, so I went outside. Within a few minutes I decided I might be more comfortable lying down, so I stretched out in the dirt beside the store and covered myself with my map to try to keep warm. After a time I opened my eyes and saw Verlen standing over me.

"What's gotten into you?" he fretted. "People are going to think you're on drugs." My energy had been drained as if someone had pulled a plug. I lay in the dirt and knew I couldn't get up.

"I haven't made my calls yet. I'm still waiting for the lines to clear," Verlen explained. He went back inside the store, apparently hoping that whatever was wrong with me would pass quickly. In an hour he was back with a sack of groceries and a can of juice for me to sip, but I didn't want any. For the first time, Verlen was helpless.

I fell asleep again, and when I woke I heard an American voice talking above me.

"She's got the bug," he said. "I've seen it a hundred times before. We'll get a taxi." Before I could turn over and look up to see who it was, Verlen had walked away with the stranger. I stayed right where I was. Ground level seemed safest. I stared at the brown paper sack Verlen had left and I looked under the steps of the grocery. In a few minutes a car drove up. I saw four tires stop and two pair of feet came toward me. I recognized Verlen's tennis shoes, and the other pair of feet belonged to the American voice. The men picked me up and folded me inside the taxi. My head lay on the lap of a bearded American. Verlen cradled my legs. My rescuer was in a hurry and talked about his ship leaving the harbor within the hour. His shirt smelled of diesel oil, and I couldn't see his face for the bristle of beard sticking out from his chin. I couldn't understand the hurried Spanish he spoke to the driver, but I knew the town was so small we wouldn't go far. Within a few minutes the taxi stopped.

"This hotel is the best place I can leave you," the American explained.

Verlen lifted me out of the car and the two men supported me as we walked through the courtyard obstacle course of clothes lines and bedding. The American propped me against a brick wall, said good-bye, and hurried back to the cab. I felt dizzy as I leaned against the building, and several identical doors seemed to be trading places with one another. I decided to lie down on the piece of cement at my feet. It took Verlen the longest time renting a room. While I wondered why he was taking so long, I watched a parade of ants walking past my nose. The courtyard rocked. The ocean swells had invaded dry land, encamping inside my stomach and between my ears.

Verlen and the hotel manager carried me to bed. Verlen looked worried, but not as worried as I was. The green corrugated ceiling undulated, ugly aqua curtains sagged at the windows, their jagged edges unhemmed. I didn't want to die there.

I would rather have been headed in the chubasco again than face the night of sickness. I had the same feeling as when we were battling the storm—it would be a long fight. Verlen stood over me handing vitamin C tablets and glasses of water. My body turned hot and then cold. Finally I rallied enough energy to retaliate, and I started to vomit and shiver uncontrollably. I remember that sometime around morning Verlen sat me on the cement floor of the shower stall and turned on cool water to rinse my sweaty body. Then I lay in bed for 15 hours before coming back to life. When I woke up Verlen was sitting beside me, stroking my head.

"I don't feel much like an explorer stuck in this aqua motel room," I said, pulling the thin printed sheet high around my neck. I soon fell asleep again, dreaming about my house in Seattle and my dog licking my face.

On the third day I was up and walking. Verlen and I were on our way to the boats when he sat down on a step, unable to move. Whatever had hit me now sneaked up on Verlen. At least I knew what to do. The manager at the hotel welcomed us back and even gave us the same room. I felt as if the trip were over and we were in a cell debriefing. For two days I sat with Verlen while he retched and shivered, trying to rid his system of the bacteria.

The fourth night it rained, and the gentle sound on the roof of the motel gave me hope. I realized this was a special place—we were separated from the ocean, and the world had stopped for us. I didn't know how we would regain the momentum of our journey, but I felt as if it were waiting for us to return. Verlen recuperated slowly. One thing I did know, I never wanted to see another refried bean again.

On the fifth day I heard roosters outside, sounding off like a string of firecrackers. When I left Verlen sleeping and walked through town, I found the streets were humming with a storm of yellow butterflies. They fluttered, danced, and dove through the streets. I sat on a stone step in the square and sharpened my pencil with a pocketknife just as Verlen had taught me so I could write a letter home. As if it were in tune with my own slow pace, a nearby car motor sputtered and died.

When I went to mail the letter to my parents, the postmaster at the correro was a young man who spoke some English. Pulling a Christmas card out from under the counter, he asked my name, then addressed the card to me and handed it over with a smile.

"Muchas gracias," I said, amazed by the man's perception of my needs. Given my first bit of holiday cheer, I caught the spirit of the season and stopped at the grocery to purchase a gift for Verlen. The most unusual thing I could find was a jar of American peanut butter, and I knew it was a gift I would like myself. I wrapped it with a piece of holiday paper I had carried in my personal bag since San Diego and hurried back to the motel. Verlen was tying his shoes when I arrived.

"You can carry this, Verlen, but don't open it until Christmas," I said, handing him the gift.

Verlen was ready to leave, so we paid the manager and told him we hoped we would not need to come back. We walked through town to our canoes without looking back.

Our absence from the boats had been costly: the manger scene had been knocked off my bow, the hatch on Verlen's boat had been pried open, a camera lens was missing, and a headlamp had disappeared. There was nothing we could do, and there was no sense getting sick all over again. The beach was littered with many fishing boats outfitted with tools, nets, motors, and oars, all apparently undisturbed but our boats were unusual and had sat unattended for days. Temptation had captured someone on the beach. The vandalism seemed more a result of curiosity than deliberate thievery.

"Few people want to be thieves," Verlen explained. "I don't believe in locking things up. If you trust someone they will usually honor it."

"You may be right, but in this case, I think we trusted too much. We didn't have much choice, but leaving these boats here all the time we were sick was just inviting trouble. I think we got off easy."

As we launched the boats I realized how tired I still was. "I'm not very ambitious today, Verlen," I said.

"I'm not either, so let's take it easy," he answered.

The easy lagoon paddling was behind us and the tide soon turned against us as we started south in Magdalena Bay, but we were both happy to be moving, even though we weren't covering much territory. For the past two months we had marked the map every night with our progress, but for the past week our trip had been at a standstill.

"Why don't we hire some sherpas?" I asked. "Other expeditions have assistance. Climbers to Everest turn back in poor weather and African explorers abort when the ammunition gets low," I explained, trying to find an excuse.

"Keep it moving, Valerie, that's the secret." Verlen smiled as he paddled by.

I dug in harder with my blade and tried to keep up.

FIFTEEN

Feliz Navidad

We landed at Belcher Point after dark and went right to work making camp. Verlen fired up the stove and I held my flashlight like a poised pencil ready to write. The text I was bearing down on was the back of a packaged soy protein entree. Why did I pause to read the instructions when I knew them by heart? What I hoped for was a variation we might somehow have missed in past preparations.

"Add contents to two cups water, bring to boil while stirring. Cover and simmer 15 minutes or until tender, stir occasionally to prevent sticking, add more water if necessary, and remember—keep your campsite clean."

I wasn't too excited about dinner: vegetable gum, tomato solids, and two cups of murky water did not a Spanish-style casserole make. Our dehydrated food was good quality, but it lost its appeal after 50 continuous days. Of half a dozen entree selections in our packaged food supply, mountain stew was my favorite, but we had run out of that one early on. I remembered that Verlen had been in charge of packing the food at the beginning of the trip, which explained why we had an overabundance of his favorite—macaroni and powdered cheese. As I stared into the cook pot I realized this was going to be another meal of necessity, not pleasure.

A group of fishermen on the far side of the arroyo were gathered in an open-air kitchen lean-to. Their cook fire was smoking and an oil lamp lit their faces around a board table.

"I bet they've got tortillas," I said, and taking my small flashlight, I ventured over to greet the men and ask for a handout. They were drinking mugs of coffee and nursing small butts of cigarettes.

"Buenas noches," I began. "Tortillas, por favor?" My expression of hunger was sufficient. One man pointed toward a stack of stiff corn rounds with bugs crawling over and through the layers. Two of the discs were set on the oil drum stove, instantly grilled, and given to my care. I took them back to the tent still steaming, but after eating only two bites, I Frisbeed the stale food into a cactus. Verlen methodically chewed his portion of soy and quietly began to lecture.

"Remember when I first introduced you to dehydrated food?" he asked.

"Yes, I thought it was great, really different," I answered.

"A person has to maintain an attitude of interest. If you believed that the food was good once you can believe that it is good again." I began to get restless.

"The boredom is all in your mind," he continued. As far as I was concerned, the boredom was in the cook pot.

"If your body was rejecting this food I could feel sorry for you, but it is only your attitude," he said, closing the subject. I closed the lid on the cook pot and decided to wait until breakfast. Looking up I saw figures approaching and two cigarettes glowing in the darkness.

"Hey," I whispered to Verlen, "they're carrying something." The visitors stopped in front of my tent and Verlen turned his flashlight toward them. The beam illuminated two men carrying an octopus. They were holding out the limp, dripping creature from the sea and waiting for us to accept it.

"Muchas buenas comidas," one of the Mexicans said. On this matter, Verlen and I were united.

"Muchas gracias, but no thank you," we said, assuring the men that we had plenty of food and no need for such a snack. As they headed back into the darkness, taking the octopus with them, I decided that my dehydrated food didn't look so bad after all.

"Do you think we insulted them?" I asked Verlen.

"I'm not sure, but I know it would insult them more if I ate it and threw up."

"I've heard that octopus is delicious." I was having second thoughts.

"Whoever told you that never put a dead octopus in their tent and tried to cook it on a camp stove in the dark."

When Verlen finished eating he walked to the sea, carrying the cook pot and spoons to wash them in the surf. He also took the remains of my meal to feed the fish. Busying myself with housekeeping chores, I arranged the gear in the corners of my tent, then took out my precious journal. This was the time of day that I coveted: the paddling was done, dinner was over, and no matter how tired I was, I took time to write every detail I could remember about the day. Though Verlen was undisputed leader of our team, when

200

I took out my journal I felt my special purpose as recorder. Verlen had utmost respect for my chronicling bent. His journal entries were brief, always less than a paragraph, noting weather and date. But I had a desire to record everything that happened, and my journal was turning into a book. I propped my knees to form a writing table and opened my notebook. Holding a flashlight in my left hand and pencil in my right, I began to write my observations of the day, December 22nd.

We had paddled 17 miles in Bahia Magdalena—the largest and safest all-weather harbor on the Pacific coast of Baja. This bay is formed by a series of large islands set into the Pacific that protect the mainland from the full force of ocean waves and wind. We had traversed the bay from the town of San Carlos, at the northeast end of the bay, to Belcher Point, a small harbor on the southern spit of Isla Magdalena. In the early part of the day the tide ran with us, helping to push us toward the mouth of the bay at Punta Entrada. We had paddled down the middle of the bay taking full advantage of the current going our way.

The tide changed direction when we were only a few miles south of San Carlos, so we paddled out of the main current and followed the mainland shore. Before reaching the widest portion of the bay we made a cautious east-west crossing of the San Carlos channel, then continued paddling toward Belcher on the far west side.

On the lee side of Isla Magdalena, I had paddled over an area alive with fish. Below me were orange rarities and sun disk specimens that reminded me of fish I'd seen while snorkeling off Maui on the Hawaiian coast. For the first time in our 600 miles of ocean travel, I could view the sea bottom outside one of the lagoons.

My flashlight began to dim, so I interrupted my writing and searched in one of my bags for extra batteries. After fixing my light, I burrowed myself back into a comfortable position and continued writing.

With the open ocean held back by the islands, the surf was reduced to a minimum surge. We had been able to stop for a bathroom break on a sandspit, and I stuck my paddle in the sand as a privacy screen while Verlen inspected a three-foot in diameter globular sea mine that had washed ashore. It was encrusted with saltwater barnacles. The mine had protruding horns, and the apparatus was apparently intact. I remembered stories about mines blowing up years after the war, so I cautioned Verlen against hitting the thing with his paddle. Scraping the metal with his knife, he appeared to be intent on breaking into the device.

In no hurry to continue paddling, I had surveyed the beach for shell treasures, filling both pockets with keepers. Verlen soon convinced me we had to go on. Not troubled by surf, I waded out into the water, guiding my canoe. The intrusion of my feet in the sand scared up dozens of bottom stingrays, and I jumped into the cockpit and paddled quickly toward deeper water.

Verlen hadn't returned from his chores, so I set down my journal and unzipped the tent screen to see where he was. When I looked out I could see the outline of his figure on the beach, still as a statue. This was a side of Verlen that didn't allow invasion. His quiet authority left no room for question. Wrapped in a thoughtful cocoon, he was waiting and listening and perhaps praying as the continued surge of the ocean tugged at the sand beneath his feet. He had an intense kinship with the outdoor world. I could respond to nature, but Verlen could communicate.

I sat back in the tent and continued recording the details from our fascinating day. Late in the afternoon we had paddled past Punta Belcher, where rusted pilings, cranes, tanks, and machinery were scattered around the beach in decay. A half-built barge dock extended into the bay, and according to the local fishermen, many a business had run aground there. The location had been abandoned because there was no fresh water on the point.

We had camped south of Belcher on the west side of Bahía Magdalena, approximately three miles north of Punta Entrada. Our plan was to exit the bay, follow the Isla Santa Margarita south, and continue 165 miles to Cabo San Lucas. Once we left the protection of Bahía Magdalena, there would be no harbors until we arrived in Cabo. This was more than twice as far as the unprotected stretch between San Ignacio and Punta Pequeña, and once we shoved off from Magdalena Bay we would be paddling for four days and three nights before going ashore. The weather had been so unstable, we didn't know if we could trust the calm to last while we made the long run.

Our map showed that sailboaters could enter the bay between Punta Entrada and Punta Redondo through a clear, deep channel 2½ miles wide. I hadn't seen any sailboats that night, but a dozen large shrimpers were anchored in the natural harbor making up our front yard. The ocean channel was visible from our landing—an avenue to the open sea.

I stopped writing and looked up when I saw Verlen's legs standing on the other side of the tent screen. He crouched down to my level and sat on his heels to talk.

"Our situation is stacking up to another delay. We've both been sick, there are 160 miles ahead with no harbor, and I've got an uneasy feeling about the weather." I had heard that tone of voice before: he must have drawn some conclusion.

"Looking at this realistically, I count four days until Christmas, five packages of food left, a few pieces of fruit and a sack of cookies from San Carlos. We've got a few canned goods, but nothing significant if we're stranded here for any length of time." I felt a pang of guilt for throwing away my dinner. My hope of being in Cabo for the holidays dimmed as he continued.

"We'll see what it's like tomorrow, but it doesn't look like we'll be shoving off right away." He said goodnight and I could hear him climbing into his tent. I stared out through the screen, beyond the land-mass shadows to the ocean. It had rained the night before, and rain again that evening seemed likely, since the sky held no stars. Another storm was apparently in the making. Across the arroyo, the light in the kitchen shack was still burning and a ring of faces glowed against the night. I set my journal aside and went to sleep.

When daylight came, the view from my tent was of a different world. Washed during the night by rain and rinsed by tide, the beach was fresh and wet. There was a rainbow shining on the horizon and wind gave a brisk kick to the air. I started to crawl out of my burrow, but the air was so cool I reached back inside for a pile jacket. Verlen was standing on the beach again, looking out to sea.

"Well, Verlen, what's the verdict today?" I called.

"We won't go. It doesn't feel right."

"You mean I've got the day off?"

"Yes, just relax." His mind was far off and brooding over our circumstances. The decision was no surprise to me, given the unstable conditions. The sky was crowded with high cirrus clouds, and the air hit our faces in gusts.

Since we were stuck for the day, I decided to explore our campsite. The arroyo that formed our landing was a sand valley cut through a rocky shore and directly across from our tents was the kitchen shack I had seen the night before. Closer to the beach, two small plywood sleeping sheds leaned against one another. These structures could hardly be accused of standing: their roofs sloped at a warped angle and one of the doors hung open. A cot took up all the cramped space, and it looked as if a person would have to climb into bed from the doorway. There was no window or light source.

Thirty feet away, three sides of scrap lumber formed an outhouse screen. Barrels, drums, timber, cans, bottles, cardboard, pieces of boats, and other trash littered the arroyo, but one small square of earth was cleared for a garden and half a dozen rows of green shoots domesticated the sandy soil.

The fishermen had a radio on in the cook shack, and "White Christmas" was playing. I recognized the tune even though it was not Bing Crosby singing, but something that sounded like chipmunks in fuzzy Spanish.

At midmorning a small plane buzzed the camp, flying low in a landing approach toward Punta Belcher. Soon afterward, a crowded open launch motored toward our beach. I could distinguish the only American from a distance by his pale complexion, pastel sport shirt, and the camera around his neck.

I watched with interest as the boat came near and landed in the sand. We figured that the American had come from the airplane. He ignored Verlen and me. Stepping out of the boat, he officiated between the fishermen and a patient interpreter who had quite a time getting a word in. I was in awe of his fancy transport and the bills he was rolling out of his pocket. This crusty man wasn't receiving from anyone; he bought what he needed. Negotiations were rapid, and the deal seemed complete—there was much nodding of heads. Only then did the American acknowledge our presence and extend his hand. I shook a palm minus several fingers. I didn't want to look down and count, but I felt the greeting of a rough and colorful story.

"Just having a little party," he said. "Taking this shrimp back to Buena Vista. Holidays you know." He sounded as if we were meeting at a corner grocery.

"Valerie and I are paddling around the Baja Peninsula," Verlen explained.

"Cabo is next," I said, but the visitor wasn't paying much attention.

"Haven't you heard?" he asked. Then, looking around at our surroundings, he answered his own question. "No, I guess not. The Golden Gate bridge was closed yesterday by one of the worst storms in San Francisco's history. The bridge has only been closed once before in 35 years. You had better stay right here—no way can you get to Cabo before this one hits. I'd take you in my plane, but you won't fit," he said with a laugh. "In fact, I took a chance coming up this way. Five states are out of power, and the storm is moving south. I suggest you paddle across the bay to the landing called Alcatraz and hop a ride on one of the motor sailers going your way. When I flew over, there were several boats refueling at the dock."

"No, we can't do that. It's not our style," said Verlen. "This trip is under our own power." The man understood style, the man understood power, but he couldn't understand why we would want to do such a thing as paddle around a piece of land where he flitted about so easily in his light plane. We obviously didn't have much in common, and he was in a hurry.

"You sure picked a rough year to take a canoe trip," he said. "The weather this year has been totally unpredictable." Escorted by his entourage, he reboarded the launch. The last we saw of him was his plane, winging south toward his holiday party. He was a reminder of how Christmas was celebrated with English-speaking friends. I stood on the beach waving good-bye to any hope of a familiar Christmas.

The visitor's weather report had confirmed Verlen's apprehension about the conditions, and we began to realize that this camp in a dried-up riverbed could be our home for the next few days.

We saw an older man on crutches hobbling toward us from the cook shack. I looked down at his limp, but was distracted by his partner, a small white dog with a spot of black fur around one eye. The short-haired dog had a skinny white tail that wrapped around his body and wagged in playful greeting. The man came slowly, weaving his way past the debris on the beach. The dog took five steps for every one the man was able to manage. When the man stood in front of us, balanced on his crutches, I could see that his blue eyes were wise with age. The dog sat beside his master's bad leg, as if protecting the weakest link of their team.

"Comidas?" he asked, offering an invitation to lunch. He put his fingers toward his lips in a gesture of eating. He seemed to understand our situation and to be making an effort to take our minds off the circumstances.

"Sí, gracias. Como se llama?" I questioned.

"José," said the man, placing his finger on his chest. "And Pepe," he continued, pointing his finger at the dog. As if on cue, the dog's ears perked up at the mention of his name. Verlen hung back, but I collected my spoon and cup to follow José to the kitchen shack. Four other fishermen looked up from their bowls and nodded a greeting, but José didn't introduce them. He just handed me a bowl and indicated that I should dig in. The food was more than edible—it was great: fresh shrimp, as many as I could eat, with lime juice squeezed over the firm meat. I stood at the worn table, brushing the flies away, cracking shells, and believing for the first time in many weeks that I was in an enviable position.

"Verlen, you are really missing a treat," I called out to my friend.

"I don't like shrimp," he called back.

"It's all in your mind," I pronounced gaily. He walked over to inspect the feast.

"What do you think about a ride to Cabo?" he asked abruptly.

"Well, this sure is a strange street corner to have our thumbs stuck out," I said.

"It's not as if I like the idea," Verlen explained.

"It's a strange proposal coming from you," I agreed.

"It's not a proposal, just a consideration," he replied. "I've never taken a ride before and I don't want one now, but let's face it—our situation doesn't look good with this unusual weather pattern. Besides, what if we paddle part way to San Lucas and this sickness we've had comes back. Our time is running out, so we should at least consider taking a ride."

José's kitchen was a meeting place for fishermen on this side of the bay, and Verlen and I were the topic of conversation. Word of our dilemma spread among the group and they already had a plan worked out for our situation. It was clear from their concern that we would need a ride to Cabo— they were adamant that we could not make it by canoe.

José's idea was to book passage on a shrimp boat and have us motored to the cape. As the men studied our maps, Verlen pantomimed a paddling stroke and pointed to Cabo on our chart. José sadly shook his head.

"Malo, mucho malo," he said, meaning it was a very bad idea. José pointed to the shrimping fleet in the harbor.

"*Erlander*," he proclaimed with a smile, singling out one of the trawlers. "Cabo uno días."

One day to Cabo aboard a shrimper rather than at least four days and three nights paddling sounded attractive, especially with the uncertain weather. José clapped his hands together and concluded, "Vamos!"

The conversation was replayed as each man stated his opinion. Even with our limited vocabulary and small pocket dictionary, we managed to communicate, probably because our situation was so painfully clear.

I ate more than my share of shrimp and stood looking at the ocean from the open side of the kitchen shack. At that moment we seemed immobilized more by indecision than by conditions.

"There really isn't anything we can do today. We wouldn't even make it to Alcatraz before dark," said Verlen. "Let's take a walk."

The cook shack, the tent, even the beach were talking on the proportions of a cage. Waiting was tiresome and the prospect of a walk beyond our present view was a cheerful motivator. We studied the terrain south of the camp and began picking our way along the sand, scrambling onto the hillside when the beach narrowed. I spent most of the excursion bent over, picking up shells and oddly shaped pieces of rock. I was burrowing away hundreds of Baja objects in the storage areas of my canoe. Verlen was not a beachcomber and frowned on my behavior, especially since to make room for my keepsakes I had transferred the water and much of our food to his canoe.

"We've put all the water in my boat. I don't mind if you take advantage of the reduced weight and paddle harder during the day, but, you can't fill up those empty spaces with shell bulk," he reprimanded.

"Verlen, I'm still paddling all my equipment. A pound of my shells is easier to paddle than a pound of water—these treasures are my memories of this place," I explained.

Verlen didn't answer, since he saw no point in arguing. He unpacked his camera and demonstrated his own method of 35-millimeter souvenier hunting in the desert. The next time I caught up with him he was climbing a rock cliff to photograph a flower.

Two hours later we shuffled back to camp and sat on the beach, watching the waves toss in restless confusion. The big ocean swells were from the west, and as they came inside the mouth of Magdalena Bay they caused considerable surf, even there on our protected sand beach. The clouds moved in sheets across the sky. Though the atmosphere tingled with the approaching storm, I tried to hold back my energy and remain patient.

"Verlen, I know it's two days before Christmas, but could we exchange our gifts now?" I asked, thinking of the crackers that were crumbling from continued repacking and the jar of peanut butter I had bought in San Carlos.

"Why not? I've got something for you, too," he said, as he headed toward his boat. Verlen dug in the bottom of his canoe and came up with his waterproof gadget box. Unsnapping the lid on the box full of tangled treasure, he poked through pens and loose change, fraying cord, lip salve, whistles, screwdrivers, and bolts to find the gift for me. He made quite a ceremony of it, having me close my eyes and open both hands. Then he laid into my palm a small yellow metal butterfly that he had carried from San Diego and kept as a surprise.

It was beautiful and sat on my finger as if it were ready to fly away until I fastened it securely to the brim of my straw hat.

"Thanks, Verlen," I said. "This is a perfect gift. Wait until you see your present." I walked over to Verlen's storage area to retrieve it. "This one is for me as well as you," I admitted, as I put the package into his hands. The holiday paper looked out of place in our tropical surroundings. "Merry Christmas," I promised. He slowly unwrapped the offering and smiled.

"Thanks for the peanut butter," Verlen said. "It's just what I wanted."

"Me too," I confessed. We sat in the sun, tugged by the wind, dipping broken crackers into the peanut butter jar. Borrowing Verlen's pocketknife, I gooed his blade and hinge with the sticky treat.

"That butterfly looks as if it has just flown down and is stopping for an instant on your crown," he said, looking up at my hat. "Funny that butterflies get anywhere at all. They seem so fragile and the strange, jumpy way they have of flying doesn't seem too logical."

For a moment we forgot about the weather and the suspension of our plans. Christmas was coming, ready or not.

Christmas Eve morning I was awake a full hour before I opened my tent to the holiday. Just by the way the tent fly flapped and tussled with the wind, I knew we wouldn't be paddling that day. The air was cold and I lay wrapped in my sleeping bag like a package waiting patiently for the special day. I thought of all the beautiful Christmas stories and knew this one would be different from all the rest. Another confirmation that we were wind-bound was the absence of any prompting from Verlen for take-off. Sitting up, I looked outside and saw my partner standing on the beach watching the shrimp boats. The fleet was huddled together in the middle of the natural harbor, where the waves rocked the boats up and down against

their anchors. Just to be certain, I called to Verlen through the screen.
"Are we going to paddle today?" He looked toward the tent and smiled patiently.

"No, but don't worry, dear girl, you'll get all you want, all you can hold."
As I settled back into my sleeping bag, I realized what a comforting thought he had given me. Perhaps he was talking about paddling and the distance ahead in the Sea of Cortez, but I took his words as a blessing for my life. I would receive more than I could ever dream.

When I lay back and propped up my head, I could just see the Mexican cook shack above my toes—a very unusual manger scene.

There had to be a reason why we were there at Belcher Point, I thought, and we probably wouldn't be moving until the lesson was learned. But I wasn't going to lie there all day waiting. I was getting hungry—what could we have for breakfast? Pulling out pieces of fruit and cookies from a plastic box in my tent, I assembled a Christmas breakfast and crawled outside to meet Verlen on the beach. We sat on the bow decks of the canoes, watching the water and studying the fluffy, delicate shore birds as they frantically pecked bits of food from the beach.

They moved in community, and even in flight, they crossed the sky in unison. I thought of myself as like the birds on the beach—moving impulsively. Verlen was just the opposite, and thought out every move in advance. I could scope out a situation and act while Verlen was still figuring, but moving quickly sometimes got me into trouble. I suspect that's what made us a good combination: we were two distinct individuals, but we accepted the same goal and shared a unique adventure.

As he thought about taking a ride, Verlen methodically reviewed every angle, taking time to watch the weather and weigh the consequences. I was flighty and ready to jump either way. But mostly, in this decision, I stayed out of the way. It was up to Verlen, since it had to be his decision if we broke with a precedent he had established over 22,000 miles. I was confident that Verlen wouldn't let ego stand in the way of his final choice. He knew bad weather could be fatal along the 160-mile unprotected stretch that lay ahead.

After we finished the few pieces of fruit and the handful of cookies, Verlen went to his tent to write a letter home. José had the radio on again in the shed, and I walked over for company, taking my journal with me. The spotted dog met me halfway and followed me into the shack. José sat quietly with his cup of coffee and a cigarette. He smiled a greeting and welcomed me to his home, then motioned that I should help myself to coffee. I poured myself a cup of hot water, mixed in some granules, chose a weathered stool in the sun just under the arch of the lean-to, and began to write. I titled a blank sheet "Peanut Butter for Christmas."

I knew my family would be going to a candlelight service at midnight on Christmas Eve. I drew pictures in my journal of Christmas as I remembered it, dreaming about the people who would fill the church, each receiving a small candle and finding a seat among the crowd. When the sermon was concluded the ushers would use the light from a large Christmas candle on the altar to light all the candles in the church, one by one. The overhead lights in the church would dim, the congregation would sing "Silent Night," and the glow of the candles would fill the church with the radiance of Christmas. In my journal I drew a Christmas tree with packages beneath, a manger scene, and a star.

The actual scene from José's kitchen shack was bleak: directly in front of me was the washstand, and the table was covered with cracked dishes and blackened pots. Several fishing lines were hung across the space and floats and ropes were tangled in discarded bunches upon the sand. Without a central dumping area, the arroyo was littered with discarded clothes, rusted cans, bottles, fish bones, and bird skeletons.

More flies gathered in the kitchen shack than I'd ever seen in my life, maybe driven in by the storm. Flies even walked on my glasses, and I crossed my eyes and stared at their bellies moving across the lenses. Flies dropped into my coffee cup—I held a spoon in one hand, ready to fish them out before they drowned. José leaned over to adjust a buckle on his boot.

"Como?" I asked, wondering about his limp.

"Langosta," he said. He went on to explain that when he was a small child he had stepped on a lobster. His foot became infected and had to be amputated.

"Sí," I nodded my head in sympathy.

I slowly gave into this place being our Christmas. Remembering a particular package in the back corner of my canoe, I walked over to the boat and dug deep into the stern. My fingers touched the rubberized waterproof pouch and I pulled the package out of storage. The smell of my cedar chest back home was released from the quilted Christmas banner as I tugged it out of the bag to breathe the ocean air. The brightly colored fabric holly wreaths brought Christmas cheer to the arroyo. I had sewn a two-inch sleeve on the back of the banner for hanging, which I threaded on a fishing line I found on the beach. Then I hung the quilt alongside the nets, fixing rocks at the bottom corners to keep the wind from whipping the banner about. Just as I sat back down on my stool to admire my decoration, a gust ripped the cloth from the line. I jumped up, rescued the banner from the sand, and carried it into my tent to lay my head upon it and dream of sugar plums dancing.

"Senorita, senorita." José called me awake from my nap about an hour later. I pulled on a jacket and climbed out of the tent, wondering what the commotion was about. With much pointing and demonstrating, José insisted that Verlen and I visit one of the shrimpers and negotiate a passage to Cabo San Lucas.

"We're going out there?" I was incredulous as I looked at the stormy sea.

"Come on, Valerie, the change of scenery will do us both good. The storm has hardly begun," Verlen said enthusiastically.

Lupe, one of the regulars in José's kitchen, was waiting, steadying an open aluminum boat with a big outboard motor. As I climbed in I realized I had forgotten my life jacket, and when I looked under the seats, I was surprised to see that there were no life jackets on board. I looked out at the shrimp boat: Verlen was right, it wasn't that far. He didn't seem the least bit concerned, and Lupe, who was controlling the outboard, looked straight ahead toward the shrimper. He took the most direct route, side-surfing on the waves and powering through the heavy seas. When I looked back to shore I saw José anxiously watching our progress. Our boat banged against the larger hull as we reached the shrimper. I reached up and grabbed the rail, bellying over the bar onto the deck. The shrimper pitched violently in the waves.

The first thing I noticed on board was a giant turtle flopped on his back and trussed in ropes. Its eyes were blinking and its neck strained at its shell collar. I understood the terror of its situation. Directly in sight of the poor creature, one of the fishermen was carving a stingray on a chopping block, and the turtle was next.

We were taken to the forward cabin to meet the captain, a big, bearded man lounging on a bunk. Lupe talked for many minutes and waved Verlen's fact sheet to emphasize our case. The captain looked at Verlen and me and then he nodded and said, "mañana."

I wasn't sure I wanted a ride on the shrimper—I just wasn't comfortable. When we walked back on deck a crew member jumped down into the ice hold and shoveled a load of shrimp from the heart of the troller up to the deck. The mound of shrimp and ice was then dumped over the side onto the floor of our boat—this was our Christmas dinner, deposited in a heap.

We shook hands with the captain, who had followed us up on deck. I couldn't bear to look at the turtle, which was being dragged into position on the chopping block. As I climbed over the rail, our boat looked very far down. I jumped in my hurry to reach my seat, and Verlen and Lupe followed. I looked up the sheer wall of the shrimper, sure that I could hear the turtle scream. A crewman threw our rope down and, set free, we powered away.

I huddled in the boat as it rose and fell on each roller. The wind roared around us, and when the boat came out of the water on each wave, the engine raced. Then, as we went down into the trough, the water flooded the exhaust. The engine gurgled and spit, lugging as if it might stop—but Lupe wouldn't let it. He seemed to know exactly how to angle the boat to give the engine air. As we got closer to the beach, the wind let up for a moment and Lupe turned the throttle for more speed. Spray and water splashed over the gunwales and soaked all of us aboard. I thought our driver would slow down to land, but Lupe went full speed ahead to the beach. I expected a jolt, but the launch just nosed gently into the sand like a lit cigarette being snubbed in an ashtray. Our roller-coaster ride was over. We hopped out, took a handful of shrimp, and walked back to the tents bent almost double against the wind.

After dinner, we spent Christmas Eve by flashlight, rereading the letters I had written Verlen from Seattle before I came on the trip. The letters were full of struggle as I had expressed my desire to paddle on the ocean. There was no struggle this night. I had arrived.

Even so, there were many places I would rather have been for this Christmas. I thought of shopping and sewing gifts. I remembered airports full of people fighting to get home for the holiday. There in the tent, Verlen read the Christmas story from the Bible. I sang every carol I knew and Verlen chimed in with his off-key bullfrog voice. I hung a polypropylene stocking from the ceiling loop of my tent with care, and hoped that St. Nicholas would find me, even there.

Early the next morning, I found my stocking elongated by two candies deposited by my white-bearded partner. I smiled as I looked at the gift hanging from my tent ceiling. Sitting up I could sense a brisk wind outside as the tent fly expanded in forceful breaths. I felt the crisp excitement of a special holiday.

The gifts were not arranged under a glowing pine tree, but spread like treasure awaiting discovery. There was no paper to rip nor bows to scatter, but instead of feeling let down, I let my imagination play Christmas. The entire world was waiting to be unwrapped. Starting with me: I unzipped the sleeping bag and folded back the nylon material. I let the tent become a large, mysterious box. There was no tape, but a zipper opening for me to undo. Outside, the world was a beautiful blue. My childhood trike was transformed into a one-person canoe resting on the sand. The 11 shrimp boats were still bridled in the harbor against the northwest wind. Rain had come in the night, and the sand was too heavy with moisture to blow.

I crawled out of the tent on all fours, anxious to make special gifts from everything in sight. My personal bag waited to be opened. Inside, my toothbrush was ready. I opened my mouth and let the bristles poke at my gums. Then I opened the canoe with expectant glee, pulling back the night cover and exposing the dark insides. I opened each stuff sack and bundle and, as I did, my heart opened to the day of Christmas.

Verlen emerged from his tent and caught me unpacking our rationed Christmas loot. The celebration gathered momentum as Verlen searched in his storage compartment for a jar of banana bread we had been saving since San Diego. When he found the can, it was puffed with fermentation. For two months we had hauled and coveted the can, and then Verlen buried it in the sand. Fortunately, my secret offering had survived.

"Open this," I said, pushing a precious can of pears toward my partner. Verlen took out his pocketknife and performed skillful surgery. In a minute the can was open, dripping with sweet pear juice.

We sat half in and half out of my tent. Both of us were quiet, lost in our own thoughts as we savored our treat. Verlen was the first to jolt to attention, when he discovered that he had eaten the last pear and reached the bottom of the can. He bent the tin lid inside the container and turned the can over in his hand as if he didn't want to let it go.

I handed Verlen the plastic bag that collected our trash.

"Why don't we clean the beach for José?" I asked, staring at the littered sand.

"Not a bad idea," Verlen agreed.

"It can be our Christmas gift to him," I said. Standing up and brushing the sand from my pants, I took the pear can from Verlen and tossed it on another can, starting a pile. Then I walked to the nearest bottle, picked it up and threw it on top of my little stack.

"Don't you think we need a plan?" Verlen asked.

"I work best on inspiration," I said. Moving faster, I picked up litter in both hands and pitched it toward my pile. Verlen positioned himself on one corner of the beach and began picking up every scrap of junk in a strict combing pattern, while I still flittered around collecting the big pieces in a haphazard manner. Within a few minutes it wasn't fun anymore. It was a bigger project than I had realized: cans, bottles, jugs, rope bits, old clothes, and junk were everywhre. I stopped picking up the pieces and took an old shovel from the lean-to. Digging a large garbage ditch, I scooped shovel after shovel full of dirt to cover the trash. I took fiendish pleasure in knowing that hundreds of flies were dying with each stroke.

When Verlen and I quit for lunch, the beach was only slightly improved—many rusty cans and cracked bottles still peeked from the sand. As José sat in the kitchen shed watching our antics, he seemed puzzled by our zeal. The beach was his home, and he accepted the clutter. In fact, an hour later, when Verlen and I had abandoned our cleaning efforts and were sitting in the lean-to, José used the last crystals of instant coffee, then threw the jar into the sand.

The afternoon had settled into an idle drone when an old man came up on the beach. His walk was unsteady, and he looked as if the wind could blow him over. I wondered how long it had taken him to hike from the fishing camp around the point. On his back was a mesh sack of collected flotsam. He set down his burden and walked into the kitchen shack, where José introduced him as Pablo.

I wanted a photo of this man, who looked as weathered as the dry hills, so I picked up Verlen's camera and pantomimed my request. Pablo nodded, then proudly straightened his soiled pea coat and adjusted his baseball hat.

José got up from his bench and poured Pablo a cup of coffee. Verlen and I could not understand all the words they spoke, but from the way Pablo looked at Verlen and me, it was clear our story was being explained. When the conversation wore out, Verlen walked over to the canoes and brought back one of our empty water jugs.

"Agua?" Verlen asked, holding up the jug.

"Sí," José replied. He got up from his seat and motioned that we should follow. Pablo stood up slowly, steadying himself on the table. José picked up a rusted shovel with a splintered, worn handle and handed it to Verlen, then headed away from the beach on the path of the arroyo. José went slowly on his crutches and Pablo walked beside, swaying as if any stone on the path might throw him off balance. Verlen and I were close behind, slowing our steps to their gait. The spotted dog brought up the rear.

About 150 feet from the beach, José stopped and pointed to a hole in the ground. When I looked in, I saw a few inches of water lying still and dead on the bottom. José took a rope from the ground, tied a knot on the handle of our jug, and lowered it to the bottom. When it came back up it was half full of discolored water.

"Not much there," I said worriedly. José looked at me.

"Poquito," I said sympathetically.

José handed Verlen the water jug and turned to walk farther up the arroyo. As we walked, José stopped frequently to reach out and touch different plants. For each plant he said a word several times in Spanish, and I soon realized we were getting a tour.

"Copal, copal," he explained, lifting the oval leaves of a small shrub. I leaned over and studied the small twigs and gray bark of the miniature trunk.

"Copal, copal!" I echoed. The spiny arms of a cactus seemed to embrace Pablo as he reached for a red fruit the size of a tennis ball blooming on the plant.

"Pitaya," he said. Pablo dissected the cactus. Removing the stickers first, he cut the bulb from the stalk and peeled the skin away. Then he cut the fruit in half and offered it to us.

"Verlen, I don't want to eat that," I said fearfully.

"Why not?" Verlen asked as he reached for his portion.

"It could be a drug." I said, looking at the small bushes around me with spines growing like hair standing on end.

"Don't you trust them?" Verlen asked, putting the fruit to his lips.

"Verlen, I've read books about this, but I don't know what peyote looks like."

"Just take a small bite," Verlen suggested, the red juice already sprinkled on his beard. I licked my half of the fruit—it tasted like a cherry watermelon but was firm, like a persimmon. José was looking at me and I saw that his eyes were kind, that he wouldn't give us anything harmful. I stopped focusing on my imagined worries and let José's patient instruction open my heart to the desert.

Long, creeping cactus vines covered the sand, the thick stems rooted in the ground. One type of cactus branched in many directions with no main trunk, and another had long tubes sprawled in a thicket of dark green stems. Some of the branches look dead and stiff, but when I looked closely enough there were small buds. As we followed our leader on the smooth arroyo path, I held the red fruit and licked again at the sweetness.

José bent over a small wire trap. There was no bait inside, just a wire cage propped open with a stick. I wondered if he had much success catching animals with that method. Before I could find the words in my dictionary to ask, we had arrived at another well. It was a rectangular hole, deep enough for a person to stand in, wide enough to swing a pickax.

"Duro," said José, "Mucho duro."

"Sí," I said looking down in the hole. The earth was very hard. The well had been chipped by hand into hardpan and bedrock in order to gain a small quantity of water not poisoned by salt or bitter minerals. There was no water in the bottom of this well, though it was just as deep as the one closer to the beach. Verlen climbed in and took several swings with an old ax that lay on the ground.

"Duro," Verlen confirmed as he climbed out. We marveled at how far the well had been dug with such worn tools and wondered if anyone had helped José with the work. The second well wouldn't give any water, and Verlen and I realized that we had a larger supply of water in our canoe than these men had in their valley. We had wanted to top-up our supply, but realized that instead we would share our water with them.

We walked back to the beach wrapped in a quiet bond of friendship with José and Pablo. The glimpse of their desert world was an unexpected gift and the jug half full of water we carried back from the crude well was more precious than gold.

As we got closer to the beach, the wind greeted us. The shrimp boats in the harbor were gone and the sun was setting in a sky pinned with stars. Slowly, the ocean turned dark with white-tipped waves. We sat with José and Pablo in the kitchen shack, drinking coffee by lantern light. The flies were asleep on the ceiling, hanging in clustered bunches. I remembered landing five days before, looking over the arroyo and seeing faces of fishermen lit by lantern glow in the same kitchen lean-to. Now Verlen and I were part of the scene. We were sitting on the inside and the lantern warmed our faces and bathed the pages of my journal in yellow light.

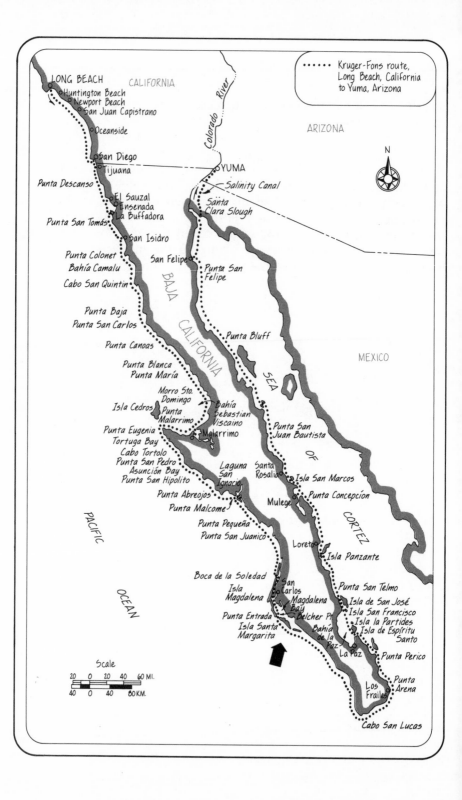

Kruger-Fons route,
Long Beach, California
to Yuma, Arizona

N

LONG BEACH CALIFORNIA
Huntington Beach
Newport Beach
San Juan Capistrano
Oceanside
San Diego
Tijuana
Punta Descanso
El Sauzal
Ensenada
La Buffadora
Punta San Tomás
San Isidro
Punta Colonet
Bahía Camalu
Cabo San Quintin
Punta Baja
Punta San Carlos
Punta Canoas
Punta Blanca
Punta María
Morro Sto.
Domingo
Isla Cedros Punta
Malarrimo
Punta Eugenia
Tortuga Bay
Cabo Tortolo
Punta San Pedro
Asunción Bay
Punta San Hipolito
Punta Abreojos
Punta Malcome
Punta Pequeña
Punta San Juanico
Boca de la Soledad
Isla
Magdalena
Punta Entrada
Isla Santa
Margarita

ARIZONA

Colorado River
YUMA
Salinity Canal
Santa
Clara Slough
Punta San
Felipe
San Felipe
Punta Bluff

BAJA
CALIFORNIA

Bahía
Sebastian
Viscaino
Malarrimo
Laguna
San
Ignacio
Santa
Rosalia
Punta San
Juan Bautista
Isla San Marcos
Punta Concepcíon
Mulege
Loreto
Isla Panzante

SEA
OF
CORTEZ

MEXICO

San
Carlos
Magdalena
Bay
Belcher Pt.
Bahía
de la
Paz
La Paz
Punta San Telmo
Isla de San José
Isla San Francisco
Isla la Partides
Isla de Espíritu
Santo
Punta Perico
Punta
Arena
Los
Frailes
Cabo San Lucas

PACIFIC

OCEAN

Scale
20 0 20 40 60 MI.
40 0 40 80 KM.

SIXTEEN

Cabo

Verlen and I sat under the arch of the kitchen lean-to discussing how to move and when. The morning wind had changed direction and blew from the northwest. Whitecaps rolled on the bay and the temperature dropped by the hour. Still anchored in the harbor were half a dozen shrimpers, but the one that had offered us a ride, the *Erlander*, was gone.

José busied himself cooking a spicy pot of fish stew with octopus suctions and other mystery ingredients.

"Calma, calma," he instructed, gently moving his hands through the air. Holding the stew spoon, he waved with the eloquent gesture of a conductor silencing the percussion section. We had become a part of José's family and he cared for us as if we were his children. Our troubles were his.

Several other fishermen crowded into the shack, sipping coffee and waiting for better weather. Pablo was particularly interested in our distress, and sat on a stool in the corner giving advice. I looked in my dictionary to translate his words: he was suggesting that Verlen and I take up fishing and stay at Belcher Point. For us, that was not an option.

We heard a motor and looked down the beach. Even though the sea was rough, a launch skittered between the waves as a lone fisherman piloted his boat to our beach. When he got within a few feet of shore, he reached for an anchor buoy and tied his boat. Gathering the rope hand over hand, he pulled the hull closer to the sand and jumped over the side into knee-deep water. It was Lupe, the capable pilot who had taken us to visit the shrimper two days before. As he walked toward the kitchen lean-to, I got up to give him my bench. We were all impatient to hear the news from the world out-

217

side our small beach. José ladled a mug full of steaming fish stew and presented it to Lupe as he entered our circle. Gratefully accepting the food, he began spooning the mixture into his mouth even as he talked.

The best we could make out was that the *Erlander* had left, and with it our chance for a ride to Cabo on the shrimper. Lupe looked exasperated, as if he felt responsible. The shrimper must have left during the night and either its captain forgot us or thought better of carrying two canoes and passengers to San Lucas. Verlen seemed almost relieved.

"Yate," Lupe said, pointing farther into Magdalena Bay. Lupe finished the hot meal, set his bowl on the wood table, and looked again at Verlen. "Yate," he repeated.

"I think he wants us to know there is a yacht in the bay," I said. Lupe made motions that he would gladly take us to see.

"We might as well go," Verlen said. "Let's meet our neighbors." After waiting six days on the beach, any possibility for diversion was worth checking out. The water didn't look at all inviting, but I collected my rain gear, picked up my life jacket, and climbed aboard the fishing boat. José balanced on his crutch at the edge of the beach and waved good-bye.

We sped over the waves, jumping from one crest to the next, seeming to take off into the air between. I almost asked Lupe to slow down, but I knew he was pushing the small boat from experience, not out of recklessness. To Lupe, this stretch of water was a highway, with the waves stacked up like heavy traffic. My body was knocked and jostled as we bounced across the surface. Finally, I gave up my seat in the bow. Holding the gunwales and keeping my weight down low, I joined Verlen in the midsection.

We motored along, a few boat-lengths from shore. It was the same route that Verlen and I had paddled nearly a week earlier and the terrain looked familiar. The land rose steeply from the shore just as I remembered, but the sun did not illuminate the water as before. Now the sea soaked up the gray light from the sky and reflected only a dark, unfriendly surface.

The village of Puerto Magdalena covered the hollow of land rimming the next harbor. Lupe was right: a yacht was anchored about 100 feet from shore. We slowed down, and as we got closer I saw the high mast and white body of a motor sailer. The port identification on the flat-ended stern read "San Francisco."

From the moment we pulled up, the reception was cool. The American captain continued fussing with a rope coil, and when he finally did look over the rail, his expression was blank. He didn't smile, and seemed to be waiting for us to explain ourselves. We hadn't said hello yet either.

"Can you give us a weather report?" Verlen called out.

"I got one earlier this morning," the man responded, "but I don't know what to make of it. I've heard two conflicting reports today. Quite a few

218

sailboats are anchored at Santa María outside the bay, waiting for the swells to settle."

"Are you going to Cabo?" Verlen asked.

"Yes," he said cautiously, as if he were afraid of what we might ask next.

"We're traveling by canoe," Verlen explained. "For us it is four days and nights of paddling to Cabo and I've got an unsettled feeling about this weather." Verlen stopped talking and looked at the sky. The sailboater didn't say a word. The boat we were sitting in bounced with the swells.

"We've been offered rides and refused them in the past, but it looks as if we may have to find one," Verlen concluded.

"I'll talk to my partners, but I don't know how we can help," the American said.

"We're camped at the mouth of the bay—been there five days now," Verlen said.

"I don't know what I can do," he warned again.

"We've never taken a ride," I explained. "It's just that we've been sick and. . . . " I stopped in midsentence. It all sounded like an excuse to me. Verlen wasn't too happy either.

Lupe turned the fishing boat around and we motored back the way we had come. Even without speaking our language, Lupe could tell that the American sailboater had not been very friendly. I went over the conversation in my mind: probably our own attitude had contributed to the poor communication. I remembered the reception we had received at the kitchen shack at Belcher Point. We usually presented ourselves like tail-wagging puppies, and the response was always the same. Who can resist bending over to pat the head of a friendly pup? Meeting the sailboater had been different. But maybe we had been different too. This time we were chasing our tails. Verlen and I had such mixed feelings about accepting a ride, that we had probably sent confusing signals. We still weren't sure what to do.

Returning to our campsite, both Verlen and I were glum, and even Lupe looked dejected. José waved from the lean-to and welcomed us back with a grin. Like a mother hen, he shuttled us into the kitchen shack and ladled out bowls of stew. When I saw the octopus suctions surfacing like eight balls, and knew I wouldn't eat my portion, but I politely sipped the broth and stirred the potion with my spoon. There we were once again, sitting in the kitchen shack. We settled back to wait.

The next morning, December 28th, the wind was strong, but the weather looked better. Verlen was still hesitant about taking off on our own—he paced the beach and I fussed with my equipment, doing unnecessary chores as I watched the swells in the harbor. A sea lion that had washed on the rocks at the end of the arroyo was methodically thrashed by waves against the shore. Its tattered body was recognizable as something that had been alive primarily by the smell. Oblivious to the ragged carcass, Verlen no longer leaned on his paddle, but stood straight, looking out to sea. He was ready to move.

"If that sailboat is going to Cabo this morning, we should see them coming out of the bay any time now," Verlen remarked, scanning the northern horizon.

"Don't you think we can make it on our own?" I asked once again, even though we had reviewed our options many times.

"It's marginal," he said. "I'm still weak from the bug and if we do run into problems, neither of us has a reserve left for fighting. One hundred and sixty miles is a long way to paddle without a harbor but we'll try if that sailboat doesn't show." Another hour passed, and the sailboat did not appear.

"Get ready to leave," Verlen said abruptly. He turned from the beach and picked up his cook kit at the tent. Walking into the kitchen lean-to, he got busier than I'd seen him in a week, making cornmeal and powdered egg pancakes to take with us. Verlen didn't ask for any help, and I could tell he wanted to be left alone. He was struggling with our circumstances more than I was. No matter who was captain for a day, Verlen was weighted with the full responsibility for our trip. He was more aware of the obstacles ahead. He knew the real dangers, while many of my fears were imagined. In a way, I was innocent. We had come this far and I figured we could make it farther. In a bravado of enthusiasm I had voted for paddling to Cabo. Now it looked as if we might try to do just that.

I was turning my canoe around in the sand, pointing it toward the ocean, when I saw the white sailboat coming from the north. It didn't look as if it would stop. I jumped into my canoe, pushed off from the beach, and paddled frantically, trying to catch the sailboat as it motored out the mouth of the bay. Remembering what Verlen had told me about tides, and knowing the sailboat was traveling at speed, I aimed in front of my target. The captain saw me coming and slowed, holding steady in the bouncing water. As I got nearer, I heard the news.

"The weather report we're receiving is marginal. A large trimaran is arriving from Santa María," the American shouted over the rail. "They'll come into the bay and pick you up on their way to Cabo. We've radioed your situation, and they should be here in a few hours." The other crew members stood on the deck, crowded around the captain. I could tell by their expressions that they were surprised to see me in the rough water. My bow rose and fell over each steep curl, and I struggled to keep my canoe upright.

"We wondered if you were coming at all," I said.

"We're going out on the tide," he shouted.

"Good sailing to you," I called, and then turned my canoe to head for shore. I was out farther than I had thought, and the excitement of the message was not enough to carry me back across the rough water without fear. The tide pulled me toward the mouth of the bay. Paddling seemed to get me nowhere, and I was almost standing still as I dug hard against the current. My boat was not weighted with gear, and without a load the canoe rode higher in the water and felt shaky. It was a wild moment: my emotions screamed panic while my common sense told me I was safe. My teammate was not beside me to help gauge the danger, but on the beach, reduced to the size of an ant.

Whatever my assessment of the situation, I knew it was up to me to paddle back. I looked toward the shore where I wanted to go: the kitchen shack was a tiny matchbox. I steered a diagonal path across the bay and stayed close to the land, where the current was reduced, working my way back to the beach.

Verlen, Lupe, José, and Pablo met me when I landed.

"Hey, you did a good job out there," Verlen said, as he slapped me on the back.

"Thanks," I replied. "I'm just glad to be back."

"Well, what's the news?" he wanted to know.

"The weather is still unstable but a trimaran is coming into the bay," I reported. "They're all set to pick us up in about an hour. Do you want to take the ride?" Verlen reached for my arm to help me out of the canoe.

"I guess we should," he decided. Ruefully shaking his head, he walked across the arroyo to take down his tent.

José, Pablo, and Lupe watched as we packed. We were sad to leave our friends, and the fishermen seemed to feel the same way. Opening my food sack, I took out everything remaining and set it on the shelves in the kitchen lean-to. I gathered wildflowers from the arroyo and set them on the table in a metal cup.

Verlen had some patches that commemorated his journey with the words "Ultimate Canoe Challenge" and a canoe embroidered on the face. I gave one to Lupe and offered to sew it on for him. I pointed to the wide space on the front of his hat, suggesting that this would be an appropriate spot, but Lupe shook his head no. I placed the patch on the upper section of his sleeve, but he shook his head again. I gave up trying and handed him the patch, watching as he placed it right in the center of his chest. Grinning with pleasure, he thumped the spot where he wanted me to sew his new badge.

The trimaran appeared at the headland and turned into our harbor. We had to go. With tears in my eyes, I hugged José, putting one arm around his shoulder and my other around his waist so I wouldn't pinch the crutch against his body. His whiskers scratched my face, and he smelled of tobacco and coffee as I put my lips on his cheek. I told him how much we loved him and I think he told me the same. I kept my arm around him as we walked to the canoes. José laid one of his crutches in the sand and helped me push my canoe into the water. I slowly began to paddle toward our ride. When Verlen caught up to me, I stopped paddling and waved to José. I took a few more strokes, then looked back and waved good-bye again.

Finally, I looked ahead to the sailboat and saw two sandy-haired Americans standing on deck, smiling and waving hello. The ship introduced itself right away with bold letters across the stern that said *Dorvida*. We paddled alongside the boat and butted our blades against the hull so we wouldn't scrape the side in the rolling water. As Verlen and I looked up from the seats of our canoes, two sunburned faces stared down.

"Hi, I'm Bob," the man said, "and this is my wife Cecilia Congdon." Even as he stretched out his hand to shake, he reached for our gear to help us on board. Kneeling on the deck, he lifted each bag as Verlen held it up.

I steadied myself against the side of the sailboat, watching the men work. Bob didn't look much past 40. His T-shirt was so faded I couldn't read the advertisement on the front, and the brightest part of him was a pair of yellow plaid shorts that seemed to illuminate his lower body and the portion of the deck he was standing on. He was totally at home on his boat.

"Call me Cec," said the woman, holding onto the deck rail and reaching for my gear. Her smile wrinkled the sides of her rounded face. As we emptied my boat, I knew I was giving up a piece of the trip by coming aboard, and I wondered again if we were doing the right thing.

Verlen climbed on the sailboat from the stern ladder and walked along the side of the deck, lining his canoe to the port bow. He and Bob lifted the canoe on board as if hauling in a big fish—except that the canoe wouldn't bend. It pivoted against the side like a teeter-totter, then settled into a perfect fit across the trimaran. Soon our two canoes were roped on deck, nosed together and ready for travel. Cec, about my height but fuller, was wearing a red and white checked muu-muu.

"How long have you been paddling?" Bob asked.

"Two months," Verlen said, pulling out his fact sheet. "We've been sitting at this harbor for five days waiting out the weather."

"That was smart," Bob said. "We sat out the last week at Santa María harbor outside the bay. The weather looks better now. The barometer is steady," he explained.

He steered the *Dorvida* out of Punta Entrada and into the ocean, where he hoisted the sails and cut the engine. Verlen sat on a high captain's stool near the stern of the boat, his feet not touching the deck. Both of us felt out of place. When Cec went into the galley to make lunch, I followed her to explain.

"We spent Christmas here at Belcher Point," I said. Recounting the events of the last week, I told her all our excuses for needing a ride.

"I've been lonely here," Cec confessed. "This is my first cruise. We left San Diego December 1st and spent Christmas without my friends and family." She handed me a plate of swordfish and crackers, then we walked back on deck. Cec's pleasure in our company eased some of my qualms about having accepted a ride. It seemed as if we needed one another.

The sailboat moved effortlessly over the territory that Verlen and I had stared at so impatiently for the past week. When I looked back to our beach, the distance across the water to Punta Belcher was widening rapidly, and I felt as if we had taken a giant leap from a diminishing platform and landed on a moving target.

Aside from our regrets, I began to relax and to realize that this was an opportunity to glimpse sailboat life. The main difference between the yacht and our canoes was that the wind pushed the sailboat along and I didn't have to paddle. I sat on the front deck with our canoes, keeping them company and watching the water rush beneath the triple hulls of *Dorvida*. Cec sprawled on the deck to deepen her tan, while Bob held the wheel and talked to Verlen about the features of the boat. Verlen couldn't seem to sit still, but kept busy with chores, airing out his canoe, looking over charts, and learning to steer the sailboat.

Cec had been trailing a fishing line from the stern and late in the afternoon she pulled in a dorado. As the beautiful green fish thrashed in protest, she thrust it into a bucket and clubbed it with a hammer.

"You treated us better when we came aboard," I observed with a laugh.

"This one is dinner," she said.

Verlen went right to work filleting the fish and handed it over to Cec in steak-sized pieces. She went into the galley and dipped the fresh meat in flour and spices, then sautéed it in oil, wine, and fresh lime juice. She cooked a pot of rice with oleo and cherry tomatoes and set out a plate of coconut cookies for dessert. I could feel myself submitting to the luxurious life.

When night came, I decided to sleep on deck with the canoes, and curled my sleeping bag and pad between the forward cabin and my familiar boat. I awoke around midnight to find that the wind had changed and gotten stronger. Water splashed over the deck, and I knew my sleeping spot wasn't safe anymore. I looked over the cabin and saw Bob's face intent and steady at the wheel.

"You'd better move," he yelled above the wind. "The weather's changing."

I didn't bother to answer, but clutched my sleeping bag and pad, hung onto the rail line, and inched my way along the deck to the stern. Bob turned the boat into the wind, then handed the wheel to Cec while he climbed forward to change the rigging. I stumbled into the cabin to get out of their way. Verlen was sleeping on the mattress, so I rolled him over to the corner and climbed in to fall asleep.

When I woke it was still dark. *Dorvida* continued to pitch, but it seemed as if the rocking was not as bad as it had been a few hours before. Bob was lying in the bunk next to ours, and I knew Cec was alone at the wheel. I climbed up the ladder to the deck, hanging onto the rungs so as not to fall backward. Cec was at the helm, her face drawn in anxiety. I knew that look: she reminded me of myself. Cec was struggling with an old friend that was really a close enemy. The fear and discomfort were part of who we both were. I sat with Cec through the rest of her watch and we fought our imaginations together.

Bob took the wheel near dawn. The wind settled and his instruments at daylight read offshore wind northeast to 25 knots. *Dorvida* settled to an 8-knot hull speed. We were halfway to Cabo, and no land was in sight.

Verlen came on deck and sat with me. He was quiet, and smiled gently as he handed me a pancake from his bag for breakfast. I wondered if I could read his mind: I figured we were both thinking about rounding the cape, and I still was not at peace with our decision to take a ride.

"Verlen, I had pictured us using our last ounce of strength to reach Cabo, and here I am sitting in shorts on the deck of a trimaran with following seas pushing us toward the harbor."

"Pride is a bad thing," said Verlen, munching his pancakes. "Maybe we're just where we should be?"

"Last night would have been rough in our canoes, but now that the morning is calm I can't help but see us out there paddling." I pointed at the calm water.

"We would have made it last night," Verlen assured me. "But it wouldn't have been real pleasant. Of course, the winds are different this far from shore. The conditions would have possibly been better close to land where we would have paddled."

"It's hard to submit to this ride, Verlen. Even though I was all for it. I guess I didn't realize what the trip meant to me until sitting here without a paddle in my hand."

"We're not a macho team," he said.

"But we're missing something big by not paddling this stretch. I've still been paddling in my mind ever since we climbed aboard."

"Try to accept the ride," he said. Then he put his arm around my shoulders. "I'm trying too," he confided.

Cec was awake and in the galley, creating a magnificent spaghetti sauce for lunch. The aroma pushed back the salt air. While it was cooking she came on deck with a handful of pictures of her children.

224

"This is my daughter," she said, holding up a color photograph. "She just got married to the nicest boy." I voiced my approval.

"Do you have any children?" she asked.

"No, but I'm pregnant with a book," I answered.

"Are you a writer?"

"I'm going to be. My children will have pages and binding instead of arms and legs." She looked at the photo she was holding.

"Is that what you want?" she asked.

"It's not something I've been searching for, or anything that took determination to find. The idea of the book is a gift. All that has happened to me is like a miracle. I really don't know how I've survived this trip, but I know I've got to write about it."

"Maybe you'll understand when you write about the journey," Cec said. "I feel pretty much the same about our sailboat experience. I wouldn't take a million dollars to have missed it, but I wouldn't take a million dollars to do it again." We both nodded in understanding. I looked at the ocean around us: still no land in sight. The water heaved around our small floating home. I bent my head back and looked at the top of the mast, following it down to the deck. A bag with an extra sail was lashed to the cabin, and I could see that the sail had separated from its binding.

"That sail needs some mending. Want me to do it?" I offered.

"Sure, that would be great," Cec said. She went inside the cabin to bring up sewing supplies. For several hours I sewed the sail corner, attaching the binding to the sheet, pushing the needle through the stiff fabric with a leather palm. I got tired and I got bored. I wanted to quit, and probably would have, but I realized that the Baja journey was changing me. Inside myself, I found a part that didn't want to quit. I knew that if I took one stitch at a time, I would eventually complete the project. I kept sewing until the sail was finished. The sewing project finally gave me some peace. However we were arriving in Cabo, we had put our minds on the goal and were getting there. Cabo was a victory, if only for the growth I had experienced already.

I woke up the second night on the sailboat just after two A.M. In the dark of the cabin I felt the vibrations of a motor and knew we were no longer sailing. When I climbed out of the cabin I saw Verlen, Bob, and Cec gathered around the wheel of *Dorvida*. The soft white light of the moon illuminated the deck, and looming behind my friends was a large dark object that looked like a giant stingray.

"What's going on?" I asked, trying to come fully awake.

"The *Cryruss*," Verlen explained, noting my confusion. "We're towing them in."

"I received a call while you were asleep," Bob added. "Their prop broke."

"Actually fell off," Cec corrected. Looking closer I realized that the shape behind our stern was another large trimaran. Bob and Cec were surely Samaritans of the sea.

"Cabo," Verlen said, pointing out a light off *Dorvida*'s bow.

"Are we there?" I asked, looking toward a faint pinpoint of red.

"By my calculations we're still 30 miles or so from the cape, but that's a navigation light sure enough," Bob reported.

"Now look up," said Cec. In the sky almost overhead I saw a dark shadow slowly retreating from the moon.

"The moon has been eclipsing now for about half an hour," Verlen said, looking at his watch.

"Well, I'm glad I woke up, I would never have believed all this in the morning," I said, taking my place at the stern. "Arriving at Cabo San Lucas is a turning point in more ways than one." *Dorvida*'s sails were down and the motor churned reassuringly. It was a beautiful night.

"If we were paddling, we wouldn't be even halfway here," I acknowledged.

I could see high shadows of land on our left and white sand mounds shining in the dark. Following the navigation beacons, we rounded the cape and arrived in the harbor of Cabo San Lucas before dawn. There were many lights on shore, each one reflected in the bay by a shimmering stripe of brightness. Mast lights marked the place of each sailboat, and these too were doubled on the dark water surface. Very slowly, we motored into the bay to safe anchorage.

On the fringe of the sleeping sailboat population, we slackened the tow line on *Cryruss*, then pulled her again to set the hook on her anchor. I saw the *Cryruss* crew for the first time as Bob shined a headlamp their way: three waving people were illuminated by the glare. Bob motored *Dorvida* into an open space and shut down the engine.

I was too excited to go back to sleep. I wanted to unload immediately and put my tent on shore, but the crew voted to rest. Bob and Cec looked as if they had just come off the night shift, and in fact, they had. Sailing more than 48 hours to Cabo had pushed their limits.

The radio woke us at dawn as it cracked with static. Bob stood bleary-eyed working the channels while Cec put the kettle on for coffee.

"Bus tour at nine sharp—meet at the laundry," a woman's voice announced.

"Two new snatch blocks—selling cheap. Call the *Halmark*," a male voice came over the wire.

"Cabo network," Bob explained.

"Sky clear today—variable winds 20 to 25 knots. . . . "

This live broadcast was the morning newspaper of the sailboaters anchored in the bay. Participants exchanged weather information, scheduled rides and chatted. Bob got on the air and announced the arrival of *Dorvida* and two canoeists from Long Beach. It was obvious from the radio that there was real life in Cabo, and I couldn't wait any longer to be part of it. Verlen and I unloaded our gear and the canoes.

"We'll see you in town," I assured Cec, as I hugged her good-bye.

"Thanks," said Verlen. He shook Bob's hand, then pulled him close into a bearhug.

We settled into our canoes—it felt great to be in the water again. Several sweep strokes and a rudder adjustment put me in line with the beach as we paddled toward shore.

The harbor was crowded with rows of colorful sailboats and motor cruisers anchored in the bay. In this floating community some of the boats were quiet, the crews still asleep, but on others people lounged on deck drinking coffee, reading paperbacks, chatting with one another, and relaxing. One small dog on a white sailboat barked wildly as we paddled by, which soon alerted many sailboaters to our presence. Verlen and I waved at the onlookers, ducked under an anchor rope, and kept paddling. A woman leaned over the rail of an orange cruiser and called hello.

"We were wondering when you would get here," she exclaimed. "Another kayaker was here a couple of days ago and asked about you." We paddled over toward the boat.

"Was the boat red?" Verlen asked.

"Yes, one man in a red boat and a fellow in a yellow kayak," the woman explained. That had to be Steve and Ed. A man came from the cabin and stood by her, staring down at us. "I don't think they're still here," she said. "I haven't seen either of them for a couple of days. Do you want to come on board?"

"No," Verlen said, "we're headed for town. Thanks for the news." Picking up his paddle, he led the way as we manuevered past the other boats.

There was one last line of sailboats before the beach, but I had stopped paying attention to them and was staring straight ahead for our landing. The surf was quiet and the beach was a gentle slope. This was the spot where 27 sailboats had washed ashore in the recent chubasco. The beach was still littered with half a dozen empty hulls, lying on their sides half-buried in the sand. As I aimed for a landing I saw that the hull closest to us was dark green with a red stripe and the word *Vagabunda* painted on the stern. Tipped toward the sea like a toy in a sandbox, the familiar boat now lay in ruins.

"Verlen, that's the Bowers' boat," I said. Pulling my canoe ashore, I ran toward the wreckage. I touched the broken hull and traced the name with my fingers. I remembered the night we had dropped off our food bag on this very ship. Where were the Bowers now? We put up our tents on the sand a few canoe lengths away from the battered hull.

To the west of our landing, the bay cut into a channel that formed an inner harbor. Between our camp and the opening were several beach restaurants. The sand leveled off to a road north of us, where a line of houses has an unobstructed view of the bay. San Lucas was definitely not a fishing camp, but a seaside resort. Many of its buildings were fancy stucco, trimmed in wrought iron.

Before leaving the States, we had arranged a mail drop in Cabo San Lucas with Mrs. Cutter, an American living on the beach road. Our instructions said we could find her house by looking for a set of full-size plastic reindeer pulling Santa in a sleigh across the roof. Sure enough, we spotted the decorations from the beach and headed toward the house.

We walked up the sandhill to higher ground and crossed the dirt road. The holiday symbols sat on a lovely home with neat flowers arranged in rows beneath painted window frames. A thin man about Verlen's age, who looked as if he had been born in the sun, stood in the driveway sorting parcels and pieces of gear. The man had a fabric wrap tied around his waist in the style of South Sea islanders. Odds and ends of clothing, water-swollen books, utensils, packs, rope pieces, and gunnysacks of walnuts lay on the cement. Before I could figure out what he was doing, a small poodle came to the screen door and began a frenzied welcome.

"Pepe, shut up," came a stern female voice from inside. The dog didn't listen, and a woman soon appeared at the door. Through the screen, I saw a bubble of red hair as she bent and shooed the pet from the entrance. Then she invited us into a spacious living room. Christmas decorations were everywhere. "We've been expecting you," she said. "Steve was here and left several days ago, heading into the Sea of Cortez. Ed wasn't going on with him—he took a bus back to the United States. They didn't leave any message for you, but I've got a box of mail for you that I've been holding."

Watching Mrs. Cutter in her comfortable home, I realized she had shaped the Baja to her needs, and had adapted to the desert as little as possible. Her house was full of conveniences, including a completely modernized kitchen and bathroom. Mrs. Cutter herself was petite and fiesty. She immediately started talking about what she would cook for us to eat, how we could shower in her decorated bathroom, and when she would show us the town.

But the first thing I wanted was my mail. When Mrs. Cutter brought out a box of letters and packages, I immediately got down on my knees and started sorting the contents. Verlen's lap was soon overflowing with letters

228

from his large family. But I couldn't complain—there were dozens of notes addressed to me. I ripped open a letter from my brother.

"When you get home," it read, "we will carry your canoe into the town hall and you can put on a program." He had enclosed an article from his small hometown newspaper that had been printing a series of stories on our adventure and quoting many of my letters. I knew these messages were treasure and I wanted to read them when I was alone. Mrs. Cutter had already put on an apron and asked what we wanted for lunch when the unusual man from the driveway came barefoot into the house.

"Have you met Bernard?" Mrs. Cutter asked.

I shook my head no and she went on.

"This is Bernard Moitessier, a writer and sailor. He gave me one of his books about sailing solo around the world." Picking up a copy of *The Long Way* from the coffee table, she hugged it to her chest. "Bernard lost his boat in the tragic chubasco. That was a horrible night here in Cabo San Lucas. Everyone from town went down on the beach and tried to help." She walked over to Bernard and patted his shoulder to comfort. "We told Bernard to come home with us," she said.

"Do you know what happened to the Bowers?" I asked. "They were the owners of the *Vagabunda*."

"No, I don't know the Bowers, but no one was hurt in the storm, I do know that. So many people lost their boats, though, and most of them are haggling now with the Mexican authorities to get their salvage out of the country. Those who had insurance are busy making claims. My husband just left for the States with a trailer of salvaged gear for several of the unfortunates."

"Do you know anything about *Gone with the Wind?*" I asked.

Mrs. Cutter thought for a moment. "No, I don't remember that name."

Bernard had settled in a chair and was smoking a cigarette.

"I'm sorry about your boat," I said, realizing that what he had been sorting in the driveway were the remains of his belongings.

"I was stupid," he said simply. "I should have taken *Joshua* out on the open sea early that day when the weather seemed wrong, but I was surrounded so closely by the other boats it would have been most difficult."

"Is *Joshua* the name of your boat?" I asked.

"Yes, my boat was named for a famous sailor, the strongest in the world," Bernard reported. "*Joshua* went twice around the world with me." He spoke as if *Joshua* had been a person. He turned around in his chair and pointed out the window to the west end of the harbor.

"There is *Joshua* now." I followed his direction to see a bare steel hull anchored in the bay. "I have sold her. I'm too old to put together the ruin."

"Will you get a new boat?" I asked, trying to be cheerful.

229

"Oh, yes," he said, and his face brightened. "My friends in San Francisco are already collecting money for my next boat."

"What will you name that one?" I asked.

"I'll name my new boat after my wife, Leana."

"Love is more important than strength," I agreed.

"Love is strength," he smiled as if we had an understanding.

When Bernard had finished his cigarette he talked about his ulcer, his publisher, the state of life in California, and the art of writing.

"Take your time when you write," he advised. "Writing will be almost as good as the journey itself."

When Verlen and I left Mrs. Cutter's house late in the afternoon, I saw the light on in the garage window. Bernard was writing, looking out over the pile of salvaged goods that now represented all his worldly possessions. It appeared that his will to express himself remained his breath of life.

The last days of 1982 brought many changes. Our tents on the beach were a strange sight amid the wreckage and disco bars. We were camped in a paradise that went on despite the destruction wrought by the chubasco. When Verlen and I were out paddling on the ocean, there was plenty of time to think over each day. In a bustling town, I felt as if everything were moving too fast. I also wanted to be off by myself. Verlen and I didn't need each other as we did when we were on the water, and reading our mail had carried each of us into the separate worlds of our friends and families back home.

Only after we had planted our tents side by side on the beach did we realize we were in a line of tourist traffic. One young couple that came over to our boats had flown down from Colorado. They talked with us for an hour about the merits of different camping gear.

"What's the best tent?" the man asked Verlen.

"And what kind of stove do you use?" the woman quizzed. I wanted to go swimming, to reread my letters, and catch up in my journal, and there we were being interviewed. I got impatient. Who were we now? We were treated as credible authorities, as if our arrival on the beach in canoes made us experts. I wondered what the trip was making of me and what type of world I was moving into.

I saw a large ferry boat pulling into the harbor, and within half an hour the population of Cabo San Lucas doubled as tourists from the ferry swarmed around the village trying to see everything in a matter of hours. I left Verlen talking with a small crowd on the beach and went exploring the town. San Lucas sat back behind the sandhills on the northwestern side of the bay. There were lots of souvenir shops with small cactus plants, straw hats, and trinkets for sale, and outdoor restaurants dotted every corner.

There were phones and ice cream cones, cars, and several grocery stores with recognizable American products. Tourists and sailboaters were more prevalent than the Mexican natives.

I found a dress shop and looked for a local costume that wouldn't clash with my red tennis shoes. For 3,111 pesos ($20) I bought a loosely woven oatmeal-colored shift with pink embroidery on the shoulders and around the skirt. I had wandered into the shop a travel-worn canoe paddler and walked back on the street a new woman—even though my tennis shoes gave me away. I wondered if Verlen would recognize me.

Then I wanted a shower, and hurried to Mrs. Cutter's house to wash off Belcher Point and the past two months of paddling. I bought a ribbon to match the dress and even considered cleaning my fingernails. When I got back to the beach, Verlen was nowhere in sight.

I got into my canoe, carefully arranging my new skirt so it would not hang on the floor. Paddling into the bay, I was drawn to the hull of Bernard's boat. Two eyes painted on the point of the bow stared boldly down into the water as if daring the sea to attack. Even in ruin this boat had a character that the other vessels were missing. The boat represented not a getaway or an experiment, but a romance between an unusual sailor and the sea. The lettering on the mangled cabin said *Joshua*. Two young men were working intently on the fractured deck. I called hello and waved before paddling on.

Turning my canoe, I paddled into San Lucas's inner harbor, where I saw more sailboats tied off at moorage. I heard Verlen's voice calling to me, and finally located him on the deck of a sailboat named *Maria II*. He had met the captain and crew, Ingrid and Jerry, and their greeting was as warm and friendly as if they had known us all our lives. I held onto their bow rope and stood up carefully in my canoe to show off my new clothes.

"Great guns, Valerie, is that you?" Verlen teased.

"Don't get that dress dirty," Ingrid said. She grabbed her camera to click a photo. "Good to meet you," she said. "From what Verlen has been telling us, your trip has been very exciting."

"That's a good word for it," I said with a laugh. "Have you seen *Gone with the Wind*?" I asked.

"I heard they survived the chubasco and crossed to the mainland over a week ago," Ingrid reported.

"We're invited to a party tonight," Verlen said.

"The sailboaters are taking over a restaurant in town," Jerry explained. "I understand you know the Bowers—they'll be there."

"You can tell us about your trip tonight," Ingrid called out. "We'll see you then."

By the time I paddled back to the tents, Verlen had walked overland and met me in camp. He disappeared into his tent to prepare for the New Year's Eve celebration. When he emerged a few minutes later, he had combed his hair with water from a canteen and put on a clean shirt. Flicking lint from his shoulders, he looked like a well-scrubbed kid. No one but Verlen can change his appearance so quickly. I think the secret is his eyes—his bright enthusiasm transforms him.

We arrived early at the party and found seats that gave us a view of the entire room. I sat enjoying my dress and looking around at the party decorations while the sailboaters filed in the door, filling the place with life and conversation. Tables had to be moved to accommodate the overflow, and for a moment I thought I should help. But then I looked at my dress and instead sat back quietly while the men shoved and rearranged the furniture in the room.

Verlen lifted a chair up and over me to make room for an additional couple at our table, and as the legs of the chair passed over my head, giant blobs of black mud and oil fell out of the chair's metal piping and dripped on my hair. The goo trickled against my neck and crept down my back, and a splatter of black blotched my new dress. Verlen was mortified and immediately began to apologize. Dismayed, I hurried to find the bathroom, which turned out to be an outhouse behind the kitchen. There was no mirror and no running water, just a room with a stool—but at least a light to see by as I cleaned my dress. I didn't want to cry. Wiping the spots dry as best I could, I straightened my shoulders, smoothed my hair, and walked back to the party.

Verlen hugged me in sympathy. It seemed ironic that after two months in salt-stained clothes, my first dress-up would be mud-spattered. But I forgot all about my dress when I saw Betty and Richard Bower walking in the door of the cafe. They immediately came over to our table with their arms outstretched in greeting. I looked into Betty's eyes and hugged her tightly. She didn't say much. We wanted to talk, but the party didn't seem to be the place for us to share the past few months and the loss of their boat.

In the restaurant there were no waves jostling me, only people. The sailboaters got loud as the celebration gathered momentum. Food was brought: giant bowls of sopa, chickpeas, tortillas, pollo, and carnitas filled the tables to overflowing.

One man had on a T-shirt painted like a tuxedo and all the women were gaily dressed. A man sitting next to me had had too much to drink. He had flown in from California and was wearing an expensive suit. He gnawed a greasy chicken leg, and between bites kissed his girlfriend, cursed the waitress, and talked about the sex and drugs he had tried. I immediately knew I didn't like the man, and Verlen was visibly uncomfortable.

When the conversation turned to our canoe trip, the man seemed very interested. He stared at me until I finally turned to confront him. When I did, he touched my back, then put his arm around me. I could feel Verlen bristle.

"You are taking this journey for me," he told me.

"Paddling on the ocean is the one thing I did for myself," I responded. But he had already stopped listening. He reached for a bowl of tortilla soup and handed another chicken piece to his girl, then ordered another beer.

I realized the roar around us was not the surf, but people talking louder and louder. The crowd was overwhelming, and the ocean seemed far away. I remembered José at the kitchen shack at Belcher Point and I thought of the miles we had to paddle ahead. I knew it was midnight when the noise of the crowd broke into cheers. As the clock struck 12 I was thinking of how far we had come and also how far it was to Yuma.

As Verlen and I walked back to our camp, traffic was heavy on the main road. Headlights glared and cars sped past as we walked on the sandy shoulder facing the traffic. At the beach I saw that even the sailboats in the bay were brightly lit and noisy with New Year's parties. Disco music filled the air, and I had to listen carefully to hear the surf lapping at the water's edge.

Verlen was captain on New Year's Day, and he decided we were leaving. The sun was bright as we took down our tents, and a beautiful boat with multicolored sails was just passing by.

"Sailing to Hawaii!" a crew member yelled, as the boat moved out like a rainbow.

Verlen and I walked up the sandhill to say good-bye to Mrs. Cutter. She was busy in her kitchen and insisted on feeding us. Before we could protest she presented two plates with eggs, toast, jam, milk, bacon, and sweet rolls. We ate a breakfast fit for a 50-mile paddling day and waddled back to our boats to shove off. As I picked up my paddle, I saw the colorful sailboat returning.

"I wonder what they forgot?" I asked, looking at Verlen.

"Let's go and see. Could be the weather," he replied. The weather was in fact the problem. The sailboat reported heavy swells out of the harbor.

"After a breakfast like that one, we've got to do some paddling anyway," I said, suffering from my overly full stomach. Verlen agreed. We paddled in the harbor, visiting the sailboats and asking about weather reports. We soon heard that another sailboat attempting to head north into the Sea of Cortez past Bahía Los Frailes had been turned back by high winds. We waited for conditions to settle, but by one o'clock we realized the day was passing and we weren't going anywhere.

"Let's paddle to the arch," I suggested. Because we had arrived at night, we had missed the most distinctive feature of Cabo. At the tip of the peninsula, a rock arch stands as an entrance to the bay. Verlen was all for the idea of seeing land's end, so we paddled toward the point, clicking photos of bathing beauties on the beach and the constant parade of small boats and dinghies cruising the harbor.

The cape itself is a dramatic congregation of rocks culminating in one 222-foot pillar rising from the sea like a bony finger to mark land's end. Several hundred feet away, La Vigia rises 550 feet and connects with one of the Los Frailes rocks to form a natural archway. Weathered and ground by the force of the waves, this pass-through is the cape's landmark.

I knew that the archway was a dangerous spot for a canoe. The ocean swells heaved and smashed against the inner walls of rock, then bounced back on themselves and collided with the next incoming wave. A boat going through the arch could be hurled against the rock unless the timing was just right.

Verlen wanted to paddle through the arch, and he asked me to take photos as he did. I was timid and stayed too far away to get the best pictures. But when he paddled through the arch, he made it look so easy, that I decided I could probably do it too. A calm came over me.

"Verlen, I'm going through," I yelled. He was surprised.

"It's tricky in there. Watch the waves, don't let them slam you to the side," he advised. "Give me the camera. I want to record this." I passed him the camera, and he got into position. I could see him on the other side through the open archway. I felt confident because I could look straight at Verlen and paddle toward him through the arch. But as I paddled nearer to the opening, the swells reared and blocked him from view. I didn't panic, but reached inside myself for more power and concentrated. With each stroke, I centered my canoe and pushed it through the arch as if I were threading a needle. All the distractions of fear vanished; I was alone in my boat with one purpose. I made it through the arch! Verlen grabbed onto my gunwales and leaned over from his canoe to hug me, pumping my hand excitedly. I shouted with pride at having made it through.

We paddled back into the bay for one last dinner on the beach. Bob, Cec, and several other sailboaters were drinking coffee in a little bayside cafe, discussing the purchases they had made in town and trading information on where to find the best prices on canned goods. The lady at the next table was nearly hysterical because she had missed the ferry back to Mazatlan and didn't know how she would be reunited with her baggage. The people at our table listened to her complain.

"How you arrive at a place makes all the difference," the woman seated next to me was saying. She had come by sailboat.

"Arriving by canoe is an even more dramatic difference," I explained. Except for the last section where we had been given a ride, I knew we had gained a unique perspective of the cape. "The distance is more than miles. I've explored inside myself."

"You're growing, kid," Verlen announced. "Let's get to bed, we've got more growing to do tomorrow—about 25 miles worth."

We said good-bye to our friends and walked down the beach in the dark. When we reached the canoes, I discovered that the weather cover had been removed from my cockpit while we had been away. I dropped down on my knees in the sand and looked quickly through my things. My hat with the tin butterfly had been on the seat, and now it was missing. That hat had been dry since Tortugas Bay. I even slept with it in the tent.

Though it was dark, I narrowed my eyes and scrutinized everyone I could see on the beach. I wasn't going to let my hat get away. A group of young Mexicans stood drinking beer at one side of the nearby restaurant, and they were looking my way. In the light from the restaurant I thought I saw one of them take something off his head. As I kept watching, everything got silent around me, just as it had when I paddled under the arch. I followed the youths, carrying my paddle. When they turned into the restaurant, I walked right in after them. The activity in the restaurant stopped as I came in the door. As I strode between the tables toward the bar, the men turned to stare at me. When they saw my purposeful expression, one of them reached behind his back and handed me my hat. The butterfly was intact.

SEVENTEEN

Turning North

On the morning of January 2nd, Verlen and I paddled away from Cabo San Lucas without looking back: we were intent on what lay ahead. Ignoring the white sandy beach curving gently eastward from the anchorage, we cut across the bay toward the lighthouse at Cabeza Bellena. We were leaving the Pacific Ocean behind and turning north into the Sea of Cortez. Compared to the life-threatening challenge of the Pacific, Verlen and I believed the Sea of Cortez would simply be a hard push to Yuma: 1156 miles to paddle in only 37 days. It had taken us 69 days to paddle the 1255 miles of Pacific Coast. The excitement of discovery and the need to hurry helped us push our canoes full speed ahead.

The sky was layered in pink and crusted with early-morning clouds. Rays of light streaked upward from the horizon, trumpeting the new day. When a sliver of brilliance emerged at the edge of the sea, I squinted to prepare for the dazzle of sunrise, but the ball of light popped into view before I could look away. It temporarily blinded me, and for a few moments, wherever I moved my head, a dark spot interfered with my vision. I pulled down the brim of my hat for shade, but only succeeded in putting a ceiling on the horizon. The space between the waterline ahead and the straw visor above my eyes was bright with glare. I kept paddling, waiting for the sun to move higher so my hat could do some good.

The point ahead was ragged and steep. An unusual conical rock rose from the shore, and I wondered if that marked the entrance to the Sea of Cortez. Even though the sun was insistent, I looked down at my compass to make sure we were headed east.

236

The map did not mark an exact dividing line between the Pacific Ocean and the Sea of Cortez, but it did show the Baja landmass clearly snubbed at the tip and rounding decidedly northeastward. Wedged between Baja and the mainland of Mexico, the Sea of Cortez or Gulf of California, is an elongated channel over 1,000 miles long, 150 miles wide at the mouth and 32 miles across at its narrowest point. From our vantage at Cabeza Bellena, no land was visible to the east, but I knew the land was there and I felt the security nevertheless.

Compared with the wild infinity of the Pacific side, the Sea of Cortez seemed manageable. The map showed the entire east side of the peninsula as one large harbor, sheltered from the Pacific Ocean. An increased number of harbors was indicated on our charts by a series of small anchors. We expected our paddling to get progressively easier as we headed north and the gulf became even more enclosed.

Our canoes were well packed with fruit, crackers, cookies, and canned juices purchased in Cabo San Lucas. We had rested for four days and eaten our fair share of tortillas and beans while exploring the tourist mecca at the cape. Now it felt good to be paddling again. We were back in business. Verlen and I had plenty to talk about—there was mail to share with one another and observations to exchange about the people in San Lucas, but we saved our conversation and remained silent, savoring a renewed sense of purpose and capability.

My skill had improved over the past two months and my arms felt strong. But, more important, the anticipation of calmer water gave me a boost of self-confidence. The Sea of Cortez offered a margin of control that had been absent on the Pacific side. The gnawing regret of hitching a ride to Cabo was finally put aside, and we anticipated the remaining 1,100 miles to Yuma as promise of redemption.

But as we pushed at the eastern limits of the bay and paddled farther north, some characteristics of the ocean followed us as if not wanting to be forgotten. Swells still bobbed our canoes and surf continued to break along the shore, but the brutal force of the Pacific was gone. The beach gave way to stretches of rock alternating with small coves of sand, as if the land itself was having a hard time making the transition between the two bodies of water.

My chart was scribbled with penciled division problems. We would need to average 30 miles a day to reach Yuma by February 8th. In Cabo San Lucas, Verlen had talked with his sponsors by phone, confirming that a plane ticket was awaiting him at the San Diego airport for a February 9th flight to Chicago. Verlen would be a celebrity at the National Sporting Goods Show, where he planned to reunite with Steve for the remainder of the Ultimate Canoe Challenge. Our biggest pressure would be meeting that deadline.

We had heard from the sailboaters that wind would be our biggest obstacle. The Sea of Cortez is plagued with prevailing northerlies that blow regularly during the winter months, and a head wind could push our canoes back almost as fast as we could paddle forward. But Verlen wasn't worried.

"There are 24 hours in a day," he explained. "The wind generally stops at night and blows from land to sea. We'll paddle when it's calm," he said, establishing a new strategy.

Verlen's appearance had succumbed to the hotter temperatures below the Tropic of Cancer. He had retired his captain's hat, and instead wore a straw bonnet with a shoelace tied from the brim around his chin. My partner didn't look nearly as authoritative as he had in the past, but I could tell by the crisp, purposeful style of his paddling that his technique was, if anything, gearing up for the final lap.

We didn't stop for breakfast, but ate between strokes. I set my paddle down only long enough to peel a carrot, then continued to paddle while I nibbled, maneuvering the vegetable farther into my mouth, using my lips and teeth to feed and hold at the same time. I wanted to stay up with Verlen—I too was bearing down for the last stretch of our journey.

It didn't take long to realize that the Sea of Cortez was offering an unexpected bonus. Because the surf was reduced, we were able to paddle within three or four canoe lengths of shore. On the Pacific side we had gotten that close only when we looked for a place to land inside a harbor. As we scanned the shore, we could see piles of rocks and sheltered coves indenting the coast, breaking up the still active surf.

I no longer looked ahead into an expanse of water with no visible end, but turned my eyes toward shore to enjoy the sights. The fishing camps we had come to expect on the Pacific side were replaced by small ranches. Although there was little to encourage settlement along the arid coast, we saw occasional clusters of worn buildings and a smattering of green that signaled a small oasis of life and probably a fresh water supply.

A large dry wash opened onto the beach at Rancho El Bledido. From my canoe I could see a cow and horse penned in a cactus-fenced corral. A highway ran along a ridge above the beach, and I spotted two houses decorating the brown hillside. We paddled past an outcrop of rocks that formed another arroyo, and when we looked up the ravine, we were surprised to see a line of camper trailers. The scene was typically American and looked out of place in the Baja that Verlen and I had come to know. But the Baja character was impossible to mask. The desert landscape dominated even here, and no hamburger or pop stands littered the beach. These tourists had ventured down the peninsular highway with their rigs well supplied and probably had a story of their own to tell about the road conditions and infrequent gas stops.

Before beginning our trip in Baja, Verlen and I had been warned that finding water would be one of our biggest concerns, but we actually had no problems with that. The solution was to always be thinking ahead and making sure to carry enough water to get us to the next supply. We usually carried about six gallons, but the amount varied with the distance, and we always allowed a reserve. With the number of miles we traveled each day, we continued to put ourselves well within range of replenishment.

I wondered how much water the campers had brought with them and how long they planned to stay. Consulting my map, I counted only a few miles from the trailers to Cabo San Lucas by road. Theirs was an ideal camp, on the outskirts of the tourist center. Cabo San Lucas's fresh water supply was good, and the supply of beer and burritos was unlimited.

The swells continued to follow us 20 miles farther north to Palmilla Point. We arrived by midafternoon and spotted a large complex of buildings sitting on the low, rocky bluff. The tiled roofs made the place look like some kind of academy, but we recognized the buildings as the luxury resort that Leland Lewis had mentioned in his *Baja Sea Guide*. This was apparently one of the first resorts built in the cape area, and it looked deserted as we paddled by. We rounded the point at about three in the afternoon, and landed on a quiet beach. Thankful for the smaller surf, we pulled our canoes ashore with no problem.

Hungry for lunch, Verlen and I walked up a sandhill north of the beach to the resort restaurant on the bluff. A maître d' dressed in a white coat greeted us at the door. The chairs were leather and the tables, arranged by windows overlooking the sea, were covered with white linen cloths and glittered with votive candles. The opulence was enhanced by lovely brass chandeliers and bright paper flowers decorating the walls. As we followed the host to a table, I noticed we were leaving sandy footprints across the carpet. When we were seated, the waiter handed us menus with a flourish. Removing my sunglasses, I untied the bandana from my neck, took off my hat, and tried to straighten my bathing suit top. Thank goodness there were no other customers in the place.

Even Verlen was not oblivious to the atmosphere. He began to freshen up by setting his elbows on the table and cleaning his fingernails with his pocketknife.

I could feel myself responding to the elegant setting and solicitous service. On the Pacific side of Baja I was never reminded that a more attractive lifestyle existed than the challenge of paddling on the sea. Now when I looked out the window and saw our canoes sitting in the sand, I experienced a conflict. I wasn't scared, tired, or bored, but some part of me was having difficulty accepting expedition life. How could I assure the waiter that I wasn't always dressed like this? I wondered how I could politely tell him of the silk dresses I had packaged at home. Could he recognize that I belonged also in his world, that I didn't always wash in with the sea?

The waiter brought us a basket of chips and my stomach brought me back to my senses. The only difference between this restaurant and all the others was that the prices on the menu were five times as expensive and there were no flies. I set the candle on the window ledge and pushed aside the unnecessary silver. We spread our map on the linen cloth and began to plot the mileage for the next day.

The meal wasn't nearly as impressive as the atmosphere. When we were finished eating, I left Verlen and hurried out the exit as if I were trying to escape. As I ran down the hill to our canoes, my heels kicked up sand that pelted my back like small arrows chasing me back to reality. I arrived panting at my canoe and snapped off the weather cover, touching the gear in my now familiar home. I knew I would make it to Yuma, but I couldn't be sure I would ever unpack those silk dresses again.

"Look at the wind," Verlen called from the top of the hill. I saw him raise his arm and point toward a small dinghy in the harbor. The boat tugged on its anchor, and within five minutes had turned 180 degrees.

"The wind is blowing south, just as we suspected," he said, making his way down the hill.

"The beach is blowing," I cried. The wind was picking up the sand on the hill and spewing it south. The sea tossed into a froth of white. It looked as if this northern wind was the one weapon the Sea of Cortez had against the Pacific swells that threatened its territory.

"No sense to fight the wind," Verlen said. "Let's make camp and be prepared to move on later, maybe even tonight." He took off his straw bonnet and pulled his captain's hat from the rear compartment of his canoe as if it were time to get serious. I never found out if the restaurant filled up that night or remained quiet. I don't even know if the owners were aware that we slept on the beach. Verlen and I were in another world, responding to the conditions of the sea. We put up our tents by the canoes and had crawled into our sleeping bags by five P.M.

It was two A.M. when Verlen woke me up. He never carried an alarm, but he seemed to know when to wake up and move. Without a protest I took down my tent and launched my canoe through the line of easy surf. Verlen came paddling right behind me. A small moon lit the sky, with an accompaniment of uncountable stars. The wind was still asleep as we paddled in the dark, edging farther from shore to avoid the outlying rocks. The ground swell and motion of the sea gave plenty of advance warning of the rocks—as the water broke over each surface, a spot of white foam burst into the darkness. Our boats were strong enough to withstand a collision, but the surge of the still-present swells could have knocked us off balance if our boats had been pushed the wrong way against a rock. Frequently I asked my partner's advice.

"Are you watching that rock?" I called fearfully to Verlen, referring to a menacing shape.

"Yes, are you watching it?" Verlen's voice came from the darkness, mocking my question. "Keep watching it," he instructed as he paddled calmly by. "If it comes after you, hit it with your paddle."

It was hard for me to comprehend the enormous amount of time Verlen had spent in his canoe. He had paddled over 50,000 miles with all his trips combined, so it was no wonder he was as comfortable there as most others would be in their living rooms. I continued to watch the rocks closely. The swells occurred in sets, and sometimes the white warnings didn't repeat for several minutes.

The northeastern horizon glowed with lights, and when I switched on my flashlight to check the map, I discovered that the town ahead had to be San Jose, a place as big as Cabo San Lucas, three miles from our present location and one mile inland on a river. The map noted a navigation light and customhouse near the shore. This town had been reported as the best watered and most fertile area in the Baja, but passing in the dark we never saw it. Just as we paddled by the last of the lights and faced the darkness again, I heard a rooster crow. The closeness of the sound surprised me. On the Pacific side, I had heard nothing but the grinding of surf; now the sounds of daily life came clearly over the water. The sound was invigorating. Verlen and I were invisible, paddling by in the night. We were not disturbing anyone's routine, not even leaving footprints, yet we had the privilege of hearing the intimate, familiar sounds.

At dawn we paddled past Punta Gorda. "Gorda" means "fat" in Spanish, and the point was fat as the name implied, curving in a squat shape against the sea. The water was shallow and laced with rocks I wanted to miss. I was glad when the sun came up and we could see better.

Now that we paddled at night, I appreciated daylight more. The moon would keep us company, but its schedule always changed. Its cool light invited us to stare. The sun, on the other hand, was a constant workhorse, not directing attention to itself except the moment it appeared and when it said good-bye. While the night was quiet, the day supported sounds of action and the well-being of warmth. I had not learned to tell time by the sun's position, but the height of its travel dictated when I could take off my coat and when I needed to slather on more sun cream. The moon gave us no such signals: remaining aloof, it glided with a court of stars against the night.

Paddling on the Sea of Cortez, I began to search the coast for interesting sights. As the sun brought our surroundings into focus, Verlen pointed out a wrecked shrimp boat half-submerged near the rocky shore. We paddled close and watched the salt water rhythmically swamp the deck, then drain back, spilling from open ports and hatchways. Teetering from every surge, the boat looked as if it would fall at any moment and completely slip below the surface. But it was firmly stuck on the rock. The metal wasn't rusted, so we wondered if the shrimper was a victim of the chubasco that had so recently devastated the sailboaters in Cabo San Lucas. The abandoned boat was a sad sight to paddle by, and we left it feeling a greater respect for the Sea of Cortez. This was big water, and it was best to be aware of its tricks. We could nearly set our watches by the predictable afternoon winds, but the violence that had caught the shrimper would be stealthy.

At midmorning, we were surprised to see a gray inflatable boat motoring toward us. As it got closer we could see two Americans and a small black dog. When they reached our canoes, the little dog went wild—standing on the pillowy sides of their boat, he strained his head in our direction and wagged his tail. As soon as Verlen reached out to grab the inflatable and hold it steady beside our canoes, the ball of fur stepped over Verlen's deck and jumped into my canoe, licking my face and making himself quite comfortable in my lap. I had never had such a visitor before, and I sat hugging the dog, hoping our new friends would stay and chat for a while. Verlen looked a little peeved by the sudden outbreak of confusion.

The people in the inflatable wore white hats and tennis shorts with T-shirts that looked as if they had been recently pressed. The things I noticed most about these people were their clean clothes, since their faces were hidden behind large darkglasses.

"We're down from San Diego," the man explained. "Camped there on the beach," he said, pointing to a small trailer in the sand.

"We come down every year," the woman added. "He sure does like you," she continued, apologizing for her dog. I was busy with my new pet, wondering if he would eat some gorp.

"How are the swells around the next point?" Verlen asked as he looked at his map.

"That's Los Frailes ahead," the man answered. Verlen showed me the map—the point, with the same name as the spot where I had paddled through the arch, was the easternmost portion of land on the Baja Peninsula.

"You won't notice the surf much past there," the man assured us. We took photos of each other and exchanged addresses, with a promise to send pictures when we got back to the States. I regretfully handed my pet back to his owners and watched the people motor away through the surf in their rubber boat. Once ashore, the dog scampered all over the place. He seemed to be happy wherever he was, which seemed like an enviable trait.

I had plenty of time to think about our unusual visitors. We paddled for several more hours, which made 28 miles before noon, and we would have reached Los Frailes Point, 11 miles farther, if the wind had not come up and blown us off the water about one in the afternoon.

We landed the canoes on a beach of rocks among piles of driftwood. I never understood why some landing spots were covered in driftwood and others were bare. The Pacific side seemed never to have much wood washed ashore, as if the heavy surf pulverized any pieces that dared make the beach. At that afternoon's camp we found plenty for a fire and could have pitched our tents on a ready-made nest.

Verlen stacked different sizes of wood for our cooking fire, beginning with twigs no thicker than toothpicks. After grading the fire starter in increasing size, he found a spot behind a large rock and drew stones together for a fire circle. While he worked, I climbed over the flat surface rocks. Many of them were hollow on top and held water from an earlier tide. Left to his own devices, Verlen naturally started a pot of his favorite dish— macaroni and powdered cheese. For a moment I wondered how anyone could actually eat the bright orange concoction, but I knew the answer— you simply have to be hungry enough.

After lunch we put the tents up in the hot sun and tried to pretend it was time to sleep.

On January fourth, we had paddled three hours before dawn when the wind came up along with the sun. We catamaraned the canoes and continued paddling. The waves weren't threatening, but we weren't taking any chances with the increasing chop. Verlen and I pushed ourselves with a brand of conservatism born from respect for the water and knowledge of how much we had to lose if either of us should capsize.

Catamaraning the canoes diminished the risk, but we then faced the hard work of fighting a head wind, and having the boats connected reduced our speed. Verlen had designed the canoes for minimum resistance to wind: the stern was only 6 inches high and the bow measured 10. The cockpit peaked at 16 inches and I was running about 4 inches deep, Verlen closer to 6. These unique specifications worked fine for a single canoe, but lost efficiency where we created a raft. Two canoes became an easy target for the wind to come against.

"Don't fight it," Verlen said, digging in with his blade. At first I thought his suggestion was a joke. With the wind hitting me in the face, I got frustrated and wanted to fight back. But as I watched, I could see that Verlen was serious about wind techniques.

"Take a longer stroke, don't scrunch up your face, relax, and pull with my stroke," he demonstrated. I watched him reaching out farther than usual, pulling deeper and slowing down his stroke rate. Then, I tried it. Verlen was right: we made much better progress when I stopped fighting and methodically measured my stroke.

Our rudder system was a real benefit. The steering was done by simply pressing our toes against the rudder control, leaving our upper bodies free to apply power on the paddle. Even though the wind worked as a steady deterrent to our forward progress, we were well equipped to keep moving. But only one of us could use the steering controls at a time. When Verlen requested that I pull my rudder out of the water and let him steer, I was disappointed, thinking that I wasn't useful. My motivation drained away. As the wind pushed against us, my strokes lost their effectiveness.

"I need you, Valerie," Verlen said as he took another long bite at the water with his paddle. "One person isn't enough to push these canoes into the wind. I can hold us, but it takes a second person to make any progress." Now that my purpose was clear, I reached down inside myself and pulled up more energy. By then we could see Punta Arena ahead. I took off my straw hat and kept my head down, hoping to streamline the canoe. At the end of each stroke, I pulled my blade out of the water and moved it forward for the entry on its edge so the broad, flat side of the paddle didn't come against the wind. Punta Arena got a little closer.

It was another six hours before we landed on the south end of the point. After pulling our catamaran ashore, I lay down in the sand beside my canoe, unwilling to move. Verlen stood by the water's edge watching three large charter boats anchor offshore. Punta Arena was giving us a firsthand view of the Sea of Cortez as a fisherman's paradise but I didn't know if I had enough energy left to care.

A man came out of a corrugated shed on the beach and looked our way, but soon was busy steadying a dinghy that arrived on shore. Several Americans stepped out on the sand, all of them in a festive mood. The catch had been good.

"A little windy out there," one American shouted toward us. He took off his cap and ran his fingers through his hair.

"Pretty bumpy ride coming back," another American observed. He looked glad to be ashore. I propped myself up on one elbow to watch what was going on. Two local fishermen were holding onto the fin of a large marlin, dragging the fish on the beach toward a waiting pickup truck. Two dorado and three dolphin fish were loaded next.

"If you don't move soon," Verlen said, looking down on me, "I may have to use that same technique." He pointed to the fish, as their tails made heavy squiggles in the sand.

"Fine with me. I'd love to be dragged up the beach, cleaned, and taken

244

to the table. But set me in a chair please, not on a plate." I got up slowly and realized I could come back to life, especially if we talked about food.

We walked over to introduce ourselves to the Americans. They were trading fish stories with one another and were eager to share the excitement of their vacation. The group looked like a bevy of backyard neighbors, but actually none of them had met before their trip to Baja.

"Word is a 250-pound marlin was caught off this very beach just before Christmas," said one of the group. A man who had introduced himself as being from Arizona grimaced in envy.

"I come here every year—love it. This place is full of fish," confirmed a Michigan vacationer.

"I heard of a 10-mile army of game fish feeding off Punta Gorda," the man from California exclaimed.

"This is fishing paradise," one of them added, taking out a measuring tape to judge his catch.

"You guys want a ride to the resort at Punta Colorado?" one of them asked.

"We guys sure do," I said. Gathering my hat and notebook, I was the first to get into the truck. As soon as we reached the resort, the fishermen headed for the bar and Verlen and I made our way to the kitchen and knocked on the door. A short Mexican woman came to the serving window, and behind her I could see large refrigerators and several other women busy making pastry.

"Comidas?" I asked eagerly.

"I speak English," she said. "We are making dinner, which will be served in two hours."

"We can't wait," explained Verlen. "We're canoeing along the coast and will be paddling later tonight."

"We're on our way to Yuma," I said. "Can you fix us anything?" I was reluctant to give up, since this was the only place to eat for miles.

"Sit down," she said patiently. "I'll see what we can do." The serving window closed, and Verlen walked toward the window while I went to look for the bathroom.

It felt good to be inside a building. My ears, eyes, and skin still tingled from the wind. I found the door marked "senoritas" and walked inside. There was a full-length mirror, and the woman reflected was different from the one I remembered. My skin was no longer sunburned, but more an all-over brown. My hair was matted, and when I took off my dark glasses I had racoon eyes where the sun hadn't reached. But I sure did look healthy. The woman staring back at me from the mirror was intensely alive—maybe that was what Verlen meant when he talked about circulation. I washed my hands and hurried back to the dining area.

Verlen had seated himself right in front of an unusual Christmas tree.

245

Looking closer, I realized the plant was an agave—the bloom had been cut and propped in the corner. I recognized the plant because my aunt had one in southern California. Agave, or century plant, grows very slowly for years, then eventually puts forth all of its energy and reserve to produce a towering stalk of flowers that looks somewhat like the flowering part of a giant broccoli. After blooming, the plant dies. I was in the middle of telling Verlen how I had lassoed the tall bloom in my aunt's back yard before it could die and fall on her house when the cook brought dinner.

First she set a basket of crackers on the table, then a plate with several spoonfuls of hash. Neither Verlen nor I was very excited. I poked suspiciously at the main dish with my fork. We ate the entire basket of crackers, but neither of us had anything good to say about the main dish that appeared to be some kind of meat. When we left, we knocked on the kitchen door to say thanks.

"What was it?" I asked.

"Special today," the woman explained. "Fried goat liver."

I was sorry I had asked.

Verlen called me awake in the middle of the night, and I stuck my head out of the tent and looked at the sea. The surface was still and yet glittered in the moonlight as if inviting me to paddle. Small waves nudged the beach in front of my tent, making a playful splash. I didn't hesitate. Packing quickly, I launched my canoe and paddled out, responding to an almost magnetic call.

True to its name, Punta Arena was a "point of sand." The low land disappeared in the darkness, and there were no bluffs or distinguishing hills. As we turned along the shore, a blinking lighthouse guided us. A mile north, a ground swell started to bounce our canoes, building a heavy surf on the point and suggesting that the area shoaled for quite a distance. But once we were past the navigation light, Punta Arena's looping point created a barrier that held back the surf and swells, and on the other side of the point the water was smooth as a lake. As we paddled farther north, all we could hear was the quiet lapping of the waves.

Within a few more miles, shadows of mountains appeared on the land side to keep us company. Bright stars shown above—it was a good night to make friends with the dark. Each paddle stroke disturbed millions of tiny phosphorescent creatures, spreading green and white sparkles like stardust. A fish swam under my boat, stirring up a stream of living light that marked its path.

Our eyes adjusted and the darkness seemed to soften. We could see quite well until Verlen and I caught sight of the lights of a town ahead—when we stared at the glow of civilization, the darkness shut us out. A line of palm trees was silhouetted against the harbor and the smell of barnyard animals came across the sea. The Pacific seemed as far away as if it belonged to another age.

The next afternoon we made a brief stop at Buena Vista, a sport fishing town that had a telephone for us to use. Verlen monopolized the lines for two hours, talking with his sponsors and assuring them that though we were behind schedule, we were alive, well, and still paddling. I spent the afternoon writing letters home and handed them to an American I met at the cafe, who promised to drop them in the mail. As the helpful young man motored our letters away on his cycle, Verlen and I walked back to the beach, headed for the sea.

The east side of the peninsula surprised us with the variety of people who had come to visit the desert. The Americans we met in the Baja were special—it takes a certain sense of adventure to cross the border into Baja and travel a sparsely populated frontier. Most of the tourists we met were there to fish and enjoy the scenery. But one renegade we met at Bahía de los Meurtos still has me wondering.

It was January 8th and Verlen and I had pulled ashore after another day of wind. I saw a flash of orange between the rocks of an arroyo, and when I walked closer, I saw the orange was a mass of fabric covering a man. A rock moved beneath my feet and the man looked up. For a moment, we stared at each other as if one of us might run. Each of us was surprised to find another person on the deserted beach. I gave him my excuse first, and explained about our canoe journey. The man didn't offer any explanation for his presence, but just went on sewing the pieces of bright orange material. He sat cross-legged in the sand.

"Small bugs sure are annoying," he explained, brandishing a large needle. Poking in and pulling out with the same continuous rhythm as my paddle strokes, the man finally introduced himself as a California professor. He had a leather dunce cap stuck on his head and the bottoms of his pants were ragged. A compact four-wheel-drive truck was parked over the rise from the beach, the back of it was crammed with supplies. He didn't say how long he had been there or how long he planned to stay, but he seemed to fit. I left him to his sewing after exchanging a few pleasantries about the weather.

The morning of January 7th we overslept and hurried to get onto the water. It was an hour after daybreak when we reached Punta Perico, a steep, rocky bluff that rose hundreds of feet into the air and overshadowed our canoes as we traveled along the base. Sharp pointed rocks littered the sea to the east, which made us hug the cliff even more tightly as we continued north.

As we rounded the point, a new piece of land appeared. which our charts identified as Isla Cerralvo. The island created a channel that funneled the water and wind toward us, and a severe bounce met us head-on as we rounded the point. The water surface chopped into a turmoil as a tidal current agitated the conditions. Our situation changed so quickly, we didn't have time to catamaran before the waves got too high for us to connect easily. I didn't even have my spray skirt on, and I was so busy trying to stay upright, I couldn't take the time to set down my paddle and arrange any precautions.

Neither of us thought about turning back, since steering forward looked less risky than trying to about-face in the crazy sea. I concentrated on each paddle stroke and jerked my head up with a start when Verlen yelled his concern.

"How're you making it?" he asked. I looked over and saw only his shoulders, head, hands, and paddle shaft above the motion of the waves. His canoe was hidden between the swells. I stared straight ahead and shut out everything around me.

"Okay. The boat is riding well," I shouted back. I had never handled seas that rough without catamaraning, and I knew the canoe deserved much of the credit. The swells were not as big as those on the Pacific, but the waves were steeper and closer together.

"Let's stay close," Verlen answered.

I didn't want to say how scared I was, so I prayed and concentrated. Forcing my thoughts to stay together, I drove off the panic and kept paddling. The more strongly I pulled forward, the more stable my canoe felt, as if the momentum of my effort could convince the waves that I was unsinkable. The canoe and I were one solid core of will, and we were making progress.

I glanced at the shore and realized the rocks were giving way to sand. The beach curved inward ahead, and a large resort sat above the sea. I stared at the hotel as if my eyes could burn through it. Paddling, paddling. I knew I would make it.

The beach was steep, and the waves made quite a show of tumbling on the sand, but I didn't let up. The momentum of getting that far should have eased so I could judge the surf, but I remained intent and kept pushing. I went in too fast and didn't think, just bore down as hard as I could. I was on top of a wave before I realized my mistake. Then I back-paddled to stay behind the break, but it was too late, I hadn't counted on how closely the next wave was coming behind me. My bow touched the shore, and just as I started to climb out of the cockpit another wave crashed over me. I fell, and the undertow dragged me back into the water. I wasn't thinking any more, it had all happened too fast. I hung onto my boat, wrestling it in the surf.

Verlen had made a better landing and was by then reaching out to pull me in. He caught hold of my bowline and tugged my boat and me up on the sand until I could feel solid ground and stand on my own.

"Good job," he said, helping me to my feet.

" I didn't make it all the way," I said, feeling disappointed and embarrassed about my messy landing.

"Yes you did," he said proudly, smacking me on the back. I sat down in the sand and started to bail my canoe. When my nerves stopped pumping adrenaline through me, I felt a wave of nausea. The day was bright and sunny, denying that anything had gone wrong.

"I'll buy you lunch," Verlen said, brushing wet sand from my deck.

"Anything but goat liver," I requested.

I laid out my gear in the sand to dry, then headed with Verlen toward the hotel. Within half an hour I had changed into dry clothes and was sitting on a tile patio with a cheese omelet, coffee, juice, and toast before me. A small puddle formed on the floor as my personal bag continued to drip.

The dining room was empty, and the owner walked out from the kitchen and sat at a table next to ours. He was a small man with stooped shoulders and a heavy stomach.

"Where are you from?" he asked in English, lighting a cigarette. Verlen told him our story.

"Well, you won't be making it north. The wind gets worse," he said. "I had guests with reservations for tonight and they will not arrive by plane today because of the wind. I hear on the radio it is windy on the entire peninsula."

"We're working around the wind and traveling at night," I answered.

"You won't make it north," he repeated. "Wait until you see the tide. When the high tide of the Pacific rises, it lifts into the Sea of Cortez. You will find currents of six knots or more when the tide moves past the middle islands farther up the coast." He paused to see if he had convinced us.

"It may be impossible to go on, but it would also be impossible for us to stop now," Verlen said patiently. The owner looked blankly at us.

"We have paddled here from Long Beach," I explained.

"That is impossible," the man decreed.

"How's business?" I asked, trying to change the subject. I looked around the empty room.

"Terrible. The peso is destroyed. And the weather this year has chased many people away." The man looked sad, and I couldn't blame him for feeling pessimistic about everything.

"Can we camp on the beach?" Verlen asked. "We do not have enough money to stay here."

"Yes," said our host, "make yourselves at home." We didn't talk much more. The owner stared at the walls of his investment and Verlen and I sat with full stomachs looking out the window to the sea. Soon we left the dining room and returned to our canoes, looking around for a good spot to spend the afternoon. At the end of the beach was a palm-thatched shelter. We took our packs and made a comfortable camp on its cement floor. The roof was shag palm, and twisted ropes circled the support poles and were tied in decorative tassels.

I sat in the shade and opened a wet paperback book. As the wind dried the pages, they began to turn. I held the book and let the pages flip like a pinwheel. I didn't feel much like concentrating—it was more fun to watch the birds. Pelicans were dive-bombing in the bay, heaving themselves from a rock, then zooming back and forth with their bellies inches above the water. Then their wings would stop as they sharply turned and hovered. When they had spied a choice morsel, they would streak again into the air, pause for an instant as if collecting their thoughts, then dive into the water, folding their wings at the last possible instant and entering the water like torpedos. Seven or eight of them poised on the rocks and flew out over the water, circling for dinner.

Verlen was busy working with the map but he looked up. "Don't let the hotel man bother you," he said.

"I was thinking about him," I admitted. "I get negative too, sometimes. I can understand him."

"He's partly right," Verlen said, sitting with his map. "With these delays, we may not make it to Yuma on time." I looked at Verlen to see if the proprietor's attitude was affecting my partner, but it wasn't something he wanted to talk about.

"I need a haircut," he said, changing the subject. He handed me a small pair of folding scissors.

I started to say "I can't," but caught myself just in time. I'd never cut anyone's hair before, but Verlen's confidence in me always made me braver. Verlen was already sitting up straight in his chair. I tucked his parka over his shoulders like a tarp and began to snip. When the damage was done, Verlen praised me for a good job. Fortunately, he didn't have a mirror.

The wind took over the afternoon, and even the pelicans stopped feeding. Verlen and I went to sleep early and planned to paddle again soon after midnight, but it was not Verlen who woke me. At eleven o'clock I sat bolt upright in my tent and knew it was not a dream: people were singing. Crawling out the door of my shelter, I woke Verlen.

"Do you hear music?"

"What?" Verlen asked. "Do you feel all right?"

"Verlen, I hear music. People are singing. Be quiet and listen." In a minute Verlen was standing in the sand next to me, putting on his cap and tucking in his shirt. We followed the song. A hundred yards from our tents a bonfire was blazing. Gathered around the light was a group of vagabundos del mar—sea gypsies of Baja—singing harmony with two box guitars. Vagabundos is both a title and a way of life. These sea drifters roamed along the peninsula with limited supplies, living off the food from the sea and what they could forage from the shoreside hills.

Verlen and I stood on the outside of the ring of light. When one of the singers saw us, a man stood up to move a sleeping child who lay on an old car seat in front of the fire. While the people continued to sing, they drew Verlen and me into the circle and welcomed us to sit down.

The air was heavy with burning mesquite and the awakened child's voice joined the harmony. The Spanish sounds were soft, reverent, and sweet. Although we couldn't understand all the words, we knew by the few we could understand that they were singing hymns of praise. We listened to several songs, looking at the warm, shadowed faces in the firelight. When they paused I knew it was time for us to participate in the singing.

"Verlen, let's sing our song for them."

"No, I can't sing," he protested.

"Come on, Verlen, you can do it." Together we sang a little ocean song that we had used for perking up our days at sea. The guitar player followed along, plucking a few chords from his instrument. When we were done the group smiled their pleasure at our contribution, then started in on another song of their own. Someone brought out a Bible and began reading in the firelight. I ran back to my tent and got my own sea-wrinkled Bible so I could follow along.

The scene filled us with new hope: surely we were meant to be in that exact spot that night, no farther from or any closer to our goal of Yuma.

EIGHTEEN

View from the Top

The morning of January 12th, I crawled halfway out of my tent and turned my head to look at the sky: low clouds bunched together in a thick gray mass and threatened rain. I stayed on my hands and knees, imagining that if I did stand up, my head might puncture the swollen cloud ceiling and bring down torrents of water. I waited quietly for the wind to touch my face, but there was no push, pull, or shove in the air. The suffocating clouds squelched all movement.

Stillness dominated the scene. Verlen's tent stood in the sand looking as if it had grown there, and I could almost believe that the darkness of night and the moisture that morning had produced the conditions necessary to form the large green mushroom shape. There was no sign of Verlen, so I knew we wouldn't be leaving right away.

Crawling back inside my tent, I zipped the door flap closed, yawned, and stretched to push the sleep from me. My hands touched both walls. I took a long drink from the gallon water jug, wadded my gear and clothing into a pile, and leaned back to write in my journal.

The day before, we had paddled 28 miles in 14 hours and landed on Isla de Espíritu Santo just before dark. The five-mile crossing had been rough, but our choices had been limited. On our lunch break at Punta Coyote, we had studied the map and proposed an island hop to Isla de Espíritu Santo, Isla San Francisco, Isla Coyote, and Isla San José before cutting back to the peninsula. This route would bypass a large bay and the town of La Paz. Our decision was a little risky, since it left us with four open-water crossings, the longest of which was 22 miles. We chose the route because time was getting short and following the shoreline around Bahiá de la Paz meant many extra miles.

Verlen had been sick again with diarrhea and stomach cramps. He never complained, but I knew something was wrong. His energy was low and occasionally he dropped behind my canoe and rode on my wake. He still had to paddle, but the wake of my canoe created a small wave and by riding the front of the short crest, Verlen's canoe got a slight boost. For the past few days he had been eating plain rice and was doctoring himself with some Mexican medicine with Spanish directions.

While I was writing, I heard the zipper of Verlen's tent opening. I didn't look up, but kept scribbling notes.

"Let's get moving," I heard him say.

"You talking to me?" I asked, continuing to write. No answer. From inside my tent I couldn't see Verlen, but I knew he was studying the sky. I stopped writing. "What about the rain?" I asked, looking up at the tent wall. Verlen unzipped my door and peeked in. He crouched in the sand, leaning on his paddle.

"The wind is from the north," he reported. "In the lee of this island the water will stay calm. All the rain will do is shrink you a little."

"Is that what happened to you?" I teased, reminding him that I was taller by three inches.

"Yep," said Verlen. Taking off his cap he scratched his head. "I'm Sanforized, but you may have more of a problem." We both laughed.

"You feeling any better?" I asked seriously.

"Yep. A little stiff around the edges, but once I get circulating that will go away. Let's get moving."

"Okay, captain. You are captain today, aren't you?" I asked, looking at the date on my watch.

"Guess I am," he said, as if it were news to him. "It's an official order then—break camp!"

"Yes, sir," I agreed. I wrote another page in my journal before closing the book and stuffing it inside my waterproof pack. By the time my tent was down, the rain had started. I pulled on my yellow raincoat and buttoned up, then I walked to my canoe and wondered how to launch. Our expedition was far different from an ordinary weekend paddling trip. Back home I'd seen plenty of canoers sloshing in water up to their knees to launch a boat, but that was not our style. Wading barefoot was reckless—contact with a jagged shell or spiny sea creature would mean injury and delay. If we waded with shoes on, we had to sit all day with wet feet. That was uncomfortable and a drain on efficiency. Because we faced day after day of paddling, we naturally found ways to make ourselves comfortable and safe. Our extended journey included sacrificing most civilized comforts, but we tried to eliminate as many inconveniences and problems as possible.

Every morning my entry was different, depending on the conditions. That morning there was no surf to worry about, and the beach was flat. I left my shoes on and pushed the canoe halfway into the water. Verlen had reinforced the deck, making it a sturdy platform. Using my paddle as a walking stick, I steadied myself, took several steps across the rear deck, and climbed into my cockpit, keeping my feet dry. Verlen had taught me that little trick, and now it was one of my habits.

Once settled in my cockpit, I looked down and saw quite a bit of sand sticking to my shoes. I drew one knee up, swung my leg out of the cockpit toward the water and knocked my heel several times on the side of the canoe. When the sand didn't all fall off, I gently placed my shoe on top of the water, letting only the sole break the surface, and rinsed the sand away. I washed my other shoe the same way and then sponged up the water on the floor of my canoe.

I pulled the spray skirt over my head and attached it to the cockpit rim so the rain wouldn't soak in on my lap. Finally, I planted my paddle in the sand below the shallow water and pushed, scooting with my hips and rocking forward to loosen my canoe from the beach. After several pushes with my paddle, my stern floated free. I was ready to go.

Before turning to paddle west, I looked past the point and saw waves and whitecaps traveling down the northeast side of the island. I liked this place right away. We had choices. Since the wind didn't affect both sides of the island the same way, we could paddle in a northerly direction on the lee side in calm water.

Rounding Dispensa Point, we cut into a small bay with a water surface like glass. Pelicans and cormorants circled in the air and roosted on the rock cliffs. A brant floated several canoe lengths ahead of us, and as we approached, the bird spotted us, then paddled its feet faster to get away. At that moment a school of sardines, spooked by our canoes, jumped out of the water. Hundreds of small silver fishes sky-rocketed in unison, and the sardine formation collided with the bird's path. The poor creature was beside itself amid the bombardment. Its head bobbed frantically, then it dove under the water.

The island looked to be a formation of volcanics, with slabs of tilted rock creating high cliffs. Huge areas had broken away, leaving the scars of erosion and exposing a salmon colored underside. The rock was porous, and much of the surface was dotted with cactus growing in cracks and crevices.

Traveling close to shore, we spied bright red crabs skittering on moss-covered boulders. These creatures disappeared underwater the minute they sensed our approach. Forming a rainbow of colors, the green moss on the rocks near the water gave way to pink slabs with brown trim. Spots of green plants and the white lime striping from birds formed the top. The colors were all the richer because of the low saturation of light on the gray day. Weather had sculpted the rocks, and many of the cliff faces were mottled with boulders, as if enormous surf and wind had pushed each spherical shape into soft putty.

I saw something white on a rock ledge and pulled my canoe for a closer look. At first I didn't know what the object was, then I realized it was a dolphin skull, washed clean by waves and bleached in the sun. The cranial dome rose steeply and almost flat at the back. The front sloped down and lengthened into a tapered point. The skull was not spooky but beautiful against the rock. A few feet away I found a cannonball-shaped rock, porous and embedded with sand particles. I strapped the skull on the stern of my canoe with an elastic bungie cord and tucked the rock into my personal bag. Feeling rich with new treasures, I climbed back into my canoe and paddled hard to catch up with Verlen.

The rain was quiet and soft until we paddled out of San Gabriel Bight. When the wind came, conditions changed rapidly—as they always do on water. The wind hit us straight on and flung the rain against us, slashing at our faces.

The quiet peace of our morning disappeared. We continued paddling, ducking into deep fingered bays for a breath of calm, then fighting our way around the point of each outlet. We stopped admiring the scenery and withdrew into a narrow world of effort.

By late afternoon we arrived at the tidal passage between Isla de Espíritu Santo and Isla la Partides. The unusual separation of these companion islands seemed a mistake of nature, and each island sent sandspits into the water as if trying to reconnect with the other. Several sailboaters were anchored in the sheltered cleft, and we paddled toward the closest boat.

"Hey, look," a figure standing on deck cried. "Kayakers!" Soon the deck was crowded with four other excited people.

"Come aboard," a pretty blond woman insisted.

"No, we've got to keep moving," Verlen answered.

"We bought some chocolate doughnuts in La Paz and I'll make you some sandwiches," the woman bribed. That did it.

"Let me at 'em," I said, as I tied my canoe to their dinghy and started aboard. Verlen followed as I climbed on deck. The faces of the *Miracle* crew were expectant and wide-eyed as they welcomed us into the main cabin. Our adventure seemed to touch them, and they wanted to hear our story. Verlen and I shared small snatches of the last few months, but our attention was on the challenge of reaching Yuma.

"What's the weather?" Verlen asked.

"Bad winds this year," the captain said. "There's a terrible storm on the mainland of Mexico this week. We're stopping here because tacking got ridiculous—one sailboat leaving Cabo San Lucas reported sailing 20 miles east to come 2 miles north. They gave up and returned to the cape."

"What's your plan?" Verlen asked.

"We're headed for Cabo. This wind is too much—25 knots is a quiet day."

"The wind hasn't been friendly with us either," I recalled, telling about our head-on battles.

It would have been easy to stay with the good company, eating more cheese sandwiches and doughnuts, but we had to get back to our canoes and paddle away. In fact, we had already stayed on the sailboat longer than we should have. Daylight was fading fast and the rain had not let up.

By the time we crossed to Isla la Partides and paddled around the next point into another bay, it was dark. But we kept paddling, groping for a campsite. From the water, the landscape was a mystery. We looked for a dent in the high silhouette of land and entered a small inlet that led to a patch of sand where we set up camp.

During the night the wind and rain continued, seeking us out even in the sheltered bay. As the turbulence pushed the warm air upwards, lumps of hail came down and pelted our tents. I lay on the windward side of the tent, and the wall pushed and billowed against me. I dreamt that I was in a floating house with large windows. Waves were pushing against the glass. Lupe and Jose paddled by in a fishing boat, and I could clearly see my yellow station wagon parked on shore.

I woke at midnight and pushed all my gear to the levitating side of my tent, hoping to weight it down. Verlen and I had planned to leave the island in the cover of darkness to complete the 22-mile crossing before the winds began, but conditions made the crossing impractical. I wrapped deeper into my sleeping bag and went back to sleep.

At first light I looked outside: low clouds blocked my view of Punta Tintorera at the north end of the island, but the rain had stopped and the wind was not reaching our hill-protected camp. We took down the tents and paddled toward the crossing.

As we rounded the last point, the wind hit us squarely in the face. The far side of the island looked wild, as if we had turned a corner into a maelstrom. Wind buffeted the island wilderness, pushing spray and surf against the cliffs. I held onto Verlen's cockpit as we bobbed in the water, reconsidering our takeoff.

"Do you want to hook the boats together and go for it?" I asked.

"No," Verlen replied. "We'll go back and make camp. That's a pretty fierce head wind." Before we reached shore, the rain started again. Verlen and I landed and hurried to set up the tents, then crawled inside. When I peeked out of the door flap, raindrops spat in my eyes. I watched the pelicans who were riding out the storm in our harbor. Once in a while the birds would shake their feathers, rearing on their legs to allow the collected water to roll off, but for the most part they sat quietly floating in the blue water.

Verlen and I snacked on peanut butter and crackers and spent the afternoon waiting. It rained all day, and the downpour got strong enough to knock down the little waves in our bay. But it didn't affect the swells farther out—we could see big surf rolling around the point, and even the clouds were being pushed around by the gusts.

By late afternoon I couldn't sit still any longer, and Verlen suggested we take a hike. We pulled on our rain gear and walked inland. The beach sand disappeared and the terrain became crumbling slabs of rock. Green tufts of scrub and brush crept along the surface.

Verlen started up a steep hillside, and pieces of the earth fell away as he climbed hand over hand. I followed Verlen's heels. Halfway up I stopped and realized that climbing mountains with Verlen was probably more dangerous than canoeing with him—we had no catamaran poles to connect us, and he would not stop until we reached the top. I couldn't look up because debris from Verlen's climb sprinkled on me, and I couldn't look down because down was very far away.

I kept climbing, concentrating on the piece of earth beside my body. A few inches from my nose was a moving carousel close-up of roots and bugs. When we did make the summit, our tents and canoes below appeared minuscule. Across the water, the entire expanse of bay melded with the sea and reached to the horizon. The view from the top was a magnificent sight!

The weather calmed down and the wind stopped. I realized we were sitting on top of a mountain and that I got there under my own power. Sitting on the rock hugging my knees, I leaned back peacefully. I remembered many years before seeing a cloth picture of a figure sitting on top of a mountain, looking over acres of land. I had wanted to purchase the print, but my companion had judged the picture amateurish. I didn't buy the picture, but I always regretted passing it up. The image spoke to me of achievement, belonging, and peace. In the Baja, on top of a mountain of my own, I was the person in the picture gazing over creation. My attraction to the print could have been a clue to the future. I had climbed a mountain to claim the image: now I was the picture.

"Worth the effort wasn't it?" Verlen said, interrupting my thoughts.

"Yes, it certainly is." I had a total sense of rightness: the Baja was becoming a part of me.

On Friday, January 14th, we pushed offshore at four in the morning. The clouds were gone and stars sparkled in the heavens. When we reached the north end of the island, I looked at the windward side as we had done two

257

days before. This time, all was quiet. In the clear darkness, I could feel no wind. To be safe, we linked the canoes and started to cross the open water. Neither of us said a word. We both paddled hard, hoping to cross the 22-mile open space before the wind could find us and attack.

At daybreak, in the middle of the crossing, Verlen and I refigured our approach to Isla San Francisco. We matched a point on the island with a landmark on the peninsula visible behind. If we kept those two references in the same relation to each other, we could remain on course. The wind came with first light and threatened our route. We angled the canoes sideways to our destination to compensate for the interference and paddled for all we were worth. San Francisco grew as we neared. I looked over my shoulder and saw Isla la Partides shrinking in size. Morning clouds swept over the horizon and waves shoved against one another. We continued paddling with long, deep, synchronized strokes. At one o'clock, we finally landed on Isla San Francisco and celebrated with a cook fire and a hearty lunch.

The next crossing was more sheltered. We paddled all afternoon and landed at Punta Salinas by six o'clock. Crabs skittered out of the way as we pulled ashore. Reviewing the map, I realized we had come 30 miles since morning. I wanted to continue, but Verlen wasn't feeling well and called a halt for the night. It was difficult for me to quit—I felt like a horse pulled up short in the middle of a race, and paced the beach before I could settle down to sleep.

On January 15th, we paddled 38 miles. The conditions were perfect—sunshine, no wind, and small swells. The sea worked with us, and the months of paddling had honed us into one powerful rhythm. Each stroke was sure and strong. A surge of confidence welled up inside me: reaching Yuma seemed possible.

We stopped for a bathroom break on an offshore rock island. Because the wind had quit, gnats were quick to welcome us, covering our bodies, biting, and crawling on our skin. Verlen leaned over to turn his boat and I brushed away hundreds of small bugs from his salt-crusted back. The bugs settled on him again and I let them be, ignoring too the swarm on my own body. As I stepped back into my boat I noticed that my shoe had broken at the edge and that my toe was peeking out, but it didn't bother me too much. The condition of our gear and the quality of our daily life had become less important than the quantity of miles covered. Quantities could be measured, and I kept track of the exact distance to our finish: 870 miles to Yuma. Mulege was 186 miles away, eight days away at our present speed.

By nightfall we had reached Punta San Telmo. The beach was a ledge of shrub, but had an open sandy spot big enough for a landing. Verlen and I were surprised to see a young man standing onshore holding the hand of a little boy.

"Buenas noches," he said, walking toward our canoes when we landed. The little boy's eyes opened wide as he looked at us. He tried to pull back as if he might like to run away and soon he was hiding behind his guardian's legs.

"Buenas noches, señor." Verlen replied. "Agua, por favor?"

"Sí." The man led the way to a village that wasn't visible from the beach. The little boy nearly stumbled as he watched us over his shoulder while he walked.

We followed a sandy path through spiny cactus and brush until an oasis appeared, where we came upon an old two-story pink stucco building rising from the desert. It was an unusual sight to see a vacant mansion presiding as a village square. Lovely palms shaded the chipped tile roof.

Verlen and I did not know the history of the village, but we could see that the people were productive. There was a small school building with a stick fence and a recess yard with swing sets made from trees. An airplane fuselage lay half-buried in the sand, and I guessed that every child in the village had logged hundreds of hours playing amateur pilot.

Each house had a small, freshly swept front yard. A group of children gathered to greet us and gave courage to the little one still holding hands with our guide. The boy knew he was the center of attention for having seen us first, and his fear disappeared as he proudly escorted the entire group.

"Tortillas, por favor," Verlen asked, holding up his wallet.

"Sí, señor." We were led to a small home sheltered beneath date palms. Clapboard windows opened onto the yard, but the inside was dark except for a glowing wood fire under a cook barrel. Mama patted tortillas on a board and her daughter pressed and grilled them on the drum. The women smiled, their hands busy with their chores.

When our transactions were complete, we carried two jugs of water and a foil pack of warm tortillas back to camp. It would have been a good night to continue paddling, but Verlen felt weak and nauseated and was soon sleeping. I fashioned a chair with my pack and took out my journal and flashlight.

I was worried about Verlen—diarrhea continued to plague his system and sap his usual strength. His efforts at doctoring himself were extreme: that day he had taken six aspirin, two Percogesic, one Lomotil, two vitamin C tablets, six Mylanta, and five drops of a special elixir he had picked up at a pharmacy in San Lucas. The medicine masked the symptoms but did not cure the problem.

Verlen's problems never shook his positive attitude. On the ocean we had paddled from harbor to harbor because the large surf kept us from getting ashore in between. There in the Sea of Cortez we could pull ashore more often, but Verlen didn't take advantage of the accessibility. We continued paddling each day until he couldn't go any farther. We had paddled 30 miles two days earlier, 38 miles the day before and 44 miles that day—not bad progress, considering the way Verlen was feeling.

As Verlen got sicker, he withdrew into stoic silence. For all his discomfort, he remained remarkably stable. I was the one who was changing: as Verlen's attention focused on his efforts to keep moving, I felt my dependency on him relax. Now I was the one who was needed. Verlen would nap while I cooked lunch and he would sleep again while I cleaned the pots and repacked camp. Warming to my increased responsibility, I was more energetic and vocal about our progress. While we were paddling that afternoon, I had pursed my lips and blown until they vibrated. At the same time I hummed, matching my stroke with the simulated sounds of an engine.

"What are you doing now?" Verlen asked.

"This is my spirit motor," I explained joyfully. Verlen smiled and kept paddling.

That night I could hear Verlen breathing peacefully. I sat nibbling tortillas as I jotted down the events of the day. I was eating without paying attention to the food, which was unusual for me. I stopped writing and looked at the tortilla in my hand. Verlen was right: food was fuel. My pleasure was paddling, and eating merely allowed me to go farther. I stoked another three bites into my mouth, then closed my journal. It was time for sleep. I wasn't tired, but it felt good to rest my arms. Earlier in the journey I would have passed out from fatigue, but by then I was more like a supervisor who wisely closes the circuits for the night. I crawled into my sleeping bag, switched off the flashlight, and fell asleep.

The next day we paddled steadily all morning, one stroke after another. My arms performed the necessary task without my having to think about it. I reached out in front of myself and pulled back, much like a hiker who walks down a trail with arms swinging briskly. But I was hiking sitting down, and my arms were striking water. Each stroke sent a current of bubbles back toward my stern. I looked over at Verlen. He was my mirror image with the same color boat, paddling stroke after stroke, trailing a widening V ripple for yards behind his stern.

The mainland was replete with offshore rocks, and the map charted a reef near our position. We had almost reached Punta San Marcial when the wind came up about 10:30. It was close to lunchtime and Verlen thought we should land south of the point, but I was captain and I saw large wind swells hitting the beach. I took time to study the map.

"We'll land north of the point," I said decisively. "It's early yet, and the wind is going to pick up rather than decrease. The landing here is bad already, and it will be worse when the wind builds up. The sea around the point is going to build. I think it will be best to get around that point as soon as we can and then find shelter. If we land here and the wind continues, we won't make it around the point for another day." Verlen was quiet, so I explained my reasoning. "I want to see what's around that next point. I'd rather not sit and wonder about it while we eat lunch on this side." Verlen still hadn't said a word. "What do you think Verlen?" I prompted, waiting for his approval.

"You're captain," he replied.

"How are you feeling?" I asked.

"Fine." His seeming lack of interest didn't help my confidence, and I began to wonder if I was wrong. Pushing for the extra miles, we paddled around the point. Midway I got more worried about my decision as the rough winds and increased waves of the point surrounded us. Landing would be tough on the north side. I kept paddling and Verlen trailed behind. I thought of all the reasons my decision might be a bad one, and wondered if we should turn around and land to the south, but I kept paddling and tried not to vacillate.

We would have had a wet landing on the north side if we hadn't come upon a small cove that sheltered a safe entry. As soon as we landed, Verlen lay on a tarp, put his straw hat over his eyes, and went to sleep. He acted as if it were natural that I should make decisions and accept a calculated risk, but I didn't see it that way. For me it was a red-letter day—I had graduated to a higher class. I had had doubts whether we could make the landing, and I was overjoyed when we did succeed. I looked at Verlen asleep on the sand. Our experience levels were so different, that what looked like a "piece of cake" to my partner was still a real challenge for me.

After Verlen's nap we loaded the boats and took off. I looked back and saw the point was a riot of white crashing breakers, but our route inside the bay was somewhat sheltered and we were able to continue paddling.

The land curved gently toward Punta Candeleros; I chose a direct route across the bay. From our distance we could see steep cliffs and narrow sand beaches on the mainland, but we were more than a mile away. We reached the point by late afternoon, then followed a stepping-stone path of rock islands to Isla Danzante. Once again we were cutting off miles of paddling by steering a direct route across the outside of the bay, but that time we had rock islands to guide us. We paddled on the protected west side of Isla Danzante only a few feet from the beach. The island looked uninhabited and barren, with only a smattering of low scrubs. At the northwest end of the island we found a suitable camp spot and set up our tents for the night.

Verlen woke me at two A.M. and we launched without taking time for breakfast. The conditions were excellent for a crossing back to the mainland, and we hurried to take advantage of the calm weather. By 2:30 we were packed and ready to paddle for Loreto. Verlen had launched when I got to the water's edge.

"Wait for me," I called, but his canoe had already been swallowed in the blackness. I understood Verlen's new strategy. He had coddled me for the first part of the trip—call it courtesy or necessary precautions, he usually made sure I was launched before taking off himself. He hadn't lost patience, but I got the distinct message that Verlen was pushing me to fend for myself. And now that he wasn't feeling well it seemed logical that I should carry more of the load. But that night was too dark for me to appreciate a lesson in self-sufficiency. I was sure Verlen wouldn't have gone far, but the darkness made me feel as if he had disappeared.

For a moment I felt very vulnerable standing on the beach alone, but Verlen had taught me well and I knew what to do. First, I surveyed the situation. The beach was moderately steep with smooth rocks. My heavy canoe glided easily as I turned it, positioning the bow for take off on the cobblestone beach. When the bow touched the water's edge, I put one foot in the boat and pushed off the rocks with my other foot. Before I could jump in, the canoe skidded into the water as if it were greased and went right out from under me. I was hanging on for dear life, screeching for Verlen and hopping alongside with one leg in and one leg out of the cockpit. As the canoe floated, it tipped dangerously to one side. I was in the water to my waist before I could stop the forward motion of my runaway boat.

"Are you all right?" Verlen's voice came from the darkness. He turned a flashlight toward me.

"Yes, I'm okay, just wait for me. I've got to start over." Browbeating myself for being in too much of a hurry, I waded back to the beach, changed my pants and socks, and tried again. Soon I was paddling off the beach and came up beside Verlen's canoe.

"Miscalculation," I admitted.

"You're doing a good job. But it doesn't pay to get in a hurry."

"Things happen pretty fast out here," I said, reviewing the muffed launching.

For an hour and a half we paddled without saying much. There was no moon, and the night settled in even more darkly. The faint stars reflected in the sea and it was difficult to know where the horizon line was. I felt as if I were paddling on a star-filled sky.

It was easy to get separated from Verlen when we paddled at night. One moment I would see him, then by the time I took a few more paddle strokes my mind wandered and the next thing I knew, I had lost him. I was in the habit of calling out to get my bearings and make sure he was near. He would answer, and just the sound of his voice reassured me that all was well.

"Verlen," I called. No answer. "Verlen." Pause. "Verlen?" No answer. "Verlen, say something. Say something so I know you are there," I called into the night. No answer. "Verlen, I need you to answer. It's like a foghorn, I need to know you are there." In a few moments I heard the response.

"Aaoooggah," Verlen boomed in a low, comic bass. He was only a few canoe lengths behind me, and I turned to see the white bow of his canoe emerging from the darkness.

When the dawn came we found ourselves paddling in a channel between the mainland and Isla Carmen. With land on both sides, it was like floating in a wide river. The bluffs on the mainland turned pink and lavender in the sunrise.

In a few more hours, Loreto came into view—a speck of white against the bright morning sunshine. Inland mountains sloped to a low plane, where the town was built. The land ahead was flat and almost disappeared in the horizon. Dolphins played with our canoes, jumping and snorting as if we were in a race for town. I couldn't get to Loreto fast enough, and dug my paddle into the water with a vengeance.

"The ocean is a highway, Verlen," I remarked, looking at the town up ahead.

"You sound like a full-fledged explorer now," he said. "Think about the time when there were no roads and people arrived at places by the sea." I was enthralled by the idea. "That's why I like the canoe," he continued. "We've got a place in history, the waterways opened up this whole continent."

"If we are on a highway, I sure would like to learn the secret of speeding," I said, paddling even faster.

"You might as well relax. You can't push that canoe past its hull speed," Verlen commented, continuing his slow, steady stroke.

"I have a problem whenever we get close to a town," I admitted.

"Pace yourself," he said. My problem was impatience: even the hint of a town could send my emotions into celebration before the fact, and once I experienced a high it was difficult to buckle down and actually reach the spot. I had to learn to hold back my expectations and keep paddling to the finish. The water got so shallow I could see the bottom.

"Slow down your stroke, Valerie," Verlen suggested. "These canoes don't move well in shallow water, you're just wasting energy."

263

A tumbled rock breakwater came into view. A cement promenade had been built on top of it with light poles fitted at intervals down the walk. When Verlen paddled left into a bay to go around some shallow water, my first instinct was to follow him, but I decided to strike out on my own and chose a shortcut to the right. My shortcut wasn't as deep as I thought, though, and soon I was forced to get out of my canoe and pull my boat over a sandbar. Pelicans squawked and splashed out of my way, and in the shallow water I saw hundreds of small fish swimming away from my feet. My race to get to town was playful competition with Verlen. The farther ahead of me he got, the more frustrated I became, even though I knew he would wait for me before going into town. He reached the breakwater before I did and was just landing when I arrived. As he held onto his bowrope and jumped out of his canoe, the surge from the waves knocked his boat against the cement, and he stuck out his paddle to keep the canoe from beating against the dock. He reconsidered the landing site and waved me farther down the breakwater to a pleasant sandy beach on the other side of a T-shaped jetty. As soon as I pulled my canoe up on the sand, I gave a sigh of pleasure.

Across a pot-holed dirt street was a rambling colonial-style hotel, with a wreath of palm trees shading a fenced patio.

"What do you think, Verlen?" I asked, pointing at the hotel. He climbed out of his canoe and nodded in agreement. It didn't take us long to gather our belongings and head for the welcoming hotel.

"Agua caliente?" was the only question I asked. Once the lady at the desk promised hot water I quickly registered. Happily clutching a room key, I took the staircase two steps at a time. Looking over the banister, I saw a swimming pool with a tiled picture of a marlin set in the bottom and a palm tree growing in a floating island. The place was a spoiler.

It hardly seemed possible that one moment I could be so dirty and frustrated and the next I could be faced with the luxury of a hot shower and clean sheets. On our trip I had learned to take advantage of siestas whenever I got a chance. This hotel was a genuine intermission.

In my room, I peeled off every piece of my dirty clothing. Sand fell from all my pockets. Where the elastic of my pants rubbed on my bare skin, there was a band of sand stuck to my belly. I went into the shower and stood for 10 minutes under the flow of warm water, soaping every part of me until I squeaked and my tan threatened to be scrubbed away. I walked out of the shower dripping, stripped the spread from the bed, and lay on the sheets with a feeling of deep gratitude. I didn't want to move. The afternoon wind came through an open window, but I didn't care what direction it blew. I only knew the breeze was gently touching my body and drying the water I had not toweled off.

Verlen knocked on my door.

"Are you ready?" he asked.

"No."

"We need to resupply here in Loreto, and I hear there is a laundry in town."

"I'll be with you in a minute," I said, spreading out even more comfortably on the bed.

"There is a little shop up the street that sells ice cream," he said, using a sure tactic. The mention of ice cream worked like a key in a lock.

"I'm coming right away," I reported. Jumping up, I dressed in an instant. When I opened the door, I could have been looking in a mirror: my partner was scrubbed and fresh. We had both been transformed by soap and water.

Together we set out to explore Loreto. Our hotel was about a quarter of a mile from the main square, and we walked through dirt streets trying to avoid puddles of water that stretched from one side of the road to the other. The low buildings seemed to be sinking into the ground from the rain received several days before. Loreto had once been the capitol of Baja, until a hurricane destroyed the site. Even now the rebuilt town looked vulnerable, with only the rock wall barrier holding back the sea. Large date palms surrounded a lazy public square, and all the park benches were occupied by elderly men.

Our first stop was the grocery, which turned out to be well stocked. There was even a shopping cart to push, so we walked up and down the aisles filling our basket. I spied a large can of orange juice and took it off the shelf.

"Please open this, Verlen," I asked, handing the can to my partner. He didn't hesitate. We both knelt on the floor and crowded around the treat as Verlen sawed into the lid with his pocket knife. Then we stood in the aisle passing the juice back and forth, drinking long swigs from the can. There was a wide variety of food, including items that we hadn't seen since San Diego. For 1,000 miles we had been looking for a sponge, and there we found a selection of different sizes. We bought batteries, new writing pads, and a bright bandana for me.

When we handed the cashier the empty can of orange juice, she looked at us in surprise.

"Bueno, bueno," I said, assuring her it had been good. "Helado, donde?"

The woman smiled knowingly and pointed to the next street. Verlen and I lugged our groceries in search of the ice cream. We found an open air cafe with a sign in English and a picture of a chocolate malt cut from a magazine. To start, we ordered two each. We didn't leave until we had quaffed a dozen between us.

Our errands used up the afternoon. There was no time for sight-seeing, but Verlen and I didn't mind. Our chores in Loreto were necessary to get us back on the water and paddling north.

Before going to the hotel we walked along the top of the seawall. The afternoon wind was up, and waves kicked at the breakwater and threw spray onto our legs. As I stood at the edge of the barrier watching the sea play its games, the wild wind reminded me of the many days we had tusseled together on the water. That afternoon my hair was clean and free to blow across my face. So many days it had matted and refused to move from my sweaty forehead.

I slowly walked back to the hotel room, where I shut out all the sunshine and wind simply by closing the door. It was like saying good-bye to a friend, but I accepted the bed and lay down. The water, the wind, the sounds, and the light were just outside, but I buried my face in the pillow. A surge came through my body telling me I should be out there, but I covered myself with a sheet and prayed for rest.

Verlen didn't wake me at midnight as we had planned. When I did open my eyes, it was morning and I knew something was wrong. I found Verlen in his room, pale and weak, doubled over with his familiar complaint of stomach cramps and diarrhea.

"You're going to a doctor," I said. "There has got to be one here in town."

"You're right," he said, finally giving in.

"We're going to get this taken care of right away," I emphasized. "You are so doggone positive that sometimes you're not very realistic." I walked down to the front desk and asked for a cab.

While we drove to the clinic I marveled at our good fortune. Though Verlen had been suffering for some time from recurring intestinal problems, I knew it was a blessing that we were now close to medical help.

At the clinic, a dozen people sat in line. There was no receptionist asking our names, no paperwork to fill out—only a friendly young doctor in a white coat diligently processing complaints.

Every time the doctor came to the main room to call another patient, he looked curiously at Verlen and me, since we were the only Americans waiting in line. Finally it was our turn, and we were ushered into a small white room. Verlen sat on the examining table, his compass hanging around his neck on a string. He still clutched his map case. I held the Spanish-English dictionary and the doctor folded his arms across his chest, awaiting our story.

It was a relief to see that many of the tools on the desk were familiar. The doctor started his examination with a thermometer. Verlen obediently opened his mouth, but the doctor picked up Verlen's wrist and put the thermometer under his armpit, then gestured to indicate that Verlen should

266

press his arm against the instrument to hold it in place. The doctor then proceeded to poke Verlen's abdomen, chest, stomach, and back. I leafed through the dictionary, pronouncing descriptive Spanish words for Verlen's ailment.

Verlen pantomimed his symptoms. All the while, the doctor nodded his head in agreement and said many words we did not understand. After a few moments, he took out a pad of paper and scribbled a prescription, then handed it to Verlen with a smile, as if to indicate the operation had been a success. He shook hands, and helped Verlen down from the examination table. The cost was 300 pesos ($1.75).

As we walked back to the hotel I started to worry.

"Verlen, you aren't going to take that medicine are you?"

"Sure I am."

"But, we don't even know what it is?" I said incredulously.

"I think he understood," Verlen said. "Maybe we can knock this bug out of me now."

"That would be nice." I was skeptical. "Do you want to rest for a few days?"

"No, I'm ready to leave."

"You can't be serious."

"I feel better already," Verlen said with a smile.

We stopped at the farmacia on the square and watched while a man measured powder into capsules and handed Verlen two mysterious bottles. One was marked Buscapiua Grageas una caja and the other coded Peutroxyl (Ampiciliua) 500 mg.

Being sick didn't hurt Verlen's appetite. We stopped at the outdoor cafe and he washed down his first dose of medicine with a chocolate milk shake. Then he loaded up his stomach with four quesadillas and three tortas.

"You'd better eat well," he explained. "We've got 796 miles to go."

"Do you think we can make it?" Verlen took one more sip of shake.

"Not if we're sitting here. Come on."

As we walked back to the hotel I looked up at the tops of the date palms. The high trees were waving back and forth—the wind had started. We hurried to get ready. It didn't take long to pack my gear, but my clothes seemed to require more room now that they were clean. The dousing at the laundry had fluffed them so that it was difficult to stuff and seal my waterproof bag. When I ran down the steps to join Verlen at the check-out desk, the palm in the middle of the swimming pool was bending and an air mattress sped from one side of the pool to the other. Wind streaks blurred the water and the colorful tile marlin on the bottom was obscured.

By the time we reached the canoes, the sea was whitecapped and unfriendly. We were used to head winds, but that wind was building into a riot. We decided to wait, but neither of us wanted to go back to the hotel and distance ourselves from the sea. We wanted to be ready to leave as soon as the wind wore itself out. Under the navigation light at the end of the beach where our canoes had been parked was an ideal spot to watch the conditions. We made a temporary camp, erecting a tent as a sun shelter. The fabric snapped and furled as we set the tent in place. Verlen finally got a chance to sleep, which gave his body time to adjust to the new medicine. I used the time to write letters home, glancing up from my writing to watch the chop and froth of the waves. I had learned to tell the severity of the wind by the distance the white tops of the waves rolled on the surface before disappearing. I counted six seconds of travel time for the whitecaps I could see. I didn't know how my observations translated into wind speed, but I knew the water was rough.

At dusk, the wind decreased. Our tents gradually stopped blowing and sagged in the calm and the flag at the end of the jetty hung limp. It would be hours before the waves completely settled, but the tension had been released and I could feel the sea relaxing.

We catamaraned the canoes, attached our spray skirts, and shoved off the beach. It was almost dark, and a navigation light signaled to us from Isla Coronados. In the next hour, the moon came up like a friendly beacon. Slowly, the waves diminished.

By midnight we no longer had to devote all our attention to staying upright, and our steady, mechanical paddling began to lull us to sleep. When my head fell forward with a nod, I jerked it back and tried to hold my eyes open. My paddling had become a steady rocking-chair motion: bending at the waist, I let the sheer momentum of my leaden shoulders keep me moving. Then Verlen's rudder flipped up from the water and plumped back with a thud.

"What was that, Verlen?" I asked, startled by the sound. I looked at the stern of his boat. The sound had not disturbed him, but my question nudged him awake.

"Must have hit a rock or something," he said, only slightly interested. In the next moment my paddle slapped a fish—I could feel the blade contacting a firm, moving body. As I followed through with my stroke, I pushed the fish into my wake. Fish were all around us, many of them jumping. In the darkness we saw flashing shadows and heard the water splash and open as if taking a breath. All of a sudden, a fish jumped up and, miscalculating reentry, flipped right into Verlen's boat. Verlen was steady, but I shrieked.

"I'd feel sorry for this fish if he landed in your boat," Verlen said. Patiently, he picked up the unexpected visitor and examined him with a flashlight. I patted my protective spray cover and clinched the zipper tighter around my waist.

"This fish will have quite a story to tell when it gets back home," he said, slipping the fish back into the water.

My body fed on adrenaline from the fish surprise until about 2:30 in the morning. I needed sleep, but we kept paddling. The moon disappeared at four o'clock, and I lost the struggle to keep my eyes open once it was too dark to see anything. My arms kept moving, offering only a token intrusion into the water.

It was the sound of a small outboard motor that chased away my drowsiness. I jogged awake and stopped paddling to search in my bag for a flashlight.

"That's not necessary," Verlen said, paddling calmly. "They won't hit us." The motor got louder.

"I don't want to be run over," I said. Finding my light, I snapped it on and waved the beam into the darkness. We heard muffled voices speaking Spanish. Then the oncoming boat swerved and motored away in another direction.

A drink of water roused me slightly, and I shook my head to convince myself I was awake. Then I heard a coyote. Its howl echoed off the hills and traveled out over the sea. The ocean had a voice—I had heard its roar often—but this coyote, barking, yapping, and howling at the stars was the voice of Baja, of the desert incarnate.

We were still paddling at dawn, and I watched the sunrise illuminate the high, rocky cliffs of shore. The land looked compacted in gigantic stone stacks. Fissures and snags made nesting places for small birds, and the air was wild with swooping dive bombers hunting for breakfast. I thought I was seeing things when a bird with blue feet flew by.

"Verlen, I really do need to stop and rest," I explained. "The last bird I saw had blue feet."

"You're okay. That's the blue-footed booby. It's real," he said, assuring me. "I've read about these birds and have been waiting to see one." He grabbed for his camera.

I was fully awake by then, and intent on finding new sights. On a high pinnacle of rock a large osprey nest hung above the sea, its lone occupant sitting stoically atop the cluster of sticks. I hoped the bird would not mistake our boats for edible fish. I concentrated so hard on identifying new birds that I almost ran into a spiny rock outcrop. I pointed out the danger to Verlen.

"Verlen, do you see that rock?"

"Oh, you mean those pelicans?"

"No, I mean that big rock."

"Oh, you mean that big pelican?"

"No, I mean those giant rocks."

"Oh, you mean those giant pelicans?"

"If you have enough energy to tease, that medicine must be working just fine. I'm going to stop feeling sorry for you and I'll keep quiet about my next bird sightings too," I threatened.

A high wall of land blocked our view on the mainland side, but the water spread out to Mexico on our right. Ahead were approximately 700 miles, and we had 21 days left. I squinted my eyes and tried to see the finish.

NINETEEN

Hurry Up and Wait

Portions of our journey had so overwhelmed me that much of my observation had focused on an inner landscape of adjustment. The environment we paddled in was a constant backdrop for my own thoughts—sometimes even a distraction from my own narrow capabilities. But as the trip became my life, I was changed by the expedition process and, more than ever, reached out to the world around me.

Baja was omnipresent: the peninsula did not disappear even when I closed my eyes at night. All the times I had wanted to quit were past. The Baja had seduced me—even if I had wanted to leave, if my spirit failed or my body became incapacitated, I believed the Baja would intercede to keep me. Cacti appeared like sentinels, blocking all ways of escape.

For all of its strength and presence, the land was vulnerable and easily defaced. Markings in this wilderness were predominantly white: the white mark of surf noted the exact line of land, white lime deposits marked the roosting perchs for the marine birds. Even our canoes had left some of their white finish on the rocks as we pulled the boats to shore. If the land was a blackboard, the surf, birds, and canoes were busy chalking graffiti.

It was just past noon on January 19th when we paddled into the south entrance of Caleta San Juanico. Outlying rocks clustered offshore and barricaded our way. As we paddled farther right to skirt the obstructions, we could see a blue fabric kayak resting on a rocky embankment. When we got closer, we saw two young men snorkeling in the clear water. Their heads popped up and they looked at us through the windows of their face masks. One of the men jerked the mouthpiece of his snorkel away from his lips.

"You're Verlen Kruger," he cried. With a few sure strokes, he reached a rocky ledge, climbed out of the water, grabbed for the bow of Verlen's canoe, and surfaced beside me with a grin. These human porpoises were bubbling with excitement.

"My name is Don Ford," the man beside me said. "We've wondered if we would see you. We've been following your big trip." If he'd had a cap I think he would have tipped it toward me. Instead, he took off his face mask and pushed a thick mass of wet hair away from his forehead. Saltwater beaded on their tanned, muscled shoulders. Diving gear, spear guns, and water jugs sat on the rocks.

"I'm Frank," the other man said. "We're from a school for outdoor leadership in Bahia Concepción. The past week a group of us has traveled on the coast. Our camp is across the bay," he said, motioning toward the peninsula.

"We heard you were coming," Don explained. "We've been looking for you."

"Where did you start from today?" Frank asked.

"By the time we reach that next point," I said, looking up ahead, "we'll have come 35 miles since midnight."

"Wow," Don said. "That's incredible. Our group takes two weeks to cover a 50-mile area."

"We don't paddle very fast because there are so many of us and we take time for fishing and snorkeling," Frank explained.

"And a lot of waiting on the wind," Don added.

"We know all about the wind," Verlen explained. "That's why we paddle at night. We can't take time to live off the land or eat from the sea. Because of all the storms this season we're behind schedule for an appointment in Yuma. That means we have to paddle pretty hard to get there."

"Do you get the feeling you're moving too fast to see everything?" Don asked.

"No," Verlen said emphatically. "We're seeing *more* of everything. In a canoe you can't move too fast, that's the nature of the beast. The speed we are traveling carries its own enjoyment. Sure, we've got a forced time limit, but that adds an excitement of its own. We have to reach Yuma by February 8th."

"How long have you been out?" Don asked.

"Almost 2½ years for me now," Verlen said slowly.

"I joined Verlen at Long Beach in October," I explained. "That makes 2½ months for me."

"And our group is trying to cram a wilderness experience into two weeks. It just seems too short," Don stated.

"A wilderness experience can happen in a moment," I mused. "It's like falling in love. I think it has to do with how receptive you are."

"Yes, that's the key—response," Verlen said. He paused. The four of us looked at each other and seemed to take a breath in unison. I was a little startled by the seriousness of our conversation, but there was no need for small talk. It had been the same with the two Americans in Ignacio Lagoon. After paddling for almost three months, we didn't have any pretense left. When a person lives in the wilderness, the appetite gets bigger, the body gets stronger, and the conversation more candid. The sea around us and the yellow rock formations were overpowered by the blue midday sky and the great outdoors.

"Well, I guess we'd better get along," Verlen said. "I'd like to make Mulege by tomorrow noon."

"It's been a real pleasure meeting you," I said.

"Same here," Don and Frank agreed. Smiling from ear to ear, we paddled alongside the rock to shake hands once again. Then we paddled away. I had to work hard to keep up with Verlen.

"Hey," I yelled. "Slow up a minute. We should have invited them to share lunch with us."

"You're right, that would have been a good idea. Too bad you didn't think of it sooner," Verlen said, paddling steadily.

"Verlen, let's go back, maybe we can still have lunch?" I implored.

"It's not very practical but..." Verlen looked over his shoulder. Don and Frank were heading toward us in the blue boat. We heard them shout and their double kayak blades beat the water with the force of a windmill.

"You need to have lunch with our group!" Frank enjoined. The two caught up with us just in time to turn us into the bay to visit their camp. Verlen and I were delighted to be chased down and intercepted. We paddled together into the cove of a sheltered anchorage, where the group of students stood clustered on the beach.

"Look what we've got," Don yelled, as if he were proudly displaying a fair catch. We came ashore on a beautiful sand beach with clear blue water sparkling in a languid cove. The students were a college-age group from Minneapolis. All seemed pleased to meet us and eager to examine our boats.

"You've got to stay for lunch," one girl exclaimed. "We've got plenty of fish." We readily accepted their offer, but Verlen couldn't be outdone. He scrounged in his canoe and brought out his own cook kit to prepare a side dish of macaroni and powdered cheese for everyone to sample.

The students were an appealing, diverse group, no two alike. One boy with red hair was dressed from ankle to head in army fatigues to keep the sun off. The others were clothed in cutoffs, halter tops, and T-shirts advertising everything from Hawaii to Grand Opera. One thing was consistent—there was not a pair of shoes in the bunch. Verlen and I were impressed by their spirit and enthusiasm. The average person does not appear on the beach in Baja with a snorkel and backpack.

"Tell us about your trip," one boy in wire-rimmed spectacles asked. Verlen explained our schedule of traveling at night and shared some of the highlights of our trip.

"This Sea of Cortez is beautiful, but we've had a rough time with the wind. Now, the Pacific side—that's a different story. The ocean is not canoe country. I wouldn't recommend it to anyone. It's just too dangerous."

"Hey, you didn't tell me that," I piped up.

"You don't think I would have told you that *before* we started do you?" Verlen quipped. Everyone laughed, but I couldn't help feeling a little nervous even though the Pacific was far behind me.

It was an interesting stop for Verlen and me: the students distilled our adventure and handed it back to us by the look in their eyes. I soaked up the compliments like a sponge, but Verlen sat, wise as an owl, returning the gift in the form of encouragement to the group.

"If I had any regrets," he said, "it would be not having done anything before in a group like you are doing." Verlen pushed the brim of his cap back from his forehead and forgot about his plate of food cooling in his lap.

"I don't regret being poor and I don't regret my limited education. I came from a sharecropper family, so poor we had to move every year to even find a place to stay. I never got the chance to be introduced to the potential of the outdoors until I was past 40—I didn't even get into a canoe until I was past 40. But an introduction is enough to stir a spark if there is one there." The group looked intently at Verlen and he smiled.

"The outdoors gives a different perspective on values. Values of enjoying nature and of being a friend and working together as a team. Helping someone with no thought of payment. Helping because you need one another." The group nodded in agreement.

"There are people who think life owes them a living. Get them out in the wilderness with a group and put them in a situation where they need one another, and a big change will occur." Verlen looked at everyone in the group.

"You are important to the group. If you don't function you lose and others lose also. Like carrying a canoe—you are needed to hold up your end. If I don't carry my share, someone else is hurting. The wilderness helps you learn that."

"If you don't eat your share, someone else will eat it for you," I laughed, pushing my fork into Verlen's plate. "The wilderness has taught me that, too." Verlen looked down at his plate, as if surprised that it was there, picked up his fork, and started eating.

"This *is* a beautiful place," one of the girls in the group said. "But I was snorkeling today and there was an apple core floating in the sea from that sailboat over there." She looked angrily at the boat that was moored at the far end of the inlet. "I almost knocked on the hull and threw it at them. The sight of that apple core floating in this paradise turned my stomach." I wondered what the sight of a dead sea lion would do to her, and I figured she would dissolve if she happened upon José's littered arroyo. Her dismay was understandable, but the issue was more complicated than she realized. The small community the group had created on the beach worked fine with everyone disposing items in garbage bags, but other problems would have arisen if they had stayed for longer than two weeks.

"This is such a delicate ecosystem," the girl went on, gesturing toward the sea. Behind her rose a large rocky hillside, completely overpowering her small frame.

I didn't know if I would call the ocean or the Baja delicate, but I was proud of her spirit and sense of protectiveness. I realized that the group's experience and class studies had given them a perspective of the ocean and the world totally different from the one where Verlen and I had lived for the past months.

"How long do you paddle?" another girl asked.

"Well, we stay out all night at times," I explained.

"How long will it take you to get to Mulege?"

"We'll be there tomorrow," I hope. Verlen kept quiet and finished his lunch. Too soon, I could tell he was ready to leave. The sun was shining and the wind hadn't started to blow. The students stood together on shore, all of them encouraging and sending us on our way. One gave the thumbs-up sign of victory, and many of them waved. The man in army fatigues applauded, one fellow flashed the high-sign, and everyone smiled.

Verlen and I paddled out of the bay with renewed purpose. The audience had a strange effect on me. I had been wondering what would happen to me after the journey, and that group told me that what I was doing was important not just to me, but for them.

The man at the New Year's Eve party in Cabo had been the first person who had told me that, but I felt more inclined to believe these students. They had sounded sincere.

"It's going to be a long night," Verlen said.

"What do you mean?"

"It's a long way to Mulege."

"We can stop and rest," I reminded him.

275

"Didn't you tell them you wanted to be in Mulege tomorrow?" Verlen asked.

"Well, it would be nice, but we don't have to," I said, feeling slightly guilty.

"We have to," Verlen said. "We are going to do exactly what you said we were going to do."

"You're right, Verlen. This adventure is big enough without inflating it." I was trapped.

The open mouth of Bahía de San Basilio lay between Punta San Basilio and Punta Pulpito. We chose our usual strategy of cutting across the open bay, but soon had to vary our direction once the wind started and we had to decide just how far to compensate for the blow. I took to the inside and Verlen strayed farther out until I could hardly see him. He allowed for the wind drift perfectly, his years of experience helping to tell him exactly the angle to approach the point. I still wanted to trust my senses and couldn't fully accept the idea of pointing away from an object I was headed for. I ended up too far to the inside of the point and had to paddle back out to clear the headland.

Verlen waited for me at the point, and when I caught up with him he was clicking photos of sea lions sleeping in the rock ledges of Pulpito. The sea lions lounged in wedges of shelter just above the surge, sleeping on top of one another. A couple of them propped up on their flippers, looking at us with big brown eyes, but most of them barely grunted as we paddled past their rookery. The point was a rocky knob projecting from the mainland. On the map it looked like a piece of jigsaw puzzle—the connecting piece had broken away and disappeared or had never been there at all.

We had been paddling for 14 hours, not counting our lunch break. The next major point of land was 16 miles away, and it was four o'clock in the afternoon. I wanted to rest. As we were debating our plan, the wind stirred up. There had been mixed winds from different directions playing on the water, but we felt a distinct south wind, the first southerly breeze in 19 days. This wind wasn't threatening, but urged us on in our decision to paddle all night. Just as the sun went down we hooked up the canoes, arranged our night provisions, and kept paddling. The south wind gave a welcome push in our desired direction.

Verlen paddled as if he were possessed.

"I want to help you set a new record for miles in a day," he explained. I sighed patiently and kept paddling. After dark the wind stopped abruptly and we slowed down. We had paddled 19 hours by then, and I began to hallucinate. I saw things glowing and hanging onto the connector poles. A squadron of pelicans flew a few inches from the surface in the dark, and I could hear their wings cutting through the air as they glided past. Their swooping black shadows haunted me until I realized they were real and simply out for a night fishing maneuver. I had a stern talk with myself. I was different now, I insisted. Highly motivated. Mulege or bust! I thought of all the changes that had been happening to me, then closed my eyes and continued paddling.

An hour later I'd had enough.

"Verlen, we've got to sleep sometime, why not take a break now?"

"We don't have to stop, needing rest is all in your mind," he said, paddling in a mechanical trance. A few moments later I tried another angle.

"Verlen, we've got to stop. I have to go to the bathroom."

"You don't have to go to the bathroom. It's all in your mind," he said, paddling on. He was a fiend.

By 11 we arrived at the next point. Verlen set his paddle down across the cockpit and looked for something to eat in his food bag. I used the short break to crawl down inside my spray cover and sleep for a few minutes. When Verlen insisted on continuing, I offered a modified plan.

"At least let's unhook the canoes. The wind has stopped and there is no advantage being hooked. I can paddle better when we're separated," I said, wanting to distance myself from his authority.

"I don't think you'll keep up. We would be hooking up again soon, and it isn't worth the effort." He knew all my tricks.

It was a dark night, but I could see the outline of land as a mass of concentrated lightning brightened the northern sky. Verlen drank a can of pop and continued paddling strongly. We had 21 hours of paddling behind us and 31 miles left to Mulege.

"Let's take a break," I suggested again.

"You are captain at midnight. If you want, we can stop at that time, but while I'm still captain, we'll keep moving," he said firmly.

I looked at my watch: there was less than an hour to wait. When midnight came, I called a halt and directed us to shore at a point past Punta Rosalia, not named on our charts. A flashing light was visible and we stopped paddling and listened for a landing place in the dark. The sound of surf on the shore warned of rocks. The waves did not lap as they would on a smooth sand beach, but jumped and bounced in the dark. When we shone our light toward the beach, we saw a bank of rocks that confirmed that our entry would be rough.

By then even Verlen was tired and agreed we needed to rest, so we carefully negotiated a landing. The beach had been pushed by the sea so that the stones were mounded together in a steep ridge, and as we pulled the canoes up and over the pyramid of stones our canoes balanced on the pivot point, with the stern hanging in midair.

We planned to sleep in the boats for a few hours and then go on. I cozied down immediately inside mine, pushing gear aside with my feet. I was halfway comfortable when Verlen interrupted me.

"We should turn the boats around," he suggested. I didn't want to cooperate—sleep was my main concern.

"Let's unhook them and pull them up to flat ground," he insisted. I climbed out of my canoe and helped pull the boats to more stable ground, then got back in and squirmed into my sleep position. Verlen was still making a production of his arrangements. I was already under my spray cover for warmth, but I could hear him moving around. When I popped my head out of my cockpit, I saw that he had taken the seat clear out of his canoe and was mopping the bottom with a sponge. He unloaded the bow to make room for his body, then pulled out his tent bag and sorted through gear looking for his mattress.

"Have you got my sleeping bag?" he asked.

"Do you realize that with all this time spent we could have more easily put up the tents?" I asked him. By the time Verlen was finally comfortable, I was wide awake and painfully aware that my seat was on a slant, sticking me in the ribs. If Verlen was going to be snug as a bug, I was too. I got out of my canoe, clumping and sputtering, put up my tent, crawled clothes and all into my sleeping bag, and began to relax. The last thing I remember was how good it felt to straighten out my aching back.

We got too comfortable: what was supposed to be a two-hour break turned into several hours of rest. When we woke, the waves on the rocks were small dumpers and we could feel the wind. Verlen was already on the water when I pulled my canoe down the steep bank. My bow sat in the water and the stern hung on the rocky beach, the midsection bridged off the ground. I knew my canoe was in a precarious position, but I was faced with a dilemma. Turning the boat sideways on the beach would not work for a launch because of the continuous dump of surf. I had to take a risk. I cleared a small channel under my canoe by removing the larger rocks on the steep bank, then carefully settled into my boat and pushed off with my paddle. My takeoff worked fine, but sand jammed under my rudder assembly and wouldn't let the blade drop. And, worst of all, my seat was still cockeyed from the night before. With the adjustable seat misaligned, the boat leaned dangerously toward the right.

There were rocks on my left, so I pushed down hard with my right foot, expecting a right rudder response, while I made strong, sweeping strokes on the left. But I was still going straight for the rocks. Sweeping frantically, the boat moved even faster in the direction I didn't want to go and crashed directly into the rocks, stopping with a dead thud. My heart was pounding. Verlen was miraculously beside me, balancing my boat and pulling my bow off the rocks as the waves jumped into my cockpit. Leaning forward, I reached back to correct my seat.

"I panicked Verlen," I admitted. As I straightened, Verlen took his bailer and emptied the water from my cockpit.

"You've got to use your control center," he said, pointing to my head. "You should have stopped paddling or back-paddled. Your panic is what pushed a little problem into a big problem"

"Do you ever panic, Verlen?" I wondered.

"Everyone has fears. I wouldn't want to be out here with someone who wasn't afraid. Just don't exercise your fears. What you exercise will dominate. Exercise the control center in your brain and you won't panic so easily."

"That's what I came here for—a brain," I reminded him.

"You're learning," Verlen soothed. "I probably would have wet my pants on that launching," he admitted.

"Thanks, Verlen, at least I didn't do that!"

As we paddled around the point in silence, large swells greeted us. These were big rollers, the likes of which we hadn't seen since the Pacific. The signs of weather were not yet in the sky, but could be read in the action of the swells: the waves were almost breaking.

"A big wind is causing these swells," Verlen predicted. "The size of these rollers means a blow is going on somewhere. If a wind does hit these waves, it will take only a few minutes to stir things up."

We paddled close to shore to be in a position for fast escape, still trying to make as much distance as possible. When the wind did hit, at midmorning, we were forced ashore on a crescent pebble beach behind a rocky point. We sat in the sun watching the wind work the ocean into a lather.

"We won't make Yuma at this rate," Verlen said. "Maybe we should call Wayne Marsula at the next phone and tell him to pick us up at San Felipe?"

I didn't say a word. Whitecaps rolled for yards before disappearing. For all our efforts, the wind had stranded us 20 miles from Mulege.

The next day we were moving again. Paddling around Punta Concepción, we ignored Bahía Santa Ines to the north and turned due west, aiming the canoes toward Mulege. My map showed a deep sheltered bay to the south, separated from the sea by a mountainous peninsula with peaks rising 2000 feet. It had taken us all morning to travel the outside coast of the rocky peninsula, so we had no time to loop inside and explore the 25-mile reach of the popular bay.

Our destination, one of the oldest continuously occupied settlements in Baja, was a patch of green set against the barren hills. The Santa Rosalia river broke through the hills and formed a narrow lagoon that opens into the gulf. As we paddled closer, I saw the lighthouse on El Sombrerito. This entrance spit of land protecting the lagoon from the sea was true to its name, rising like a Mexican sombrero from the water.

We entered the river channel and paddled up a lazy stream into a tropical oasis of palm trees and flowering shrubs, a scene that seemed unreal compared to the desert surroundings. We parked our boats on the river bank and walked into town on a dusty one-lane street.

The intersection of Highway 1 seemed to be the center of activity in town. Motorcycles, trailers, pickups, dusty campers, and vans with surfboards all merged at a wide spot in the road. A truck burdened with a bellowing steer strapped in the back was pulled over with its hood up. On the opposite side of the road an old man was hawking tomatoes from the open trunk of his beat-up car. A wrecker wheeled to a stop with an uprooted cactus harnessed in the tow strap.

There were two restaurants to choose from, competing on either side of the street. We passed up the purple one and chose the one painted green. The walls inside were the same color. The print tablecloths looked cheerful, but the one covering our table was sticky with food from the previous dinner guest and stuck to my elbows when I sat down. Each chair was broken in a different place. Verlen rocked his from left to right on the uneven floor, and my chair creaked as if it begrudged my weight and might dump me any moment. A bicycle leaned in the corner against an icebox and a mop and pail sat beside the window. A small altar decorated with plastic carnations and melting candles was directly across from me. The kitchen was hidden behind a fingerprint-smeared swinging door. We changed our minds about dinner and just ordered pop with no ice. We drank out of the bottle, refusing the water-spotted glass, then headed back into town to search for a grocery.

We found a well-stocked tienda and selected a pile of food to take to the check-out.

"Helado?" I asked.

"Sí," the woman at the desk said, pointing toward a freezer at the back of the shop.

Inside the deep freeze was a carton of half-melted ice cream and a scoop. Plastic cups sat on a nearby shelf. I helped myself to a large serving and we both walked back through the check-out counter transfixed. Verlen was right behind me with a scoop just as big.

Carrying our groceries, Verlen and I walked back to the boats and paddled down river to Skipper's Boat Landing. We set up our tents on a dock near the mouth of the river and fell asleep soon after the sun went down.

When Verlen woke me at 2:30, the thought of the 50 miles ahead to

Santa Rosalia sent me burrowing into my sleeping bag, pleading for more time. I closed my eyes again but a persistent dock light shone through the thin fabric of my tent and lit my sleeping space as if it were morning. Verlen was already packing his gear.

I crawled out of my tent yawning and walked to the edge of the dock to look at the water. Usually the sea looks bright and reflective against a dark night, but that early morning the artificial dock light blackened the water and the space beyond looked impenetrable. Moving like a sleepwalker, I loaded my boat and climbed into my canoe by force of habit. I wondered if I was still dreaming.

The navigation light at El Sombrerito guided us into Bahía Santa Ines. There were so many lights on shore that it was difficult to fix the exact location of Punta Santa Ines. We used our compass and headed due north. Swells rolled into the bay from the northeast and a heavy offshore wind swept the bay from the west. An unsettling two-way chop resulted until daylight, when the wind swung northwest and herded the swells in its own direction.

We worked for every one of our miles that morning and came ashore at Punta Santa Ines tense and hungry. A deserted motel sat on the hill above the beach, many of its windows broken and some of them boarded. Verlen and I walked up a set of stone steps to explore. Several trailers were parked in a wide space of sand next to the building, and when we looked into one of the rooms we saw six Americans making use of the facilities, sitting at a card table drinking pop and playing cards.

"Hi," I said, waving in the open window.

"Shall we deal you in?" one of the women asked cheerfully.

"No, don't let us disturb you. We're just stopping on the beach," Verlen explained. We walked back to the beach and sat in the hollowed dent at the bottom of a sandhill. Protected from the wind, I busied myself cooking breakfast, while Verlen bent over the map with his compass and pencil. I looked up and saw a man, woman, and dachshund coming down the beach. At first I thought they were out for a stroll, but realized they were headed our way.

The man was the leader of their investigation. He had a camera around his neck and walked purposefully, his shoulders braced against the wind, plowing with sure steps through the deep sand. Half a pace behind came the woman. She couldn't walk as fast as the man and seemed to rely on him pulling her along. The dog was low in the middle and had a terrible time traveling, dragging its stomach in the sand with every step of his short, stubby feet.

"Could I take your photo?" the man asked when he got close enough to be heard.

"Sure, it's okay with us," Verlen said, looking at me for confirmation. We both looked up and smiled.

"No, I want a pose," the man explained. "This picture has to be just right. Could you sit on your canoes over here?"

We did just as he asked.

"That's good. Now move your arm a little to the left," he said to me, guiding my arm into position. "Could you cross your legs at the knee? Good. Now, just relax and look natural. Look as if you're having a good time."

I felt like a mannequin. He took so long adjusting his camera that my smile froze on my mouth. To him we were a curiosity, something to tell the folks back home about. He didn't ask any questions, and I wondered if he understood what we were doing.

"Would you like one of my fact sheets?" I asked.

"Sure, that would be wonderful . . . " he accepted the sheet of written description I had printed three months earlier. The woman looked over his shoulder and he began to read aloud.

"Complete circumnavigation of the Baja Peninsula, 2,411 miles of salt water beginning at Long Beach, California . . . to paddle 2,411 miles I believe you have to want to. . . . My whole being is focused and determined to finish the distance and experience this Baja journey. . . . The why is becoming clearer with each paddle stroke—closer in touch with my womanhood, my spirit, my mind and body, my God and His World. . . . "

I sat in the sand, listening to the words and hearing them as if for the first time.

"Verlen, we've got to make it to Yuma," I said positively.

"Is this you?" the man interrupted excitedly.

"We can if you want to badly enough," Verlen answered me. "You'll have to make friends with the wind and bust your butt paddling."

"Could I take one more picture?" The man was awestruck. I looked at Verlen and then I looked at the sea.

"Just smile." Click. "Thank you very much," the man said, backing away. He put his arm around the woman and firmly pulled on the dachshund's leash. The trio slogged through the sand toward the vacant resort, the dog leaving a flat brushed trail in the sand all the way up the hill.

Verlen and I ate two pots of food, repacked our boats, and pushed off the beach. Paddling toward Punta Chivato, we made a sharp turn west, following the coast. As soon as we were beyond the protection of the point, the north wind hit with a vengeance, blowing steadily. My canoe bobbed like a cork in the mounting swells, and I swung the paddle high on each return to avoid slapping the oncoming waves and splashing water on myself. My glasses were already wet and streaked with salt. I had no opportunity to clean them, because as soon as I put my paddle down my canoe was weather-vaned sideways and pushed backwards. When I rested the paddle across the cockpit, even for a moment, the wind caught the blade in a twirl, rolling the shaft on the cockpit rim. The heavy-ended blade dipped overboard, and I grabbed to save it.

It was going to take a lot more than being friendly to keep moving against the wind, and giving all my effort wasn't helping much either. We needed a strategy. The offshore island of San Marcos presented a special advantage since its west side would be protected from the northeast wind. Crossing to the island made sense—the southwest tip was hardly out of our way and the lee side of the island would be calm enough to keep paddling.

The crossing was rough, and every stroke counted. Verlen and I didn't talk but stayed busy paddling. He didn't offer to hook up, and I didn't ask. It was the biggest water I'd been in as a single. I kept paddling and put the possibility of rolling over out of my mind—like a window-washer who refuses to look down.

Even before we reached the island, it began to protect us from the wind. The sea calmed a quarter of a mile from shore as the high island hills blocked the air currents. As we paddled closer, I noticed the hills were not solid but had been ripped and gouged. At first I thought it was natural erosion, but then I realized that excavation had scarred the terrain—the island was a gypsum mine.

Several miles north, we spotted a loading dock jutting into the sea and pulled ashore on a beach far removed from the wilderness. The sand was pressed and marked with the tracks of earth movers, dock lights and powerlines. We had landed in a company town. The houses were set close together and loud sirens blasted to tell the time. A work launch arrived just as the sun went down, with Chinese bosses directing the Mexican workers in unloading cargo from the boat. From the way the supervisor looked at Verlen and me while we were putting up our tents, I wondered if we were going to be conscripted. But he didn't say a word.

Before dawn we were awakened by a loud airhorn signaling the beginning of another shift. It was the morning of January 23rd, and the wind had died down during the night. We packed and climbed into the canoes as if we too were answering the call of another work day.

We crossed the open water back to the mainland, heading for Santa Rosalia, and were caught once again in a heavy wind coming from the north. After seven hours of hard paddling against the wind, the sight of town was a welcome relief. Santa Rosalia had no natural harbor, but an artificial boxed harbor had been constructed of slag and waste from an adjacent copper mine operation. The rough sea was held back very effectively within the breakwater, but even inside it there were whitecaps on the water from the wind.

Verlen and I paddled through the channel opening and were grateful to find the wind's force partially blocked within the rectangular enclosure. Many others had also taken advantage of the protection, and navigation buoys tried to keep the peace between fishermen, ferry service, and industrial transport, all coexisting behind the breakwater. The beach was a narrow sidewalk of sand that totally disappeared in places where trucks and supply sheds congested the harbor.

A small fleet of fishing boats motored into the opening behind us and tied next to one another near the customshouse. Gathering armloads of nets from their boats, the fishermen sloshed ashore on a partially submerged wooden pier. Verlen and I were still looking for a place to land when a fishing boat pulled up beside us.

"Mucho mal olas," a fisherman called out, reporting the rough conditions of the sea. His eyes were shaded by a moth-eaten fur hat and his large body was covered in a yellow rubberized rainsuit. He shut off the motor and glided his boat between two other fishing boats, squeezing into the already crowded space.

As the boats shifted position, we saw a small patch of sand between a supply shed and a broken truck. There was room enough for only one tent and the bows of our canoes; the stern ends floated in the water at the edge of the small landing.

Stepping out from behind the truck, a little boy and girl looked at us curiously. The way her grubby hand held tightly to his, I assumed they were brother and sister. The boy was about five years old and swaggered toward our camp spot as if he owned the place. A shapeless T-shirt hung almost to his knees, his face was dirty, and his bare feet stuck out from beneath a pair of stained blue jeans. His little sister was barely out of the toddler stage and appeared to be at the mercy of her big brother's baby-sitting techniques.

The boy was fascinated with my boat and he touched everything that moved, popping the elastic shock cords and pulling the strings on my spare paddle tie. He was just the kind of child who wouldn't be still even if someone sat on him.

Verlen sat on a tarp and pulled his map out of the plastic case. He was quiet for a quarter of an hour and then looked up.

"We've got to face our problem," he said. "There are 380 miles to go and only 13 days left. That averages 30 miles a day, and I don't know if it's possible to finish the distance with the wind stopping us so regularly."

"How are you going to make your plane?" I asked.

"Wayne could pick us up here in the Baja. In fact, I should call him and have him standing by to pick us up at San Felipe. Then, when I come back after Chicago, I would just put back in at San Felipe and continue paddling from there."

"It's not so easy for me, Verlen. I can't wait at San Felipe for you to get back, and I can't see staying with Wayne for three weeks while you're gone. The only way I could finish the trip would be for me to go alone into Yuma." That thought quieted me down considerably.

I didn't want to agree with Verlen, but there wasn't much I could say. Our journey had turned into a race. We walked into town together and found a phone booth in the pharmacy. I sat down on a step to bring my journal up to date while Verlen stepped into the booth and began making calls to Wayne and his home. I could tell his mind was on reentry. Mine was on the possibility of failure. Way back at Ignacio, I had declared I would finish solo if necessary, but now I wondered if I should consider going alone. San Felipe was more than 150 miles south of Yuma.

While I waited for Verlen, a young man about 20 came into the store, and when he saw that the phone booth was occupied he sat down beside me on the step.

"You waiting for the phone?" he asked in a heavy French accent.

"No, my partner is making some calls," I said. "It will take him a while. It usually does." I smiled absentmindedly and went back to work in my journal.

To my surprise, the young man took out a journal of his own and began to write. I looked at him more intently. He was shorter than I, compact and sunburned. The desert had weathered him in an attractive, rugged way. He caught me staring and looked back with bright blue eyes.

"I'm Pietro Biondo," he said in greeting.

"Hi, I'm Valerie Fons."

"I'm unicycling through Baja," he announced. Taking out a map, he began to show me the route. His head bent over the chart as he intently traced the highway on which he had come.

"Hey, I'm paddling around the Baja." I took out my map and showed him where we had come and where we were going.

We looked at each other and recognized ourselves. Both of us stuck out our hands to shake. The characters were different, the vehicles were not alike, the dangers did not balance, but Pietro's story was similar to mine. When he talked about his legs aching, I thought about my arms. When he mentioned the desert hills, I knew he was talking about my waves.

"You've got to meet Verlen," I said, standing up and knocking on the phone booth door enthusiastically. I opened the door.

"Yes, Wayne, just a minute," Verlen interrupted his call. I pointed toward Pietro.

"He's unicycling through Baja!" I said incredulously. Verlen smiled and held up one finger to indicate he was almost finished. I shut the door on the booth and sat down again by Pietro.

"Where's your bike?" I asked.

"At the hotel on the square. I've been camping out, but I wanted a shower—maybe I should say I needed a shower. It's been several weeks since I had one," Pietro explained.

"You don't have to explain," I laughed knowingly. "Have you found any ice cream in town?" I asked.

"No, but I'm looking." He smiled with immediate understanding.

People we had met outside our experience wanted lots of information of why and how, but talking to Pietro, I was able to share the satisfaction of our experience in a special way.

"People are lucky to be doing what they like," I observed.

"They aren't lucky," he said sensibly. "They work at making it work."

"Yes, I guess we do."

When Verlen finished on the phone, he enthusiastically shook hands with Pietro. We had dinner together at a nearby restaurant, and spent most of the evening talking about routes, preparation, planning, problems, joys of traveling, and thoughts of home. But even as we compared notes, Verlen kept a close eye on his watch and soon announced our curfew. We planned to wake at midnight and continue north.

We only got a few hours sleep, and by one o'clock we were paddling out the harbor, passing the green and red navigation lights at the head of the entrance channel. Even as we headed out the channel we knew there was trouble—big swells rolled under us, some of the waves were breaking, and frills of white spotted the darkness.

Turning north, we paddled along the narrow breakwater. The waves got bigger and rolled down the slag mole, scalloping in a severe amplitude. The wind blew gently on our faces, teasing us to take a chance, but it wasn't good sense to take off at night with so many signs running against us. On the coast ahead the landing spots would be unfriendly, dark, and flooded with surf. We turned back, seeking refuge once again in the harbor of San Rosalia. But our practice run had not been futile: the effort of dismantling camp and leaving the harbor assured us that we were trying our best. We pitched our tents again and got a few more hours sleep.

At daybreak, we walked to Pietro's hotel room to see if he would like to eat breakfast with us, but he had already gone. The same wind that stalled us was helping to push our new friend south.

We walked to a bus station a block away from the dock for breakfast. The waiting room was like all stations in the world: sleepy-eyed passengers were nodding by their suitcases, listening for the announcement of their coach, little children sat on mama's lap and leaned on papa's shoulder. A woman in a faded housedress slowly mopped the linoleum floor and emptied the ashtrays. People sat at a worn lunch counter drinking coffee and waiting with their bags stacked at their feet.

Verlen and I sat at the counter and ordered fried eggs and tortillas. We watched as the buses came and went, picking up passengers and leaving others. The announcement of the bus for San Felipe reminded Verlen and me of our predicament.

When we got back to the canoes, we saw that the fishermen had not gone out either. Several of them stood repairing nets while the others chatted, marking time. The wind was up, sending ripples over the water inside the harbor. Spray coming over the breakwater gave us a clue to the turmoil on the other side.

I went to lie down in the tent, but stopped for a minute by my canoe when I noticed that the elastic shock cords were gone. I knew immediately who had taken them—and sure enough, the small dirty-faced bandit was sitting behind one of the trucks, looking quite proud of himself as he snapped the elastic and showed off to his sister. He took one look at me, stuffed the loot into his little sister's pockets, and then ran down the beach, leaving the little girl in tears. I took to comforting the innocent accomplice, traded her a cookie for our cords, and encouraged her to go home.

All morning we sat in the tents, not getting anywhere. We simply had to wait. Life in Santa Rosalia was going on behind us, a confusion of cars, buses, people, and activity. Verlen and I sat on the edge, waiting for the wind to let us continue and watching our time running out.

TWENTY

Meretz

The sea is a champion of movement. Even in the quietest part of night, when everything comes to rest and the earth seems to stand still, the movement of the sea diminishes but never stops. We learned not to curse the sea, but tried to imitate it. Our journey was an expression of movement: when we were still, it was only in preparation for moving again.

Our two-day wait in Santa Rosalia came to an end when the tempo of the sea softened several hours after midnight on January 25th. Verlen and I saw our chance and paddled away from the navigation lights in the harbor. Following the breakwater north, we drove hard, dipping our paddles boldly in the darkness. The sea was docile, as if the band of moonlight dancing on the surface were quieting the water.

I couldn't help but think of the various conditions of the sea as its different moods. I knew when the sea was angry and I knew when it was being coy. The sea played by its own rules, and to succeed Verlen and I had to accept them. I had not been able to change the sea one bit, but it was changing me.

My canoe was the part of me that belonged to the sea. The unique vehicle allowed me to move with the water, gliding in a continuous fluid breath. I wanted to believe that my canoe was an effective camouflage so that the sea would think me one of its own, but the sea was not fooled. The wind came and waves reared like a herd of broncos, kicking to buck us off the water before noon on January 26th.

Verlen and I had made good progress: we had paddled 70 miles in 36 hours since leaving Santa Rosalia when we pulled ashore at Punta San Juan Bautista on a patch of sand beach.

The desert seems best suited to bite and prick and is not thought of as a friendly place, but throughout our journey the desert had offered us rest. The desert is a masterpiece of stillness, and it was when we were being still that we best understood the definite progress our movement had brought.

I was too tired to put up my tent, but just lay my sleeping pad on the sand and pulled a tarp over myself. I woke a few hours later with a feeling of foreboding. As I held still and looked from right to left, I saw a coyote. The shadow that had serenaded us many nights, the animal that was ever present but rarely seen, was prowling the beach. As I watched this one search the beach for dead fish, he came within a canoe length of my resting spot and still was not scared off. The animal's body was taut and scruffy, its coat dry and matted, its eyes wild. The coyote seemed to view me as part of the desert. It was my boat that finally spooked the animal—the strange 17-foot white fish lying on the beach sent him trotting into the brush.

Sitting up on my sleeping pad, I looked at the desert around me and felt as if I truly belonged. Maybe I could finally begin to understand the secrets that had eluded me. I lay back down and stayed quiet. Moving closer to the edge of the pad, I turned my head and put my face close to the sand, studying the granules. The breath from my nostrils moved the small particles.

A few inches away, I noticed a small funnel shape indenting the sand, and at the bottom of the funnel a mysterious hole. I watched as a careless ant walked to the rim of the harmless-looking dimple. The grains of sand began a minilandslide and the ant slid toward the bottom of the hole. The more frantically the ant tried to climb back to level ground, the faster the sand carried it to the bottom. I never saw the trap's villain, but a quick movement like the snapping of a hinge sucked the victim into its jaws.

Time was a funnel trap for Verlen and me, and we were falling into failure.

"Verlen, we've got to get moving," I said, shaking his sleeping body. "Wake up, we've slept enough."

"There's no hurry," he said. Groggy from sleep, he rolled over and shielded his eyes from the sun with an outstretched hand.

"The wind is letting up," I said excitedly.

"Settle down," he cautioned, looking at his watch.

"I know we can make it to Yuma," I said eagerly. I was watching another ant sliding into the sand funnel, and he followed my gaze, leaning closer to look.

"Verlen, could you and Steve do it?"

"What?"

"Could you and Steve make it to Yuma?"

"Yep."

"Could you do it if you were alone?"

"Yep."

"Then we can make it to Yuma."

"Nope." I looked at him with exasperation. "Valerie, I've been paddling since 1963. You were 12 years old when I got my first canoe. Since then I've raced every long distance race in North America. I've won some of the toughest ones. There are a couple of races that I've finished that aren't even run anymore because they were too difficult. My total paddling mileage is somewhere close to 50,000 miles."

"Verlen, I can't measure up to your experience. You knew that when I started, but I have gotten to be a much better paddler."

"Yep. You're the strongest woman paddler I've seen."

"Well?"

"You can give more." I was quiet for several moments.

"We can make it to Yuma." I repeated.

"How do you propose to do that?" Verlen asked. He was already getting up.

"Remember when you said I didn't have to sleep, that it was all in my mind?"

"Yep, I remember."

"And when you said I didn't have to go to the bathroom, that it was all in my mind?"

"Yep, I remember that one, too," he said with a laugh.

"Well, Verlen, I think you've been right all along and now I know something you couldn't teach me."

"What's that?" he asked.

"We can make it to Yuma if we believe it in our hearts."

"Face the facts, Valerie. We would have to average better mileage than we planned," Verlen said, rolling his sleeping pad.

"Facts are nothing compared to vision," I said resolutely. "Will you try?" I asked, staring up at him. He pulled closed the draw cord of his personal bag and threw the pack over his shoulder.

"Will you try?" I asked again. He walked to the canoe and turned the boat to face the sea. Then he looked at me.

"I've never quit," he said with a smile. "If you are willing to push, let's go." I scrambled to my feet and hurried to pack.

Over the next few days my journal entries were brief. We would pull ashore to eat and sleep for an hour, and I would write only a word or two, noting our location and the time. We were haunted by desire. Verlen took caffeine tablets and still fell asleep while paddling. We never put up the

290

tents, for fear of getting too comfortable and oversleeping. We caught naps on the sand and woke sore and stiff when the cold of night chilled us, or sweaty and dazed when the heat of day threatened to fry us.

We watched the moon go down and the sun come up in different parts of the sky. We floated and nodded and drifted as we tried to pull ourselves together enough to continue paddling. After 48 hours we had gone another 85 miles.

Just past Punta Las Animas, during a brief lunch break, I found a large tortoise shell. It was a beautiful shape, a roundish oval with scalloped edges and a hump of platelets on the back. The shell fit perfectly on the front of my canoe, over the peak of the deck.

I laughed out loud looking at my tortoise shield. The dolphin skull was strapped on the stern, just above my life jacket. My canoe had certainly changed since takeoff nearly 3½ months before. The lettering I had applied to my boat in Long Beach was worn and frayed, and many of the characters were missing entirely. Patches of gel coat had chipped and abraded, exposing the Kevlar fiber underneath, but there was not one dent or hole in the hull from the months of abuse. My dear boat was surviving the journey well.

As we continued north in the Sea of Cortez, a new condition developed that we needed to consider: the tide increased, and I envisioned the 1,000-mile length of the Gulf as 1,000 railroad cars piled in a collision, pressing one another and compacting. The overflow, the bursting at the seams, caused a rise in the level of water on the beach.

On the Pacific side, the tide had acted to strand our boats and increase the surf. The tide in the Sea of Cortez was not nearly as dangerous, but potentially more of a problem because it was bigger. We had been told to expect 20- to 25-foot tides at the head of the gulf, which didn't affect us much in our present location because we were staying ashore only a short time and moving on. But we could see the efforts of the high tide on the beaches where we stopped. A line of flotsam and jetsam would be pushed toward the top of the beach and the sand would be swept clear when we arrived. In places, the tide left the sand corrugated in ripples. When we landed in high tide, the beach would be minuscule, with water lapping the line of debris.

As we neared the Bahía de los Angeles, the Sea of Cortez squeezed between the peninsula and the offshore island of Ángel de la Guarda, a passage about 45 miles long and 10 miles wide, and the tidal current was significant in the reduced space.

The tide itself did not produce a great action in the sea, but when the wind interfered the reaction was explosive. When the northwest wind came down on the incoming tide in the channel, the nap of the water was rubbed the opposite way, and the sea would agitate and jump like crazy water. The stricture of the channel, the current, the wind, the phase of the moon, and the depth gradient all stressed the sea until the water fairly boiled. This set of circumstances was dramatically different from anything else we had seen: the waves were short, choppy, swirling, and rough. As we approached Punta Gringa, conditions got even worse, creating what Verlen called a riptide coursing past the headland. Fortunately, we had already catamaraned to face it. The waves jumped up, over, and into my canoe as if they themselves were trying to escape the turmoil. We got wet but kept paddling north.

On January 29th I leaned against a rock wall, huddling under a tarp just before sundown. It was raining and we had found the skeletal remains of a fishing camp past Punta Bluff and pulled ashore to rest.

Verlen built a fire in the shelter of a rock overhang and we ate spaghetti by flashlight. I didn't think about what I was eating, but kept putting one bite after another in my mouth, swallowing to get it down. At that stage in our journey there were only a couple of things I wouldn't eat—tuna, for one, because of an open can I had lost inside my boat for two weeks, and cornmeal, because it reminded me of being seasick at La Buffadora.

Thinking back, I could count on my fingers the number of hot breakfasts we had had since we started out. I decided to count this spaghetti meal as a breakfast because we had just slept an hour and were preparing to travel all night. As I chewed, I watched the rocks in the bay disappear under waves and then rise again as the water fell away.

As we sat in front of the fire we planned our strategy for the final miles. I fantasized about calling Wayne from San Felipe and announcing that we were going all the way to Yuma.

Verlen seemed cranky and preoccupied. He claimed the fire was putting smoke in his eyes, and he kept changing his position in the cramped space. He talked about the closeness of home, and I could sense the inevitable separation of our team.

Whenever I thought about saying good-bye to Verlen a scene from an old Shirley Temple movie came to mind. The little girl was in the care of a white-bearded lighthouse keeper named "Cap" until foster parents came to take her to a new home in the city. When the little girl left in an open motor car with her new family, the lighthouse keeper held his cap in his hand at the gate. Shirley cried pitifully and leaned out the window waving good-bye.

Verlen was like that lighthouse keeper to me. He had been an encouraging teacher, prodding me to do my best, and the closest friend I had ever had. I felt like a child being driven away by the conclusion of our trip.

The rain stopped in the early evening and we paddled away from camp, our fire still burning on shore as we drifted into the darkness. I wanted to say good-bye to Verlen on the water. He was paddling up ahead, and I knew he couldn't hear me, but I looked over my shoulder at the gold glow of the fire on shore and whispered good-bye. Tears rolled down my cheeks.

I had seen a lot of power in the Baja. The ocean was gigantic, the winds were fierce, the storms wild with energy. I had endured many hardships, including the ferocious chubasco. But I knew as I paddled away from the beach that what I would remember as the greatest power of all was the love Verlen had given to me.

Verlen's positive thinking would have to be called love, and bordered on the irrational. He believed in me even when I failed. He had seen me through and he had seen through me. We had not only shared the Baja experience together, we had shared ourselves. What had taken me to the Baja was the lure of high adventure. What had kept me there was the satisfaction of growth.

I had learned the necessary skills of expedition life: I could put up a tent in 2½ minutes and start a fire with very little wood. I could paddle all night, ride out rough storms in my canoe, and brace when the waves caught me unaware. I had learned to survive, but I had also learned how to live. The experience transformed me: I knew I was capable of feats that I could not have imagined before. I had a new sense of confidence and purpose, and the sure knowledge that nothing worthwhile is gained easily.

My values had changed, too: I had traded a 4,000-square-foot home for a 17-foot boat and the out-of-doors. Facing the challenges of paddling the Pacific Ocean and the Sea of Cortez had improved the quality of my life. There is a Hebrew word for energy of endurance from beginning to end—*meretz*. This was my style now. The Baja experience had developed within me a durability that was not something I would say good-bye to. I would live with this blessing the rest of my life.

When we pulled ashore in the early evening we were approximately 130 miles from San Felipe. The beach bordered a gently curved cove pebbled with marble-sized rocks. We tugged the canoes about 15 feet up from the water's edge and I got busy fixing a pot of stew for supper. Both of us were tired. After eating, Verlen didn't follow his usual habit of making a trip to the water's edge to wash his bowl; he just leaned back against his pack and fell asleep. I walked over to my boat and pulled out a tarp and sleeping pad.

We overslept, and woke around midnight. I was the first to realize something was wrong.

"Hey, Verlen," I said. "Did you turn your boat around before you went to sleep?"

"Huh?" he said, sitting up and squinting toward the water.

"Verlen, your boat is turned around." We hurried to the water's edge, where we found Verlen's canoe turned completely around on the stones and settled into a hollowed trough facing the water. Verlen's straw hat which had been sitting beside his boat, was partially buried, the brim had entirely disappeared under a covering of stones. A small food bag was missing, and his paddle was gone. Tide was the culprit, and we berated ourselves for having been so careless—we could easily have lost a boat. My canoe was a few feet higher on the beach, and hadn't been disturbed. As I started to untie my spare paddle to give to Verlen, he walked the beach with his flashlight, unable to believe that he had lost his last paddle. When he had almost given up, his shoe unearthed a bit of yellow, and he knelt and scooted rocks with his hands until the paddle appeared, several inches below the surface.

Still smarting from our mistake, we packed our canoes and headed off into the darkness. I had said good-bye, but the trip wasn't over yet.

On the afternoon of January 31st we saw the high mountains of San Felipe ahead. By the time the sun went down I had memorized the distant outline of the hills. I paddled on, waiting impatiently for the moon to appear and shoo away the blackness. We followed the shore faithfully, steering for the shadow of the distant headland. Paddling into a gently curving bay, we were mesmerized by several lights on shore. Before we knew it, we had drawn too close to land and were caught on a shoal. My paddle touched bottom about a foot under the surface. The boat moved slower and almost stopped, bogged down in the shallow sea. We were probably paddling on top of a tide-flooded beach, and tried to compensate by steering farther to the right.

Fish jumped around me. Ahead, I saw a sandspit, where current ripped past the low point. As we paddled closer, the sea bounced in the darkness and it was difficult to keep my balance. I leaned to the right, then to the left, and got used to feeling the bottom with my blade. Then with the next stroke, I reached for the security of sand and couldn't touch it. Just as I came around the point, a fish jumped into my boat. With the cockpit so close around me, it was as if the fish had jumped down my dress.

"Verlen, get it out, get it out," I cried, screaming in alarm. I was wearing shorts, and the fish was flipping, flopping, and jumping between my bare legs.

"Verlen, get it out. I can't touch it . . . Oh!" I shrieked as the wet creature flipped its tail against my leg. Verlen paddled over and shined a flashlight into my boat, highlighting an ugly green fish that was gasping for breath.

"Poor fellow," Verlen said calmly. "He doesn't want to be here, either."

Verlen leaned over my deck, reached down between my feet to pick up the displaced fish, and returned it to the water. I immediately regretted my panicky reaction and tried to excuse it.

"Look, I'm sorry, Verlen. I know it is silly to get so upset. It wasn't such a big fish," I consoled myself. "I'm just tired and my nerves are shot," I said, laughing nervously. "I apologize."

I concentrated on my paddling. There was plenty of water by then, and I was just getting the rhythm of my strokes back and starting to relax when another fish jumped into my boat. I panicked again.

"Verlen, get it out, get it out." The fish startled me worse than someone tapping me on the shoulder in a dark alley. This new fish was ricocheting off my ankles and the sides of the canoe.

"You're bigger than the fish," Verlen said. "You can get him out."

"Verlen . . . " I was shocked at my unstrung behavior, but the fish shocked me more. I wasn't a hero and couldn't pretend to be one, but once I got over the fright, I figured I could handle a fish. But the creature had by then flipped under my seat, so I had to get out my flashlight to locate it. Then I realized I didn't want to touch it, so I pulled out my plastic cookie box, scooped up the fish, and flipped it overboard.

I didn't say another word to Verlen, but rode a high wave of adrenaline 10 more miles until we could see the lights of San Felipe. A glow began at the horizon and a giant orange ball rose from the sea and into the sky: the moon had come at last.

Twelve miles from San Felipe, we heard a small engine and saw a fishing boat approaching with a light on the bow. I quickly reached into my pack and took out my flashlight, pointing it ahead.

The engine was suddenly quiet, and we paddled toward the light. When we got closer, we saw a fisherman leaning over the side of his boat, hauling in lobster traps from the sea. When he saw us, he waved and spoke excited Spanish.

"Dos horas, mucho mal tiempo," he said, gesturing toward the sky and warning us of a storm.

"Sí, muchas gracias," we exclaimed, grabbing onto the side of his boat.

"Radio Ensenada," he continued. We did not understand every word but the fisherman made it clear that we would be safe at San Felipe. Verlen and I thanked the man again and paddled toward the lights of town.

I wondered if he was right in predicting that a storm was coming—he must have been sure to come out in the middle of the night to secure his traps. I checked the signs: there were no swells to warn us, no wind. But as we paddled farther into the bay at San Felipe, I could see clouds flying in to smother the moon.

We heard the fishing boat coming up behind us. The engine slowed, and the fisherman accompanied us into the harbor. The town beach was a block-wide mud flat glistening in the darkness as it reflected the lights of town. The tide had created a long, shallow expanse where the dark hulks of fishing boats were anchored in sand and tipped on their sides at the keel line as the water moved out from under them. The fisherman motoring with us struck bottom a long way from dry ground. He took off his shoes, rolled up his pant legs, and jumped into the shallow water, then walked to high ground to plant his anchor.

Our canoes drafted only a few inches, so Verlen and I were able to continue paddling farther in. When my blade touched sand, I pushed off the bottom so I wouldn't have to wade. As my canoe slowed down my wake caught up with me, creating a wave that traveled all the way to the beach in a white roll. This alerted me that the water was only a few inches deep, that there was no way I could make dry ground by floating. The sand eventually stopped my canoe and I had to climb out and drag my boat out of the water.

We reached San Felipe on February 2nd. I wanted to find a phone and call Wayne immediately with the good news that we were ahead of schedule, but it was two o'clock in the morning. A wind had started, and the palm trees on the beach were swaying. San Felipe looked vulnerable and quiet. Most of the residents were sleeping, unaware of the storm advancing from the sea. Our friendly fisherman was the only one in sight, and he was soon hurrying down the street to shelter.

Verlen and I worked quickly to set up camp on the beach side of a stone retaining wall separating San Felipe from the sea. I put my tent next to an old wooden fishing boat and tied a line to my canoe. Then I crawled into my sleeping bag with a sigh of relief. In the past eight days we had averaged 46.2 miles a day. The joys of relaxing in a tent were indescribable.

When I awoke, it was immediately obvious that we weren't going anywhere. My tent walls were sagging with moisture, and through the fabric I could see rivulets of rain running down the outside of the dome. I opened the tent zipper and peeked out. The clouds were stacked and rolling as if preparing to crash like surf on the shore, and the beach was congested with fishermen securing their boats from the storm. Using a four-wheel-drive jeep, they were busy moving their boats away from the water's edge.

By the time I had put on my rain gear and climbed out onto the sand, Verlen was digging a trench around my tent with his paddle to keep the water from puddling inside. To steady our tents, we tied additional lines from all corners to the boats around us. Then Verlen and I walked through the rain into town.

San Felipe was the closest thing we'd seen to a familiar town since we'd left the States. It was not a fancy tourist resort area, but a business community with many shops marketing trinkets to Americans crossing the border.

There were small stores with glass windowfronts displaying straw hats, belts, and Mexican shirts. San Felipe had a paved main street and a set of stoplights. A cactus growing in a patch of dirt next to a street lamp reminded me that the desert was not far away.

A cafe with an honest-to-goodness phone booth outside was our first stop. We ordered tortillas, beans, and omelets, then sat cozily in a booth as the rain poured down outside. Many others had taken the same shelter: local fishermen sat at the lunch counter smoking cigarettes down to their last half-inch, and a man in the kitchen kept poking his head out through the swinging door, keeping track of the customers and ringing the cash register.

A picture made of seashells hung over the lunch counter. I had never liked that kind of art before, but that day I looked at the shells and thought they were beautiful. I slipped my hand in my pocket and touched the shell I had picked up at our last lunch spot many miles back. I knew those shells on the wall: I had slept on them, touched them, and treasured them. I knew just where they were from because I had been there.

A map of the Baja decorated another wall, and I stared at the length of the entire peninsula. I was willing to bet that no one else in the cafe had been the distance—except Verlen, who sat across from me in the booth, both elbows on the table, cap still on his head, looking at his map in the plastic case that he always carried when he left the canoe, figuring now, even so close to the end, just how many miles were left and wondering if we would make it with the rain.

A picture of Jesus hung by the kitchen door. I recognized Him right away even though I'd seen other pictures that showed Him differently. I felt He had been with Verlen and me on our journey.

A calendar with a pretty blond in a skimpy bathing suit hung over our table. I looked at her red painted fingernails, then studied my own broken, dirty ones. I had heavy calluses where the paddle rubbed my palms, and the backs of my hands were tanned and freckled. I looked up at the smiling blond and smiled back. I had been somewhere she would never go.

The rain came down even harder, as if the sky would burst. A small crowd of Americans hurried into the restaurant for shelter, carrying the rain inside on their jackets and shaking the weather off on the floor. One of them had a newspaper—the first I'd seen in three months. We heard that the highway was flooded out, that the tourists in San Felipe were stuck.

I would have gone over to their table to visit if our breakfast hadn't arrived just then. As I looked at the eggs, cheese, tortillas, and beans, the cafe itself disappeared into the background and the voices became a blur.

When we had eaten our fill, Verlen and I stood at the phone booth. Holding a tarp over our heads, we called Wayne.

"Hello," Wayne's voice came over the wire.

"Wayne, do you know what day this is?"

"Valerie?"

"We're in San Felipe. We're going all the way to Yuma," I said excitedly. "Here, talk to Verlen, he'll tell you the details."

"Don't get excited, Wayne," Verlen began. "Yes, I know, Valerie's like that," he said laughing on the phone and smiling at me. "We're in San Felipe and ahead of schedule, but this weather could blow our success." Pause. "Oh, it's raining there too? I see." Pause. "This rain is cutting off our margin. We've still got more than 150 miles to go." Verlen's comments were soon reduced to responses to Wayne's many questions.

As I waited under the eave of a building, I watched the man sweeping his roof, hoping to save it from collapse. I realized I could use some cleaning up. Being in a city, I began to feel my dirt. On the ocean, the dirt never seemed so bad, and when it did I could just wade into the water. I knew that when I cleaned up again I would be at the end of my journey.

"Time for the big finish," I heard Verlen say. "Good-bye, Wayne." He hung up the phone and walked over to me.

"Steve is ahead of us and he's gone up the Colorado River. First time the Colorado has been running water into the gulf in about 20 years," he said. "Wayne tells me the river is in flood. Steve found a body tangled in some brush." I stared at Verlen, letting the information sink in. He was quiet.

"Is that the way we're going?" I asked.

"No, just because the river is running doesn't mean we have to change our plans. I did quite a bit of research on the salinity canal before you arrived at Long Beach, and I think we should stick to the original plan," Verlen said. We stood there at the phone booth, lost in thought for a few minutes, then walked toward a grocery to buy food and a jug of water, preparing to continue our trip.

When we got up the next day at dawn, the storm was over and the surf lapped gently on shore. One by one, the fishermen came out after the storm, checking their boats and preparing to launch. Several dogs romped on the beach, nipping at the water. Birds were feeding and flapping, stretching their wings after the rain. One pelican got a whole fish in its mouth, then reared on its legs and lifted its body out of the water to wiggle and slither the fish down its long throat.

We had five days left and more than 150 miles to go, with little information as to what problems we might yet encounter. It would be close, but we were going to do everything possible to reach Yuma. Church bells were ringing in town and the world was waking up. Verlen took down his tent, and I knew I had to get out of my sleeping bag and move.

To reach Yuma, we would need to find the Santa Clara Slough, north of the gulf, paddle across it, and enter the Wellton Mohawk Canal—a salinity bypass canal that flows into Yuma. No two maps agree on the exact boundaries of the Santa Clara Slough, but the area is described as swamp and is pictured as an inland lake located between the Rio Colorado and the highway to El Golfo de Santa Clara.

On February 3rd, Verlen and I crossed the northern end of the gulf, snubbing against land at the head of the oversized bay, and paddled east, to El Golfo de Santa Clara on the mainland of Mexico. From there we paddled north, staying close to shore and looking for an opening into the slough.

We stopped paddling soon after dark and set up camp—even though we were in a hurry, it would be easy to miss the opening of the slough without sufficient light. We expected to find a drainage channel leading into the slough, and the next morning, just south of Isla Pelicano, we came upon a sluggish, narrow river. We detected a flow of current emptying into the gulf and assumed it was the channel into the slough. We paddled upstream, excited and happy, knowing we were on the right track.

The sand shore disappeared and the banks of the channel turned to mud. There was no way to pull ashore, since the sloping mud banks leveled off above our heads in a layer of brush and grass. Instead of widening out into a slough, the channel we were following began to narrow, and I wondered if we were going the right way. The current increased and the water churned white. Soon the channel became so tight that I could touch my paddle on either side of the bank. Walls of mud seemed to close around us.

Eventually I could no longer paddle against the increasing current. Verlen was still working against the flow, wedging his paddle into the mud bank and pushing himself forward. I got out of my canoe with intention of walking and pulling from the bank, a technique called "lining." It was lucky that I had a firm grasp on the bowrope when I climbed out, because my canoe was instantly sucked back the way I had come. I scrambled up the bank, slipping in the mud and falling back one step for every two I took forward. I quickly realized that my bowrope was not going to reach from the canoe to the top of the bank, so I went back down the incline and held my boat against the current while I looked inside my pack for an extra length of rope. As I squatted on the bank, pieces of mud fell away and I had to keep retreating even as I searched for the rope, inching backwards, until I was sitting on my bottom in the mud with both feet sliding out from under me. I tied the extra length to my bowrope and started up the mud bank again, using my paddle as a staff to pull myself up the bank.

The lining was tricky. As I walked at the top of the bank holding the rope, the bow of my boat pulled forward and caught in an outcrop of mud. I let the boat float backward, then pulled it forward again, hoping to slide it over the mud. This procedure was fairly successful, but every once in a while I would have to climb back down the hill and muscle my boat over a mud hump before climbing back up the mud bank and pulling again.

Verlen was by then on the mud bank too. We were making slow but steady progress, and had come several miles from the gulf when I saw a four-foot waterfall ahead. The increased gradient meant we had certainly discovered a path to the slough. Working together, we dragged the heavy canoes against the current and over the falls.

When we had tugged both canoes over the waterfall, we stood in the mud among several small channels that braided for about a quarter of a mile, then joined a large body of water. As far as the eye could see to the north and west was water. To the east, grey mesas crowded the sky. We pulled the canoes through one of the channels to what we knew must be the slough.

Mud caked our paddles, covered our legs, and smeared the white hulls of the canoes. The channel I was wading in widened as I pulled my canoe forward, pushing a wake of mud with my bow. It took both of us to pull each canoe the last 100 yards. The slough was ahead and I kept moving, thinking happily about paddling again.

We stopped for lunch at the edge of the pool, where there was only an inch of water underneath the boats. I washed my hands in the slough and tried to wipe the mud off my legs, then sat on my deck with my feet planted in the mud and just the slightest ripple of water coming up past my shoe bottom. Verlen and I congratulated ourselves for having found the slough.

We dragged our canoes for over an hour trying to find deeper water. Then, getting into the canoes, we tried poling and pushing off the bottom with our paddles. We shoveled mud for several hours, hoping for the slough to get deeper, but it didn't. When I looked down at the bottom I could see flaps of dried mud curling and fraying as we disturbed the sediment.

In places, the water got even shallower, and soon Verlen and I were out of our canoes, the bowropes tied around our waists, pulling and wading in ankle-deep water. We kept following our compass northwest in the giant tidal mudflat.

"I thought you researched this area," I said suspiciously.

"I did," Verlen responded. "I even saw aerial photos of the slough, but those didn't show how deep the pool was. My guess is that the photos must have been taken during a monthly high tide, because it didn't show all the mudbank we crossed."

At first our spirits remained high because shoveling mud in the slough was new and different after paddling for 3½ months on the ocean. But it soon became clear that we were stuck in the mud, and that there were 30 miles of slough ahead before we could hope to find the opening into the canal. Our enthusiasm flagged as we continued to drag our canoes in the few inches of water. In places the canoes didn't float at all, but lodged in mud, so that we had to pull and jerk to make them move. The mud almost brought us to a halt, but we still hauled, putting our life jackets underneath the rope around our waists to keep the weight we were tugging from cutting into our skin.

We were still pulling our canoes when the sun went down. I have never seen such a bleak scene: as far as I could see ahead was the thin layer of water over mud. I felt discouraged, but I prayed and promised that I would not give up.

Verlen and I sloshed on into the night, pulling our canoes through the water and mud by starlight. I let Verlen get ahead, but it was an eerie sight to see him walking on the water. I called for him to wait up, and when I reached him I took his hand and we walked together, leaning heavily on our ropes.

At midnight we agreed to rest. We stuck our paddles into the mud, tied the bowropes to the makeshift posts, and climbed into our cockpits to sleep. With my weight in the boat, my canoe settled into the mud as firmly as if I were on dry ground. When I gazed at the stars, they looked close enough to touch in the black sky. Yuma seemed farther away.

We woke before dawn and stepped out of our boats into the cold slough water. I harnessed up like a horse ready to plow and started on again, dragging my canoe. At midmorning we came to a series of poles stuck in the mud, with wire strung between dotted with plugs and tubing. Someone must have put them there for a purpose, but we couldn't tell what it was. We followed these unusual markers until they ran out. By early afternoon we had reached what we thought was the end of the slough, but we had another problem: the opening into the canal was nowhere in sight.

We stuck our paddles into the mud and wrapped our life jackets around the handles so we wouldn't lose sight of our canoes, then waded into the dead-end corridors at the top end of the slough looking for the canal. We found no opening.

Since our attempts were getting us nowhere, we decided to turn around and try to locate the road leading into El Doctor that had to run at the base of the mesas. Possibly there we could get some information. We pulled our canoes back the way we had come, and by early evening arrived at the poles stuck in the slough. When I saw people among the poles, at first I thought it was a mirage. But as we got closer, I saw a dozen men with cables and wire coiled around their shoulders setting more poles into the mud. I was excited and tried to hurry, but it was impossible in the mud. I dropped the rope of my canoe and started to run.

"Settle down, Valerie," Verlen cautioned. "If you want to get to Yuma, I would suggest you put on your long pants and not startle these guys." He was right. The workmen were surprised to see us pulling our canoes through the mud, and would have been even more startled to see me running toward them in my undershorts.

"Buenas noches," I began. "Dos días," I explained, pantomiming our sledging through the slough. "Wellton Mohawk Canal, donde?" I questioned.

The men began to talk at once. Several of them handed their cables to others in the group, took my bowrope from me, and began pulling my canoe toward the mesas. I reached into my boat and took out several bundles to help make the boat lighter. From what Verlen and I could understand, the men were setting seismic lines for oil exploration in the slough.

Near shore, our group came to the end of the shallow water and faced only mud ahead. The men hesitated for a moment, then four of them lifted my canoe on their shoulders. They were trying to be polite and helpful, but I knew how heavy the canoe and gear were. I walked alongside clucking and fretting that they were attempting too much.

The mud got deeper, and soon the men were sinking to their knees as they carried my boat on their shoulders. Verlen worked with several men carrying his boat. The effort was extraordinary—I could hardly walk in the sucking mud with my own light load. Verlen and I tried to make them understand that we would camp on the mud and see them in the morning, but they insisted on helping us get the boats to higher ground. One of the men stopped and told the group he was dropping out, but his friends wouldn't let him quit and soon he was back underneath my canoe, lifting the burden with the rest of them.

We came to a line of brush and a small shack beyond on solid ground. The men put down our canoes with relief and congregated at a small pond filled with water, where they washed the mud from their legs and clothing. While several of the men built a fire, I unpacked my canoe and handed out candy bars and fruit to our helpers, wishing we could do more.

It was dark by then. Verlen took out his flashlight and talked to several of the men about the location of the canal. Verlen and I had three nights left and we were about 80 miles from Yuma. I fell asleep even as Verlen looked at the map once more.

When I awoke in the morning, I unzipped the door of my tent and saw my first shark: it was staring from the front of a small-size T-shirt. As I opened the tent flap, a cluster of children gathered closer. Their hands were in their pockets and they waited quietly, looking in at me and my belongings.

The men already had a fire going and were standing around drinking coffee, waiting for another work day to begin. Their tools and cables sat on the dirt at the edge of the mud. As soon as Verlen and I were ready to leave, the men picked up our canoes and headed out into the slough once again. We formed a parade, slogging along in the mud. When we reached the shallow water, the men set down our canoes and pointed out the way to the missing canal: the day before, we had been too far to the west. Then they set off to their own work. By midday we found the canal and dropped our canoes over the spillway into a concrete-lined channel.

The current was fast. Verlen paddled steadily upstream, but I gave up almost immediately and walked on top of a sandy ledge, lining my boat. Within a few minutes, Verlen realized I had chosen the more efficient way to make progress on the canal. We tied the two boats together, then one of us walked along the top of the canal pulling while the other sat in the rear canoe steering. We worked in shifts.

I had just completed a two-hour stint and Verlen was pulling when we arrived at the border crossing. There was a high wire fence over the canal, but we saw a way of getting through to the other side by careful maneuvering. Verlen was nervous.

"Verlen, what do we do here?" I asked.

"Shh," he said tensely.

"Verlen, that's silly. We've been making all kinds of noise."

"Well, we don't want to alarm anyone. We don't want to get held up here at the border. We don't have time for an international incident, nor do we have time to find a customs officer."

"Relax. We have nothing to hide," I reminded him.

"This canal is not a recreational waterway. If the wrong official catches us, we may be asked to leave, and I don't see any buses going by here to Yuma," he pointed out.

Verlen insisted we both put our canoes into the canal and paddle to reduce our visibility, at least until we were out of sight of the border crossing.

"Don't look suspicious, Verlen," I chuckled, making fun of his alarm.

By late afternoon we had put aside our fears of a border incident and were pulling our canoes again, making steady progress up the canal. We had stopped to eat a bite of lunch when a green jeep came speeding along the dirt path beside the canal. Our visitors turned out to be the Border Patrol. Pulling a flat iron sled that smoothed the sand and made an even surface for spotting footprints, the jeep stopped right in front of us. A young patrolman got out and headed determinedly toward us. I expected trouble. Verlen cleared his throat and stood up to shake hands.

"Hi, I'm Verlen, Verlen Kruger, and I'm exploring the North American continent by canoe."

The patrolman's expression suddenly changed. "Hey," he said excitedly.

"I know you! I'm from Michigan. My mom's been sending me newspaper clippings so I can keep up with the progress of your trip. I sure am pleased to meet you." Grasping Verlen's hand, the patrolman grinned from ear to ear. So did we. After we exchanged stories about our journey, the patrolman detailed the problems with illegal aliens at the border, then went on to describe the gates and bridges up ahead that we would have to go around. Then he waved as Verlen got into his canoe and I slipped the towrope around my waist to haul the boats north.

Verlen and I took turns pulling the canoes, agreeing to take two-hour shifts. I was doing the walking when the sun went down, and it felt easier to keep going than to stop. When I looked back at the boats, I could see they were riding about a foot from the edge. Verlen was supposed to be steering, but he fell asleep after dark. I didn't wake him. When my midnight shift was over, I kept on walking. I figured that Verlen had paddled me way back in the beginning of the journey, and now it was my chance to help him to Yuma.

I felt calm and happy walking along toward Yuma. The only barrier in front of me was fatigue, and I had dealt with that one before. If I could just get something to eat, I knew a surge of energy would take hold and I'd be able to go farther. When I stopped to get a cookie from the boat, Verlen woke up.

"Go back to sleep," I told him. "I'm not ready to quit."

"Hey, it's my turn," Verlen said after looking at his watch.

"I want to walk a little farther. I'm really enjoying this."

"No way, I don't want to be pulled into Yuma. It's my turn. You get in the canoe," Verlen ordered.

"Verlen, after all this distance, I'm not going to let you pull me into Yuma," I said hotly.

"So you want to be the one who gets us to Yuma, do you?"

"I haven't worn out from walking, and I think it's only fair. You paddled me at the beginning of the journey when I was seasick," I reminded him. "It's poetic justice, Verlen."

"Well, I'm not seasick," Verlen retorted. "And no expedition is run on poetic justice. We're going in as a team."

Ahead was a gate where the road crossed the canal, and a dirt embankment blocked our progress. I couldn't pull the boats any farther by myself anyway. Verlen climbed out of his boat, and it took both of us to muscle the canoes out of the channel. We slipped a paddle through the bowrope of the lead canoe. Working as a team, with one of us on each side of the shaft, we pulled forward. We dragged the canoes until we reached the top of the embankment, and then we could see the lights of Yuma, twinkling like a thousand jewels in a star-studded crown.

Epilogue

Verlen arrived at the San Diego Airport on February 9, 1983, 10 minutes before his plane took off for Chicago. After the National Sporting Goods Show, he joined Steve Landick to paddle *up* the Grand Canyon, setting another record for the team. The two men then continued another 4,800 miles before they arrived home in Lansing, Michigan, to conclude the 28,000-mile Ultimate Canoe Challenge on December 15, 1983.

Valerie did not return to her home in Woodinville, but went on to race in the World Championship Au Sable River Marathon in Michigan. During its 36 years of existence, the race had never been completed by a woman's team in qualifying time. In July of 1983, Valerie and her partner, Anne Renaud, finished the 240-mile race in 16 hours and 50 minutes, placing tenth in the men's professional division (there was no women's division).

In April of 1984, Valerie paddled with Verlen again and raced the entire 2,348-mile length of the Mississippi River in 23 days, 10 hours, and 20 minutes. They set a new world record for the fastest time canoeing downstream on the Mississippi and earned a listing in the Guinness Book of World Records, beating the previous record, set by the British Royal Air Force, by 19 days.

Three years after they completed their Baja trip, Valerie and Verlen were married, on April 3, 1986, and in June 1986 they departed from Inuvik, Northwest Territories, en route to Cape Horn, Chile, beginning the Two Continent Canoe Expedition. They are observing and documenting the land, people, and water quality of the western hemisphere on this 21,000-mile voyage of discovery.